Lecture Notes in Information Systems and Organisation

Volume 50

Lecture Notes in Information Systems and Organization—LNISO—is a series of scientific books that explore the current scenario of information systems, in particular IS and organization. The focus on the relationship between IT, IS and organization is the common thread of this collection, which aspires to provide scholars across the world with a point of reference and comparison in the study and research of information systems and organization. LNISO is the publication forum for the community of scholars investigating behavioral and design aspects of IS and organization. The series offers an integrated publication platform for high-quality conferences, symposia and workshops in this field. Materials are published upon a strictly controlled double blind peer review evaluation made by selected reviewers.

LNISO is abstracted/indexed in Scopus

More information about this series at http://www.springer.com/series/11237

Stefano Za · Augusta Consorti ·
Francesco Virili
Editors

Organizing in
a Digitized World

Individual, Managerial and Societal Issues

 Springer

Editors
Stefano Za
Department of Management
and Business Administration
University of Chieti-Pescara
Pescara, Italy

Augusta Consorti
Department of Management
and Business Administration
University of Chieti-Pescara
Pescara, Italy

Francesco Virili
Department of Economic
and Business Sciences
University of Sassari
Sassari, Italy

ISSN 2195-4968   ISSN 2195-4976   (electronic)
Lecture Notes in Information Systems and Organisation
ISBN 978-3-030-86857-4   ISBN 978-3-030-86858-1   (eBook)
https://doi.org/10.1007/978-3-030-86858-1

This Springer imprint is published by the registered company Springer Nature Switzerland AG
The registered company address is: Gewerbestrasse 11, 6330 Cham, Switzerland

Contents

Looking at the Digitized World from Different Perspectives

Stefano Za[1(✉)], Augusta Consorti[1], and Francesco Virili[2]

[1] DEA—Department of Management and Business Administration,
University "G. d'Annunzio" of Chieti-Pescara, Pescara, Italy
{stefano.za,augusta.consorti}@unich.it
[2] Department of Economics and Business Administration, University of Sassari,
Via Muroni 25, 07100 Sassari, Italy
fvirili@uniss.it

1 Introduction

We are living disruptive times, experiencing unprecedented large scale societal emergencies that are amplifying the combined pressures of high potential digital enablers. The sudden gigantic adoption of distance working and distance learning at a global scale, with the consequent hybridization of local/remote, presence/distance, human/machine relational dimensions [1]; the ever-increasing proliferation of smart and connected objects, feeding the expansion of big data [2], together with the diffusion of edge computing and commercial, wide-scale AI systems [3]; the expanding presence and relevance of open digital platforms and digital ecosystems [4] are reshaping our traditional ways of living and organizing at all levels: individual, managerial, and public.

Also, our traditional Conference of the Italian Chapter of AIS, while celebrating its XVII edition (ItAIS 2020) held at the University of Chieti-Pescara on October 16th–17th, 2020, was directly affected by sudden - and to some extent uncertain - patterns of digital hybridization. Specifically, by adopting a combination of multiple digital platforms supported by the flexibility and adaptive openness of participants, the conference was successfully - and safely - held in hybrid mode, allowing the collaborative participation of conveners, local participants, and remote attendees.

The 17 chapters contained in this volume are a revised version of selected contributions presented at the conference, as developed through a double-blind review process. They draw a fresh and novel picture of organizational transformations underway in contemporary times, providing a plurality of views that makes this book particularly relevant to scholars but also to practitioners, managers, and policymakers. Three major areas emerge from this research debate. The first area (Part 1) is focused on the central role of individual responsible behavior in the ever-evolving digital work practices that are reshaping organizations [5, 6]. The second one (Part 2) relates to the analysis of managerial challenges connected to immaterial values and intangible assets within organizations. Finally, the third area of interest (Part 3) is centered around the analysis of governance and political issues connected with innovation patterns in the public sector and academic research institutions.

S. Za et al. (Eds.): ItAIS 2020, LNISO 50, pp. 1–7, 2022.
https://doi.org/10.1007/978-3-030-86858-1_18

2   Part1 – Individual Perspectives. Engaging Individuals in Digital Working Practices

Any collective phenomenon is founded and formed by individuals. As shown in the opening contribution of Part1, newly emerging phenomena such as citizen science can be understood by looking at individuals and how they are attracted and engaged in collective action. Sorrentino and Palumbo propose a conceptual analysis of citizen science projects, i.e., research collaborations where tasks are performed by members of the public. Building upon recent developments in the literature on public management and service science, the authors consider the applicability of a service logic to citizen science, seen as a kind of knowledge co-production. Such new conceptual framework is proposed as a new and promising way to understand and analyze individual motivations, engagement factors, and value production mechanisms of a new phenomenon by applying conceptual tools from different disciplines in a novel way.

If collective action is often understood by investigating individual motivations, similarly it is often by looking at individual working practices that interesting organizational explanations can emerge. Pascarella and Bednar investigate the actual implementation of organizational sustainability in individual work practices, focusing on SMEs. Their empirical investigation involved 148+86 employees in 40+26 SMEs in two stages. With a series of semi-structured interviews, framed according to the Socio-Technical-Toolbox [7], sustainability work practices were investigated in four areas: economic, social, environmental, and technological sustainability. Their analysis shows that employee empowerment in rethinking their own work practices is crucial for the effective implementation of sustainability in SMEs. To this end, much distance is yet to be covered to actually engage SMEs' workers towards the effective integration of sustainability in daily work practices.

Complementing socio-technical studies, HR investigations of the complex universe of personal traits and behavioral characteristics reveal another dimension that is fundamental to the effective redesign of work practices, particularly in smart working contexts. The study conducted by Cori, Sarti, and Torre highlights the crucial importance of specific personal characteristics (i.e., responsibility and self-regulation) in the smart/remote working experience experienced by workers during the Covid-19 lockdown. The analysis, based on a survey of 254 employees in Italy, shows how organizational, superior, and peer support can enable, stimulate, and enhance positive, proactive behaviors in smart working, offering interesting stimuli for the open debate on the evolving patterns and implications of smart working in HR.

An HR perspective on the role of individual traits is also offered by de Gennaro, Adinolfi, Piscopo, and Cavazza, with a focus on job crafting/personalization experiences in digital work practices. Again, individual differences are shown to be relevant: through a qualitative pilot study and a quantitative study, the authors show the relevance of positive personal attitudes towards technology in facilitating job personalization and self-redesign in an is increasingly digitized working context, suggesting optimal behaviors and functioning within organizations resulting from positive and proactive attitudes and traits of individuals.

Besides job crafting, smart working, sustainability practices, and citizen science, coworking is another relevant context for investigating digitized work. But, as suggested in the chapter by Toraldo, Tirabeni, and Sorrentino, the role of individuals in coworking cannot be fully understood when neglecting technology itself. The authors propose a scoping review of the relatively young literature on coworking, showing that in the vast majority of coworking studies, investigators rarely go beyond a metaphorical (rather than analytical) use of technology. The high level of abstraction means that, paradoxically, technology disappears from the analytical attention. They therefore claim that it is crucial to explicitly bring technology into the analysis to better understand how coworking 'works.' This could be done by considering coworking as a 'work-oriented infrastructure' and recognizing its dynamic complexity and its technical features and aspects in use. We are reminded here that in socio-technical analyses, achieving a balance between social and technical dimension is often challenging, but crucial to the research outcomes.

3 Part2: Managerial Perspectives. Coproducing Intangible Assets and Values in Organizations

The contributions presented in this part discuss organizational and managerial issues focusing on intangible assets and values (such as Intellectual Capital, Corporate Reputation, Corporate Social Responsibility, and Corporate Social Innovation) and security issues.

Castelnovo focuses on Corporate Social Innovation. It has emerged over the last two decades as a way for firms to exploit societal needs as an opportunity to generate innovative ideas under the assumption that unsolved social problems may result in higher costs for them. Work integration of people with disabilities is one such critical social issue. The paper explores the implementation of disability management as a corporate social innovation process with reference to a selected set of enterprises often cited as international best practices for the integration of people with disabilities in the workplace. These cases have been analysed based on a grid defined by comparing disability management guidelines published by international organizations generally considered as important reference points for the occupational integration of people with disabilities. The grid helps identify and classify different factors that should be considered in the design, implementation, and evaluation of disability management. The mapping of the results can allow a comparison of different strategies that enterprises can follow in implementing the disability management function as a process of corporate social innovation.

Demartini, Trucco, and Beretta explore the relationship between Intellectual Capital Disclosure (ICD) and audit and non-audit fees (NAF), in the Global Financial Crisis (GFC) period, by analyzing data on UK listed companies collected by Thomson Reuter for the years 2004, 2008, and 2011. Starting from the assumption that under conditions of uncertainty the distinction between AF and NAF is not really clear, the authors decide to consider the GFC period to test whether different economic conditions affect this relationship. The authors provide some preliminary results, describing the limitations of their study and proposing further research developments.

An aspect often related to Intellectual Capital is the Corporate Reputation (CR) of the company. This is the topic debated by De Nicola and Anees. Specifically, they consider Corporate Social Responsibility as one of the main elements affecting CR. In this chapter, the authors investigate the mediating role of CR on the relationship between CSR perception and customer citizenship behavior (CCB), by employing a sample of 278 fast fashion customers. They found that CSR perception has a direct positive effect on CCB, and CR acts as a mediator in the relationship between CR and CCB.

An issue often connected to Corporate Social Responsibility is represented by sustainability performance [8]. Specifically, Kashif et al. provide a preliminary analysis of the accounting literature by selecting papers published in top journals. They explore the discourse on sustainability and performance in the accounting field, developing a taxonomy of the literature discussing both sustainability (social, economic, and environmental) and sustainability performance management aspects (such as auding, accounting, reporting, and assurance), seeking to identify the connections between these two dimensions. The analysis reveals that the reporting aspect covers the social, economic, and environmental sustainability equally, while on the accounting side, much attention is given to environmental over social and economic sustainability. Assurance was found to be the emerging topic in the accounting field.

Another relevant topic frequently considered as an aspect related to the CSR concerns security issues [9]. Sparrius and Sadok focus on security policy in the education sector, analyzing the security policies of 100 UK schools. Their purpose is to examine the extent to which these policies address the security risks faced by schools. This investigation has the potential to assess the effectiveness and relevance of security policies. The key findings show that many security policies are primarily centered on traditional technology-focused solutions and not on threats targeting the human elements in their organizations. In addition, they are also not easily accessible to staff. The authors propose that a socio-technical approach to information security would potentially result in a better understanding of the role and application of security policies in schools, and therefore improved information security.

Baskerville et al. focus on cybersecurity governance by suggesting an approach based on design thinking and pragmatism. The chapter draws on pragmatism because, from its earliest formulation, pragmatist thinking was anchored to a dual interest in ethics and science. Under this lens, pragmatic ethics cannot exist as a set of rules or principles, but rather requires a cyclical, empirical process whereby ethical principles and context interact to promote justice among stakeholders in the search for reliable solutions during the unravel of critical events. Design thinking sheds light on the ongoing interaction between relevant actors (bearing different, often conflicting interests and values) and their competing ideas to co-produce appropriate solutions in a given social and technical context. As a result, a Pragmatic Ethical Reasoning (PER) process approach is proposed for managing unexpected critical events when organizations need to learn ethical and design solutions on the fly.

Salvi and Spagnoletti's contribution close this part. The authors focus on High Reliability Organizations (HRO). These specific organizations need to devise and implement organizational processes aimed at minimizing the risk of failure while facing high risks and high stakes. Specifically, in their contribution the authors examine the case of military HRO operating under Mission Command principles. Mission Command is a doctrine that was developed to address unforeseen circumstances through diffused leadership. However, digitally-enabled Command and Control (C2) systems may challenge this doctrine. Remote-control technologies, automatic weapon systems, and tracking tools have seen widespread application in modern warfare. Such advancements may foster purely vertical approaches whereby commanders can monitor and control the battlefield from afar. The authors investigate the tensions between digitally-enabled Mission Command and Control systems and the centripetal force of purely vertical C2 structures. This scenario contrasts with Mission Command in that leaders can veer to more task-oriented approaches, which in turn may lead to a progressive decrease in subordinate accountability. This is problematic for the entire command pyramid. The authors contribute to the HRO literature by shedding light on the paradoxical role of digital technologies in mission-oriented organization.

4 Part3: Public Perspectives. Exploring Issues in Public Government and Research

The third part of this book discusses governance and political issues concerning the public sector and interesting topics related to the research activities of academic communities.

Berardi and Ziruolo debate the managerial approach in the public sector, and how the adoption of digital technology can foster Smart Governance practices. Specifically, the authors focus on the analysis of the digitization process of the public sector in Italy, known as the Digital Administration Code (CAD). Through the analysis of reports from national agencies such as AGID and data elaborations from AGICOM, the authors describe the Italian public sector's state of the art in terms of digitization and adoption of new technologies. Despite the efforts made by the central government, the results highlight that the Italian public administration has enormous difficulty in exploiting the potential of the new digital technologies, making the transition towards the adoption of a stronger Smart Governance approach problematic.

Krumay et al. focus on the potential risk arising from the use of digital technology in organizations providing critical infrastructure, which are held accountable by governments to ensure sufficient protection. Typically, governments require information to monitor cybersecurity levels of critical infrastructure providers over time, which are currently subject to the respective national legislation in developed economies. Following design science research guidelines, this study offers a generic framework that supports continuous monitoring and benchmarking of an organization's cybersecurity status. It is generic and allows for application by different critical infrastructure providers and usage by government institutions to help achieve national cybersecurity status oversight. The design proposition is supported by an extensive review of academic literature, consultation of relevant industry standards, and two main rounds of field interactions. The framework includes 15 major risk areas, and a collection of associated metrics and controls, which cover material and social mechanisms. Finally, the authors highlight that the specific domain of study would require more design work targeting knowledge accumulation spanning academic research and industry practice.

Sohail et al. focus their attention on political connection and board interlocking across firms. While the influence of political connections and board interlocking is theoretically evident, its detection and disclosure appear very difficult. The idea behind the research is that network science theories and data visualization techniques might be suitable for political connection and board interlocking detection and disclosure. To this end, the authors use social network analysis (SNA) to explore the hidden relationship between corporate organizations. Using the data of Pakistan stock exchange for the period from 2009 to 2015, this work discovered the deep penetration of political connections and analyses the board interlocking. Furthermore, they found the web of networks in which corporations build their relationship with politically connected firms for valuable resource access. More than 70% of the investigated firms were found to be interlocked across consecutive years. The results were found to be stronger as the number of political connections in the board increased.

Francalanci and Giacomazzi discuss the characteristics and limitations of the search mechanisms provided by online platforms classifying the academic literature. Specifically, they inquire whether and to what extent academics perform their online search, use current advanced search mechanisms, and what role online search plays in the different stages of the research process. With this in mind, the authors present the results of an empirical survey conducted with academics in the MIS field. The results from 326 respondents unveil interesting insights into the literature search habits of academics and, overall, indicate that despite the consensus on the low quality of current online search mechanisms, only a tiny minority of users seems to be willing to trade search simplicity for relevance.

Bertolotti et al. investigate how the systematic adoption of research evaluation systems in the Italian academic context may influence research outcomes. The authors propose a conceptual framework that can identify, define, and describe the relevant entities involved in the evaluation process, their measurable properties and relationships. Afterwards, they present the first draft of an ontology derived from an existing ontology concerning the academic world, and the criteria for its design. The authors report the steps taken to modify the received ontology in order to suit specific purposes, with an interdisciplinary contribution to the selection and adaptation of entities. Novel considerations about the use of formal conceptual systems and the contribution of this work to the socio-technical view are finally drawn, and some further directions of the project are proposed.

References

1. Sako, M.: From remote work to working from anywhere. Commun. ACM **64**(4), 20–22 (2021)
2. Hajjaji, Y., Boulila, W., Farah, I.R., Romdhani, I., Hussain, A.: Big data and IoT-based applications in smart environments: a systematic review. Comput. Sci. Rev. **39**, 100318 (2021). https://doi.org/10.1016/j.cosrev.2020.100318
3. Zhou, Z., Chen, X., Li, E., Zeng, L., Luo, K., Zhang, J.: Edge intelligence: paving the last mile of artificial intelligence with edge computing. Proc. IEEE **107**(8), 1738–1762 (2019). https://doi.org/10.1109/JPROC.2019.2918951
4. Wang, P.: Connecting the parts with the whole: toward an information ecology theory of digital innovation ecosystems. MIS Q. **45**(1), 397–422 (2021)
5. Aguilera, R.V., Waldman, D., Siegel, D.S.: Responsibility and organization science: integrating micro and macro perspectives. Organ. Sci. (forthcoming). https://doi.org/10.2139/ssrn.3760065

6. Jiang, W.Y.: Sustaining meaningful work in a crisis: adopting and conveying a situational purpose. Adm. Sci. Q. 0001839221994049 (2021). https://doi.org/10.1177/000183922199 4049
7. Bednar, P.: Sociotechnical Toolbox: Information System Analysis and Design. Craneswater Press Ltd., London (2020)
8. Strand, R., Freeman, R.E., Hockerts, K.: Corporate social responsibility and sustainability in Scandinavia: an overview. J. Bus. Ethics. **127**, 1–15 (2015). https://doi.org/10.1007/s10551-014-2224-6
9. Ridley, G.: National security as a corporate social responsibility: critical infrastructure resilience. J. Bus. Ethics. **103**, 111–125 (2011). https://doi.org/10.1007/s10551-011-0845-6

Individual Perspectives. Engaging Individuals in Digital Working Practices

(Co-)Producing Knowledge out of the Academic Box. A Service-Based View of Citizen Science

Maddalena Sorrentino[1]([⊠]) [iD] and Rocco Palumbo[2] [iD]

[1] University of Milano, Via Conservatorio 7, 20122 Milan, Italy
maddalena.sorrentino@unimi.it
[2] University of Rome "Tor Vergata", Rome, Italy

Abstract. This qualitative paper sets out to build upon recent developments in public management and service science literatures to better understand the increasing engagement of individuals and communities in the co-production of knowledge within Citizen Science (CS) projects, i.e., research collaborations where tasks are performed by members of the public. Mapping the scattered geography of contemporary CS, the study focuses on two cross-cutting make-or-break factors: the role of ICT and the individual motivations to participate in CS. The paper argues that a broader appreciation of CS informed by a 'service' view becomes itself a potential source of new insights not limited to the CS field. In particular, the study proposes that framing CS as a 'service ecosystem' can provide public decision makers and IS designers with essential insights for the broader understanding of conditions, processes and outcomes of citizen's online experience.

Keywords: Knowledge co-production · Citizen science · Value co-creation · Crowdsourcing · Service logic

1 Introduction

In a seminal book, the social theorist David Beetham [1] depicts public services as inclusive goods which are subject to public scrutiny and are developed according to a norm of public ethos that values citizen participation. Embracing this perspective, citizen science (CS) – i.e. the involvement of non-expert (lay) people in scientific discovery, monitoring, and experimentation [2] – can be understood as a public service which is aimed at generating and disseminating scientific knowledge.

The increasing role of CS across many research fields is widely referenced [3–5]. Its value is increasingly acknowledged by national governments in the United States and Australia. Global NGOs, including the United Nations Environment Programme (UNEP), have also voiced their support [6]. In the European Union, CS has gained wider attention since the launch of specific research and innovation funding programmes, such as Digital Agenda, Digital ERA, and Horizon 2020 [7].

Basically, voluntary involvement in CS projects requires lay people to co-produce knowledge with (public) research institutions, and in partnership with expert scientists. As the word "citizen" suggests, participation is open to the general public without any

S. Za et al. (Eds.): ItAIS 2020, LNISO 50, pp. 11–25, 2022.
https://doi.org/10.1007/978-3-030-86858-1_1

formal training in science [8]. Citizen science is often considered a form of crowd-sourcing applied to science, capable of producing scientifically sound data, as well as unexpected insights and innovations [9]. Most of the CS projects stand on public funding [7].

The interrelated conditions of emergence of collaborative scientific ventures include, on the *macro* side: the erosion of the separation between public and private spheres; the new societal dynamics, namely the new relationship between society and science; the radical rethinking of innovation models and research practices [10]; and ICT-related developments. These latter are of particular relevance, thanks to: the ubiquity of Internet and the diffusion of ICT resources across the population; the availability of tailored web-based platforms to support data collection and sharing between government, citizens, civil society, and the private sector [11] (OECD, 2019, p. 27); the affordability of user-friendly devices that allow volunteers to access online CS platforms anywhere, anytime; and the affirmation of the 'hacker-scientist mindset of the computer age' [12]. On the *meso* side, the conditions of emergence of CS include: the scale and scope of the research projects (often too cumbersome and expensive for one single research institution alone, especially in what is known as the field of 'Big Science'); the role and the variety of the non-academic stakeholders; and the configurations of the field of research in terms of project design, lab facilities, training tools, and other resources to support research and participation goals.

Three key rationales make the co-production of scientific knowledge of interest to public management research. First, citizen science provides occasions for the public officials to use science to address community-driven needs and issues [13] and to involve citizens in monitoring the changes taking place around them [14]. Second, data collected in these 'new spaces for citizen action' [5] can potentially contribute to informed policy-making [15]. Third, from the viewpoint of the public research institutions, implementing CS means expanding the in-house knowledge production boundaries and addressing crucial questions about resource management and implementation decisions. Hence, CS requires the public decision makers to make a 'deliberate design' effort [16] about aligning goals, outcomes and trade-offs.

At this critical point in time, disciplines such as information systems, public management, and service science need to dialogue and reciprocally merge, meld and inform co-production of knowledge in CS environments. In this study we see CS as a joint knowledge production endeavor performed in an 'ecosystem' [17: 161], i.e., "a community of interacting entities – organizations and individuals that coevolve their capabilities and roles and depend on one another for their overall effectiveness and survival". The following pages elaborate on these issues. More specifically, the purpose of this paper is to (1) assess the degree to which a service lens can be applied to CS and (2) outline the ensuing implications, in terms of value creation, for the relevant actors. Regarding the first aspect, we believe it is essential and timely to recognize the multilevel nature of activities performed by organizations and laypeople. With reference to the second aspect, understanding the citizen's value creation process is fundamental to co-production design and implementation because it allows for the determination of the appropriate configuration of resources for individuals and communities.

Overall the paper makes three contributions. First, we extend the influential ideas originally proposed by Osborne and Strokosch [18], on the co-production of public services (or the mix of activities that both public officials and citizens contribute to the provision of public services: "the former are involved as professionals, or 'regular producers,' while 'citizen production' is based on voluntary efforts by individuals and groups to enhance the quality and/or quantity of the services they use" [19: 1002]), applying these to a domain (CS) that remains under-appreciated in the organizational debate. Second, combining the 'service' logic (i.e., a logic which emphasizes the centrality of the user's experience and the systemic vision of public service delivery) with an organizational perspective, we explore the potential of a service-based view of knowledge co-production practices. Finally, we outline key areas deserving further investigation for both the practice and the theory.

For the purpose of this paper, the terms 'citizen(s)', 'volunteer(s)' and 'lay people' are used as synonyms, even though insightful distinctions have been proposed by the extant literature, including [20–22]. However, it is not intended to be the definitive interpretation, given that the proposed discussion is the first step of an ongoing research project aimed at reframing the practice of knowledge co-production and building new bridges among disciplines.

Accordingly, the paper (Sect. 2) offers a panoramic view of the current studies on citizen science but mainly focuses on two landmark features: the role of the ICT and individual motivations to participate. Section 3 illustrates the chosen qualitative research approach. Section 4 provides an interpretation of CS informed by a service logic; this analytical key highlights the centrality of citizen scientists as value creators, the systemic vision of citizen science and the dual role of the ICT (i.e., as both operand and operant resource) in CS projects. Section 5 discusses the practical and research implications. Section 6 sets out the conclusions.

2 Related Work

Citizen science is a term that lacks a precise definition [23]. In general, the label describes scientific activities – from the virtual to the physical – in which individuals who are not professional researchers in a particular field actively participate in a research project in partnership with scientists or on their own. Thus, individuals' engagement can vary dramatically, from collecting data for someone else's project to working alongside researchers to develop and execute nearly every part of a project [24].

The variety of terms describing the larger space of public participation in science demonstrates the diversity of both the research disciplines in which CS is applied, and also those interested in understanding citizen science (*e.g.*, public understanding of science, science and technology studies, Internet studies, human-computer interaction). Increasingly, the term citizen science is used to refer to all of these variations on scientific collaboration with the public [25].

According to a recent scientometric article [23], the main fields of study employing CS are biology, ecology and conservation research. Moreover, the social sciences and geography have increasingly started to invite volunteer contributors to research. In quantitative terms, the largest scientific output is to be found in the fields of ornithology, astronomy, meteorology and microbiology [23]. However, it should be noted that most CS projects fall outside the scope of scientometric evaluation, since scientific output is not a main goal.

Literature has generated valuable knowledge in identifying and understanding citizen science. Extant research documents the rise of CS in various geographical contexts and levels, illustrates diverse empirical cases and offer accompanying theoretical reflections. Space limitations mean that, here, the thematically structured overview will focus on the two key aspects that affect CS in the public realm: ICT developments and citizen motivations to participate. Here we examine the relevant literature from an organizational perspective rather than from a purely technological perspective.

2.1 The Role of the ICT

There is a wide consensus in attributing the impetus for citizen science to the progress of the ICTs [26] and, in particular, to the Web 2.0 movement, "in which individuals are no longer passive browsers but active contributors" [27: 418].

The technologies required to leverage the power of non-scientists to collect and analyze data vary. For instance, in Kenya, researchers have developed Hotspotter, an image recognition software which can identify individual zebra by their barcode-like stripe pattern and body shape. In 2015, hundreds of volunteers participated in photographing zebra using GPS-enabled cameras. Images were then run through Hotspotter which led to the identification of 2350 unique animals [11, 28].

The spread of the Internet into everyday life has substantially increased CS projects' visibility, functionality, and accessibility [13]. Further, user-friendly interfaces "….have made participation possible for groups that previously were not reached or well served by citizen science, such as those with literacy or numeracy skills that are not text based" [13: 1436]. Similar to what happens in crowdsourcing contexts, the 'focal agent' (e.g., a research institution) "…broadcast[s] problems to crowds so that potential solvers can decide whether to self-select and solve problems" ([29: 368]. It is remarkable that the focal agent does not evaluate each potential solver to choose a qualified one. At the same time, "…not every member of the crowd that self-selects to solve the problem is in the right position to solve it" (ibidem).

Social media and the Internet also have enabled citizen science projects that can be accomplished only through online platforms. People who are passionate about a subject can quickly locate a relevant CS project, follow its instructions, submit data directly to online databases, and join a community of peers. eBird, for example, engages the global birdwatching community to collect more than 5 million bird observations every month and to submit them to a central database where they can be analyzed to document the quantity and distribution of bird populations [13]. Another good example is *Zooniverse*, an online platform that currently hosts more than eighty active CS projects and has more than 1.5 million registered volunteers [30]. Professional scientists use Zooniverse to crowdsource the analysis of unprecedented volumes of data by asking volunteers around the world to classify or transcribe pre-existing evidence (e.g. sound files, videos, or pictures, such as the millions of images of galaxies, moon craters, and particle collisions). A frequently mentioned Big Science project is Higgs Hunters. Launched in 2014, it helps physicists search for *exotic* particles in data from CERN's

(European Organization for Nuclear Research) Large Hadron Collider in Geneva, the world's highest energy particle accelerator. The quality of the volunteers' contribution to and participation in this online research effort (hosted on the Zooniverse platform) has been recognized by the scientific world several times [13, 31].

Citizen science activities are often structured around campaigns, where volunteers gather and annotate a specific type of data [32]. Further, some projects are bounded by a specific time or place. In contrast, eBird and Higgs Hunters solicit the inputs of the citizen scientists continually and without geographical constraints.

Public engagement in science ventures can take a variety of forms. According to [24: 1–3], CS range along a spectrum of contributory, collaborative, and co-created projects. The former are generally designed by scientists, and members of the public contribute primarily through data collection. While collaborative projects are also designed by scientists and involve data contributions by the public, volunteers may be involved in project refinement, design, data analysis, or the sharing of results. Co-created projects are designed by scientists and members of the public working together, where at least some of the participants are actively involved in most, if not all, steps of the research process. Co-created citizen science projects – also called "Community Science" [33] – represent the highest level of volunteer engagement, and alongside collaborative projects may provide a platform to reach new audiences with topics and approaches that are relevant to individual and community interests. As such, "community science initiatives may have the greatest potential to achieve a wide range of public understanding impacts" [33: 9]. However, the move of currently engaged volunteers from projects that are largely contributory toward more co-created projects is slow [24].

The need to support the volunteers in the transition from the role of simple data collectors to that of co-creators of meaningful citizen science projects leads to the second key aspect of CS: the motivations to participate.

2.2 Motivations to Participate

The value of CS to scientific institutions is clear. According to Bonney and colleagues [13: 1437], CS projects "…truly do science – that produce reliable data and information usable by anyone, including scientists, policy-makers, and the public, and that are open to the same system of peer review that applies to conventional science". Some drawbacks to co-created projects include a higher investment of time required by those managing the project and serving in supporting roles (e.g., scientists, subject-matter experts, platform managers) [24].

No less meaningful is the value of CS to volunteers. Citizen scientists have always been a highly composite category in socio-demographic and cultural terms. Indeed, in CS projects, the maximization of diversity and inclusion is considered the best means to foster in-depth scientific learning-by-doing [6]. Also, the new spaces opened up by the ICT developments is set to increase the variety of the sites and contexts of application in which knowledge co-production occurs. This heterogeneity 'by design' has an influence on the ways citizen scientists perceive the value to be gained from entering the project and the value of their experience.

Extant research shows numerous possible outcomes for individuals, in terms of, for example, increased knowledge, skills, scientific literacy [24]. Participation in co-created projects also may provide lay people with a greater understanding of the scientific process, their community structure, social context, and opportunities to communicate their findings to the public [33]. Increased social interactions are often necessary in co-created projects to deepen understanding and sustain engagement, and these may be viewed as either a motivation or barrier to participation.

In general, managing the motivation and self-efficacy of lay people in citizen science projects is tricky. Motivation to participate is multifaceted [34]. Research reveals a range of intrinsic and extrinsic motivators, and also highlights great diversity in what drives active participation. According to Deci and Ryan [35] and Cappa et al. [8], intrinsic motivation is connected to self-determination in participating due to satisfaction in performing a valuable scientific task and in increasing their understanding of scientific issues, while extrinsic motivation is related to the intention to contribute based on some reward. Research has highlighted the importance of both intrinsic and extrinsic motivations for the success of virtual communities, as some people may participate mainly due to their self-interest or to contribute to a social aim, while others are primarily interested in the reward they can obtain.

Empirical research on factors that motivate participation and retention in citizen science projects distinguishes between motivations for participating in field-based versus online ventures. While the demographics and motivations of virtual citizen scientists working on field-based projects have long been studied by sociologists, and the mechanics of user contributions to such sites have been extensively examined by data scientists, it is only relatively recently that the philosophers of science have taken an interest in this theme [36].

Studies of local, community-based citizen science projects – reported by [24] – have shown that opportunities for in-person social interaction among participants and fulfilment of a general interest are common motivators for participation. In contrast, research into online citizen science projects has shown that contributing to scientific research and bolstering participants' online reputations are key motivators [37]. Online CS projects show extraordinary turnover rates. Moreover, participant motivations have been shown to fluctuate over the course of an online project and to differ based on the quality or quantity of participation in online environments. Many of these purely online projects are broadly focused on science, technology, engineering and mathematics (STEM) topics, while community-based projects tend to address local issues (e.g., environment protection, the monitoring of at-risk areas).

"Matching project activities with volunteer motivations may be the best method for achieving volunteer satisfaction and retention and also may enhance recruitment" for individuals with diverse interests and backgrounds [24: 2]. CS projects that align with participants' hobbies, previously existing interests, or previous engagement in other activities are believed to be the most likely to keep levels of motivation high (Bonney et al., 2009, p. 47). Once individuals are recruited, effective training and collaborative learning, often using online training tools, may enhance engagement, especially in co-created projects, and connectedness.

Research to date suggests it is important to streamline online training and collaborative resources as much as possible, to ensure that they are easy and fun to use and to directly link them to a tangible project of interest to participants [24].

In a nutshell, ICT developments and citizen motivations to participate are two key drivers and mainstays of citizen science. The ICTs provide the research institutions with unprecedented opportunities to involve the public in scientific work and knowledge co-production (and vice versa), but the true make-or-break factor of success is the citizen motivations to participate, which are difficult to detect and govern. Influencing citizens' personal motivation remains "a complex task, due to their often highly individual nature" [38: 301]. Despite this, ICT and motivations hold similar promise for the broader case of co-production in the public realm.

To recap, by considering CS as an established field, the above selective review offers a novel perspective in which the co-production (of scientific knowledge in this case) is not only popular and on the rise, but which already offers empirically significant and scientifically valuable experiences at different scale, is supported by authoritative public research organizations the world over, and is institutionalized.

In what follows, the two key, interlocking, make-or-break factors are more closely analyzed and reframed.

3   Research Approach

The previous section references many of the historically crucial topics for co-production in public services. The central issues and concerns for management scholars include: the joint working between service users and service providers, where each player is given a well-defined role in different times and places and in a specific phase of the 'production process'; the various modes of interaction, enabled by ICT-based tools and infrastructures; and the challenge of securing the recruitment and retention of volunteers. An additional and recurrent factor in the managerial research on co-production is the prevalent instrumental position – which Osborne and Strokosch [18] call an 'add-on to service delivery' – attributed to the members of the public in relation to the service professionals in public agencies, an aspect that typically emanates from a New Public Management (NPM) perspective.

For some years now, the public management research has started to break with the mainstream thinking, in particular with the notion that the service user is merely a provider of additional input on a voluntary basis. For instance, exploring the nature of value creation in public services from a service perspective led Osborne and colleagues [18, 39] to propose a rethinking of co-production in the public realm. Its basic premise is that co-production is intrinsic to any service experience [39: 18–19]. This theoretical revisit has allowed, among other things, to directly link co-production to service innovation and to the co-creation of value in public services. Interestingly, framing co-production in a New Public Governance (NPG) perspective implies concentrating on both processes and system [39].

In the following we use this insightful work as a springboard to reframe CS. Basically, we assume that CS can be considered a form of nonscientist engagement aimed at generating and disseminating valuable scientific knowledge within the academic community and society at large. As a phenomenon, CS overlaps with crowdsourcing and is sometimes called "crowdsourcing for science", but in fact only some citizen science projects are akin to crowdsourcing, while others are not, due to scale or structure [25]. These and other features of CS make it an interesting context for studying such wide-ranging topics as participation, relationships between laypersons and scientists, knowledge dissemination. Here, however, our concern is solely on the affinities to co-production of public services. In this view, the role of service user and that of service provider are covered by, respectively, the citizen scientist – i.e., a self-selected volunteer that engages in the research work without the hierarchical bureaucracies or formal leadership structures – and the research institution – i.e., a public sector organization (or PSO) that partners with volunteers. This tentative exercise has the goal of teasing out new insights that can broaden our understanding of the nature and role of ICT-mediated knowledge co-production in online contexts.

Methodologically, we analyze CS through the lenses of service management because we believe that useful lessons can be learned from this perspective. The next section reviews the central elements of a service-based view ([17, 18, 39–41]) then transposes this analytical key to the context of citizen science. Section 5 explores the practical and theoretical potential of this exercise.

4   A Service-Based View of Citizen Science

Citizen science depicts a composite "…socially distributed knowledge production system" [42: 10]. Culturally heterogeneous, it can be likened to a 'service ecosystem' in which multiple forms of interaction and exchange take place among social actors [17: 161]. According to Lusch and Nambisan a service ecosystem is "a relatively self-contained, self-adjusting system of mostly loosely coupled social and economic (resource-integrating) actors connected by shared institutional logics and mutual value creation through service exchange" [17: 161]. The social actors are also forming a kind of virtual community capable of self-adjusting and integrating resources. The central theme is how research institutions try to unlock volunteers as 'complementary assets' [43]. Common structures (or 'shared institutional logics') permit the creation of the 'service' (singular) in conjunction with some entity, whereby "…service involves applying resources for the benefit of others or oneself" [17: 158]. According to Lusch and Nambisan, service ecosystems, service platforms, and value co-creation are the three core components (or pillars) of service innovation.

The service platform is 'the place' where the user (the citizen scientist) meets the provider (the research institution). Service platform is a broad term that can be applied to various types of PSO-provided resources, tangible or intangible (including websites, ad-hoc forums, software artefacts, back-office facilities, and datasets), relatively stable or emergent. Thus, the service platform hosts the iterative interactions that drive new knowledge creation and forms the fulcrum of the service ecosystem, meant as 'the venue for innovation' [17]. The connections among the elements may be loose, "as when a variety of off-the-shelf software systems are used separately to support various project goals", or tight, as in a project website that offers multiple functionalities, including data collection tools, visualization components, blogs, news feeds, email, forums, project information, "in a unified way" [34: 168].

Interestingly, Grönroos [40] differentiates between user service logic and provider service logic, and suggests that the value creation and co-creation processes must support each other. Specifically, in tune with the service logic, it is always the user (not the provider) that creates value: first, "…using all resources available to them" and contributing their time, effort and expertise "…to achieve specific goals in a way that is valuable to them" [40: 5]; and, second, independently (i.e., in isolation) from the service provider. This latter circumstance arises, for example, when a citizen scientist interacts in person or digitally with their peers on social media. The dyadic interaction can generate positive, negative or neutral impacts on the value creation process [41].

In contrast, a provider service logic permits us to observe how the public sector organization (e.g., a research institution) plays the role of enabler and resource supplier. In that sense, the PSO ensures the availability of a supportive environment (e.g., an accessible online platform) designed specifically for the citizen scientists, or 'users' in the classic sense. This platform is a 'social information system', i.e., an information system based on social technologies and open collaboration [44]. As in the case of service logic, the idea is to achieve specific goals in a way that is valuable to users [40]. This is the approach found when, for example, a CS platform offers a variety of user tools, such as blogs, chats, educational materials, and mobile gamified apps to encourage, motivate and retain contributors from the millennial generation [32].

In essence, according to Grönroos, although the output is fundamental, the process is the defining feature of the service. This shift of focus from output to process has two important implications: for how the quality of service is perceived by the users and, therefore, also for the development and management of service: "…To be valuable help to the users, the resources, processes and competences provided by the service organization must be *"aligned* (our emphasis) with the resources, processes, and competences the service users require" [40: 6].

In the event of discrepancies, the users will, first of all, perceive low or even inadequate service quality. Secondly, this low quality will translate into inadequate value for them [40]. The two claims clearly illustrate the relationship between expectations, subjective experience and actual performance, but they also illuminate the potential reasons for non-scientist members of the public dropout in CS projects. The relationship means that expectations, subjective experience and actual performance, in turn, affect the process and outcomes of engagement in research collaborations. As service users, citizen scientists are motivated to engage in an interaction with the research institution to the extent to which they realize value from their 'situated experience' [45] with science and the knowledge they bring to the project. Importantly, value is emergent and differs between individuals and the situation in which an evaluation occurs [46].

Thus, from the PSO perspective, the effective design of the service is a necessary but not sufficient condition for a successful service delivery [47] and positive outcomes. The elusiveness of the value, the variety of motivations that underpin participation and retention, and the unpredictability of the contexts (physical and virtual) in which interactions are taking place [46] mean that what happens in the service system cannot be fully and deliberately planned by the provider. At the same time, a process of co-production that is meaningful for the relevant actors can emerge only when it is both enabled and shaped by purposeful managerial action.

To citizen science, a service-based view recognizes ICT as an integral element of the ecosystem in which a CS project is conceived and developed. Lusch and Nambisan [17: 157] highlight the dual nature of information and communication technology: *operant* resource (as the agent that acts on other essential resources, and triggers or initiates the innovation) and *operand* resource (that on which an operation - e.g., the access to an online database - is performed). As operant resource, the digital tools create novel opportunities for knowledge integration or enhance the understanding of citizen scientists beyond basic data collection. Examples of operand resources include digital infrastructures, user interfaces or smart technologies that can help hold together diverse actors and enable collaboration within the service ecosystem.

5   Potential Implications

Viewing CS through the lenses of service management is a valuable way of conceptualizing and understanding citizen's engagement in co-production. A service-based view emphasizes the centrality of the user's process logic and experience, the systemic vision of public service delivery and the dual role of the ICT in support of resourceful actors, three concepts that plot an alternative course to that taken by the NPM-inspired mainstream.

Now, as a preliminary and non-exhaustive exercise, we try to identify which areas could be deserving of further investigation and development on both the practical and the conceptual fronts. The considerations below refer to the public services organizations (PSOs), in the general sense of the term, willing to realize the potential of co-production initiatives in various fields of application.

5.1   Implications for the Practice

Firstly, if the imperative for public organizations is to reinvent themselves as "service" organizations [48], then the shift in thinking calls for the PSOs to pay more attention to "...the organization and its service processes and leadership such that the required fit is achieved" [40: 6]. From a management perspective, a preparatory step to maximize the expected outcomes of co-production is to identify what resources are required at the individual, organizational and systemic levels. This tripartite, in turn, provides a foundation for designing multidimensional systems of performance assessment.

Secondly, PSOs need to design better features for user-centric platforms and supporting tools. Because co-production efforts such as CS initiatives are predicated on the contribution of a large number of participants (or 'complementary resources'), user engagement and willingness to contribute are critical issues that software designers must take into account when developing, testing and implementing artefacts. Put simply, designers who want not only to limit user dissatisfaction but also to encourage continued use of web platforms should be aware of two categories of technical features: i.e., *satisfiers* and *motivators*. The former include functionalities whose absence will cause a participant to experience dissatisfaction with a website. The latter are those which add value to a website [34: 169–170]. An iterative approach to the design is essential to ensure the constant alignment of the features of the artefacts with the personal interests and needs of the users. That said, public decision makers should always be mindful of the dual role of ICT as both operant and operand resource. In the former case, the organizational units involved include information systems, service innovation and knowledge management. In the latter, the most interested units are those in charge of network management, standards and organizational routines.

Thirdly, the locus of knowledge creation and sharing is destined to move progressively toward the periphery of PSOs. The continuous redefinition of the ecosystem's geography will effectively require information systems and organizational members to take on more complex roles. The aim is to allow for continuous scanning by the PSOs to identify the signals that indicate when boundaries should be crossed and reconfigured and when they should not [49: 1401]. In this respect, PSOs face an enormous challenge in dealing with an environment that lacks physical sites and often includes anonymous participants.

5.2 Research Directions

Citizen science demonstrates more heterogeneity than other co-production fields of application, e.g. the public involved in CS is heterogeneous 'by design' (see Sect. 2.2). To gain significant traction in understanding under what conditions and constraints co-production is likely to succeed or fail, it is necessary, first, to delve into the intrinsic motivations of the members of the public. A concept that promises interesting developments for understanding the willingness to interact in CS ecosystems is that of psychological distance (or 'the perceived closeness to an experience') that Holmqvist et al. [46] recently applied to different aspects of value creation in services.

Second, the dual (operand and operant) role of ICT takes on considerable meaning in the studies dedicated to the innovation potential of technologies deployed in co-productive practices. As operand resource, the analytical attention must be placed on the capabilities of the technologies to support the coordination of the processes, the sharing of knowledge and the accumulation of the data. As operant resource, the research focus must favor the potential of the ICT to shape the design and the content of the services.

Finally, the data flows produced by the online CS platforms offer unprecedented possibilities for process tracing, which, in turn, affects actor, process or task transparency. Interestingly, the wealth of freely available information can help to plug the primary methodological gap - i.e., the absence of co-production evidence in large N settings - that challenges the researchers (e.g., [50]) and that has, until now, limited the generalizability of the findings of many empirical studies. A further important step in capturing the factors shaping motivation in ICT-mediated contexts is to keep detailed logs of most interactions among community members.

6 Final Remarks

In this paper we consider the applicability of a service logic to citizen science (CS), seen as a kind of knowledge co-production. Building on Grönroos' work, we also propose that the experiential process of value co-creation by lay people affects the process and outcomes of engagement in research collaborations. In addition, teasing out and combining these insights has shined a light on several lines of action that can aid the successful practice and outcomes of ICT-based co-production in the public realm. This preliminary exercise has also demonstrated that the integration of insights from distinct theoretical perspectives (information systems, public management, and service science) enables these disciplines to learn from each other, and could even help reinforce the understanding of CS and its implications.

Overall, our paper makes a valuable contribution to the debate about how to spur citizen participation through technology, specifically how to encourage co-production through experiential value co-creation. Nevertheless, implementing co-production remains challenging for public service organizations and this circumstance limits its development in practice.

The present study's focus on the two primary factors of success, i.e., the role of ICT and the citizens' motivations to participate in CS as a specific form of co-production, is a clear limitation. This is further hindered by the use of only a service logic as interpretive key which, despite being an efficacious tool to conceptualize the research institution as a service provider and value co-creator, and to highlight the centrality of the user as value creator in the service system, is, poorly equipped to give us a full understanding of the political and policy context of public service [51].

Hence, Citizen Science offers great promise for scholarly enquiry on co-production. We believe that there are many opportunities for interdisciplinary research on these issues. The availability of empirically significant and scientifically valuable experiences, the institutionalization of the engagement of the volunteers, and the systematic use of assessment and measurement practices compared with other application fields in the public sector, characterize CS as a more mature co-production domain. However, it goes without saying that further research is required before the current CS can be considered as a likely scenario for public service co-production in the long run.

The paper presents the initial findings of an ongoing research endeavor. As such, it does not provide definitive answers but instead offers a more elaborate set of issues relating to co-production supported by ICT platforms. What this study shows is that, in the case of designing co-production platforms, attention should be focused on the unique characteristics of the citizens that use them. The paper addresses complex problems in a conventional way, but one, nevertheless, that has the potential of rewarding us with a far richer understanding of co-production in public settings.

Acknowledgement. Our sincere thanks go to our colleagues Massimo Florio and Stefano Carrazza who took the time and interest to discuss an earlier version of this paper with us.

References

1. Beetham, D.: Bureaucracy. Open University Press, Buckingham (1987)
2. Callon, M.: The role of lay people in the production and dissemination of scientific knowledge. Sci. Technol. Soc. **4**(1), 81–94 (1999)
3. Franzoni, C., Sauermann, H.: Crowd science: the organization of scientific research in open collaborative projects. Res. Policy **43**(1), 1–20 (2014)
4. Hadj-Hammou, J., et al.: Getting the full picture: assessing the complementarity of citizens science and agency monitoring data. PLoS One. **12**(12), 1–18 (2017)

5. Jasanoff, S.: Ordering knowledge, ordering society. In: Jasanoff, S. (ed.) States of Knowledge: The Co-Production of Science and the Social Order, pp. 13–45. Routledge, London (2004)

6. Hecker, S., et al.: Citizen Science: Innovation in Open Science. Society and Policy. UCL Press, London (2018)

7. Holocher-Ertl, T., Kieslinger, B.: White Paper on Citizen Science in Europe (2013)

8. Cappa, F., et al.: Bring them aboard: rewarding participation in technology-mediated citizen science projects. Comput. Hum. Behav. **89**, 246–257 (2018)

9. Wiggins, A.: Crowdsourcing science: organizing virtual participation in knowledge production. In: Proceedings of the 16th ACM international conference on Supporting Group Work. ACM (2010)

10. Nowotny, H., Scott, P., Gibbons, M.: Introduction: "Mode 2" revisited: the new production of knowledge. Minerva **41**(3), 179–194 (2003)

11. OECD: Using digital technologies to improve the design and enforcement of public policies. In: OECD Digital Economy Papers. OECD, Paris (2019)

12. Rothstein, M.A., Wilbanks, J.T., Brothers, K.B.: Citizen science on your smartphone: an ELSI research agenda: currents in contemporary bioethics. J. Law Med. Ethics **43**(4), 897–903 (2015)

13. Bonney, R., et al.: Next steps for citizen science. Science **343**(6178), 1436–1437 (2014)

14. Hecker, S., et al.: Innovation in citizen science–perspectives on science-policy advances. Citizen Sci. Theory Pract. **3**(1), 1–14 (2018)

15. Liu, H.-Y., Kobernus, M.: Citizen science and its role in sustainable development: status, trends, issues, and opportunities. In: Ceccaroni, L., Piera, J. (eds.) Analyzing the Role of Citizen Science in Modern Research, pp. 147–167. IGI Global, Hershey, Pennsylvania (2017)

16. Shirk, J.L., et al.: Public participation in scientific research: a framework for deliberate design. Ecol. Soc. **17**(2), 29 (2017)

17. Lusch, R.F., Nambisan, S.: Service innovation: a service-dominant logic perspective. MIS Q. **39**(1), 155–175 (2015)

18. Osborne, S.P., Strokosch, K.: It takes two to tango? Understanding the co-production of public services by integrating the services management and public administration perspectives. Br. J. Manage. **24**(S1), S31–S47 (2013)

19. Parks, R.B., et al.: Consumers as co-producers of public services: some economic and institutional considerations. Policy Stud. J. **9**(7), 1001–1011 (1981)

20. Alford, J.: Why do public sector clients co-produce? Towards a contingency theory. Admin. Soc. **34**(1), 32–56 (2002)

21. van Eijk, C., Gascò, M.: Unravelling the co-producers. Who are they and what motivation do they have? In: Brandsen, T., Steen, T., Verschuere, B. (Eds.) Co-production and Co-Creation Engaging Citizens in Public Services, 63–79. Routledge, New York (2018)

22. Voorberg, W.H., Bekkers, V.J.J.M., Tummers, L.G.: A systematic review of co-creation and co-production: embarking on the social innovation journey. Public Manag. Rev. **17**(9), 1333–1357 (2015)

23. Kullenberg, C., Kasperowski, D.: What is citizen science? – A scientometric meta-analysis. PLoS One. **11**(1), 1–16 (2016)

24. Frensley, T., et al.: Bridging the benefits of online and community supported citizen science: a case study on motivation and retention with conservation-oriented volunteers. Citizen Sci. Theory Pract. **2**(1), 1–14 (2017)

25. Wiggins, A., Crowston, K.: Surveying the citizen science landscape. First Monday. **20**(1), 1 (2015)

26. Yuan, Q.: Co-production of public service and information technology: a literature review. In: Proceedings of the 20th Annual International Conference on Digital Government Research, pp. 123–132.. Association for Computing Machinery, Dubai, United Arab Emirates (2019)

27. Zhao, Y., Zhu, Q.: Evaluation on crowdsourcing research: current status and future direction. Inf. Syst. Front. **16**(3), 417–434 (2012). https://doi.org/10.1007/s10796-012-9350-4
28. Berger-Wolf, T., et al.: The Great Grevy's Rally: The Need, Methods, Findings, Implications and Next Steps. Technical report, Grevy's Zebra Trust (2016)
29. Afuah, A., Tucci, C.L.: Crowdsourcing as a solution to distant search. Acad. Manage. Rev. **37**(3), 355–375 (2012)
30. Jackson, C.B., Crowston, K., Østerlund, C.: Did they login? Patterns of Anonymous Contributions in Online Communities. In: Proceedings of the ACM on Human-Computer Interaction, p. 77 (2018)
31. Barr, A.J., Kalderon, C.W., Haas, A.C.: 'That looks weird'— evaluating citizen scientists' ability to detect unusual features in ATLAS images of LHC collisions. ATLAS NOTE, **ATL-COM-OREACH-2016–017** (2016)
32. Bowser, A., et al.: Using gamification to inspire new citizen science volunteers. In: First International Conference on Gameful Design, Research and Applications ACM Stratford, Canada, pp. 1825 (2013)
33. Bonney, R., et al.: Can citizen science enhance public understanding of science? Public Underst. Sci. **25**(1), 2–16 (2016)
34. Prestopnik, N.R., Crowston, K.: Citizen science system assemblages: understanding the technologies that support crowdsourced science. In: iConference 2012, 7–10, February 2012, ACM, Toronto, Ontario, Canada, pp. 168–176 (2012)
35. Deci, E.L., Ryan, R.M.: The "What" and "Why" of goal pursuits: human needs and the self-determination of behavior. Psychol. Inq. **11**(4), 227–268 (2000)
36. Watson, D., Floridi, L.: Crowdsourced science: sociotechnical epistemology in the e-research paradigm. Synthese **195**(2), 741–764 (2016). https://doi.org/10.1007/s11229-016-1238-2
37. Nov, O., Arazy, O., Anderson, D.: Scientists@Home: what drives the quantity and quality of online citizen science participation? PLoS ONE. **9**(4), e90375 (2014)
38. Brandsen, T., Steen, T., Verschuere, B. (eds.): Co-production and Co-creation: Engaging Citizens in Public Services. Routledge, New York (2018)
39. Osborne, S.P., Strokosch, K., Radnor, Z.: Co-production and the co-creation of value in public services. In: Brandsen, T., Steen, T., Verschuere, B. (eds.) Co-Production and Co-Creation: Engaging Citizens in Public Services, pp. 18–26. Routledge, New York (2018). https://doi.org/10.4324/9781315204956-3
40. Grönroos, C.: Reforming public services: does service logic have anything to offer? Public Manage. Rev. **21**(5), 775–788 (2018). https://doi.org/10.1080/14719037.2018.1529879
41. Grönroos, C., Voima, P.: Critical service logic: making sense of value creation and co-creation. J. Acad. Mark. Sci. **41**(2), 133–150 (2013)
42. Gibbons, M.: Science's new social contract with society. Nature **402**(S6761), C81–C84 (1999). https://doi.org/10.1038/35011576
43. Teece, D.J.: Profiting from technological innovation: Implications for integration, collaboration, licensing and public policy. Res. Policy **15**(6), 285–305 (1986)
44. Schlagwein, D., Schoder, D., Fischbach, K.: Social information systems: review, framework, and research agenda. In: Thirty Second International Conference on Information Systems ICIS, Shanghai (2011)
45. Jefferies, J.G., Bishop, S., Hibbert, S.: Service innovation through resource integration: an empirical examination of co-created value using telehealth services. Public Policy Admin. **36**(1), 69–88 (2019). https://doi.org/10.1177/0952076718822715
46. Holmqvist, J., Guest, D., Grönroos, C.: The role of psychological distance in value creation. Manag. Decis. **53**(7), 1430–1451 (2015)

47. Osborne, S.P., Radnor, Z., Torfing, J., Triantafillou, P.: The new public governance and innovation in public services: a public service-dominant approach. In: Torfing, J., Triantafillou, P. (eds.) Enhancing Public Innovation By Transforming Public Governance, pp. 54–70. Cambridge University Press, Cambridge (2016). https://doi.org/10.1017/CBO978131610533 7.003
48. Lusch, R.F., Vargo, S.L., O'Brien, M.: Competing through service: insights from service-dominant logic. J. Retail. **83**(1), 5–18 (2007)
49. Yoo, Y., et al.: Organizing for innovation in the digitized world. Organ. Sci. **23**(5), 1398–1408 (2012)
50. Brandsen, T., Verschuere, B., Pestoff, V.: Taking research on co-production a step further. In: Pestoff, V., Brandsen, T., Verschuere, B. (eds.) New Public Governance, the Third Sector and Co-Production, pp. 381–388. Routledge, Abingdon (2012)
51. Osborne, S.P., Radnor, Z., Strokosch, K.: Co-Production and the co-creation of value in public services: a suitable case for treatment? Public Manage. Rev. **18**(5), 639–653 (2016)

Sustain the Abilities of the Future SMEs' Empirical Study

Lucia Pascarella[1(✉)] and Peter Bednar[1,2]

[1] University of Portsmouth, Portsmouth, UK
peter.bednar@port.ac.uk
[2] Lund University, Lund, Sweden

Abstract. Sustainability of the enterprise is crucial to support long-term business survival and development. Unpredictable events such as Covid-19 highlights sustainability issues in enterprises. This empirical study aims to investigate sociotechnical sustainability in real world work practices. The focus is on employee involvement and problems in work practices concerning the economic, environmental, social, and technological area. The study draws on findings from the 2019 and 2020 analyses on sustainability development in employees' work practices. Overall, there seems to be a lack of integration of sustainability in work practices and this does not support the employees in their efforts to co-create a sustainable future for the enterprise.

Keywords: Empirical study · Sustainability analysis · Work-practices · Sociotechnical analysis

1 Introduction

The research focuses on sustainability in small and medium enterprises (SMEs) based on empirical study. The study draws on findings from two studies one in 2019 and another in 2020 discussing then possible concerns with the current epidemic situation. The continuous development of abilities is a priority challenge in SMEs to sustain their long-term future development. Pandemic and crises situations, for instance, the Corona Virus (Covid-19), demonstrate the need for the business to support multiple sustainability aspects of SMEs in both the present and the future. Due to Covid-19, the flexibility' necessity to build a new way to work from home, tested enterprises' ability to sustain the business [1]. Therefore, the situation highlighted weaknesses to sustainable development.

In this context, technologies combined with social involvement in work-practices seem to increase their relevance to support the enterprises' sustainability. Integration and equilibrium between technologies and employee' knowledge seem to be crucial to adapt to changes [2]. From a socio-technical perspective, appreciation of both social and technological aspects is essential to remain flexible and competitive in a continually evolving context [3]. Hence, the document focuses on an empirical study where sustainability in the economic, environmental, social, and technological area in employee work

S. Za et al. (Eds.): ItAIS 2020, LNISO 50, pp. 26–40, 2022.
https://doi.org/10.1007/978-3-030-86858-1_2

practices, were analyzed. Moreover, the study explores sustainability by emphasizing both employee involvement and problems that they face in their work-practices.

The 2020 study is based on dataset resulting from individual trainee analysts project. The project involved 26 trainee analysts, each of whom engaged a different SME. The primary purpose was to gain real world understanding of work practices in SME's. Trainee analysts' investigation developed through semi-structured interviews based on multiple preset questionnaires to develop useful information directly from employees.

Therefore, each trainee analyst interviewed at least two employees (2–4), multiple times, from the same SME to explore enterprise' work practices. Overall, 26 trainee analysts interviewed 86 employees from January 2020 until April 2020 in 26 different enterprises. This analysis relies on data gained thanks to the sustainability questionnaire from Socio-Technical Toolbox (STT) 2020 [4], which tried to incorporate a systemic approach in the research. The questionnaire is composed of 46 questions, set up to be asked directly at the employee, divided into four parts: economic sustainability, social sustainability, environmental sustainability, and technological sustainability.

Additionally, this research also concerns the previous 2019 sustainability analysis project. This was conducted in a similar fashion as the 2020 study, but based on a dataset which contains information about 148 employees in work practices in 40 different SME's, involving 46 individual trainee analysts. That information relied on semi structured interviews, observations and a sustainability' questionnaire of STT 2018 [5], which was based on Triple Bottom Line sustainability vision [6]. Hence, questionnaire 2019 composed of 24 questions divided into the following parts: economic sustainability, social sustainability, and environmental sustainability.

Although the two studies are based on different years' datasets there is the possibility to discuss and compare results regarding sustainability problems. Including the analysis of the level of attention to the creation of value for the future concerning the environmental, economic, and social sphere. Nevertheless, the time gap between the two analysis, the differences in enterprises and involved individuals, the results are similar between the studies.

The next section will describe the background of the STT project and outlines how previous work provided the basis for the empirical study. Subsequentially, the authors will show the empirical study, which started with a comparison between 2019 and 2020 analysis. Then the analysis will focus on the investigation of employee involvement and problems that they face in sustainability work practices. Furthermore, the last part of the analysis will explore employee suggestions to solve the problems that they face in work practice. The paper will then conclude discussing the findings and potential for further work.

2 Background

The analysis purpose is to explore employee work practices to uncover sustainability' issues to change them in orientation to business excellence. Hence, to achieve the scope of the project, STT is the guideline base of the empirical study as offers *"a collection of tools, techniques, and methods which can be used to support organizational change in practice"* [5:3]. This toolbox aims to give tools to discuss work-systems which is the primary concern of organizational change. Furthermore, STT has been used on SMEs, which are the core of this analysis, and other types of businesses over two decades. The STT has approximately 30 variety of method analysis to support the exploration of work-systems (Sustainability Analysis is one of these). Additionally, to support the methods of the analysis, STT comprises five main areas of study each of them has its questionnaire of interest [interaction, sociotechnical, sustainability, change-potential, information, and cyber-security].

The empirical study relies only on the sustainability part of the toolbox. In this regard, STT's sustainability questionnaire and analysis were modified after the first sustainability analysis done in 2019 in order to develop the current second analysis, which relates to the new 2020 version of the toolbox. The graph (see Fig. 1) shows the process described above, which concern the sustainability questionnaire 2020' creation that is the base of this empirical study. The main changes concern the introduction of technological sustainability and systemic perspective in sustainability analysis and related questions in the questionnaire (one reason to make it explicit was that we experienced that analysts and employees tended to take the sustainability of the technology aspect for granted and thus also often forgot about it).

Following the sociotechnical approach, technological sustainability should be an essential focus as it concerns *"how work practices in a Human Activity System are related to and influence use and change of technological resources"* [4:38].

Technology which is not appropriate and integrated into work could create an issue in practice to the whole system. Therefore, not just development of technology but in particular development of technology use, must be integrated into the social employee and business context, if they are intended to support work in practices and systemic sustainability.

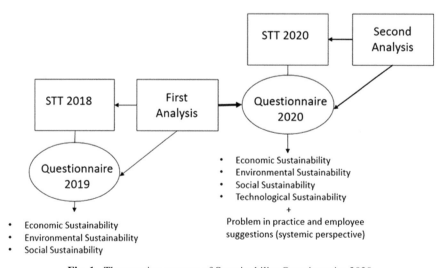

Fig. 1. The creation process of Sustainability Questionnaire 2020.

Systemic perspective in sustainability analysis emphasizes the importance of taking into consideration (integrated) interaction and interconnection of different sustainability areas related to employee' work (in context of the actual work practice). Systemic perspective highlights the need to understand the problematical situation of sustainability in employee' everyday work practices, to change them to improve the whole (work) system starting from employees' point of view. Hence, the sustainability questionnaire includes questions that investigate the problems in employees' work practices and their suggestions on solutions in each of sustainability' area.

3 Empirical Study

The empirical study relies on sustainability' questionnaire contained in STT 2020 [4]. The primary aim of the analysis is to understand if enterprises pursue sustainability in practice. Subsequentially, the analysis focuses on the involvement of employees in sustainability' areas work practices emphasising their point of view.

Hence the analysis explores employees' vision on problems that they face in sustainability practices and their suggestions to solve them. To achieve these scopes, authors focused on the meaning that specific questions aimed to investigate. All employees' responses were categorised and collocated in a range schema according to the question coherence. More employees show coherence and personal involvement in answers, and higher should be the integration of sustainability in practices.

The authors used the same categorisation and ranges method used in the previous first analysis to facilitate the findings' comparison [7]. Therefore, conforming to the previous categorisation, each employee answer was collocated to a range' schema. Subsequentially, to the specific answer, was attributed the mean value of its belonging range (for instance 10, 30, 50, 70 and 90). Thus, more as the answer shows more coherence and personal involvement in sustainability practices higher is its range value. The range schema used in ascending order is the following:

- 0 – 20,
- 20 – 40,
- 40 – 60,
- 60 – 80,
- 80 – 100.

Subsequentially, to evaluate the behaviour of the whole business for each question, the mean was calculated using the number of employees and their average range values. The resultant value was then, re-placed in the range schema describing the general question-related behaviour of the whole enterprise.

3.1 Second Sustainability Analysis

The first approach to the analysis was to investigate the behaviour of enterprises concerning sustainability in their current practices. The study started analyzing questions (see Table 1) intending to uncover the level of problems in all sustainability' areas. The

Table 1. Questions that aim to identify the problem in all sustainability areas.

Sustainability area	Question
Economic	Is local budget surplus carried over to next year?
Social	Is there someone else who can do your job if you are away?
Environmental	Does your job require specific environmental considerations?
Technological	Does your job require specific technological knowledge?

level of the problem is reflected in the knowledge of employees in practice regarding economic, social, environmental, and technological sphere.

The results show a minimum gap between that economic area with 60,87% and environmental area with 57,69%. Those areas present the most significant sustainability problem compared to the other areas. Instead, the social area shows the lower problem having a percentage of 19,23%. Furthermore, analysis concerning technological area ranks the latter in the middle of the four problematical sustainability areas and shows that this field has almost the same percentage (30%) between answers placed in the highest and lowest range.

Despite the different sizes of the sample examined compared to the previous analysis, the economic and environmental areas, which are usually the primary perception of sustainability, maintain their minimum gap still being the most problematic areas. Likewise, social sustainability is still the area which presents the minimum problem in enterprises' sustainability behavior. In this context, as the etymology of word sustainability suggests that it is essential to sustain the ability of the enterprise to create value to achieve long-term future development. Hence, to achieve this information, the analysis focuses on the questions below (see Table 2).

Table 2. Questions that aim to identify the ability to create future value in all sustainability areas.

Sustainability area	Question
Economic	Are you expected to keep spare financial reserves/resources?
Social	Do you get personal mentoring by an expert in your job?
Environmental	Do you get training/advice in environmentally friendly practices?
Technological	Do you get update training on the new technology?

The analysis shows that the technological area has the most considerable attention in the sustainment of employees' ability to create future value with the respective percentage of the high of 45,57% and medium-high 44,30% ranges. The environmental sphere ranks right behind the technological one having a percentage of 45%, and then there is the social area with 30% of high attention to the future. However, considering the percentages in the medium-high and lowest range, the social area in comparison to environmental (respectively having 5% and 20% in the lowest range) presents a higher ability to create value for the future. Instead, the economic sphere has the most critical situation having 36% in the lowest range, and further none of employees interviewed highly expect to keep spare financial resources as shows the miss presence of values in the highest range.

In comparison to 2019 findings, the economic field still results to be the area with critical attention to the future having the lowest results. In a pragmatic sense, economic value is the one that allows the development of the enterprise, but results show on the contrary that is the last to be pursued. Basically this suggests that there is a lack of incentive for employees to be financially prudent with business budgets. However, enterprises seemed to increase their attention to the environmental area on the one hand while at the same time decrease it in the social area on the other hand. Overall, despite factors such as test sample, size sample, time pass, there are only small differences in the results, the overall findings from 2019 and 2020 analysis seem to be coherent with each other.

3.2 Involvement in Practice

The involvement of each employee in sustainability practices is essential in the evalua-tion of sustainable practices of the whole enterprise. The authors hypothesize that if the employee, who is the smallest part of the enterprise' system, is involved in all sustainabil-ity areas in work practices, there is the interconnection between all areas and integration of the sustainability concept in practice. Hence, if the involvement exists in employee work practices, the enterprise should be oriented toward sustainable development.

Table 3. Questions that investigate the involvement of employees.

Sustainability area	Question
Economic	Is your work involving financial decisions?
Social	Are you involved in training of others in your job?
Environmental	Are you personally involved in recycling as part of your job?
Technological	Do you personally use technology in your job?

Questions in the table above (see Table 3) lead to uncovering if the employee is personally involved in sustainability practices in his/her job. The graph below (see Fig. 2) highlights that sustainability in economic and environmental areas have the lowest involvement of employees in work practices. Instead, analysis shows that the technological area presents the highest employee' involvement placing 22 enterprises on 26 in the highest range.

The environmental and economic sphere, in comparison to 2019 analysis, seems to decrease its involvement in practices. In 2019 the environmental area showed the highest number of enterprises which have the highest level of involvement of employee in practices (15 enterprises on 40) sub sequentially followed by the economic sphere. Instead, the social area seems to increase the level of involvement of employee in work practices. Overall, even though different sizes of samples affected the comparison, none of the enterprises showed the highest involvement of employees in each sustainability area instead both samples present a low number of enterprises in the highest involvement levels ranges.

Compared to results concerning future value, the technological area, which involves the most employees in practices is also the one on which the enterprises pay the highest level of attention to the creation of value for the future development. Furthermore, from a systemic perspective, the employee could be considered the smallest part who personifies the entire system. Therefore, if the employee is not involved in all four areas, effective sustainability is not pursued in practices as they miss the interaction between the different single sustainability areas, which together as a whole could improve and benefit the development of enterprise. In this context, analysis emphasizes that only 2 out of 26 enterprises involve each employee in all the areas of sustainability. Half of those enterprises additionally show a medium-high level of attention directed towards the creation of value for the future.

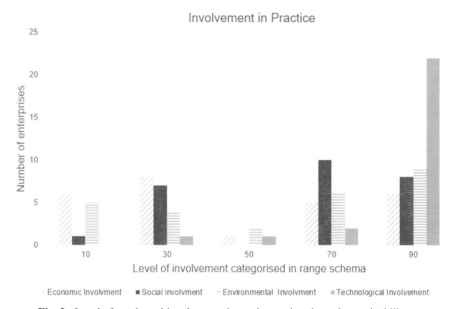

Fig. 2. Level of employee' involvement in work-practices in each sustainability area.

3.3 Problem in Practice

This area of the study relies on the new area' inquiry concerning 2020 research. In the previous paragraph, the problem was analysed under enterprise vision to sustainability to future development (see Table 2). Here, the authors intend to investigate the problem in work practices from employees' point of view. Hence, the focus is to understand if there is any problem in employees' sustainability work-practices and if they think to act in their job following sustainable practices analyzing questions below (see Table 4).

Furthermore, problems observed in all sustainability areas will be compared to problems in practice.

The graph (see Fig. 3) shows that the problem in the environmental area is serious as employees think that their job does not need specific environmental considerations. However, employees also assert to conduct their job respecting the environment showing low problems in practice. In this case, there could be a double problem deriving from enterprise and context, including a disconnection between aspiration and practice.

Table 4. Questions that investigate problem in practice.

Sustainability area	Question
Economic	Do you think to have the appropriate grade of freedom and responsibility in the work-related resource management?
Social	Do you think that your work is done respecting the environment?
Environmental	Do you think that the enterprise gives you the appropriate training for the various work activities?
Technological	Do you have any problem in the use of technology?

Enterprise seems to be unable to convey environmental sensitivity and knowledge concerning environmentally friendly practices to their employee. Additionally, employees, affirm to develop eco-friendly work while, at the same time, they do not express any environmental consideration about their job, do not pay attention to the environment also in their life context. Therefore, the whole context that surrounds the employees seems not to involve them to pursue environmental consideration from their personal to the enterprise context.

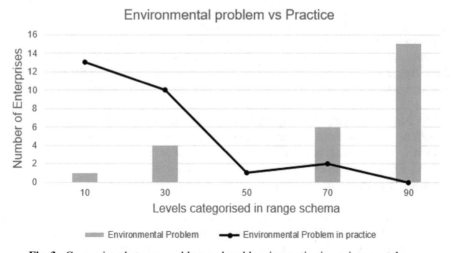

Fig. 3. Comparison between problem and problem in practice in environmental area.

The analysis illustrates that the economic area, as the environmental one, shows (see Fig. 4) a high sustainability problem and a problem in practice placed in the lowest range from employees' perspective. Indeed, even though employees believe to have the appropriate grade of freedom and responsibility in their job, they have low freedom on the financial and resource. Hence, employees seem to be passive as they do not want responsibility concerning the economics sphere, as they are used to receiving orders and passively using the information and resources received.

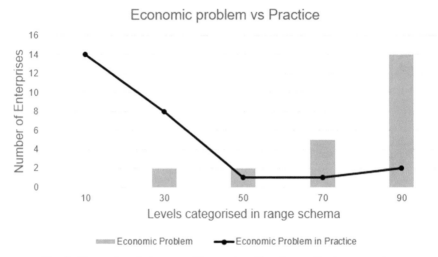

Fig. 4. Comparison between problem and problem in practice in economic area.

The technological area (see Fig. 5) highlights that the problem in employee work practices is lower than sustainability problem for the enterprises. Although employees do not show knowledge concerning technology used in their work practices, they affirm to use those technological tools do not experience any issue. Therefore, enterprises seem to give intuitive technology tools but not the appropriate knowledge to use it.

Furthermore, the graph below (see Fig. 6) describes the relationship between involvement in practice, decision making related to the technological field and the problem that employees have in practice. The graph shows two different scenarios:

- The case of "β" and "ε" enterprise highlight that if employees are fully involved in both work-practice and decision-making process which concerns technology to use in their job, problems in practice seems to lower as are placed in the lowest range.
- In contrary, enterprises "α", "γ", and "δ" underline that when the employees' involvement in decision is low problems in practice tend to increase.

Hence, the involvement of employee in the decision concerning technological tools seems to be a crucial point to avoid problems and increase collaboration in practice.

The analysis on social area shows (see Fig. 7) coherence between results from the sustainability problem and problem in practice. Furthermore, even if there is a high

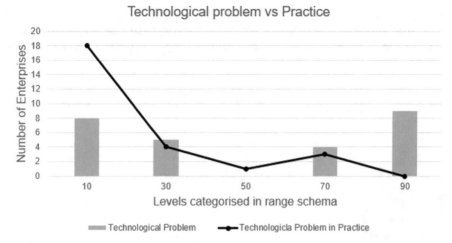

Fig. 5. Comparison between problem and problem in practice in technological area.

involvement of the employee in social sustainability work-practices and a large number of enterprises placed in the lowest range concerning the problem, the percentage of the enterprises with great attention to future social value seems to be low.

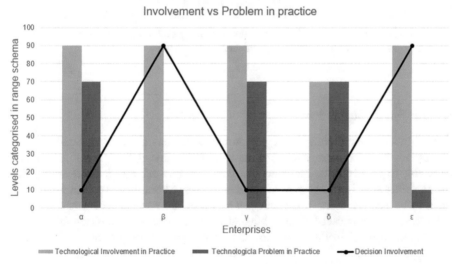

Fig. 6. Involvement of the employee in decision making and work-practice compared to the problem in practice concerning technological area.

However, upon closer inspection, there is a high involvement of employees in only a part of social sustainability work practices. Accurately, employees receive personal mentoring from an expert and are involved in training others; however, enterprises do not seem to include employees to external-stakeholder collaboration. Indeed, results show a high percentage of enterprise which do not collaborate with the local community and neighboring business. This lack of collaboration could underline the lack of attention of the enterprise to community relationship and ultimately loss of local support for their business.

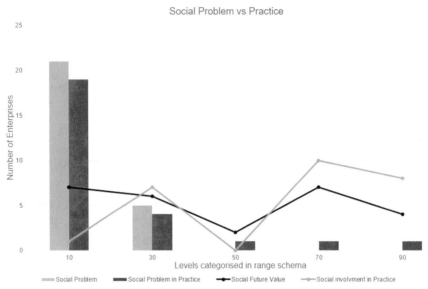

Fig. 7. Involvement of the employee in decision making and work-practice compared to the problem in practice concerning technological area.

3.4 Employee' Suggestions

The study will then directly investigate problems that employees underlined and their suggestions to solve them, aiming to improve their working life. Overall, employees were able to point out the problems that they face in work-practice concerning each sustainability area; however, they do not give any suggestions to solve them. Employees seem to be passive users in the enterprise as they are used to receiving orders and implementing them instead of being integrated into a proactive and collaborative vision.

This managerial method does not allow employees to be proactive. Instead, this method could lead them to be inactive, and thus they could become insensitive to give any suggestions. This perspective could be a problem for the enterprise as it could impede collaboration and integration practice. However, some employees gave some suggestions.

Concerning the economic area, employees suggest increasing the communication between them and management in order to make management understand their real work needs. Furthermore, employees suggest having more financial and resource freedom to deal with less bureaucracy to achieve their work needs and work better. Regarding the social sphere, the employees' suggestion is to receive full training. Employees require extended time and knowledge, and further, they seem to prefer individual training as the information received will be more effective. Concerning the environmental area, employees suggest incrementing the re-cycling policy reducing the paper waste. In this regard, employees propose to reduce prints having a technological work device. In the technological area, only three employees out of 88 proposed suggestions to possible solve problems. They suggest having external service for the enterprise concerning technologies and having additional training on them.

4 Discussion

Unpredictable events highlight the importance of resilience and flexibility of enterprises and human systems. Covid-19 causes dangerous respiratory diseases and, the vector of transmission is people. The virus, due to its facility of transmission epidemic, caused the lockdown in the world. Findings in Sect. 3 highlight the disconnection to sustainability, and this has an impact on every crisis. The world pandemic situation stood out the *"lack of planning and preparation for the lockdown which has starkly demonstrated the importance of resilience: the ability for human systems to anticipate, cope, and adapt"* which is sustainability roots [7]. Besides, this event sheds light that we are all part of the system being interdependent [8]. Hence, the virus points out lacks which could undermine sustainability in enterprises' practice. Covid-19 affected each area of systemic sustainability, highlighting their inter-dependencies.

Concerning the environmental area, researches seem to confirm that virus is carried out in pollution environments where there is a particulate matter [9, 10]. The particulate matter is in the air and develops in industrially polluted areas increasing the spread of the Covid-19 [10]. In this context, the lockdown of the world has potentially made us more conscious of the environmental damage that enterprises cause. Given the closure of enterprises reduced their pollutant work-practices, finding alternative ways to implement their business, pollution decreased, affecting the environment positively. Hence, there are ways to reduce pollution in favor of the environment. Enterprises have to focus on environmentally friendly work practices and understand the importance to have a healthy environment. Additionally, not only enterprises but the entire context to reduce crowding in closed space, for instance, metro and bus, encourage the use of bicycles to both the health of the environment and the individual. However, plastic pollution, concerning virus protective clothing, for instance, plastic gloves, is increasing due to the unsustainable behaviors of single individuals in their life context.

In this scenario, Covid-19 points out the importance of the social sphere highlighting the fundamental attention to the individual that enterprises and communities should have. Due to the pre-existent lacks in social sphere difficulties in the relationships between employee and enterprise increased. The pre-existent missed communication leads to an increment of the level of stress of employees. Therefore, the lack of presence of physical interaction demonstrates problems regarding employees' involvement and mental health in both life and work context. If an employee feels understood and comfortable and safe in their work context, he is likely to contribute passionately in his work. This dangerous situation before any pragmatical concern for enterprises highlights the value of employees. Enterprises who are adopting physical security measures or adapting their work in smart ways through technology highlight that they care not only for their business but also for their employees. Hence, employees became the central focus of enterprises valuing their health and knowledge to work together for a common goal. Each brick is crucial to building a house, so do each employee to the business, but this is only possible if the business is robust enough to cope with the changed business situation.

Besides, the complexity' of the situation underlined the importance of care to local communities and the importance of all stakeholders. For instance, Versace, Prada, Gucci, and Armani converted their business to produce useful materials for the world emergency, increasing their social value in the community [11, 12]. Giorgio Armani affirmed that "*the moment we are going through is turbulent, but it also offers us the unique opportunity to repair what is wrong, to regain a more human dimension*" which pursues the authenticity focusing not only on profit but also on different value creation [13].

Regarding the economic sphere, Covid-19 captured the no presence of economic sustainability showing most problems in practices. Economic sustainability, under a pragmatic perspective, is the first to be pursued. Hence, when there is a miss in practices is also the first area to be affected. Enterprises are not prepared to face the pandemic situation under economic sustainability perspective as they do not have sufficient diversification and flexibility in their business model and practices. Businesses which are based and dependent only on physical shops or services suffer majorly do not having the possibilities to carry on their activities. However, businesses that have an online presence do not seem to be affected in the same grade by the crisis. Economic sustainability could be achieved following the Nintendo example, which invests in different kinds of businesses involving managers in long-term prospects treat them as family members in the company and trusting of their teams [14].

In this context, technology use and adaptation seems to be essential to pursue business goals. Covid-19 pushed the limits of technologies, highlighting ways how technology could be useful to pursue sustainability in practice. This pandemic period accelerated technological innovation in almost every field, effecting long term changes in businesses [15]. Technological tools, now more than ever, are crucial to reducing distances to able smart working to increase social sustainability and individual health. Overall, from the pandemic situation caused by Covid-19 emerges the need to develop businesses under a more sustainable vision underlying lacks and possible changes to implement in practice. In this context, a holistic and socio-cultural approach based on dependencies to context is crucial to pursue organizational changes.

5   Conclusion

One of the main themes coming out of this research was that employees are not involved directly in key decision-making aspects within the context of their professional work. Abilities and capabilities in practice are the essential concern that underpinned competitive advantage designed to support enterprise development in incessant changes a context full of un-predictable events. One of the events which caused changes and had the most influence is the Covid-19 virus. The latter highlighted the missing ability and capabilities of enterprises to face critical situations pointing out their sustainability lacks. In this context, abilities, capabilities, and the involvement of each stakeholder in practice are crucial to achieving a common development goal. The involvement, capability and the ability of each employee are essential to able flexibility. Hence, employees should have responsibilities, resources and be valued in their practices both in knowledge and abilities to trigger their proactive actions which could be essential to sustain and support the business in the long term.

The study emphasizes the lack of proactivity of employees, highlighting that the current managerial approach could be counterproductive as a way to support the business resilience and robustness long term. Employees overall suggest increasing knowledge sharing and communication, which are the fundamental factors underpinned to collaboration. Collaboration is the base for community support, evolution and progress being essential to develop competitive advantages. In the movie "Beautiful mind" Nash suggests that *"best result will come when everyone in the group doing what's best for himself and the group"* [16]. Hence, enterprises need to work together and collaborate with their stakeholders into the respect of sustainability goal. However, analysis of employee vision underlined that they are not fully involved and integrated into sustainability work practices and emphasize a significant lack of collaboration in practice.

In future research, it could be interesting to understand how and at what level employees feel involved in sustainability introducing direct questions in the future oriented questionnaire. It could be useful to understand in what way employees would like to be involved in each sustainability areas. A question aims to explore the level of involvement, for instance, could be "How much do you feel involved in the economic sphere to a scale from 1 to 5? And How?". Furthermore, a future analysis could concern how Covid-19 impact on sustainability in practices comparing the current and future practices from employees' point of view. To this scope, questions that could be integrated into the 2021 questionnaire will focus on the development of any changes in sustainability practices. For instance, "Do you notice any changes regarding environmental practices before and after Covid-19? If yes, can you describe it?".

In conclusion, enterprises do not seem to integrate sustainability in work practices in any significant way, and used technology solutions do not seem to be integrated into an overall business oriented sustainability vision.

According to sociotechnical perspective, balance technology and the human factor enables the development of enterprises. Employees knowledge join to technological tool permits enterprises to be flexible and capable to face a critical situation. Therefore, it is crucial to involve employees to co-create and have a future regenerative development [17]. This inclusion could improve not only enterprise context but also employee life context introducing sustainable vision to the whole system. Enterprise benefits on drawing on the full knowledge and support of employees. Hence to sustain the capability and the ability of each part of the enterprise's system, and to favor co-creation, shall designate the development of sustainability in practice.

References

1. Craven, M., Singhal, S., Wilson, M.: Risk Practice COVID-19: Briefing Note, April 13, 2020 Our Latest Perspectives on the Coronavirus Pandemic. McKinsey & Company (2020)
2. Mumford, E.: Designing Human Systems for New Technology - The ETHICS Method (2020)

3. Mumford, E.: Redesigning Human Systems. IRM Press, Hershey (2003)
4. Bednar, P.: Sociotechnical Toolbox: Information System Analysis and Design. Craneswater Press Ltd., UK (2020)
5. Bednar, P.: Sociotechnical Toolbox: Information System Analysis and Design. Craneswater Press Ltd., UK (2018)
6. Elkington, J.: Enter the triple bottom line. In: Henriques, A., Richardson, J. (eds.) The Triple Bottom Line: Does It All Add Up?, pp. 1–16. Earthscan, London (2004)
7. Pascarella L., Bednar, P.: Systemic sustainability analysis in small and medium-sized enterprises (SMEs). In: The XVI Conference of the Italian Chapter of AIS (ITAIS), Naples, Italy (2019)
8. Florizone, R.: Three Ways the Coronavirus is Shaping Sustainable Development. IISD (2020). https://www.iisd.org/library/coronavirus-shaping-sustainable-development. Accessed 13 May 2020
9. Moss, K.: The Coronavirus Pandemic Could Give Business Leaders a Broader Mandate for Sustainability. World Resource Institute (2020). https://www.wri.org/blog/2020/04/corona virus-pandemic-could-give-business-leaders-broader-mandate-sustainability. Accessed 13 May 2020
10. Setti, L., et al.: Searching for SARS-COV-2 on particulate matter: a possible early indicator of covid-19 epidemic recurrence. Int. J. Environ. Res. Public Health 17, 2986 (2020)
11. Setti L., et al.: Relazione circa l'effetto dell'inquinamento da particolato atmosferico e la diffusione di virus nella popolazione, simaonlus (2020). https://www.simaonlus.it/wpsima/wp-content/uploads/2020/03/COVID19_Position-Paper_Relazione-circa-l%E2%80%99e ffetto-dell%E2%80%99inquinamento-da-particolato-atmosferico-e-la-diffusione-di-virus-nella-popolazione.pdf. Accessed 14 May 2020
12. Repubblica, D.: https://d.repubblica.it/moda/2020/03/23/news/coronavirus_brand_di_moda_producono_mascherine_gucci_prada_valentino_lvmh_kering-4701373/. Accessed 13 May 2020
13. Repubblica, D.: https://d.repubblica.it/moda/2020/04/15/news/intervista_a_giorgio_armani_la_moda_deve_rallentare-4713385/. Accessed 14 May 2020
14. How to survive the first 100 years of business- Lessons from Nintendo, Medium. https://medium.com/@japanesebusinessconcepts/how-to-survive-the-first-100-years-of-business-lessons-from-nintendo-f9657a0432a5. Accessed 14 May 2020
15. Elavarasan, R.M., Pugazhendhi, R.: Restructured society and environment: a review on potential technological strategies to control the COVID-19 pandemic. In: The Science of the Total Environment, 138858 (2020)
16. Wikiquote. https://en.wikiquote.org/wiki/A_Beautiful_Mind_(film). Accessed 3 June 2020
17. Hutchins, G., Storm, L.: Regenerative leadership: the DNA of life-affirming 21st century organizations (2019)

How Smart is This Working? Traces of Proactivity in the Italian Experience During Covid-19

Enrico Cori[1(✉)], Daria Sarti[2], and Teresina Torre[3]

[1] Department of Management, Polytechnic University of Marche, Ancona, Italy
e.cori@univpm.it
[2] Department of Economics and Management, University of Florence, Florence, Italy
daria.sarti@unifi.it
[3] Department of Economics and Business Studies, University of Genoa, Genoa, Italy
teresina.torre@economia.unige.it

Abstract. The purpose of this study is to analyse the adoption of proactive behaviours by smart workers and the role played by the remote support provided to employees in encouraging such behaviours during the COVID-19 lockdown. In detail, it aims at examining how two dimensions of proactivity, responsibility and self-regulation, can be fostered by the support from superiors, co-workers, and organisation. These topics are present in the debate on smart working (SW) among scholars and practitioners in the fields of human resource management and organisational behaviour and have assumed greater significance due to the sudden and unplanned switch to SW during the lockdown. A survey was carried out on a sample of 254 employees in Italy in May 2020. The findings demonstrate the importance of support from organisation and co-workers in encouraging proactive behaviours, as well as the positive role that such support, in turn, plays in reinforcing support from superiors.

Keywords: Proactive behaviour · Smart working · Organizational support · Superior's support · Co-workers' support · Responsibility · Self-regulation · COVID-19

1 Introduction

In recent times, new and alternative working styles are becoming more common as the traditional ways of working no longer meet the needs of organisations and their employees. In the early 2000s, the concept of smart working (SW) came into focus in Italian [1, 2, 3] as well as international [4, 5, 6] scholarly literature, as a new work arrangement challenging the conventional work modes and traditional systems of hierarchical

S. Za et al. (Eds.): ItAIS 2020, LNISO 50, pp. 41–58, 2022.
https://doi.org/10.1007/978-3-030-86858-1_3

control[1]. The main features of SW are greater flexibility in terms of working location and work timings [7, 8], greater discretion in work activities, and increased accountability. Organisations providing such SW practices are believed to elicit better performance from employees and foster positive competitiveness [9, 10], which is essential for the survival and growth of the organisation [11]. Such improved productivity reinforces the value of newly adopted SW models [12].

At the same time, as Morgan [13] remarked, many interesting technological changes are happening that have a relevant impact on work modes. The unexpected acceleration in the development and diffusion of new technologies supporting communication, collaboration, and social networking, together with the pervasive dissemination of powerful and easy-to-use mobile devices, has enabled the growth of portable workspaces [14, 15]. Such technologies have given rise to innovative solutions that allow workers to freely determine when to work, where to work, and how to work. It is now possible to work in relaxing conditions with better performance – which is the ideal form of SW according to a certain rhetoric associated with the SW model [16].

Even before the lockdown, some enterprises had been experimenting with SW as a feasible solution that balances conflicting needs, such as the company's need for efficiency and productivity and the individual's need for flexibility and work-life balance [17, 18]. Often, combined solutions were proposed which suggested that workers could go to work on most days of the week and do smart working on the remaining working days [5, 6]. However, smart working remained a niche practice, with smart workers only representing a small percentage of the total working population in Italy [19].

It was in this situation that Italy came to face with the COVID-19 pandemic. One of the first decisions of the Italian government was to kick-start the switch to SW across industries (and also to modify existing laws to facilitate its implementation). Suddenly, SW became the new normal, at least for those who were in occupations that could be performed remotely. Even enterprises that had never used SW suddenly had no choice but to embrace it. However, one of the basic characteristics of SW – the choice to work anywhere – was not feasible anymore because in the lockdown the only choice was to work at home, with all the inevitable implications it entailed.

This new scenario offered the possibility of observing the dynamics traditionally associated with SW in a context where elements that are considered fundamental for the success of SW were absent or not sufficiently present. These elements are: the planned and controlled transition from office working to smart working, the voluntary adoption of SW by employer and employee, an agreement between employer and employees regarding the expectations from such an arrangement, and the division of working time between the office and remote workplace.

In particular, the sudden and obligatory switch to SW without no preparation whatsoever persuaded us to focus on the role of perceived support in promoting high performance and full acceptance of SW. Furthermore, the urgency and inevitability of the

---

[1] Although we are aware that the term 'remote working' is the most used in the international literature, and that this expression is sufficiently generic to indicate any form of work carried out far from the institutional workplace, in this paper we prefer to use the expression 'smart working' since it is commonly used in Italy, and it has been used by the Italian Government during the COVID-19 lockdown to indicate it as the primary working mode.

transition to the new way of working led us to investigate some behavioural dynamics, such as the propensity to act proactively.

Traditionally, research on SW experiences focused primarily on its perceived benefits, such as better work-life balance and the impact on individual wellbeing. However, this study privileges the perspective of work analysis, with the aim of shedding light on organisational behaviours and its determinants in SW conditions. In particular, we think interesting and significant findings can be uncovered by investigating the relationship between support and employees' proactivity, which is, according to the literature [20, 21, 22, 23, 24, 25], one of the most critical features for the evolution of work.

We wonder if and to what extent, in the SW experience during the lockdown, support from superiors, colleagues, and organisations may have fostered the adoption of proactive behaviours in terms of perceived responsibility and self-regulation.

In order to pursue the goal of this study, the paper is organised in the following manner. In the second section, the theoretical background is presented, and our hypotheses are introduced. In the third part, we present the analysis and its most relevant results. In the last section, some preliminary suggestions in relation to our question are introduced together with the main limitations of our research; considerations useful for future development are also proposed.

2   Theoretical Background

The choice to focus on the analysis of the organisational behaviour of workers rather than on the perceived advantages and limits of SW during the lockdown has shaped the definition of the theoretical frame of reference.

Among the numerous studies that have focused on the earliest teleworking experiences up to the most recent initiatives inspired by the 'smart' or 'agile' work philosophy, we have selected those addressing the issues of superior-subordinate relations and peer relations, in terms of perceived support, as well as those focusing on the emergence or accentuation of proactive behaviours as a consequence of the detachment from the traditional workplace.

Studies on supportive and proactive behaviours in work contexts find their roots in numerous organisational theories. Nevertheless, the socio-cognitive perspective can be acknowledged as a common root, with particular reference to Social Cognitive Theory [26, 27] and Social Exchange Theory [28, 29]. However, the analysis of such behaviours in work situations assisted by technology recalls some of the main cornerstones of the socio-technical approach, such as those relating to the work system as a unit of analysis, to the idea of increasing organisational variety, and finally to the importance of discretionary behaviours compared to prescribed behaviours [30].

2.1   Perceived Responsibility and Self-regulation as Dimensions of Job Proactivity

Whereas the focus on control is naturally associated with the analysis of the achievement of predefined objectives or the adoption of behaviours in line with assigned tasks, the emphasis on supportive climate evokes the possibility that individuals adopt proactive behaviours.

We think that the work situations that arose during the lockdown period, characterised by the lack of physical contiguity with superiors and colleagues, could turn out to be propitious opportunities to foster the development of proactive work behaviour. Hence, our choice was to investigate whether this type of behaviour actually occurred and what are the antecedents and conditions that specifically enabled it.

The proactivity construct has been defined in various ways by scholars, depending on the adopted research perspective. Fundamental distinctions have been drawn between proactivity as a motivational state, as a process of generating goals and striving to achieve them, and finally as an outcome [31, 32, 33]. In addition, proactive personality has been identified as an antecedent of proactive behaviour [20, 32, 33]. A further distinction is proposed between different behavioural categories: proactive work behaviour, proactive person-environment fit behaviour, and proactive strategy behaviour [23]. For the purposes of this study, we consider those behaviours as proactive that are oriented towards taking initiative, anticipating events or problems, and exploring innovative paths and methods.

In turn, proactivity at work is considered capable of determining a series of outcomes, both at the individual and organisational level [21, 34, 35]. Bateman and Crant [21] observe that individuals who behave proactively can achieve higher job performance and significant career advancements, along with the gain of recognition of leadership skills by colleagues and subordinates. Moreover, companies reap benefit from the proactive behaviour of their employees such as better work relationships, development of anticipatory strategies, and the ability to initiate actions to gain competitive advantage rather than simply react to the moves of others.

In this study, we direct our attention towards two specific dimensions of proactivity at work: perceived responsibility and orientation towards self-regulation. These two dimensions often appear in organisational studies on proactivity [36, 37, 33].

Goodman and Svyantek [38: 259], with reference to the responsibility perceived by the employees in carrying out their job, describe responsibility as 'the feeling of being your own boss, not having to double-check all your decisions; when you have a job to do, knowing that it is your job'. In most studies, perceived, often referred to as felt, responsibility is regarded as an antecedent of proactive behaviour [39, 34, 35, 36, 37]. In particular, Parker, Bindl, and Strauss [32: 838] argue that 'felt responsibility for change also reflects employees' internalisation of values relevant to change and, as such, predict proactive work behaviour'. However, only in the conceptual model proposed by Wu and Parker [33], responsibility perception is explicitly indicated among the motivational mechanisms, which, in turn, induce processes for defining and pursuing proactive goals.

Similarly, the orientation towards self-regulation is considered to be a pre-requisite to the development of proactive behaviours [41, 32]. Given the numerous theoretical perspectives that have been applied to the topic, it is very difficult to trace back a shared meaning of the term self-regulation. For the purpose of this study, we consider self-regulation as a process that enables an individual to engage independently in goal-directed activities or feedback loops [42, 43, 44, 45, 45, 46]. According to Bandura and Woods [48: 408], 'self-regulation of motivation and performance attainments is governed by several mechanisms operating in concert (such as) affective self-evaluation, perceived self-efficacy for goal attainment, and personal goal setting'.

Among the studies on proactivity at work, a greater emphasis on this construct is placed by Frese and Fay [34: 170] who define their own conceptualization of personal initiative as 'one aspect of a general theory of self-regulation' and state that 'there is no personal initiative without self-regulation'. According to Parker, Bindl, and Strauss [32: 830], 'to understand what prompts, stifles, and shapes proactivity, one can look to motivation theories, particularly to self-regulation theory'. At the same time, they complain that, nonetheless, 'little attention has been given to the self-regulation process during proactivity' [32: 847] and underline its relevance in the goal generation and striving process.

Methodologically, a valid contribution to self-regulation studies is offered by Ten Brummelhuis, Halbesleben, and Prabhu [48], who proposed the 12-item New Ways of Working Scale, aimed at measuring the degree of control employees have over their work in terms of content, work times, work location, and communication tools.

2.2 Organisational Support, Superior's Support, and Co-workers' Support

The rapid spread of the COVID-19 pandemic has resulted in a sudden and forced change in the working space-time modalities from one day to the next. Thus, the particular contextual circumstances persuade us to focus our attention on employees' perceptions about the support offered by superiors, co-workers, and the organisation during the lockdown period in a condition where a gradual preparation for change was not possible.

The concepts of organisational support, superior's support, and co-workers' support have been studied since the late 1970s, especially within the socio-cognitive theoretical perspective, particularly in the context of the social exchange theory [28, 29]. Such studies have progressively aimed at deepening meanings, reciprocal relationships, and relationships with possible outcomes of the three identified levels of support at work.

In their first study, Eisenberger et al. [49: 501] defined perceived organisational support as 'the beliefs concerning the extent to which the organization values their contributions and care about their well-being', and asserted the existence of a positive relationship between perceived organisational support and absenteeism, arguing that 'perceived organisational support is assumed to increase the employee's effective attachment to the organization and his or her expectancy that greater work effort will be regarded' [49: 504]. Already in this seminal contribution, the idea therefore began to materialise that a high perception of organisational support can determine what a few years later, at the end of the 90s, was conceptualised as a proactive attitude at work. However, a subsequent study by Rhoades and Eisenberger [50: 702] stated that the perception of organisational support is more clearly linked to the assumption of greater responsibilities than those formally assigned, thus configuring extra-role behaviour.

At least in the early studies, it is difficult to distinguish the meaning of a superior's support from that of organisational support [50]. Babin and Boles [51: 60] define superior's support as 'the degree to which employees perceive that superiors offer employees' support, encouragement and concern' and verify the existence of a positive relationship between supervisory support and job satisfaction.

In line with Fuchs and Prouska [52: 8–9] we look at perceived superior's support as 'the degree to which employees believe that their superiors care about them and value their work contributions', and perceived co-workers' support as 'the degree to which employees perceive that their co-workers care about their well-being and respect their contributions to the organization'. Organisational support is defined as the extent to which 'the organization cares about their employees and values the relationship to them' [53: 102], a definition that strongly recalls that of Eisenberger et al. [49].

In the early studies, co-workers' support is considered one of the three forms of 'social support', together with superior's support and support from family and friends [54, 55]. Scholars especially emphasise its ability to mitigate occupational stress caused by job-related strain and health concerns in an even more pervasive way than superior's support, without assuming a relationship between the two forms. Once it gained dignity as an autonomous object of study, the role of co-workers' support is pointed out in one of the pioneer studies on telework, by Teo, Lim, and Wai [56], before even the support from superiors and the organisation was investigated. They considered superior and work colleagues' support among the variables that can significantly influence the decision to telework. Almost 20 years later, another study on telework, precisely on the effects of this on the well-being of workers, jointly considers superior's support and co-workers' support as elements of perceived social support, distinguishing the latter from that of perceived organisational support [57: 208]. Finally, it is worth noting the study by Collins et al. [58], in which the selective preference of teleworkers to seek the support of co-workers rather than superiors is highlighted in a relationship pattern that evolves over time and in relation to the intensity of the teleworking experience.

Among the studies on the constructs of organisational support, superior's support, and colleagues' support, many authors find evidence to support relationships with dimensions of the firm's performance and workers' well-being. Wayne, Shore, and Liden [59] suggest a significantly positive relationship between perceived organisational support on the one hand, and organisational citizenship behaviours and affective commitment on the other. Stinglhamber and Vandenberghe [60] identify a link between perceived superior support, affective commitment to the superior, and turnover. Kowalski and Swanson [61] underline how the impact on the performance and satisfaction of teleworkers is determined by mutually reinforcing relationships between trust, communication, and superior's support. Fuchs and Prouska [52] demonstrate that perceived organisational support, perceived superior support, and perceived co-workers' support all correlate positively with change evaluation. Bentley et al. [57] find that perceived superior, co-worker, and organisational support are positively related to job satisfaction and negatively related to psychological strain and social isolation. Finally, Sungu et al. [62] demonstrate that perceived organisational support positively influences job performance and job satisfaction both directly and indirectly through the mediating role of affective organisational commitment.

However, to the best of our knowledge, with the exception of the aforementioned contribution by Rhoades and Eisenberger [50], no study has investigated the mediating roles of the three variables – organisational support, superior's support, and colleagues' support – in predicting proactivity.

2.3 Hypotheses and Model

Despite the large number of studies acknowledging the effect of these three variables together on different individual and organisational outcomes, the relationships between the three single levels of support are scarcely investigated in the literature and univocal indications by scholars are not always provided. Specifically, literature on the relationship between superior's and co-workers' support is very scant. Only a few studies have investigated their relationship purposefully and found sound evidence. For example, a significant and positive correlation between superior's support and co-workers' support has been shown by Yang et al. [63], while studying the effects of superior's and co-workers' support on job stress and presenteeism. However, the evidence from this study is limited, since the survey is circumscribed to older employees. Other authors in the investigation of the relationship between the two variables [64] found a positive and significant correlation between perceived superior and co-workers' support; however, they failed to demonstrate a positive interaction between the two variables in predicting a specific outcome, that is, service recovery performance in the hospitality industry.

Despite this lack of empirical evidence, we believe that the confirmation of this relationship is useful in investigating the determinants of proactive behaviour.

Thus, we posit:

Hp1 – Superior's support has a positive and significant relationship with co-workers' support.

For their part, Newman et al. [65] found a significant and positive relationship between co-workers' support and organisational support. In their study, aimed at analysing how the support of bosses and superiors influences the intention of employees to leave the company, they verify how the relationship between the support of superiors and colleagues on the one hand, and turnover intention on the other are mediated by perceived organisational support. In particular, the authors highlight that employees who possess greater expressive network resources, that is relationships with co-workers providing psychosocial support and feedback, feel more supported by their organisation [65: 14]. Furthermore, they find a positive relationship between perceived superior support and organisational support, also demonstrating the mediation effect of perceived organisational support in the relationship between perceived superior's support and affective commitment [65]. In addition, some studies demonstrated that perceived organisational support was influenced by a number of variables, including perceived coworkers' support [66] and co-workers' quality of communication [67].

Thus, we posit:

Hp2: Co-workers' support has a positive and significant relationship with organisational support.

As far as the relationships between the three forms of support and the outcome dimensions are concerned, previous studies have proven a fair variety of links. Parker, Williams, and Turner [31] show a relationship between co-workers' trust and proactivity at work, where co-workers' trust is seen as having the effect of peers encouraging personal initiative. Furthermore, a positive relationship is hypothesised between leadership support, co-workers' support, and proactivity at work by Parker, Bindl, and Strauss [32], where supportive behaviours are considered context variables having a positive impact on proactive motivational states, proactive goal generation, and proactive goal striving (including self-regulation). However, only Rhoades and Eisenberger [49] implicitly refer to the existence of a relationship between perceived organisational support and proactivity. In fact, they observe a relationship of medium intensity between organisational support and 'actions favourable to the organization that go beyond assigned responsibilities' [49: 702]. The study of Martinez-Sanchez et al. [8] indirectly supports the link between perceived organisational support and proactive behaviour. Although the variables related to organisational support and job proactivity do not explicitly appear in their conceptual model, the authors suggest how 'HR development practices favour the adoption of discretionary efforts by employee (…) through its impact on the organisational support that employees perceive' [8: 211], where the adoption of discretionary efforts can be associated both with the willingness to assume greater responsibilities than those assigned and with the propensity to self-regulation.

Thus, we posit:

Hp3 - Organisational support has a positive and significant relationship with perceived responsibility.

Hp4 - Organisational support has a positive and significant relationship with self-regulation.

The weak relationship between superior's support and proactive behaviours highlighted in the literature has led us to argue the possible existence of both a direct and an indirect link between support by superiors and the two outcome dimensions representing proactivity.

In this vein, we argue that during the COVID-19 pandemic, superior's support is positively related to proactivity both directly and indirectly. Considering the favourable effect of the social dimension of the job on individual attitudes (e.g. [68, 69]) and our previous hypotheses, we argue that the superior's support experienced during the pandemic may increase the perception of co-workers' support, which, in turn, increases work proactivity. In addition, using the same rationale, superior's support is positively related to the perception of organisational support, which in turn is related to work proactivity. Thus, in addition to these two simple mediation processes, we also posit a sequential, mediated process in which both co-workers' support and organisational support serve as mediators between superior's support and proactivity. Therefore, we hypothesise the following:

Hp5: The positive relationship between superior's support and the outcome variable (perceived responsibility) is sequentially double-mediated by co-workers' support and organisational support.

Hp6: The positive relationship between superior's support and the outcome variable (i.e. self-regulation) is sequentially double-mediated by co-workers' support and organisational support.

The hypotheses are presented in Fig. 1, with the total effect representing the sum of the direct and indirect effects of superior's support on the dependent variables.

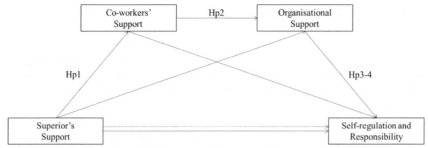

Hp5: Superior's support → Co-workers' support →Organisational support → Responsibility
Hp6: Superior's support → Co-workers' support → Organisational support → Self-regulation

Fig. 1. The research model. Direct (continuous lines) and total (dashed line) effects.

3 Empirical Analysis

3.1 Method

A questionnaire was administered to employees adopting SW during the COVID-19 lockdown period. A quantitative method was used for the analysis of the survey data. The rationale for choosing a quantitative approach for this study is based on the recognised advancements in the research on SW; the debate on SW is rich in emerging constructs and empirical contributions investigating its individual and organisational outcomes as well as the individual and organisational conditions enabling SW implementation [4]. In addition, the constructs that are herein investigated – such as proactivity (e.g.[35]) and measures of organisational, superior's, and co-workers' support [56] – have been already studied in the literature of managerial psychology and human resource management, and statistically validated measures are available.

Thus, the empirical research was based on the data gathered through an original questionnaire developed using both established scales (see variables table) and new items (useful to deepen other aspects of the workers' experience). It was distributed across a population of smart workers during the COVID-19 pandemic lockdown in Italy, using the software Lime Survey.

For the purpose of this analysis, we considered the following variables: perceived responsibility, self-regulation behaviours, and the three dimensions of perceived support.

A total of 320 questionnaire access codes were distributed and 254 people fully completed the questionnaire; thus, the response rate was 79.4%.

3.2 Variables

The dependent variables used are employees' *self-regulation* and employees' *perceived responsibility*. They are measured using two validated scales already present in the literature. Cronbach's alpha was used as the scale reliability coefficient.

For the variable *self-regulation*, the scale was previously used by Ten Brummelhuis, Halbesleben, and Prabhu [70]. The range of responses was based on a five-point scale ranging from 1 = 'decreased a lot' to 5 = 'increased a lot'. Cronbach's alpha was .869.

For *perceived responsibility*, the scale was taken from the previous study of Goodman and Svyantek [38]. The range of responses was based on a five-point scale ranging from 1 = 'decreased a lot' to 5 = 'increased a lot'. Cronbach's alpha was .877.

The independent variable *superior's support* was measured with four questions taken from a previous study by Teo, Lim, and Wai [56]. The range of responses was based on a five-point scale ranging from 1 = 'decreased a lot' to 5 = 'increased a lot'. Cronbach's alpha was .952.

The mediating variable *co-workers' support* was measured with four questions taken from a previous study by Teo, Lim, and Wai [56]. The range of responses was based on a five-point scale ranging from 1 = 'decreased a lot' to 5 = 'increased a lot'. Cronbach's alpha was .941.

The mediating variable *organisational support* was measured with 7 questions taken from previous studies by Teo, Lim, and Wai [56] and by Selart, Johansen, and Nesse [53]. The range of responses was based on a five-point scale ranging from 1 = 'decreased a lot' to 5 = 'increased a lot'. Cronbach's alpha was .918.

In addition, some control variables were included considering their possible impact on the dependent variables in the analysis. These were *age* (1 = 25–34, 2 = 35–39, 3 = 40–44, 5 = 50–54, 6 = 55 and higher), *gender* (1 = female, 2 = male), and *education level* (ranging from 1 = high school education to 7 = tertiary education, advanced level) (Table 1).

Table 1. The variables used in the study: name, number of items, reference, example of items, and Cronbach's alpha.

Variable name	Nr. of items	Reference	Example of item	Cronbach's Alpha
Superior's support	4	[56]	I was able to rely on my supervisor/boss for assistance when I encountered difficulties	.952
Co-workers' support	4	[56]	I was able to count on my work colleagues to help me solve any problems	.941
Organizational support	7	[56] [53]	I am satisfied with the information received regarding how my company is facing this crisis	.918
Self-regulation	4	[70]	I was more free to decide how to do my job	.869
Responsibility	8	[38]	I have been led to take on more responsibility than those assigned to my job	.877

3.3 Analysis and Results

Data were empirically analysed using SPSS and the PROCESS macro developed by Hayes and Emerson [71] in order to test the research hypothesis previously reported.

The sample in this study was composed of 44.8% females. Of the respondents, 39% were between 25 and 34 years old, 12% between 35 and 39 years old, 8% between 40 and 44 years old, 9% between 45 and 49 years old, 14% between 50 and 54, and 18 were aged 55 or more. Approximately 35% of respondents held a high school diploma, 21% had a bachelor's degree, 41% held a master's degree, and 3% had a PhD.

Evidence resulting from the analysis and depicted in Figs. 2 and 3 shows that perceived superior's support positively and significantly affects co-workers' support (Hp1), which in turn affects organisational support (Hp2). Thus, both Hp1 and Hp2 are confirmed.

Further, it is demonstrated that organisational support affects both responsibility and self-regulation, thus supporting Hp3 and Hp4.

The results also demonstrate that both superior's support and co-workers' support indirectly affect positive employee outcomes in conditions of crisis through the effect of the perception of organisational support. Specifically, the data highlighted in Figs. 2 and 3 demonstrate the absence of a direct effect between the predicting variable (superior's support) and dependent variables (responsibility and self-regulation) in the two models. Thus, we have an indirect-only mediation effect [72]. The indirect effect is significant in the absence of a direct effect for both dependent variables measuring employees' positive attitudes, that is, responsibility and self-regulation. Thus, Hp5 and Hp6 are supported.

In other words, the effect of superior's support on both perceived responsibility and self-regulation operates fully and only through the intervening variables of co-workers' support and organisational support. Perceived superior's support positively affects organisational support perception, which, in turn, positively affects the outcomes investigated here.

Therefore, the specific relationships between the three variables of support present in any organisational context are demonstrated. Moreover, this result reinforces the importance of the social and relational dimensions of the organisation, which become even more relevant in the absence of physical proximity.

In addition to the double mediating effect, the results of our study have shown that there are two mediating effects, one for each model: superior's support→ organisational support→ perceived responsibility (Fig. 2) and superior's support→ organisational support→ self-regulation (Fig. 3).

Thus, for responsibility (see Fig. 2), the indirect effect is significant for superior's support → organisational support → responsibility and superior's support → co-workers' support → organisational support → responsibility. As for self-regulation, (see Fig. 3) the indirect effect is significant for superior's support, organisational support, and self-regulation.

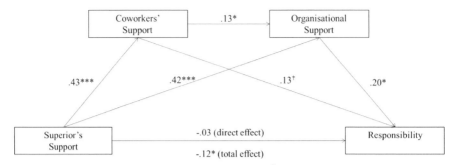

Dashed lines are used for insignificant relationships.

Fig. 2. Effects of organisational support on employees' perceived responsibility.

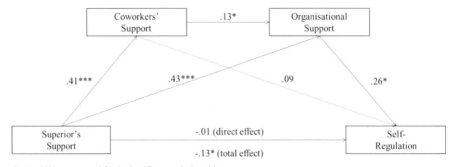

Dashed lines are used for insignificant relationships.

Fig. 3. Effects of organisational support on employees' self-regulation.

4   Conclusions, Limitations, and Further Research

The aim of this study was to investigate whether and how the full immersion in the SW experience lived by workers during the COVID-19 lockdown enhanced the development of their proactivity. Furthermore, we argued whether and how this effect can become long-lasting or at least produce new lessons for future practice.

The study brings attention to the influence of three forms of workplace-based support – organisational support, superior's support, co-workers' support – on two dimensions, perceived responsibility and self-regulation, which are key-components of employees' proactivity.

We think that the sudden and unavoidable switch to SW may have encouraged many workers to strengthen their propensity to take responsibility and to express a greater capacity for self-regulation. Therefore, we examined those tendencies as outcome variables. The choice of support as an independent variable was based on the consideration that it (in the different forms it assumes) represents a fundamental element in promoting proactive behaviours, and this is especially true when the SW is performed without preparation, as it was the case during the COVID-19 pandemic.

The results of our study represent a first step forward in understanding conditions that boost proactive behaviours when working remotely.

The analysis shows that the absence of a planned transition from the traditional way of working to SW did not inhibit the ability of workers to perform their task effectively and to cope with uncertain situations and associated problems, contrary to the expectation that a sudden and haphazard change forced by a pandemic would hamper effectiveness. We believe that this result can be explained by the pre-existence of favourable organisational conditions for SW. We can reasonably assume that these conditions are primarily traceable to an organizational culture, in which the value of cooperation is strongly shared and a managerial style emphasizing the role of superiors as those helping employees to perform their work and tasks so to pursue the organizational goals is recommended.

With regard to the opportunities offered by better and motivating conditions, it is noteworthy that despite the fact that SW was not chosen voluntarily but imposed upon workers, virtuous behavioural dynamics oriented towards proactivity at work were activated, offering interesting insights in favour of an ongoing adoption of SW.

In particular, our results highlight the importance of encouraging all kinds of supportive actions investigated here as enablers of employees' positive attitudes at work. This is relevant in the awareness that supportive actions at the organisational level, during a period marked by social distancing and isolation may be considered more important by employees compared to other kinds of support, which, rather, in 'normal' conditions, are proven to directly affect employees' behaviours and attitudes. However, the need of a 'behind the scenes' strategy put in place by superiors is also required for ensuring that the positive perception of organisational support enables employees' positive behaviours. When people are present in the workplace, the physical proximity with colleagues and superiors makes it easy for them to perceive the supportive environment of the organisation; but when they are far away from the workplace, this perception becomes weaker.

The current study is intended to help find opportunities of developing and reinforcing proactive behaviours associated with different modes of SW. In this sense, our research confirms the importance of companies carefully monitoring and maintaining the social and relational tissue of their organisation. Particularly, a general attitude of co-workers' mutual support encouraged by superiors' positive attitudes towards cooperative behaviours is suggested. Companies must encourage supportive behaviours, suitably managing both cultural and organisational dimensions. Indeed, this seems to be the most significant indication for entrepreneurs and managers, who during the lockdown period experienced this way of working for the first time, and who wished to continue in using it as a normal practice. The findings of this study could serve as evidence on the basis of which companies can implement policies and training interventions aimed at raising awareness of the importance of social support and at creating effective organization-employee communication channels for supportive purposes, the effect of which can be really beneficial and appreciated especially in emergency conditions like the COVID-19 pandemic.

The present study has some limitations. First, as the study was limited to a sample of Italian employees, generalised conclusions regarding the model's predictions cannot be made. Second, as the variables were measured via a common method and source, there may be some systematic bias in asking the same respondents about both dependent and independent variables. In addition, the cross-sectional design adopted is a limitation that precludes any causal conclusions. However, in order to guarantee the anonymity of the respondents on such sensitive issues, the chosen method is the only viable one for collecting such data. The use of multiple sources and longitudinal analysis is thus impossible in this context.

Further research may be primarily oriented to extend the survey to a larger sample of the population involved in SW during the lockdown, in order to obtain greater data reliability. A second line of development could concern an in-depth analysis searching to understand the different forms of support, whether it can be mediated by technology or whether it should involve face-to-face contact, and the amount of support that is ideal for eliciting proactive behaviours. In this sense, a qualitative approach could be used fruitfully to enquire about personal experiences and to get more detailed information; this seems particularly useful since individual perceptions are to be investigated. For example, through a focus group, it would be possible to make a comparison between significant experiences in different sectors, detecting common traits and substantial differences. Moreover, it is important to verify to what extent the positive effect on the propensity to assume greater responsibility and self-regulation is determined by the combination of the three types of support. It is possible that emotions linked with stepping up to face a crisis facing the company and the entire community may have played a non-marginal role in the proactive attitude assumed by many SW employees during the pandemic.

References

1. Boorsma, B., Mitchell, S.: Work-life innovation, smart work. a paradigm shift transforming: how, where, and when work gets done, San Jose, CA, Cisco Internet Business Solutions Group (IBSG) (2011). https://www.cisco.com/c/dam/en_us/about/ac79/docs/ps/ps/Work-Life_Innovation_Smart_Work.pdf. Accessed 25 Jan 2021
2. Chartered Institute of Personnel and Development - CIPD and Capgemini: Smart working: The impact of work organization and job design. Research insight. London, United Kingdom (2008)
3. Lee, J.: Cross-disciplinary knowledge: desperate call from business enterprises in coming smart working era. Technol. Econ. Dev. Econ. **19**(sup1), 285–303 (2013)
4. Gastaldi, L., Corso, M., Raguseo, E., Neirotti, P., Paolucci, E., Martini, A.: 'Smart working: rethinking work practices to leverage employees' innovation potential'. In: Proceedings of 15th CINet Conference 'Operating Innovation - Innovating Operations', Budapest (Hungary), September 7–9, pp. 337–347 (2014)
5. Torre, T., Sarti, D.: Into smart work practices: which challenges for the HR department? In: Ales, E., Curzi, Y., Fabbri, T., Rymkevich, O., Senatori, I., Solinas, G. (eds.) Working in Digital and Smart Organizations, pp. 249–275. Springer, Cham (2018). https://doi.org/10.1007/978-3-319-77329-2_12
6. Torre, T., Sarti, D.: Themes and trends in smart working research: a systematic analysis of academic contributions. In: Imperatori, B., Bissola, R. (eds.) HRM 4.0 for Human-centered Organizations, pp. 177–200. Emerald Publishing Limited (2019). https://doi.org/10.1108/S1877-636120190000023014

7. Brewer, A.M.: Work design for flexible work scheduling: barriers and gender implications. Gend. Work. Organ. **7**(1), 33–44 (2000)
8. Martínez-Sánchez, A., Pérez-Pérez, M., De-Luis-Carnicer, P., Vela-Jiménez, M.J.: Telework, human resource flexibility and firm performance. New Technol. Work. Employ. **22**(3), 208–223 (2007)
9. Haines, V.Y., III., St-Onge, S.: Performance management effectiveness: practices or context? Int. J. Human Resour. Manage. **23**(6), 1158–1175 (2012)
10. Wood, S., Van Veldhoven, M., Croon, M., de Menezes, L.M.: Enriched job design, high involvement management and organizational performance: the mediating roles of job satisfaction and well-being. Human Relations **65**(4), 419–445 (2012)
11. Matejun, M.: The role of flexibility in building the competitiveness of small and medium enterprises. Management **18**(1), 154–168 (2014)
12. Chiaro, G., Prati, G., Zocca, M.: Smart working: dal lavoro flessibile al lavoro agile. Sociologia Del Lavoro **138**, 69–87 (2015). https://doi.org/10.3280/SL2015-138005
13. Morgan, J.: The Future of Work: Attract New Talent, Build Better Leaders, and Create A Competitive Organization. Wiley, Hoboken, NJ (2014)
14. Ahuja, M.K., Chudoba, K.M., Kacmar, C.J., McKnight, D.H., George, J.F.: IT road warriors: balancing work-family conflict, job autonomy, and work overload to mitigate turnover intentions. MIS Q. **31**(1), 1–17 (2007)
15. Barnes, S.J., Pressey, A.D., Scornavacca, E.: Mobile ubiquity: understanding the relationship between cognitive absorption, smartphone addiction and social network services. Comput. Hum. Behav. **90**, 246–258 (2019)
16. Clapperton, G., Vanhoutte, P.: The Smart Working Manifesto. Sunmakers, Oxford, UK (2014)
17. Felstead, A., Henseke, G.: Assessing the growth of remote working and its consequences for effort, well-being and work-life balance. New Technol. Work. Employ. **32**(3), 195–212 (2017)
18. Torre, T., Sarti, D.: Innovative approaches to work organization and new technologies. first insight from the Italian context. In: Baghdadi, Y., Harfouche, A., Musso, M. (eds.) ICT for an inclusive world. LNISO, vol. 35, pp. 133–145. Springer, Cham (2020). https://doi.org/10.1007/978-3-030-34269-2_11
19. Politecnico di Milano: Osservatorio Smart Working, report dei risultati della ricerca 2019. Politecnico di Milano, Milano (2019)
20. Bateman, T.S., Crant, J.M.: The proactive component of organizational behavior: a measure and correlates. J. Organ. Behav. **14**(2), 103–118 (1993)
21. Bateman, T.S., Crant, J.M.: Proactive behavior. meaning, impact, recommendations. Bus. Horiz. **42**(3), 63–70 (1999)
22. Parker, S.K.: From passive to proactive motivation: the importance of flexible role orientations and role breadth self-efficacy. Appl. Psychol. **49**(3), 447–469 (2000)
23. Parker, S.K., Collins, C.G.: Taking stock: integrating and differentiating multiple proactive behaviors. J. Manag. **36**(3), 633–662 (2010)
24. Bindl, U.K., Parker, S.K.: Proactive work behavior: forward-thinking and change-oriented action in organizations. In: Zedeck, S. (ed.) APA Handbook of Industrial and Organizational Psychology. Vol. Selecting and Developing Members for the Organization., pp. 567–598. American Psychological Association, Washington (2011). https://doi.org/10.1037/12170-019
25. Bakker, A.B., Tims, M., Derks, D.: Proactive personality and job performance: The role of job crafting and work engagement. Human relations **65**(10), 1359–1378 (2012)
26. Wood, R., Bandura, A.: Social cognitive theory of organizational management. Acad. Manag. Rev. **14**(3), 361–384 (1989)
27. Bandura, A.: Social cognitive theory of self-regulation. Organ. Behav. Hum. Decis. Process. **50**(2), 248–287 (1991)

28. Emerson, R.M.: Social exchange theory. Ann. Rev. Sociol. **2**(1), 335–362 (1976)
29. Cropanzano, R., Mitchell, M.S.: Social exchange theory: an interdisciplinary review. J. Manag. **31**(6), 874–900 (2005)
30. Trist, E.: The evolution of socio-technical systems. a conceptual framework and an action research program (1981). https://www.lmmiller.com/blog/wp-content/uploads/2013/06/The-Evolution-of-Socio-Technical-Systems-Trist.pdf. Accessed 25 Jan 2021
31. Parker, S.K., Williams, H.M., Turner, N.: Modeling the antecedents of proactive behavior at work. J. Appl. Psychol. **91**(3), 636–652 (2006)
32. Parker, S.K., Bindl, U.K., Strauss, K.: Making things happen: a model of proactive motivation. J. Manag. **36**(4), 827–856 (2010)
33. Wu, C., Parker, S.K.: 'Proactivity in the Work Place: Looking Back and Looking Forward' in The Oxford Handbook of Positive Organizational Scholarship, pp. 84–96. Oxford University Press, Oxford (2011)
34. Frese, M., Fay, D.: 4. Personal initiative: an active performance concept for work in the 21st century. Res. Organ. Behav. **23**, 133–187 (2001)
35. Crant, J.M.: Proactive behavior in organizations. J. Manag. **26**(3), 435–462 (2000)
36. Thomas, J.P., Whitman, D.S., Viswesvaran, C.: Employee proactivity in organizations: a comparative meta-analysis of emergent proactive constructs. J. Occup. Organ. Psychol. **83**(2), 275–300 (2010)
37. Tornau, K., Frese, M.: Construct clean-up in proactivity research: a meta-analysis on the nomological net of work-related proactivity concepts and their incremental validities. Appl. Psychol. **62**(1), 44–96 (2013)
38. Goodman, S.A., Svyantek, D.J.: Person-organization fit and contextual performance: do shared values matter. J. Vocat. Behav. **55**(2), 254–275 (1999)
39. Morrison, E.W., Phelps, C.C.: Taking charge at work: extra-role efforts to initiate workplace change. Acad. Manag. J. **42**(4), 403–419 (1999)
40. Grant, A.M., Parker, S.K.: 7 redesigning work design theories: the rise of relational and proactive perspectives. Acad. Manag. Ann. **3**(1), 317–375 (2009)
41. Fay, D., Sonnentag, S.: A look back to move ahead: New directions for research on proactive performance and other discretionary work behaviours. Appl. Psychol. **59**(1), 1–20 (2010)
42. Kanfer, F.H.: Self-regulation: Research, issues and speculations. In: Neurunger, C., Michael, L. (eds.) Behavioural Modification in Clinical Psychology, pp. 178–220. Appleton Century Crofts, New York (1990)
43. Karoly, P.: Mechanisms of self-regulation: a systems view. Ann. Rev. Psychol. **44**(1), 23–52 (1993)
44. Vohs, K.D., Baumeister, R.F.: 'Understanding self-regulation. An Introduction' in Handbook of Self-regulation, pp. 1–13. Guilford Press, New York (2004)
45. Zimmerman, B.J.: Attaining self-regulation. In: Boekaerts, M., Pintrich, P., Zeidner, M. (eds.) Handbook of Self-regulation, pp. 13–35. Academic Press, San Diego (2001)
46. Porath, C.L., Bateman, T.S.: Self-regulation: from goal orientation to job performance. J. Appl. Psychol. **91**(1), 185–192 (2006)
47. Bandura, A., Wood, R.: Effect of perceived controllability and performance standards on self-regulation of complex decision-making. J. Pers. Soc. Psychol. **56**(5), 805–814 (1989)
48. Ten Brummelhuis, L.L., Halbesleben, J.R.B., Prabhu, V.: 'Development and validation of the new ways of working scale. In: Annual meeting of the Southern Management Association, Savannah, GA (2011)
49. Eisenberger, R., Huntington, R., Hutchison, S., Sowa, D.: Perceived organizational support. J. Appl. Psychol. **71**(3), 500–507 (1986)
50. Rhoades, L., Eisenberger, R.: Perceived organizational support: a review of the literature. J. Appl. Psychol. **87**(4), 698–714 (2002)

51. Babin, B.J., Boles, J.S.: The effects of perceived co-worker involvement and supervisor support on service provider role stress, performance and job satisfaction. J. Retail. **72**(1), 57–75 (1996)
52. Fuchs, S., Prouska, R.: Creating positive employee change evaluation: the role of different levels of organizational support and change participation. J. Chang. Manage. **14**(3), 361–383 (2014)
53. Selart, M., Johansen, S.T., Nesse, S.: Employee reactions to leader-initiated crisis preparation: core dimensions. J. Bus. Ethics **116**(1), 99–106 (2013)
54. La Rocco, J.M., Jones, A.P.: Co-worker and leader support as moderators of stress-strain relationships in work situations. J. Appl. Psychol. **63**(5), 629–634 (1978)
55. La Rocco, J.M., House, J.S., French, J.R.: Social support, occupational stress, and health. J. Health. Soc. Behav. **21**, 202–218 (1980)
56. Teo, T.S., Lim, V.K., Wai, S.H.: An empirical study of attitudes towards teleworking among information technology (IT) personnel. Int. J. Inf. Manage. **18**(5), 329–343 (1998)
57. Bentley, T.A., Teo, S.T.T., McLeod, L., Tan, F., Bosua, R., Gloet, M.: The role of organisational support in teleworker wellbeing: a socio-technical systems approach. Appl. Ergon. **52**, 207–215 (2016)
58. Collins, A.M., Hislop, D., Cartwright, S.: Social support in the workplace between teleworkers, office-based colleagues and supervisors. New Technol. Work. Employ. **31**(2), 161–175 (2016)
59. Wayne, S.J., Shore, L.M., Liden, R.C.: Perceived organizational support and leader-member exchange: a social exchange perspective. Acad. Manag. J. **40**(1), 82–111 (1997)
60. Stinglhamber, F., Vandenberghe, C.: Organizations and supervisors as sources of support and targets of commitment: a longitudinal study. J. Organ. Behav. **24**(3), 251–270 (2003)
61. Kowalski, K.B., Swanson, J.A.: Critical success factors in developing teleworking programs. Benchmark. Int. J. **12**(3), 236–249 (2005). https://doi.org/10.1108/14635770510600357
62. Sungu, L.J., Weng, Q.D., Kitule, J.A.: When organizational support yields both performance and satisfaction. Pers. Rev. **48**(6), 1410–1428 (2019)
63. Yang, T., et al.: Effects of co-worker and supervisor support on job stress and presenteeism in an aging workforce: a structural equation modelling approach. Int. J. Environ. Res. Public Health **13**(1), 1–15 (2016)
64. Guchait, P., Paşamehmetoğlu, A., Dawson, M.: Perceived supervisor and co-worker support for error management: Impact on perceived psychological safety and service recovery performance. Int. J. Hosp. Manag. **41**, 28–37 (2014)
65. Newman, A., Thanacoody, R., Hui, W.: The effects of perceived organizational support, perceived supervisor support and intra-organizational network resources on turnover intentions. Pers. Rev. **41**(1), 56–72 (2012)
66. Hayton, J.C., Carnabuci, G., Eisenberger, R.: With a little help from my colleagues: a social embeddedness approach to perceived organizational support. J. Organ. Behav. **33**(2), 235–249 (2012)
67. Allen, M.W.: Communication and organizational commitment: perceived organizational support as a mediating factor. Commun. Q. **40**(4), 357–367 (1992)
68. Op den Kamp, E.M., Bakker, A.B., Tims, M., Demerouti, E.: Proactive vitality management and creative work performance: the role of self-insight and social support. J. Creat. Behav. **54**(2), 323–336 (2020)
69. Schreurs, B.H., Van Emmerik, I.J.H., Günter, H., Germeys, F.: A weekly diary study on the buffering role of social support in the relationship between job insecurity and employee performance. Hum. Resour. Manage. **51**(2), 259–279 (2012)
70. Ten Brummelhuis, L.L., Halbesleben, J.R.B., Prabhu, V.: Development and validation of the new ways of working scale. In: The Annual Meeting of the Southern Management Association, Savannah, GA (2011)

71. Hayes, E.A.F.: PROCESS: a versatile computational tool for observed variable mediation, moderation, and conditional process modeling [White paper] (2012). http://www.afhayes. com/index.html
72. Meule, A.: Contemporary understanding of mediation testing. Meta-Psychology **3**, 1–7 (2019)

Work Digitalization and Job Crafting: The Role of Attitudes Toward Technology

Davide de Gennaro[1](✉), Paola Adinolfi[2], Gabriella Piscopo[3], and Marianna Cavazza[4]

[1] University of Salerno, Via Casa Rosa 35, 80063 Piano di Sorrento, Italy
ddegennaro@unisa.it
[2] University of Salerno, Fisciano, Italy
padinolfi@unisa.it
[3] University of Salerno, Salerno, Italy
gpiscopo@unisa.it
[4] Bocconi University, Milan, Italy
marianna.cavazza@unibocconi.it

Abstract. Responding to recent calls in literature, this article aims at investigating the effect of digitalization and information and communication technologies (ICT) on job crafting, a proactive behavior defined as work personalization or individual job redesign. More specifically, through a qualitative pilot study, we examine the attitudes toward technology – namely the individual's collection of beliefs which determines whether or not to engage in certain related behaviors – leading to these "do it yourself", unstructured, and self-targeted practices in a working context that is increasingly digitalized. The inductive qualitative research with 28 interviews suggests the mediating role of two variables in the smartphone and general social media usage. Implications for theory and practice, suggesting optimal behaviors and functioning within organizations arising from positive and proactive attitudes and traits of individuals, are discussed.

Keywords: Job crafting · Attitudes toward technology · Smartphone usage

1 Introduction

The organizational culture and behavioral dynamics of the past 20 years have had to deal with a "do it yourself" (DIY), unstructured, and proactive approach toward work called job crafting [1]. This can be defined as "work personalization" or "individual job redesign": these are changes made independently by workers to make their job more stimulating and motivating [2], but also to improve work engagement and meaning-fulness [3]. With job crafting employees actively modify the meaning of their job by shaping activities or relations in order to experience and live their job in a different way [4].

Job crafting captures the physical and cognitive modifications individuals implement in the task or relational boundaries of their work [1]. It consists of three proactive individual behaviors enabling employees to modify their jobs to fit more their natural

S. Za et al. (Eds.): ItAIS 2020, LNISO 50, pp. 59–72, 2022.
https://doi.org/10.1007/978-3-030-86858-1_4

skills, preferences, and inclinations at work: (i) physically altering the task boundaries to increase, reduce, or simply modify the activities to be carried out, (ii) changing the relationship style by investing in or avoiding high quality relationships with co-workers, supervisors, customers, and so forth, and (iii) rethinking the cognitive nature by mentally reframing one's job in more positive terms. For example, a personal trainer behaves in task crafting when choosing a different environment from the usual gym to train customers [5], an accountant behaves in relational crafting when preferring to participate in social initiatives rather than focusing on the traditional job [6], and the cleaning staff of a hospital behaves in cognitive crafting when attributing to the own work a wider and more significant meaning in relation to the contribution made to the healing process of patients [7].

The literature on the topic has grown a lot together with the new organizational dynamics that have taken hold at work, but at the same time some points remain unsolved. First, despite it has long been predicted that digitalization and information and communication technologies (ICT) are fundamentally changing the way we work and live [8], just few authors have dealt with issues related to ICT – such as the use of technology or other information systems to change the processes of work [9], to maintain increased flexibility [10], or to perform one's own tasks in more innovative ways [11] – so scholars did not define any specific technology-related crafting forms and the contributions on the subject are scarce [12], although a need for studies on the behavior of individuals in this new perspective is feld [13]. Moreover, the analysis of the antecedents of job crafting is still overlooked [14], even if job crafting literature examined personality, work, and demographic determinants such as proactive personality [15], general self-efficacy [16], work engagement [17], job performance [18], and job satisfaction [19]. Furthermore, a shortcoming of current research concerns the overemphasis on the task and relational dimensions of job crafting and the little scholarly attention towards the cognitive one, as testified by the fact that most of the scales to measure job crafting do not even include items to measure the cognitive dimension [20]; the use of scales that include all three variables are preferable since none of the sub-topics should be underestimated [6], but a large part of literature does not think so. Finally, in our knowledge also studies in the public sector are scarce, except for a few examples [21, 22], although they are pre-scribed jobs with well-defined tasks, expectations, and positions in which the behavioral practices of job crafting could creep in [23].

To fill these gaps, this study aims at investigating job crafting in a "technological" perspective, that is to identify – within a central public administration of a region of southern Italy – how the positive attitudes toward technology affects these proactive behaviors. Through a qualitative pilot study with 28 interviews, this study tries to shed light on the neglected relationship between work digitalization and job crafting, also contributing to literature by advancing research on antecedents and "digital" causes that can lead to changes in one's job and by considering all the three facets of job crafting. The spread of ICT technologies is profoundly changing the world of work and people's lifestyle habits [24] and the possibility that proactive workers' behavior is also changing as a consequence cannot be excluded. The new processes connected to ICT, in addition to creating new job opportunities and improving their quality, can also determine the emergence of new risks that must be identified and assessed with a view to well-being and undesired behaviors at work. The mediating variables of this relationship, which emerged from this pilot qualitative study, suggest that the positive attitudes towards technology leads to job crafting behaviors through the use of smartphones and social media. Implications for theory and practice are discussed.

2 Theoretical Framework and Hypothesis

The job crafting expression was proposed in 2001 by two psychologists – Amy Wrzesniewski and Jane E. Dutton – in an attempt to describe a possible magic: that of transforming the work you have into the work you love. It is about actions undertaken from a bottom-up approach that generates greater work engagement and higher performance [3], and that employers should recognize in order to guide workers behavior towards positive actions [25]. Work engagement, for example, is defined in terms of high levels of energy and involvement in the own work [26]: engaged employees often experience positive emotions, i.e. happiness, enthusiasm, knowledge, or self-efficacy and they are fully connected and in line with their job [27]. Indeed, when employees mobilize resources through job crafting behaviors, they can create a work environment that meets their needs and that is more in line with their abilities [2].

Job crafting is an activity that employees spontaneously undertake to meet their needs and preferences in the workplace [28]. It's a behavior that requires an adaptation to the challenges and to the constraints imposed by an employer [23] and it represents a strategic advantage for individuals and for the organization as a whole, although these changes are not always in line with the organizational goals and needs [29]. These are changes which can have a structural (physical or procedural), social, or cognitive form [1] and which are self-targeted and volitional [30].

Wrzesniewski and Dutton [1] argued that individuals are motivated to engage in job crafting behaviors because they are guided by three types of needs: the control over work, the social relations individuals experience in the workplace, and the attractive image. Based on these needs, many scholars distinguish "personal/individual" and "contextual" antecedents of job crafting [31], i.e., respectively, the self-efficacy [2] and the work context [32]. The personal/individual determinants affect person's behaviors, such as the Big Five personality traits and the proactive personality [33, 34] and the orientation to action [35]. Nevertheless, personal/individual factors influencing job crafting behavior cannot do without contextual factors – such as leadership [36] and colleagues [3] – referring to the environments condition where work activities take place. As already mentioned, despite these studies, the literature has somewhat neglected the deepening of the antecedents of job crafting [6, 14].

The pioneering conceptualization of job crafting by Wrzesniewski and Dutton [1] saw a further ramification in 2010 when some authors examined the concept through the lens of the Job Demands-Resources model (JD-R) [2]. This approach enables consideration of the relationships between resources and demands associated with one's particular job in the job crafting process. More specifically, the authors argue that (challenging and hindering) job demands are the aspects of the job that drain an individual's resources, while (structural and social) resources acquired with one's job can help individuals address specific job demands. In this paper, we have decided to rely on the initial framework by Wrzesniewski and Dutton since the JD-R model does not consider the cognitive dimension of job crafting at all, conceived as not relevant because it is not about shaping the boundaries of one's work" [2]. Conversely, the cognitive job crafting represents a proactive strategy for achieving fit with the work environment through changing the meaning of work and work identities [14], but also the starting point of the entire job crafting process [23, 37], therefore including it in our study may have relevant and interesting implications.

Drawing on job crafting theory and responding to recent calls in literature [12, 38] this study aims at identifying an antecedent of job crafting in digitalization, since behaviors could be oriented towards the technological aspect of work [39]. The advent of technology has changed the landscape so that almost all activities can be carried out via a portable device or with a laptop; for example, thanks to Wi-Fi, people can have access to the Internet, e-mails, and many different types of applications anywhere and at any time of the day, and this undoubtedly influences the way people carry out their work [40]. The design and nature of knowledge work is changing due to work digitalization [24], since digital technologies are supposed to increase the automation of different work tasks, resulting in job destruction [41]. Consequently, also employees' behaviors are affected by digitalization with tremendous positive, but also negative potential for the organization and individuals [13].

Within this framework, the goal of this study is to investigate the attitudes towards technology, and in this way to understand what are the digital tools and ways through which individuals behave like job crafters. Attitude represents an individual disposition toward performing a certain behavior [42] and it is influenced by the perception of utility and ease of use [43, 44]. It is a concept of three-dimensional nature, involving cognitive, affective, and behavioral components [45], and it is primarily an interplay of affect and cognition to be then a behavioral tendency [46]. Among the studies on the topic, an attitude toward a concept, such as technology [47], is the individual's collection of beliefs which determines whether or not to engage in certain behaviors [48]. Attitudes toward technology may include enthusiasm and at the same time boredom interest in the subject [49] and this dual perception of the phenomenon translates into numerous contributions on the topic in the literature of the last years [50–52]. Nevertheless, in our knowledge, so far it has not been studied in depth in relation to proactive behaviors.

Since job crafting is mainly based on personal factors – and the "attitude" has been shown to lead to an improvement in job characteristics and a perception of person-job fit due to engaging in job crafting [16, 31] – a relationship with ICT tools may exist. It is therefore possible that the positive attitudes toward the use of technology influences and determines job crafting behaviors.

3   Method

The proposed study represents the first of the two phases in which it was conceived. It is a qualitative pilot study useful for formulating hypotheses and subsequently measuring them with a quantitative methodology to be referred to the entire organizational population to give greater rigor to the results. The use of a pilot study is fundamental for a good study design as it can provide interesting and unexpected insights from a study object [53, 54].

3.1 Data and Procedures

In this pilot study, we adopted an inductive qualitative approach [55, 56], by employing a qualitative research method based on different sources in order to reduce the impact of potential biases [57]. In line with this, empirical data are based on formal documents, such as appointments decrees and job descriptions, which gave us an overall overview of the organizational and work situation of the public administration object of the study, and workshops and focus groups organized to develop our initial insights with a sample of volunteer workers involving 3 to 5 participants.

Data were collected through semi-structured interviews conducted with workers of a central public administration in southern Italy dealing with healthcare. Healthcare organizations in recent years embraced the digital paradigm and they are characterized by a high degree of complexity because of the heterogeneity of healthcare professionals' mindsets, networks, and decision-making processes [58]. Since there is a growing awareness that recognizes the need for healthcare professionals to take a proactive role in shaping their future jobs to improve healthcare systems [18], this sample may be particularly interesting to investigate these behavioral dynamics. The interviews lasted about 45 minutes and took place in respondents' office. As part of a work process reorganization study, it has been possible to recruit 28 participants including managers, employees, and interns.

Participants were informed that a team of researchers was conducting a study on technology, ICT, and proactive workplace behaviors and was looking for participants. The average age of participants was 48.4 years ($SD = 8.74$) and gender was almost equally distributed (13 women and 15 men). All interviews were audio-recorded and then transcribed for the qualitative analysis.

3.2 Coding and Analyzing

We followed the Gioia Method [59], which is a systematic approach useful for bringing "qualitative rigor" of inductive/abductive research. The study's approach depended on a generic research question, i.e. "we wished to explore attitudes, beliefs, and behaviors about work digitalization and the use of technology at work". The interviews were administered without a structure of questions, but rather as if they were informal conversations within which it was possible to range over all the topics that concerned attitudes and working behaviors of public workers. According to this method, we did not aprioristically impose any constructs or theories to our study; for instance, we did not talk about the concept of job crafting and we did not describe the features of this technique to the participants. Indeed, we found that respondents never used the term "job crafting" in their claims.

In analyzing the interviews, we used both a grounded theory approach [60] as well as Gioia method [59], and this analysis process involved three phases that systematically moved from unprocessed data to theoretical assumptions. In the first stage, the focus was on finding recurring themes in interviews based on respondents' answers. The notes from the interviews was uploaded into an online software for qualitative data analysis, Dedoose; then two researchers independently coded all the transcribed interviews and subsequently compared personal codes by engaging in a discussion when disagreements emerged. We used Cohen's [61] κ coefficient to estimate the level of agreement between the coders, following an iterative approach [62] and continuously iterating between our data and the emerging conceptualizations. By comparing codes and by engaging in a discussion when disagreements emerged, the final consensus reached the value of κ=.90, reflecting excellent agreement between the raters [63]. Subsequently, we discerned patterns in the data with the aim of bringing out concepts and relationships and then of formulating them in theoretically-relevant terms [59], giving particular attention to nascent concepts that seemed to have no adequate references in the literature. Once we identified all the relevant first-order recurring themes and codes and the second-order concepts and relationships, we assembled them into a data structure that can be presented as a visual representation (Fig. 1).

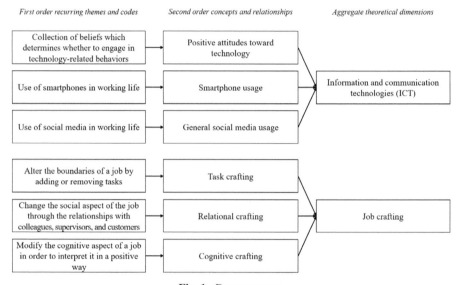

Fig. 1. Data structure.

4   Results

As above mentioned, none of the public workers interviewed was familiar with the concept of job crafting; however, the majority of them revealed to regularly engage in a series of proactive behaviors that were aimed at modifying some aspects of their job which fit with the task, relational, and cognitive techniques described by Wrzesniewski and Dutton in their seminal contribution [1].

With reference to the attitudes towards technology, the interviewees showed different (and also diametrically opposed) opinions, without any particular correlation emerging on the basis of demographic variables:

I believe that technology is fundamental for our lives and for our work; to date it is unthinkable to live without! (Respondent #3, example of positive attitudes toward technology)

The human mind is not replaceable by machines; indeed, we should reclaim its centrality. (Respondent #8, example of negative attitudes toward technology)

On the one hand, some interviewed workers claim to have positive attitudes toward ICT since they use these tools to improve their work:

Without technology, most of the current jobs would be ineffective and, at the same time, thanks to technology, I can do all my tasks without unnecessary waste of time. Just think of what it meant to make an account 100 years ago. Technology, smartphones, and fast communication allow us to do great things. (Respondent #14, example of positive attitudes toward technology)

This positive approach refers both to the performance of work activities (*"e-mails, for example, make communication effective and eliminate barriers and distances typical of our bureaucracies"*, Respondent #17), and to the place where these are implemented (*"I can practice smart working on certain days of the month and for me it is a very pleasant way of working"*, Respondent #24).

On the other hand, others prefer the "traditional" work that does not include technology, showing negative attitudes toward it:

Our life has been destroyed by technologies: we are always connected, there is no privacy, we are increasingly dependent on the smartphone and we do not even realize this problem. (Respondent #6, example of negative attitudes toward technology)

The world was better when technology did not exist, starting from relationships to lifestyle. (Respondent #12, example of negative attitudes toward technology)

Although the latter do not present particularly relevant results from the point of view of job crafting, interestingly those who show a positive attitude towards technology are also those who modify their work proactively. In line with the job crafting literature, findings indicate that workers were motivated to craft their job by the desire to increase the resources and relations at their disposal, to introduce new challenges to work activities that were considered as too "boring", and to seek improving the external prestige of their work that was particularly denigrated in recent years. Indeed, workers claimed to change the characteristics of their work thanks to technological tools according to approaches that are reminiscent of job crafting and it is interesting to note that almost every respondent talks about two main tools, namely social media and smartphones, in crafting his/her job:

Thanks to technology I am able to carry out activities other than traditional ones (...), for example I have set up a data archive that had never been put in order (...). Technology is also useful as it allows me to avoid many superfluous activities and sometimes with my smartphone I monitor the progress of tasks. (Respondent #27, example of task crafting)

I think technology is fundamental (...), for example I can use the smartphone at any time of my day to interface with colleagues and experts and thus I can improve my work performance (...). I also use Facebook to follow groups of colleagues, take a cue, and answer questions. (Respondent #10, example of relational crafting)

Citizens must be aware of the work we do (...). I often share my experiences and activities on social networks in order to make everyone participate in my work and feel myself even more appreciated. (Respondent #21, example of cognitive crafting)

The positive attitudes toward technology, therefore, could prove to be an antecedent of job crafting as the actors who show this cognitive and behavioral predisposition proactively modify the characteristics of their work to make it more stimulating and motivating. Moreover, since they are reported in almost all the interviews, smartphones, as a technological tool, and social media, as a virtual "place", appear relevant in this possible linear relationship and could represent mediating variables capable of explaining the previous relationship and ensure a greater understanding of the phenomenon. On the contrary, respondents who showed a negative attitude toward technology or who did not express themselves in this regard were found to be less proactive and not actively committed to changing the characteristics of their activities, relationships, and cognitive perception.

5   Discussion

The aim of the present study was to examine the relationship between the attitudes toward technology and job crafting. Using a qualitative method approach and laying the foundation for a quantitative validation, our results suggest the presence of a linear relationship, perhaps mediated by smartphone usage and general social media usage.

Our work offers several contributions to theory and research. First, we address the call from Zhang and Parker [64] and Niessen and colleagues [14] to provide new insight on both the antecedents of job crafting beyond individual dispositions and on cognitive crafting, a dimension that has been little examined in the job crafting literature. A study of all the components of job crafting, therefore including cognitive job crafting, helps investigate the behavioral dynamics that lead to a shift in work meaning, work identity, and emotions [65]. Moreover, in line with prior studies that have shown job crafting to be a contextually embedded phenomenon [64], we have demonstrated that individuals' attitudes represent significant drivers of the entire job crafting process. More specifically, we demonstrated that the workers who have a positive attitude towards technology are the same workers who reinvent themselves to modify their job and make it more pleasant. The positive attitudes toward technology translates into flexibility, critical spirit, creative dissonance that feeds on diversity to create a new amalgam that favours a richer decision-making process and therefore better work performance. This insight can open up new avenues in research on antecedents of job crafting, as it is possible that the personal characteristics of individuals play a critical role in the changing process that has not yet been fully investigated.

Second, by integrating digitalization and ICT into job crafting literature, we have demonstrated that the new organization of work and the new working practices evolve hand in hand with workers' trends and behaviors. Lazazzara and colleagues [12] had identified this literature gap, but no study had gone so far in investigating these dynamics. Interestingly, smartphones and social media have been shown to be critical tools and virtual places for practicing job crafting and some studies had already foreseen this future trend. An example is characterized by locational crafting, which has been defined as the possibility for an individual to carry out one's work tasks in different locations [10, 66]. This is also in line with the definition of "challenging job demands" giving the opportunity to stimulate employees, to reach more difficult goals, and to develop skills and knowledge by creating a more challenging work environment [3, 15], for example by actively pursuing new opportunities (creating a new project) and opening up to new developments and changes (being the first to work with a new tool) [30].

Furthermore, the study of job crafting in a prescribed work context such as that of the public sector is also an interesting contribution for literature. Identifying a "stable" work as a sample, from the point of view of its characteristics and duration over time, is undoubtedly a rigorous way of doing research because it allows not to suffer distortions due to improper contextual factors.

5.1 Practical Implications

Practically, this study suggests that a positive attitude toward technology makes workers more motivated and satisfied, so managers should increase their performance and well-being by facilitating job crafting behaviors and helping them developing digital skills, knowledge, and competencies needed to expand their tasks. Managers in fact play a critical role in motivating individuals to undertake proactive behaviors by supporting initiatives and experimentation [67] or assisting them in pursuing their unanswered callings [23]. It could be also useful providing opportunities to participate in job crafting interventions and sharing "what works" could be the kick-off toward improving healthcare [18].

Furthermore, it has been shown that social support and organizational culture, also through appropriate and innovative solutions with employees [66], are decisive for the implementation of job crafting, so leaving more autonomy to workers could generate positive consequences for the organization from the individual [68] and collective [69] points of view.

Finally, but it is more appropriate to discuss this in the following paragraph about future research, given the possibility of distraction and distorted uses of technology [70, 71], managers should pay close attention to these behavioral practices to ensure that they are in line with business objectives. When an individual perceives supportive personal factors (e.g., increased self-confidence), approach crafting is associated with positive experiences, such as meaningfulness, esteem-enhanced occupational identity, and job satisfaction [72–74]; on the contrary, constraining personal/contextual factors along the job crafting process means that even job crafting may result in negative experiences [66, 74, 75] or that people do avoidance crafting [12], i.e. limiting positive behaviors and refraining.

5.2 Limitations and Future Research

This study has several limitations. First of all, it is a qualitative pilot study which draws inspiration and formulation of the hypotheses from an exploratory and semistructured investigation, so that the results may appear to be partial and not theory-founded. Although there is a strong methodological rigor, it is indeed important to proceed with the quantitative investigation by developing the hypotheses and further deepening the concepts emerged in this first phase. Moreover, this study focuses on one of the aspects of technology, which refers to workers' attitudes, but does not deepen all its facets, for different reasons. Through an analysis of the attitudes it is indeed possible to investigate the behavioral predispositions of individuals, but surely some issues related to the digitization of work remain undervalued, therefore it is important for future research to deal with these topics. Furthermore, future research may measure the consequences of job crafting in terms of technology and digitalization, also by not excluding any of the three components of job crafting to avoid partial studies. Finally, since the literature to date has mainly focused on the positive outcomes, not considering the dysfunctional consequences – such as the frustration resulting from not being able to meet proactive goals generates negative experiences [73, 74] or the shift towards an interest in crafting in other domains [10] – of job crafting [12, 16], studies on the subject should not overlook these aspects, especially when it comes to technology.

6   Conclusion

To the best of our knowledge, this study is the first to respond to recent calls in literature by investigating the effect of work digitalization and ICT on job crafting via the attitudes of public workers toward technology. Attitude represents an individual disposition toward performing a certain behavior and it is influenced by the perception of utility and ease of use. Through an inductive qualitative research with 28 interviews, it has been suggested the role of smartphone usage and general social media usage in this relationship. A subsequent quantitative analysis will try to give greater rigor to the present study, assuming a relationship with two mediators and thus enriching the literature on the antecedents of job crafting. Our work offers several contributions to theory and research, suggesting optimal behaviors and functioning within organizations arising from the positive traits and attitudes of individuals in an ICT's perspective.

References

1. Wrzesniewski, A., Dutton, J.E.: Crafting a job: revisioning employees as active crafters of their work. Acad. Manage. Rev. **26**(2), 179–201 (2001). https://doi.org/10.5465/amr.2001.4378011
2. Tims, M., Bakker, A.B.: Job crafting: towards a new model of individual job redesign. SA J. Indust. Psychol. **36**(2), 1–9 (2010)
3. Tims, M., Bakker, A.B., Derks, D.: The impact of job crafting on job demands, job resources, and well–being. J. Occup. Health Psychol. **18**(2), 230–240 (2013). https://doi.org/10.1037/a0032141
4. Vuori, T., San, E., Kira, M.: Meaningfulness-making at work. Qual. Res. Organ. Manage. Int. J. **7**(2), 231–248 (2012). https://doi.org/10.1108/17465641211253110
5. Grant, A.M.: Relational job design and the motivation to make a prosocial difference. Acad. Manage. Rev. **32**(2), 393–417 (2007). https://doi.org/10.5465/AMR.2007.24351328
6. Buonocore, F., de Gennaro, D., Russo, M., Salvatore, D.: Cognitive job crafting: a possible response to increasing job insecurity and declining professional prestige. Human Resour. Manage. J. **30**(2), 244–259 (2020). https://doi.org/10.1111/1748-8583.12270
7. Ghitulescu, B.E.: Shaping tasks and relationships at work: Examining the antecedents and consequences of employee job crafting. Doctoral dissertation, University of Pittsburgh (2007)
8. Beno, M.: The four major factors impacting on the future of work. In: Rocha, Á., Adeli, H., Reis, L.P., Costanzo, S. (eds.) WorldCIST'19 2019. AISC, vol. 930, pp. 12–24. Springer, Cham (2019). https://doi.org/10.1007/978-3-030-16181-1_2
9. Bruning, P.F., Campion, M.A.: A role-resource approach-avoidance model of job crafting: a multimethod integration and extension of job crafting theory. Acad. Manage. J. **61**(2), 499–522 (2018). https://doi.org/10.5465/amj.2015.0604

10. Sturges, J.: Crafting a balance between work and home. Human Relations **65**(12), 1539–1559 (2012). https://doi.org/10.1177/0018726712457435
11. Grant-Vallone, E.J., Ensher, E.A.: Re-crafting careers for mid-career faculty: a qualitative study. J. Higher Educ. Theory Pract. **17**(5), 10–24 (2017). https://doi.org/10.33423/jhetp. v17i5.1533
12. Lazazzara, A., Tims, M., de Gennaro, D.: The process of reinventing a job: a meta-synthesis of qualitative job crafting research. J. Vocat. Behav. **116**, 1–18 (2019). https://doi.org/10.1016/j.jvb.2019.01.001
13. Nöhammer, E., Stichlberger, S.: Digitalization, innovative work behavior and extended availability. J. Bus. Econ. **89**(8–9), 1191–1214 (2019). https://doi.org/10.1007/s11573-019-009 53-2
14. Niessen, C., Weseler, D., Kostova, P.: When and why do individuals craft their jobs? The role of individual motivation and work characteristics for job crafting. Human Relations **69**(6), 1287–1313 (2016). https://doi.org/10.1177/0018726715610642
15. Bakker, A.B., Tims, M., Derks, D.: Proactive personality and job performance: the role of job crafting and work engagement. Human Relations **65**(10), 1359–1378 (2012). https://doi.org/10.1177/0018726712453471
16. Rudolph, C.W., Katz, I.M., Lavigne, K.N., Zacher, H.: Job crafting: a meta-analysis of relationships with individual differences, job characteristics, and work outcomes. J. Vocat. Behav. **102**, 112–138 (2017). https://doi.org/10.1016/j.jvb.2017.05.008
17. Lichtenthaler, P.W., Fischbach, A.: A meta-analysis on promotion-and prevention-focused job crafting. Eur. J. Work Organ. Psychol. **28**(1), 30–50 (2019). https://doi.org/10.1080/135 9432X.2018.1527767
18. Gordon, H.J., Demerouti, E., Le Blanc, P.M., Bipp, T.: Job crafting and performance of Dutch and American health care professionals. J. Personnel Psychol. **14**, 192–202 (2015). https://doi.org/10.1027/1866-5888/a000138
19. De Beer, L.T., Tims, M., Bakker, A.B.: Job crafting and its impact on work engagement and job satisfaction in mining and manufacturing. South Afr. J. Econ. and Manage. Sci. **19**(3), 400–412 (2016). https://doi.org/10.17159/2222-3436/2016/v19n3a7
20. Weseler, D., Niessen, C.: How job crafting relates to task performance. J. Manage. Psychol. **31**(3), 672–685 (2015). https://doi.org/10.1108/JMP-09-2014-0269
21. Bakker, A.B.: A job demands–resources approach to public service motivation. Public Admin. Rev. **75**(5), 723–732 (2015). https://doi.org/10.1111/puar.12388
22. Tuan, L.T.: HR flexibility and job crafting in public organizations: the roles of knowledge sharing and public service motivation. Group Organ. Manage. **44**(3), 549–577 (2019). https://doi.org/10.1177/1059601117741818
23. Berg, J.M., Wrzesniewski, A., Dutton, J.E.: Perceiving and responding to challenges in job crafting at different ranks: when proactivity requires adaptivity. J. Organ. Behav. **31**(2–3), 158–186 (2010). https://doi.org/10.1002/job.645
24. Vuori, V., Helander, N., Okkonen, J.: Digitalization in knowledge work: the dream of enhanced performance. Cogn. Technol. Work **21**(2), 237–252 (2019). https://doi.org/10.1007/s10111-018-0501-3
25. Petrou, P., Demerouti, E., Peeters, M.C., Schaufeli, W.B., Hetland, J.: Crafting a job on a daily basis: contextual correlates and the link to work engagement. J. Organ. Behav. **33**(8), 1120–1141 (2012). https://doi.org/10.1002/job.1783
26. Bakker, A.B., Albrecht, S.L., Leiter, M.P.: Key questions regarding work engagement. Eur. J. Work Organ. Psychol. **20**(1), 4–28 (2011). https://doi.org/10.1080/1359432X.2010.485352
27. Bakker, A.B.: An evidence-based model of work engagement. Current Direct. Psychol. Sci. **20**(4), 265–269 (2011). https://doi.org/10.1177/0963721411414534

28. Kira, M., van Eijnatten, F.M., Balkin, D.B.: Crafting sustainable work: development of personal resources. J. Organ. Change Manage. **23**(5), 616–632 (2010). https://doi.org/10.1108/09534811011071315

29. Van den Heuvel, M., Demerouti, E., Bakker, A.B., Schaufeli, W.B.: Personal resources and work engagement in the face of change. Contemp. Occup. Health Psychol. Global Perspect. Res. Pract. **1**, 124–150 (2010). https://doi.org/10.1002/9780470661550

30. Tims, M., Bakker, A.B., Derks, D.: Development and validation of the job crafting scale. J. Vocat. Behav. **80**(1), 173–186 (2012). https://doi.org/10.1016/j.jvb.2011.05.009

31. Wang, H., Demerouti, E., Bakker, A. B.: A review of job-crafting research: the role of leader behaviors in cultivating successful job crafters. In: Parker, S.K., Bindl, U. K. (eds.) Proactivity at Work: Making Things Happen in Organizations, p. 95. Routledge, New York, NY (2017). https://doi.org/10.4324/9781315797113-12

32. Vera, D., Crossan, M.: Strategic leadership and organizational learning. Acad. Manage. Rev. **29**(2), 222–240 (2004). https://doi.org/10.5465/amr.2004.12736080

33. Parker, S.K., Bindl, U.K., Strauss, K.: Making things happen: a model of proactive motivation. J. Manage. **36**(4), 827–856 (2010). https://doi.org/10.1177/0149206310363732

34. Wu, C.H., Li, W.D.: Individual differences in proactivity: a developmental perspective. In: Parker, S.K., Bindl, U.K. (eds.) Proactivity at Work: Making Things Happen in Organizations, p. 226. Routledge, New York (2017)

35. Xanthopoulou, D., Bakker, A.B., Demerouti, E., Schaufeli, W.B.: The role of personal resources in the job demands-resources model. Int. J. Stress Manage. **14**(2), 121–141 (2007). https://doi.org/10.1037/1072-5245.14.2.121

36. Leana, C., Appelbaum, E., Shevchuk, I.: Work process and quality of care in early childhood education: the role of job crafting. Acad. Manage. J. **52**(6), 1169–1192 (2009). https://doi.org/10.5465/amj.2009.47084651

37. Yin, K., Xing, L., Li, C., Guo, Y.: Are empowered employees more proactive? The contingency of how they evaluate their leader. Front. Psychol. **8**, 1802 (2017). https://doi.org/10.3389/fpsyg.2017.01802

38. Lee, J.Y., Lee, Y.: Job crafting and performance: literature review and implications for human resource development. Human Res. Dev. Rev. **17**(3), 277–313 (2018). https://doi.org/10.1177/1534484318788269

39. Parker, S.K., Morgeson, F.P., Johns, G.: One hundred years of work design research: looking back and looking forward. J. Appl. Psychol. **102**(3), 403–420 (2017). https://doi.org/10.1037/apl0000106

40. Rosen, L.D., Whaling, K., Carrier, L.M., Cheever, N.A., Rokkum, J.: The media and technology usage and attitudes scale: an empirical investigation. Comput. Human Behav. **29**(6), 2501–2511 (2013). https://doi.org/10.1016/j.chb.2013.06.006

41. Timonen, H., Vuori, J.: Visibility of work: how digitalization changes the workplace. In: The 51st Hawaii International Conference on System Sciences, p. 5075 (2018). https://doi.org/10.24251/HICSS.2018.634

42. Davis, F.D., Bagozzi, R.P., Warshaw, P.R.: User acceptance of computer technology: a comparison of two theoretical models. Manage. Sci. **35**(8), 982–1003 (1989). https://doi.org/10.1287/mnsc.35.8.982

43. Pynoo, B., van Braak, J.: Predicting teachers' generative and receptive use of an educational portal by intention, attitude and self-reported use. Comput. Human Behav. **34**, 315–322 (2014). https://doi.org/10.1016/j.chb.2013.12.024

44. Teo, T.: Unpacking teachers' acceptance of technology: tests of measurement invariance and latent mean differences. Comput. Educ. **75**, 127–135 (2014). https://doi.org/10.1016/j.compedu.2014.01.014

45. Breckler, S.J.: Empirical validation of affect, behavior, and cognition as distinct components of attitude. J. Personal. Soc. Psychol. **47**(6), 1191–1205 (1984). https://doi.org/10.1037/0022-3514.47.6.1191
46. Bagozzi, R.P., Burnkrant, R.E.: Attitude organization and the attitude–behavior relationship. J. Personal. Soc. Psychol. **37**(6), 913–929 (1979). https://doi.org/10.1037/0022-3514.37.6.913
47. Ankiewicz, P.: Perceptions and attitudes of pupils toward technology. In: de Vries, M.J. (ed.) Handbook of Technology Education, pp. 1–15. Springer, Cham (2018). https://doi.org/10.1007/978-3-3-319.38889-2_43-1
48. Ankiewicz, P., van Rensburg, S., Myburgh, C.: Assessing the attitudinal technology profile of South African learners: a pilot study. Int. J. Technol. Des. Educ. **11**(2), 93–109 (2001). https://doi.org/10.1023/A:1011210013642
49. Ardies, J., De Maeyer, S., Gijbels, D., van Keulen, H.: Students attitudes towards technology. Int. J. Technol. Des. Educ. **25**(1), 43–65 (2014). https://doi.org/10.1007/s10798-014-9268-x
50. Cai, Z., Fan, X., Du, J.: Gender and attitudes toward technology use: a meta-analysis. Comput. Educ. **105**, 1–13 (2017). https://doi.org/10.1016/j.compedu.2016.11.003
51. Hsiao, M.H.: A conceptual framework for technology-enabled and technology-dependent user behavior toward device mesh and mesh app. Future Bus. J. **4**(1), 130–138 (2018). https://doi.org/10.1016/j.fbj.2018.03.003
52. Sunny, S., Patrick, L., Rob, L.: Impact of cultural values on technology acceptance and technology readiness. Int. J. Hosp. Manage. **77**, 89–96 (2019). https://doi.org/10.1016/j.ijhm.2018.06.017
53. Kim, Y.: The pilot study in qualitative inquiry: Identifying issues and learning lessons for culturally competent research. Qual. Soc. Work **10**(2), 190–206 (2011). https://doi.org/10.1177/1473325010362001
54. Van Teijlingen, E.R., Hundley, V.: The importance of pilot studies. Soc. Res. Update **35**, 1–4 (2001)
55. Höglund, L., Holmgren Caicedo, M., Mårtensson, M., Svärdsten, F.: Strategic management in the public sector: how tools enable and constrain strategy making. Int. Public Manage. J. 1–28 (2018). doi: https://doi.org/10.1080/10967494.2018.1427161.
56. Thomas, D.R.: A general inductive approach for analyzing qualitative evaluation data. Am. J. Eval. **27**(2), 237–246 (2006). https://doi.org/10.1177/1098214005283748
57. Bowen, G.A.: Document analysis as a qualitative research method. Qual. Res. J. **9**(2), 27–40 (2009). https://doi.org/10.3316/QRJ0902027
58. Karamitri, I., Talias, M.A., Bellali, T.: Knowledge management practices in healthcare settings: a systematic review. Int. J. Health Plan. Manage. **32**(1), 4–18 (2017). https://doi.org/10.1002/hpm.2303
59. Gioia, D.A., Corley, K.G., Hamilton, A.L.: Seeking qualitative rigor in inductive research: notes on the Gioia methodology. Organ. Res. Methods **16**(1), 15–31 (2013). https://doi.org/10.1177/1094428112452151
60. Glaser, B.G., Strauss, A.L.: Discovery of Grounded Theory: Strategies For Qualitative Research. Routledge, New York (2017)
61. Cohen, J.: A coefficient of agreement for nominal scales. Educ. Psychol. Measur. **20**(1), 37–46 (1960). https://doi.org/10.1177/001316446002000104
62. Locke, K.: Grounded Theory in Management Research. Sage, London, UK (2001)
63. Carey, J.W., Morgan, M., Oxtoby, M.J.: Intercoder agreement in analysis of responses to open-ended interview questions. Field Methods **8**(3), 1–5 (1996). https://doi.org/10.1177/1525822X960080030101
64. Zhang, F., Parker, S.K.: Reorienting job crafting research: a hierarchical structure of job crafting concepts and integrative review. J. Organ. Behav. **40**(2), 126–146 (2019). https://doi.org/10.1002/job.2332

65. Grant, A.M., Campbell, E.M.: Doing good, doing harm, being well and burning out: the interactions of perceived prosocial and antisocial impact in service work. J. Occup. Organ. Psychol. **80**(4), 665–691 (2007). https://doi.org/10.1348/096317906X169553

66. Van Wingerden, J., Derks, D., Bakker, A.B., Dorenbosch, L.: Job crafting in schools for special education: a qualitative analysis. Gedrag en Organisatie **1**(26), 85–103 (2013)

67. Lazazzara, A., Quacquarelli, B., Ghiringhelli, C., Nacamulli, R.C.: The effect of autonomy, skill variety, organizational learning culture and HRM on job crafting. In: Academy of Management Proceedings, p. 17635. Academy of Management, Briarcliff Manor, NY (2015). https://doi.org/10.5465/ambpp.2015.17635abstract

68. Lyons, P.: The crafting of jobs and individual differences. J. Bus. Psychol. **23**(1–2), 25–36 (2008). https://doi.org/10.1007/s10869-008-9080-2

69. Mattarelli, E., Tagliaventi, M.R.: How offshore professionals' job dissatisfaction can promote further offshoring: organizational outcomes of job crafting. J. Manage. Stud. **52**(5), 585–620 (2015). https://doi.org/10.1111/j.1467-6486.2012.01088.x

70. Brooks, S.: Does personal social media usage affect efficiency and well-being? Comput. Human Behav. **46**, 26–37 (2015). https://doi.org/10.1016/j.chb.2014.12.053

71. Gill, P.S., Kamath, A., Gill, T.S.: Distraction: an assessment of smartphone usage in health care work settings. Risk Manage. Healthc. Policy **5**, 105–114 (2012). https://doi.org/10.2147/RMHP.S34813

72. Fuller, A., Unwin, L.: Job crafting and identity in low-grade work: how hospital porters redefine the value of their work and expertise. Vocat. Learn. **10**(3), 307–324 (2017). https://doi.org/10.1007/s12186-017-9173-z

73. Kossek, E.E., Piszczek, M.M., McAlpine, K.L., Hammer, L.B., Burke, L.: Filling the holes: work schedulers as job crafters of employment practice in longterm health care. Indus. Labor Relations Rev. **69**(4), 961–990 (2016). https://doi.org/10.1177/0019793916642761

74. Meged, J.W.: Guides crafting meaning in a flexible working life. Scandinavian J. Hospit. Tour. **17**(4), 374–387 (2017). https://doi.org/10.1080/15022250.2017.1330845

75. Gascoigne, C., Kelliher, C.: The transition to part-time: how professionals negotiate 'reduced time and workload'i-deals and craft their jobs. Human Relations **71**(1), 103–125 (2018). https://doi.org/10.1177/0018726717722394

When Technology is Taken for Granted: The Paradox of Co-working

Maria Laura Toraldo[1] (ID), Lia Tirabeni[2] (ID), and Maddalena Sorrentino[1(✉)] (ID)

[1] University of Milano, Milan, Italy
{marialaura.toraldo,maddalena.sorrentino}@unimi.it
[2] University of Milano-Bicocca, Milan, Italy
lia.tirabeni@unimib.it

Abstract. Co-working is an exemplary case for exploring the organisation and significance of work. Two main thrusts prompt co-working arrangements: the idea of exploiting information and communication technology (ICT) to share experiences and knowledge, and the idea of joining forces to survive economically. Drawing upon a scoping review, this qualitative paper argues that the role of ICT artefacts in studies on co-working takes a back seat. Invoking technology 'in name only' prevents research from connecting the social to the technological. We claim it is crucial to bring technology into the analysis to better understand how co-working 'works'. We could do that by considering co-working as a 'work-oriented infrastructure' and recognising its dynamic complexity.

Keywords: Co-working · Information technology · Workspace · Technology artefacts

1 Introduction

Recently, we have been observing significant changes in the way, and larger context, in which work is carried out [1]. The conventional understanding of work, as something individuals perform at an office site with workload and schedules marked by office hours is gradually being replaced by the idea that productivity is decoupled from physical location and set hours [2]. A blurring of traditional boundaries between life and work, production and consumption, and paid and free work is altering work practices and redefining frames of workplace interaction [3]. Unlike 'traditional work', new work configurations are frequently implemented outside the well-established and institutionalised practices ways of employment [4] leading to a variety of work configurations with respect to where and how work is performed [5].

The freedom to work anywhere is a dominant trait of the contemporary gig economy and this is supported by discourses that celebrate the entrepreneurialism of independent workers and the idea of 'being their own boss' [6]. It is in this context that we observe the global emergence and growing popularity of 'co-working spaces' [7], spaces that reinterpret the open office plans by crafting work experiences for mobile and self-employed workers [8].

© The Author(s), under exclusive license to Springer Nature Switzerland AG 2022
S. Za et al. (Eds.): ItAIS 2020, LNISO 50, pp. 73–86, 2022.
https://doi.org/10.1007/978-3-030-86858-1_5

The emergence of work settings such as co-working spaces are enabled in no small measure by the affordances of information and communication technology (ICT). The ubiquity of mobile technologies and real-time information—always available once a smart device or a laptop is plugged in—have created a window of opportunity for alternative work arrangements [7–9].

In this paper, we are interested in the role of technology and how it is positioned and addressed across academic debates (discourses) around co-working.

Much research on co-working has emphasised the opportunities heralded by digital technologies in reconfiguring the temporal as well as the spatial dimension of work. For example Van Dijk [10: 470] defines co-working spaces as workplaces shared by different individuals and businesses or organisations, with digital technologies facilitating this 'working apart together'. As this definition seems to suggest, the very existence of such spaces is made possible thanks to the current power of ICT applications and platforms. Richardson [9] observes that "co-working offices are workspaces enabled by digital technologies and sometimes producing 'born digital' businesses" and, as she continues, "this work is thus 'digital' in that it occurs through software, hardware and connectivity affording the possibilities of smaller, self-organised producer units" [9: 2].

Digital technologies, and more generally, digitalisation processes, are so widespread and part of an ongoing debate that some scholars have noted that the consequences that introducing such technologies may have on organisations tend to be divided into two polarised positions: an alarmist and an optimistic one [11]. In this debate, techno-deterministic narratives alternate with a triumphalist spirit. Both views propose technology as either an enemy to be fought and beaten, or the messiah to be glorified and encouraged. In both cases, the protagonist is always the same: technology, with the human as the subordinated subject.

However, and quite interestingly, in our opinion, technology has become so ubiquitous that, at least in some cases, it tends to disappear—it is now so taken for granted as to be, in effect, invisible. While in many cases, we may see the use of the word 'technology' as a buzzword without any specific meaning, in few other accounts it never enters the discourse. As recently stated by Beverungen, Beyes and Conrad [12: 621]:

> While the hype around digital technologies and 'digitalization' continues unabated in both its main variants of uncritical affirmation and dystopian diagnoses, digital media themselves have become pervasive, ubiquitous and so utterly mundane that we barely take note of them.

1.1 Research Aim and Contribution

Here we use co-working as a 'revelatory case', being a paradigmatic example of novel way of working in the digital economy, to investigate whether and to what extent technology appears as an issue in academic studies.

As an umbrella term, co-working refers to the activity of different professionals (including freelancers, startuppers and self-employed individuals) hosted in a *neutral* office-related environment where they can telecommute and/or work by themselves. Taking such an understanding as our point of departure, our two-step research question can be formulated as follows:

What are the main debates around co-working (RQa), and how is technology situated within those debates (RQb)?

The present paper is a first step towards building better conceptualization with regard to ICT artifacts in co-working studies. Our aim is, thus, twofold: first, we summarise and interpret the research related to technology and co-working. Here, the reframing of the relevant literature is aimed at identifying the boundaries of co-working, its temporal and spatial expressions, and defining the main themes. Second, we assess the role of technology and the extent to which the majority of studies frequently evoke it, but rarely provide deep explanations on how technology informs organisational design and practices. Thus the paper raises awareness on the vague use of the notion of ICT in the debate on co-working. It also makes an effort to place the interplay of ICT and co-working within the wider context of the relationship between technology and organisations.

In the next pages, we outline our research patbh (Sect. 2) and then identify and summarise the major themes emerging from a selective review of co-working studies (Sect. 3). Section 4 gives a preliminary answer to our questions. The discussion that follows (Sect. 5) highlights the analytical gains that a conception of co-working as 'work-oriented infrastructure' yields. Finally, the paper identifies interlinked areas worthy of further attention.

2 Method

Given the multifaceted and unstable character of co-working, the research approach must necessarily be interdisciplinary. It must draw on insights from different lenses to capture the ambiguities, dilemmas, and contradictions that emerge in the field of co-working. Accordingly, we performed a scoping literature review with the aim of mapping research streams and identifying areas worth further investigation.

By definition, a literature review is based on a rigorous and transparent methodology [13] and can be adopted for different reasons and with different approaches depending on the aim of the review and the topic under study. As with any empirical research, a review process generally consists of at least three phases: data collection, data analysis, and synthesis. However, according to Wolfswinkel et al. [14: 1] "compared with the vast and deep breadth of literature on empirical research methods and philosophical approaches to science, there are in contrast very few instructional texts for conducting a solid literature review". Among them, we can mention the well-established PRISMA model that has been employed primarily in medical settings [15]; the method developed by Denyer and Tranfield [16] encompassing five steps in producing a systematic review; other scholars proposed the 'scoping' study as an alternative review method that comprises a further type of literature review [17, 18].

In general, a scoping review represents a special technique to 'map' relevant literature in a given field of interest. Different reasons underpin the adoption of a scoping review [18]: it can be seen as a first step within an ongoing process of reviewing with the ultimate aim to produce a full systematic review. The scoping approach might be also conceived as a method in its own right able to identify knowledge gaps. In this latter case, it may or may not lead ultimately to a full systematic review. However, in comparison with other review methods, a scoping review is distinguished by its ability to rapidly map the field under study and quickly identify the emergent gaps.

After formulating the research question(s) to be addressed (stage 1) - i.e., W*hat are the main debates around co-working (RQa),* and *How is technology placed within those debates (discourses) (RQb)? -* we identified the relevant studies (stage 2). Our mapping of the contributions started with an initial exploratory review of academic papers on the topic. First, fundamental keywords have been identified. To avoid issues concerning, for example, plural forms, wildcards have been used; the ultimate keywords adopted in our research are: 'future of work', 'co-working', 'technology'. Keywords were searched for throughout the whole manuscript. The type of article searched has been limited to published or in press articles with an English version available. Conference papers were not included in the search because conference papers usually have tight constraints on length, which limit authors' contribution. Last, the databases to be consulted were chosen; to include as many results as possible, the same search was performed on Scopus, Web of Science, Proquest and JSTOR.

Then, a list of contributions fitting the criteria was downloaded from each of the selected sources. We restricted the search to articles published between 2005 and 2020. Preliminary data cleaning has been performed to merge papers from multiple sources into a single entry. This step generated a list of about 100 articles. We then performed a second check on the bibliographies of studies found through the database searches to identify further references to be included. A further step consisted in the study selection (stage 3). We reviewed 62 relevant papers from different disciplines, including economic geography, urban planning, cultural and communication studies, management and organisation studies. This enabled us to achieve an initial understanding of the phenomenon, identifying the key themes and discussions associated with co-working. We performed the open coding phase: each author separately assigned one or more conceptual labels to each paper of the sample basket. Through the axial coding, the main concepts were grouped into coherent conceptual categories. Again, this was made by each author separately. Then, we discussed together the defined categories and reconciled them. Finally, the conceptual categories were connected one to the other in a coherent scheme. We proceeded to chart the data (stage 4) and, finally, collect, summarise and report the results (stage 5), which we present in the following section where the main debates around the co-working paradigm are grouped into thematic areas.

3   Results

3.1   Definitions and Foundations of Co-working

The notion of co-working has recently gained increasing attention amongst scholars from different disciplines, including economic geography, urban planning, business studies (e.g. [8, 19–21]) which have offered accounts of how co-working emerged and what its distinguishing features are.

It is generally recognised that the first co-working space was opened up in San Francisco in 2005. Brad Neuberg – a member of the open-source movement [22] - laid the groundwork for what it would spread out to later in most of the major cities: a space in-between a formal office and a private home, mixing professional activities with collaborative leisure-like activities in an informal space ([19, 21, 23, 24]).

A broad strand of studies on co-working from a diverse set of disciplines (including information systems, urban planning, management, cultural studies, sociology) is primarily concerned with the reconstruction of the phenomenon and consequently with its illustration and definition ([8, 25–28]).

For example, in their account on novel work arrangements, Spreitzer et al. [29] define co-working as "membership-based workplaces composed of a diverse group of people who do not necessarily work for the same company" (p. 491). As such, one of the defining features of co-working is that here different professionals get together to work on individual projects [8] and that such a diversified group of professionals often belong to different fields. The authors observe that co-working contexts respond to the need for working from alternative and more informal spaces, yet they provide a sense of connection to individuals. Professional affiliation and identity markers are, therefore, key aspects offered by co-working.

As further outlined by Merkel [23], the very structure of these spaces—conceived as informal, flexible and open—underpins a "normative cultural model that promotes a set of values such as community, collaboration, openness, diversity, and sustainability" [23:124]. In sum, co-working is "not just about working 'alone together' or 'alongside each other' in a flexible and mostly affordable office space" (p. 124). It is, rather, a social practice that needs to be situated within the structural changes in the general labour market and in the organisation of work [23: 125]. Overall, ideas about work that circulate in coworking discourse tend to focus on individual experience [30].

3.2 The Collaborative Dimension: Community, Collaboration and Knowledge Exchange

A growing body of literature on co-working addresses the issues of social community and relationality by illustrating how community feelings emerge in these spaces [19, 24–26, 31]. For example, Robelski, et al. [32] observe that interacting remains a primary reason for choosing to work in a co-working facility. Interestingly and paradoxically, how and how often interaction takes place seem to follow an opposing dynamic if compared to more traditional working settings. For example, if on the one hand, the co-working 'amplifies the relationality among members' also through emotional connections [33]— in the hope that users share knowledge or cooperate across their respective projects [34]—on the other hand, the openness of co-working does not necessarily mean open communication [35: 248, 36].

A further connection is also made between interaction and knowledge exchange in these spaces. Butcher [37:339] highlights how the temporary spatial proximity between coworkers provides opportunities to combine and disseminate knowledge from different domains at particular times. However, Parrino [38] notes, social proximity alone is not sufficient to create the interactions and knowledge flows that can lead to innovation.

Much of the appeal of co-working lies in its capacity to foster social relations. [39] look at how a feeling of community emerges within shared locations when people establish bonds and a sense of common purpose. Along these lines, scholars [40] have focused their attention on the affective quality of social atmospheres, investigating the aesthetic dimensions of co-working spaces.

As reported by Foertsch [41] in the 2019 Global Coworking *Survey*, for 56% of the members, interaction with other members and a strong community are still the most important deciding factors for co-working. In a recent article published by *Organization Studies*, Garrett et al. [19] observe that co-working fosters community relationships. Such ways of working act as an antidote to the sense of loneliness which sometimes affects independent workers. As emerged from interviews conducted with co-working individuals, in these contexts the community is actively co-constructed through daily interaction and the creation of a sense of purpose.

Along similar lines, Spinuzzi [26] and Capdevila [21] found that feelings of isolation, inability to build trust and relations experienced in home offices are among the reasons that lead people to co-working. The authors take a step further by investigating the connection between community and collaboration. Collaboration is seen as the engine that enables the feeling of community to emerge. This point is reiterated in many studies that have looked at the benefits coming from cooperation ([21, 24, 42]).

Research has argued that collaboration increases the chance of knowledge exchange, which ultimately fosters creativity, innovation and value creation [10, 31, 42]. Much of this literature implicitly suggests that the very coexistence of freelancers and microbusinesses with complementary skills fosters knowledge sharing. The knowledge that is shared by coworkers is a "crucial way to provide the diversification and collaboration required for innovation" [31: 7]. And, by the same token, Moriset [43] and Kopplin [44] observe that serendipitous encounters and the probability of meeting with people from diverse backgrounds is the rationale behind bringing different professionals together.

3.3   The Aesthetic Dimension: Workspace Design, Creativity and Innovation

Co-working is often set against traditional work arrangements. To a certain extent, co-working challenges but does not replace standard facilities. According to Turkle [36: 122], 'the spaces themselves become liminal, not entirely public, not entirely private'. Therefore, spaces in these, what one might call 'technologically dense environments' [45] are continually reconfigured by the multiple meanings of practices, giving rise to hybrid organisational forms in which the boundaries between the individual sphere and the context become mobile and cannot be predetermined. For instance, Bandinelli and Gandini [46] use the term 'collaborative individualism' to capture the ambivalence of co-working and coworkers' sociality, and the coexistence of entrepreneurialised and individualised conduct with an ethical framework of sharing and collaborating.

Furthermore, it is suggested that aspects of physical structure, i.e. location, layout and proximity to others, shape patterns of work coordination, and can be correlated with organisational outcomes such as efficiency and performance. Accordingly, physical spaces can be instrumentally designed to serve organisational purposes [35: 240]. For instance, co-working is meant as logistic support and reference point to knowledge workers becoming independent contractors and freelancers as a consequence of organisational downsizing and outsourcing processes [22: 111]. In turn, the outsourcing of physical structures offers built spaces that can be tailored to individual needs and budgets. Also, locating co-working spaces near influential stakeholders, such as funding institutions or universities engaged in research, can be a strategy to manage organisational dependency on scarce and critical resources. Overall, the above streams of research assume a relation between organising and how the physical layout and spatial dimension are orchestrated [34].

Overall, coworking is more than just a third space [47]. Research argues that effective collaboration, among other things, requires arranging for appropriate configurations of the workspace (e.g. [20]). As observed by de Vaujany et al. [48], aesthetic codes, atmosphere, and spatial configurations shape the constitution of people's experiences and work activities. Gregg and Lodato [49] refer to ambience management as the activity of setting the stage for work and arranging the conditions that enable people to casually interact, connect and avoid sources of friction.

The design of the available space itself is attractive for specific users, such as freelancers. A good number of studies on co-working have argued that co-working is designed to enable independence, autonomy and free collaboration (e.g. [50]). Such values point to an entrepreneurial dimension that seems to be central in these novel workplaces. The entrepreneurial spirit is facilitated by infrastructure as well as an absence of hierarchy [51] which provides opportunities for the development of personal networks. Several studies have observed that innovation (e.g. [52]) can also be triggered through careful workspace design ([43, 51]). According to Capdevila [31], managers should orchestrate the conditions to enable innovation: social innovation, user-based innovation and open innovation are just some of the forms of innovation that can be triggered within these spaces.

Besides the rhetoric of workers' autonomy, innovation and self-fulfilment, a further connection is made between co-working and its effect on urban renewal. The fact that in many cities such spaces are appearing either as corporate spaces or as part of public initiatives can be explained as broader interventions in urban contexts. As noted by Merkel [23: 124], co-working can be assimilated to phenomena such as 'community gardens, neighborhoods councils, and artistic interventions', all initiatives emerged as forms of re-appropriation of underused city spaces. As such, co-working is deemed to contribute to creative districts and creative cities, more generally.

3.4 The *Place* of Technology Within the Debate on Co-working

What exactly is the place of technology within those discussions and debates on co-working? To address this question, here we draw from the five broad clusters (or 'views of technology') illustrated by Orlikowski and Iacono [53] in their highly influential article: *Desperately seeking the "IT" in IT research. A call to theorizing the IT artifact*, i.e. Tool view; Proxy view; Ensemble view; Computational view; Nominal view. We adapted and applied this classification to our set of codified publications (Table 1).

A first glance at the most-cited studies on co-working leads to the general observation that ICTs are deemed critical variables (or enabling resources) for the diffusion of more flexible forms of work, outside of traditional workspaces [19]. The latest technologies are seen to be an integral part (a 'strong presence') of co-working [54]. However, recent research on the emergence of 'liquid consumption' [56] patterns seems to challenge the rational *tool view* of technology. According to Bardhi and Eckhardt [56], for example, in social and economic conditions characterised by professional precarity, people tend to access rather than own consumption resources and rely on high-tech, portable technologies and digital communication tools. From this perspective, ICTs are seen as tools

Table 1. Conceptualization of ICT in co-working literature (based on [53])

Cluster	Conceptualization of technology	Examples from the paper analysis
Tool view	Artefacts are expected to do what its designers intend them to do	[19, 54]
Proxy view	Key aspects of technology may be captured through surrogate measures	[55]
Ensemble view	ICT is analysed in association with organizational context of use	[19, 40]
Computational view	The focus is on technical features (e.g. modelling capabilities) of artefacts	[7, 44]
Nominal view	References to technology are either incidental or used as background information	[9, 33]

with which coworkers (as *liquid consumers*) manage to reconcile their jobs and social relationships.

Second, consistent with a *proxy view,* co-working exemplifies the convergence of macro-trends that characterise post-industrialism and the information society. Simply put, technological advances are the engine of nonstandard configurations of working. In this view ICT artefacts are usually regarded as devices that enable independent workers and teleworkers, teams and groups, and organisations to realise business opportunities and performance benefits (*computational view*). A recent quantitative study [55] has delineated inputs, outputs and outcomes of co-working in UK. In both the proxy and computational views 'technology' is largely taken to be physical artefact or collection of attributes which have direct and readable effects on behaviour [57: 15].

Third, the increasing dependence on the internet and mobile technologies not only to enable communication but also to facilitate the sharing of data and ICT tools across time, space and platforms is underlined in studies that highlight the social content of co-working. For instance, spatial, social and digital elements [40] co-shape creative processes. Studies typically compare the effects of ICTs with those of face-to-face communication. Turkle's original point of view, summarised in the phrase [36: 122]: "The connectedness that 'matters' is determined by our distance from available communications technology", offers two further points for reflection. First, it allows us to observe that what people want out of public spaces is that they offer a place to be private with tethering technologies. Second, and interestingly, it highlights that participation in the technologies of everyday practices as well as social relations, production processes and activities [58] are necessary to become a full member of a community of practice [37: 331]. The common wisdom, ICTs help build a sense of community [19]. However, more skeptical commentators argue that it is nothing beyond the mediated performance [33: 9]. Also, technology has given rise to networked individualism [59]. To better support the task of setting up a new company or a freelancing project, members are required to co-develop local digital architectures. Working across multiple platforms and channels has been labelled *digital bricolage* [40]. It denotes an *ensemble view* of technology.

The *nominal view* of technology, on the other hand, refers to all those contributions (the majority) where technology is absent or undertheorised. Generic terms – including: digital technology, technological change, 'digital technologies for connectivity' [9], ICT, digital platforms - are used as mere background information. Furthermore, in many studies that engage with technology minimally, the main focus is elsewhere, e.g.,: on entrepreneurialism, socioeconomic change, sharing economy [55], business innovation [52]. The space for the conceptualization of artefacts is therefore limited. It should be noted that there are also contributions – e.g. [40] - that interpret the role of technology in a critical way, that is, with the aim of capturing the ambiguities, tensions, and contradictions that lie under the surface of co-working practices [33]. Studies connect pervasive digitalization of work with rising job insecurity [29] and precarisation [30]. Questions of power and control have somehow been left aside in mainstream approaches to the study of technologies and new forms of work [27].

4 Discussion

Information and communication technologies are an integral aspect of the global phenomenon of co-working. However, judging from our review, the conceptualization of ICT is underestimated. This is consistent with the original study by Orlikowski and Iacono [53]. Simply put, little has been done so far to explore how ICT artefacts play out in practice in these settings. Extant research that engages with co-working has explored ICT only in a cursory 'nominal' way [53], so technology takes a back seat.

Commentators rarely go beyond a metaphorical (rather than analytical) use of technology. The high level of abstraction means that, paradoxically, technology disappears from the analytical attention. Even where ICT is mentioned, the primary emphasis of the authors is elsewhere. The upshot is a conceptualisation in which the space for 'technological choice' is very limited. Invoking technology 'in name only, but not in fact' [14: 128], in turn, prevents analysis from connecting the social to the technological. Consequently, the understanding of the key issues that co-working raises on organizing is narrow and misleading. First, the analytical separation between the technological sphere and the social sphere leads us to consider - erroneously - technology no longer as a choice, but as a 'contextual' element with respect to organizational choices. Second, this delimitation reduces the perception of the relevance and interest of the IT/IS scientific community in co-working studies. It is not coincidence that only a small number of the papers selected for scoping review have been published in journals included in the AISeL Library. Third and finally, considering technology as a reified element and also an external constraint prevents a reliable account of the exceptions, ambivalences and 'hybrid' situations that are encountered in practice (see examples in Sect. 3).

The predominant 'nominal' view of technology is really surprising if we consider that numerous theoretical perspectives that have sought to illuminate the organisation-technology interactions actually date back to the past century. Neglect of ICT artefacts and platforms in research on co-working is difficult to explain in light of the current spread of digital technologies in workplaces and all domains of life. As nicely written by Orlikowski and Scott [60: 88]:

Work today always entails the digital; even where the work itself doesn't directly involve a computing device, most contemporary work relates to digital phenomenon. What we mean by this is that most work practices involve digital technology to a greater or lesser extent — whether through digital networks that transfer email, cellular communications, and webpages or the computers that process financial transactions [...], and handle logistics so parcels can be delivered on time. [...] all work is today being reconfigured in relation to digital technologies [...].

Let us take a step back to better understand this point.

Early on Star and Ruhleder [61] emphasised the importance of approaching IT artefacts as complex infrastructural formations. According to Tilson et al. [62: 756–758], the infrastructure-turn calls us to critically review the categories that have so far helped us make sense of the sociotechnical reality we study. Indeed, while research on organisations has mainly focused on organisational structures, a growing body of literature, particularly within the field of science and technology studies [63, 64], places 'universal service infrastructures', including water systems, electricity or information systems, at the centre of the analysis.

Here, we do not consider infrastructure as "some kind of purified technology, but rather, in a perspective where the technology cannot be separated from social and other non-technological elements" [65: 349]. Actually, in our scoping review, we found only scant discussion about complex infrastructural formations supporting the new working practice in shared spaces. Thus, while we recognise that several studies on co-working highlight the essential role of both human and social elements, along with other non-technological factors (e.g., physical spaces), not the same attention has been given to the technological elements.

One more question then arises: how can conceiving co-working as 'work-oriented infrastructure' [65] help a fuller appreciation of what is currently at stake? Due to space limitations, only sketchy considerations will be outlined here.

To begin with, we can say that technology becomes transparent when its use and functioning can be taken for granted, namely when social and technical relationships are firmly established [66]. Put simply, we may say that technology is invisible because it is *consolidated* and opaque. The former property is rooted in a process of "deep ecological penetration" [65: 359] by which the interdependencies of artefacts and technologies become embedded into the practices of the infrastructure and vice versa. The opaqueness originates from the ubiquitous nature of technologies that support specific and highly complex work tasks. Deep penetration implies that *even* the co-workers are 'unconscious about the properties' [65: 365] of the infrastructures they use. Following Kornberger and Clegg [67: 1095] co-working spaces can be thought of as "material, spatial ensembles" that organise in unanticipated ways the flows of communication, knowledge, and movement between heterogeneous groups of users.

The above arguments appear as an optimistic and comfortable understanding of the technology's absence from the mainstream debate on co-working.

However, we could also—and certainly more critically—observe that by seeming innocuous, co-working spaces and related technologies "normalize power relations by fixing them in undeniable material reality" [68: 262]. Based on this observation, we claim that consolidation and opaqueness are not neutral; rather they entail a potential imbalance in power between those who provide the (work-oriented) infrastructure and those who use it. The former actors dictate the rules of the game and will try to use technologies to govern and control organisational processes in a non-coercive way, however little they are subject to claims and conflicts. The latter come into contact with digital artefacts and facilities, and, where possible, appropriate them through subjective knowledge and purposive action. In other cases, the constraints conveyed by the artefacts will shape co-workers' choices.

All of which suggests that thinking about co-working as being infrastructurally mediated means putting the link between technology and social regulation processes at the centre of reflection. Conceptually, an interpretation informed by such a view offers an analytical tool to untangle the invisible work [69] performed by the users of co-working spaces, as well as the invisible work made by the providers and designers of the infrastructure (of which technology is one element) to incorporate users' needs.

5 Concluding Remarks

In the words of Orlikowski and Iacono [53], here, we were desperately seeking technology in the co-working literature. Drawing on a preliminary scoping review we discovered that mainstream research on co-working tends to engage with technologies only minimally. We also noticed that this 'nominal view', paradoxically, has reduced the weight of ICT as an issue of specific reflection, pertinent to the organisational study field. Therefore, we argued that a fuller appreciation of the relationship between technology and co-working requires a reflection on social regulation processes which take place in a broader context where "no single actor can design and govern the structure" [70: 156].

The predominance of the nominal view of technology in co-working research suggests that there are opportunities for considering more elaborated views and conceptualizations. In particular, the infrastructural lens brings our attention to actors' divergences, and to the presence of a variety of regulative regimes that produce new constraints, alignments, and new opportunities for the different categories of actors. This alternative perspective also offers a way to recognize the complex dimensions of co-working, thus acknowledging the multiplicity (along with invisibility) of practices, and rejecting unidimensional visions of technology, virtual organizing and distributed work configurations.

Starting from these preliminary results, further research should consider together the points of view of employers, co-workers and providers of co-working facilities. Future efforts should adopt mixed methodologies, i.e. qualitative and quantitative analysis at a micro, individual level. We acknowledge several limitations related to the chosen study design. For example, as we said at the outset, the review of co-working scholarship is not meant to be exhaustive or even necessarily representative. We also point out that the tags used by the different studies do not always have the same meaning. Moreover, the inclusion and classification criteria are the personal choices of the authors of this paper.

Our discussion can only remain open and must necessarily be enriched with contributions from other scholars who share its assumptions. The challenge has just begun, yet promises to be highly rewarding.

References

1. Halford, S.: Hybrid workspace: re-spatialisations of work, organisation and management. New Technol. Work. Employ. **20**(1), 19–33 (2005)
2. Gregg, M., Kneese, T.: Clock. In: Beyes, T., Holt, R., Pias, C. (eds.) The Oxford Handbook of Media, Technology, and Organization Studies, pp. 95–105. OUP, Oxford (2020)
3. Fineman, S.: Work: A Very Short Introduction. OUP, Oxford (2012)
4. OECD: Embracing Innovation in Government. OECD, Paris (2018)
5. Ropo, A., et al.: Why does space need to be taken seriously in leadership and organization studies and practice? In: Ropo, A., et al. (eds.) Leadership in Spaces and Places, pp. 1–24. Edward Elgar, Cheltenham (2015)
6. Luckman, S., Andrew, J.: Online selling and the growth of home-based craft micro-enterprise: the 'new normal' of women's self-(under) employment. In: Taylor, S., Luckman, S. (eds.) The New Normal of Working Lives, pp. 19–39. Palgrave Macmillan, Cham (2018)
7. Waters-Lynch, J., et al.: Coworking: a transdisciplinary overview, pp. 1–58. SSRN (2016)
8. Gandini, A.: The rise of coworking spaces: a literature review. Ephemera **15**(1), 193 (2015)
9. Richardson, L.: Sharing as a postwork style: digital work and the co-working office. Camb. J. Reg. Econ. Soc. **10**(2), 297–310 (2017)
10. van Dijk, S.: At home in the workplace: the value of materiality for immaterial labor in Amsterdam. Eur. J. Cult. Stud. **22**(4), 468–483 (2019)
11. Meyer, U., Schaupp, S., Seibt, D.: Digitalization in Industry. Palgrave, Cham (2019)
12. Beverungen, A., Beyes, T., Conrad, L.: The organizational powers of (digital) media. Organization **26**(5), 621–635 (2019)
13. Greenhalgh, T., et al.: Diffusion of innovations in service organizations: systematic review and recommendations. Milbank Q. **82**(4), 581–629 (2004)
14. Wolfswinkel, J.F., Furtmueller, E., Wilderom, C.P.: Using grounded theory as a method for rigorously reviewing literature. Eur. J. Inf. Syst. **22**(1), 45–55 (2013)
15. Harris, J.D., et al.: How to write a systematic review. Am. J. Sports Med. **42**(11), 2761–2768 (2014)
16. Denyer, D., Tranfield, D.: Producing a systematic review. In: Buchanan, D.A., Bryman, A. (eds.) The SAGE Handbook of Organizational Research Methods, pp. 671–689. Sage, London (2009)
17. Pham, M.T., et al.: A scoping review of scoping reviews: advancing the approach and enhancing the consistency. Res. Synth. Methods **5**(4), 371–385 (2014)
18. Arksey, H., O'Malley, L.: Scoping studies: towards a methodological framework. Int. J. Soc. Res. Methodol. **8**(1), 19–32 (2005)
19. Garrett, L.E., Spreitzer, G.M., Bacevice, P.A.: Co-constructing a sense of community at work: the emergence of community in coworking spaces. Organ. Stud. **38**(6), 821–842 (2017)
20. Salovaara, P.: What can the coworking movement tell us about the future of workplaces? In: Ropo, A., et al. (eds.) Leadership in Spaces and Places, pp. 27–48. Edward Elgar Publishing, Cheltenham (2015)
21. Spinuzzi, C., et al.: "Coworking is about community": but what is "community" in coworking? J. Bus. Tech. Commun. **33**(2), 112–140 (2019)
22. Bodrožić, Z., Adler, P.S.: The evolution of management models: a neo-Schumpeterian theory. Adm. Sci. Q. **63**(1), 85–129 (2018)
23. Merkel, J.: Coworking in the city. Ephemera **15**(2), 121–139 (2015)
24. Rus, A., Orel, M.: Coworking: a community of work. Teorija in Praksa **52**(6), 1017–1038 (2015)
25. Brown, J.: Curating the "Third Place"? Coworking and the mediation of creativity. Geoforum **82**, 112–126 (2017)

26. Spinuzzi, C.: Working alone together: coworking as emergent collaborative activity. J. Bus. Tech. Commun. **26**(4), 399–441 (2012)
27. Aroles, J., Mitev, N., de Vaujany, F.X.: Mapping themes in the study of new work practices. New Technol. Work. Employ. **34**(3), 285–299 (2019)
28. Blagoev, B., Costas, J., Kärreman, D.: 'We are all herd animals': community and organizationality in coworking spaces. Organization **26**(6), 894–916 (2019)
29. Spreitzer, G.M., Cameron, L., Garrett, L.: Alternative work arrangements: two images of the new world of work. Ann. Rev. Organ. Psych. Organ. Behav. **4**(1), 473–499 (2017)
30. de Peuter, G., Cohen, N.S., Saraco, F.: The ambivalence of coworking: on the politics of an emerging work practice. Eur. J. Cult. Stud. **20**(6), 687–706 (2017)
31. Capdevila, I.: Joining a collaborative space: is it really a better place to work? J. Bus. Strateg. **40**(2), 14–21 (2019)
32. Robelski, S., et al.: Coworking spaces: the better home office? A Psychosoc. Health-Related Perspect. Emerg. Work Environ. **16**(13), 2379 (2019)
33. De Vaujany, F.-X., Leclercq-Vandelannoitte, A., Holt, R.: Communities versus platforms: the paradox in the body of the collaborative economy. J. Manag. Inq. **29**(4), 450–467 (2019)
34. Cnossen, B., Bencherki, N.: The role of space in the emergence and endurance of organizing: how independent workers and material assemblages constitute organizations. Human Relations **72**(6), 1057–1080 (2019)
35. Hatch, M.J.: Organization Theory, 2nd edn. OUP, Oxford (2006)
36. Turkle, S.: Always-on/always-on-you: the tethered self. In: Katz, J. (ed.) Handbook of Mobile Communication Studies and Social Change, pp. 120–137. The MIT Press, Cambridge (2008)
37. Butcher, T.: Learning everyday entrepreneurial practices through coworking. Manage. Learn. **49**(3), 327–345 (2018)
38. Parrino, L.: Coworking: assessing the role of proximity in knowledge exchange. Knowl. Manag. Res. Pract. **13**(3), 261–271 (2015)
39. Waters-Lynch, J., Duff, C.: The affective commons of Coworking. Human Relations, 1–22 (2019). (in press)
40. Toivonen, T., Sorensen, C.: The Creative Process in Coworking & Collaborative Work: Insights for Executives, Managers & Designers (2018)
41. Foertsch, C.: 2019 State of Coworking: Over 2 Million Coworking Space Members Expected. Deskma (2019)
42. Cabral, V., Van Winden, W.: Coworking: an analysis of coworking strategies for interaction and innovation. Int. J. Knowl. Based Dev. **7**(4), 357 (2016)
43. Moriset, B.: Building new places of the creative economy. The rise of co-working spaces. In: 2nd Geography of Innovation International Conference 2014, Utrecht January 23–25 (2014)
44. Kopplin, C.S.: Two heads are better than one: matchmaking tools in coworking spaces. Rev. Manage. Sci. 1–25 (2020). (in press)
45. Bruni, A., Pinch, T., Schubert, C.: Technologically dense environments: what for? What next? Tecnoscienza **4**(2), 51–72 (2013)
46. Bandinelli, C., Gandini, A.: Hubs vs networks in the creative economy: towards a 'collaborative individualism.' In: Gill, R., Pratt, A.C., Virani, T.E. (eds.) Creative Hubs in Question. DVW, pp. 89–110. Springer, Cham (2019). https://doi.org/10.1007/978-3-030-10653-9
47. Krause, I.: Coworking spaces: windows to the future of work? Changes in the organizational model of work and the attitudes of the younger generation. Foresight STI Govern. **13**(2), 52–60 (2019)
48. De Vaujany, F.-X., et al.: Experiencing a new place as an atmosphere: A focus on tours of collaborative spaces. Scand. J. Manage. **35**(2), 101030 (2019)
49. Gregg, M., Lodato, T.: Coworking, hospitality and the future of work. In: Röttger-Rössler, B., Slaby, J. (Eds.) Affect in Relation. Families, Places, Technologies, 1–22. Routledge, London (2018)

50. Bouncken, R.B., Reuschl, A.J.: Coworking-spaces: how a phenomenon of the sharing economy builds a novel trend for the workplace and for entrepreneurship. RMS **12**(1), 317–334 (2016). https://doi.org/10.1007/s11846-016-0215-y
51. Bouncken, R.B., Fredrich, V.: Good fences make good neighbors? Directions and safeguards in alliances on business model innovation. J. Bus. Res. **69**(11), 5196–5202 (2016)
52. Cheah, S., Ho, Y.-P.: Coworking and sustainable business model innovation in young firms. Sustainability **11**(10), 2959 (2019)
53. Orlikowski, W.J., Iacono, S.C.: Research commentary: desperately seeking the "IT" in IT research—a call to theorizing the IT artifact. Inf. Syst. Res. **12**(2), 121–134 (2001)
54. De Paoli, D., Sauer, E., Ropo, A.: The spatial context of organizations: a critique of 'creative workspaces.' J. Manag. Organ. **25**(2), 331–352 (2019)
55. Clifton, N., Füzi, A., Loudon, G.: Coworking in the digital economy: context, motivations, and outcomes. Futures, 1–16 (2019). (in press)
56. Bardhi, F., Eckhardt, G.M.: Liquid consumption. J. Consum. Res. **44**(3), 582–597 (2017)
57. McLaughlin, I.: Creative Technological Change. Routledge, London (1990)
58. Lave, J., Wenger, E.: Situated Learning: Legitimate Peripheral Participation. Cambridge University Press, Cambridge (1991)
59. Wellman, B., Boase, J., Chen, W.: The networked nature of community: online and offline. IT & Soc. **1**(1), 151–165 (2002)
60. Orlikowski, W.J., Scott, S.V.: Digital work: a research agenda. In: Czarniawska, B. (ed.) A Research Agenda for Management and Organization Studies, pp. 88–96. Edward Elgar, Cheltenham (2016)
61. Star, S.L., Ruhleder, K.: Steps toward an ecology of infrastructure: design and access for large information spaces. Inf. Syst. Res. **7**(1), 111–134 (1996)
62. Tilson, D., Lyytinen, K., Sørensen, C.: Research commentary—digital infrastructures: the missing IS research agenda. Inf. Syst. Res. **21**(4), 748–759 (2010)
63. Winner, L.: Upon opening the black box and finding it empty: social constructivism and the philosophy of technology. Sci. Technol. Human Values **18**(3), 362–378 (1993)
64. Kallinikos, J.: Recalcitrant Technology: Cross-contextual Systems and Content-embedded Action. LSE, London (2002)
65. Hanseth, O., Lundberg, N.: Designing work oriented infrastructures. Comput. Support. Cooper. Work (CSCW) **10**(3–4), 347–372 (2001)
66. Bruni, A., Gherardi, S.: Studiare le pratiche lavorative. IL Mulino, Bologna (2007)
67. Kornberger, M., Clegg, S.R.: Bringing space back in: organizing the generative building. Organ. Stud. **25**(7), 1095–1114 (2004)
68. Hatch, M.J.: Organization Theory. OUP, Oxford (2018)
69. Star, S.L., Strauss, A.: Layers of silence, arenas of voice: the ecology of visible and invisible work. Comput. Support. Cooper. Work (CSCW) **8**(1–2), 9–30 (1999)
70. Bygstad, B.: Generative mechanisms for innovation in information infrastructures. Inf. Organ. **20**(3), 156–168 (2010)

Managerial Perspectives. Coproducing Intangible Assets and Values in Organizations

Disability Management as a Corporate Social Innovation Process

Walter Castelnovo$^{(\boxtimes)}$ (iD)

University of Insubria, Varese, Italy
Walter.castelnovo@uninsubria.it

Abstract. This exploratory paper discusses disability management as a corporate social innovation process, based on the mapping of selected cases of enterprises often cited as international best practices. The aim of the study is to identify some critical success factors firms should consider when developing their disability management programs. To this end, the selected cases are analyzed based on a grid defined by comparing disability management guidelines published by international organizations generally considered as important points of reference for the job integration of persons with disabilities. The contribution of the paper is twofold. On the one hand, the results of the mapping can help firms to identify and classify different strategies and measures they can adopt to develop their disability management programs. On the other hand, the paper contributes to the bridging of a gap still present in the literature since disability management has so far received little attention in the literature on both corporate social responsibility and corporate social innovation.

Keywords: Disability management · Corporate social innovation · Persons with disabilities · Work integration · Work retention

1 Introduction

According to the United Nations Industrial Development Organization, social innovation "refers to a novel solution to a social problem that is more effective, efficient, sustainable, or just than current solutions [1]. Mulgan, Ali, Halkett and Sanders [2] define social innovation as "the development and implementation of new ideas (products, services and models) to meet social needs" (p. 9). It amounts to a "complex process of introducing new products, processes or programs that profoundly change the basic routines, resource and authority flows, or beliefs of the social system in which the innovation occurs" [3, p. 235]. The International Labor Organization [4], relates the social value of innovation to the capacity of determining social transformations, fostering social development, increasing welfare and reducing social inequalities. Hence, the main goal of social innovation is to identify and satisfy social needs emerging not only from the traditional situations of hardship and marginalization, but also from new challenges posed by the contemporary world, e.g. sustainability, quality of life and quality of work.

© The Author(s), under exclusive license to Springer Nature Switzerland AG 2022
S. Za et al. (Eds.): ItAIS 2020, LNISO 50, pp. 89–103, 2022.
https://doi.org/10.1007/978-3-030-86858-1_6

Social innovation has been traditionally discussed mainly with reference to not-for-profit organizations. To refer to the firms' responsibility for the impacts of their decisions and activities on society and the environment the term Corporate Social Responsibility (CSR) in used, instead [5]. However, organizations and business entities are more and more expected to move beyond the traditional CSR to a new and different paradigm that can cope with the demands and needs of the present dynamic economic environment [6]. Kanter [7] defines Corporate Social Innovation (CSI) this new paradigm that aims at commercially driven benefits and at the same time contributes to the development of human well-being and societal quality and quantity of life [8]. This particular role of enterprises for social innovation has been explicitly acknowledged in the Social Innovation Europe initiative that is based on the idea that "social innovation can and must come from all sectors – the public sector, the private market, the third sector, and individuals/households – meaning that also firms have a role on it" [9, p. 19].

In the continuously growing literature on CSI, corporate social innovation is generally defined along the lines of the traditional definition of social innovation [8, 10]. Much of the research on CSI has focused on various aspects of corporate social innovation – e.g. the dimensions of innovation, the scope of change and how change is generated. However, less attention has been paid to the implementation process of corporate social innovation programs and to key organizational aspects, including the impacts on operational structures and processes and the role of organizational culture [11]. These aspects are critical as, different from CSR, "CSI involves deeper collaboration across functions within a firm and with external parties to co-create something new that provides a sustainable solution to social ills" [12, p. 5014].

Employment of persons with disabilities (PWD) extends social responsibility of corporate organizations [13–15] and represents a real opportunity for CSI. In fact, by increasing the level of diversity in the workforce, disability management represents a significant innovation opportunity for firms, one that can contribute to the firms' success and sustainable competitive advantage [16]. Notwithstanding this, the issue of PWDs' employment is still relatively less explored [17] and the role of business enterprises in supporting the employability of PWDs has rarely been reported in a clear manner [18, 19].

The paper discusses the establishment and development of the disability management function by firms as an example of CSI. By focusing on disability management, the paper aims at exploring some organizational aspects of the implementation of CSI programs, including the role of the management, the organizational culture and climate, the workforce composition, and the accommodation of working conditions. To this end, the paper considers how disability management has been implemented in a selected set of enterprises often cited as international best practices. The selected cases are analyzed based on an analysis grid defined by comparing disability management guidelines published by international organizations generally considered as important points of reference for the job integration of PWDs. The grid includes some of the most relevant organizational aspects of the development of corporate disability management. By using the grid to map the selected cases, different strategies and measures emerge that firms can adopt for the development of their disability management programs.

The contribution of the paper is twofold. On the one hand, the analysis grid can be seen as providing a guideline for a structured process for the development of the disability management function within firms. In fact, the mapping of the cases discussed in the paper allows the identification of some critical points that an organization should consider in designing and developing its disability management function, which is of practical importance. On the other hand, the paper contributes to the bridging of a gap still present in the literature, since disability management has so far received little attention in the literature on both CSR and CSI [15, 20, 21].

The paper proceeds as follows. The next section introduces disability management as a corporate social innovation process. Then the methodological approach is described, and the analysis grid is introduced. In the section that follows the analysis grid is applied to map the selected cases and the results of the mapping are discussed. Finally, some conclusions are drawn from the mapping and some limitations of the study as well as some future research directions are presented.

2 Disability Management as a Corporate Social Innovation Process

With the increasing differentiation of the workforce during the '90s, diversity has been suggested to enhance problem solving capabilities of a group, to provide better service to a diverse customer base, and to boost organizational creativity [22]. This led firms to start developing diversity management programs to transform possible problems deriving from workforce heterogeneity into opportunities [23]. According to Thomas [24] 'diversity management' refers to management practices implemented to deal with the issues of workplace inequality and diversity. Key to diversity management is that no person's competence and character should ever be overlooked or undervalued on account of race, sex, ethnicity, origins, or physical disability. Said differently, "diversity management is concerned with acceptance of a multicultural workforce comprising employees with diverse ethnic, racial, religious and gender backgrounds" [25, p. 249], as well as chronically ill and disable workers. This presupposes an open and inclusive organizational climate and an organizational culture that promotes workers for their merits and makes professional growth opportunities available for all [14, 15, 26].

Disability management, as well as chronic disease management, has occasionally been incorporated into diversity management. This is done based on the view of disability as a form of social diversity. However, there are some relevant differences between diversity management and disability management. Shrey and Lacertes [27] define disability management as "a proactive process that minimizes the impact of an impairment on the individual's capacity to participate competitively in the work environment" (p. 5). On the other hand, diversity management can be defined as "the voluntary organizational actions that are designed to create greater inclusion of the employees from various backgrounds into the formal organizational structures through deliberate policies and programs" [28, p. 208]. From this point of view, although diversity management and disability management share a common focus, there are important differences between the two. Diversity management "focuses more heavily on integrating different groups or units of employees", whereas for disability management the basic issues are "related to prevention, accommodation, being injured and the resulting return-to-work process.

Thus, disability management primarily deals with actual physical barriers arising from health issues. It focuses on the individual employee" [23, p. 87].

In general terms, it is now common to consider disability management as a broad and variegated set of practices aimed at promoting and supporting work integration and re-integration of people with disabilities. Disability management represents an increasingly relevant organizational function. Due to medical advances and increased life expectancy, the percentage of workers suffering from different non-ability conditions (including disabilities) is continuously increasing. Often these people are too young to retire and not sick enough to take disability leave. Moreover, they also want the self-esteem that comes from making ongoing contributions, and the social benefits that work relationships can offer [29]. Too often organizations are unaware of the chronic illness or disability conditions that impact on an employee's work life and the risk is that the situation only becomes apparent when it is too late for any intervention. As pointed out in [25], increasing organizational awareness of these issues helps to retain talented workers and allows people with chronic illness and disabilities to continue to contribute to the organization.

Disability management represents a corporate approach to enable organizations to take an active stance in maintenance and optimal functioning of employees with disability problems. Increasing participation of employees with disability or handicap, employing workers with partial work disability and offering them a new chance at labor participation is one of the major goals of re-integration policies [25]. Hence, disability management not only helps organizations to retain talented workers or to transform possible problems deriving from workforce heterogeneity into opportunities, but also contributes to fulfil more general social needs by promoting inclusion and improved quality of life for people in conditions of hardship. Disability management can thus be considered a relevant, and sometime even critical, component of the corporate social innovation activities.

Despite the increasing importance of disability management for firms and society at large, the concept is still broad and nebulous [30]. This makes it difficult for firms to identify the most appropriate disability management strategies and measures to adopt in their specific context. A structured analysis of how disability management has been implemented by firms considered as international best practices can thus help to identify and evaluate alternative solutions and guide firms in the development of their disability management programs.

3   Methodological Approach

The research reported in this paper has been conducted in two phases. In the first phase a search on the website of government agencies and international organizations generally considered as important point of reference for the job integration of PWDs has been performed. The search involved the following organizations:

- International Labour Organization
- World Economic Forum
- World Bank
- World Health Organization
- United Nation Department of Economic and Social Affair
- OECD
- International Disability Alliance
- Disability Management Employer Coalition (DMEC)
- European Disability Forum
- European Foundation for the Improvement of Living and Working Conditions
- European Association of Service Providers for Persons with Disabilities
- PATHWAYS Project – "Participation To Healthy Workplaces And Inclusive Strategies in the Work Sector"
- U.S. Centers for Disease Control and Prevention

From the comparative analysis of documents (guidelines, white papers, policy briefs, reports, and recommendations) published by the organizations above, the most important aspects to consider in the implementation of disability management as an organizational function have been identified. These elements, that can be considered as critical success factors for the implementation of disability management, have been codified in a grid that has been used in the second phase of the research to map some well-known international successful cases of disability management.

The components of the grid have been grouped according to a logic corresponding to the steps of an ideal structured approach to the implementation of disability management as a specific organizational function. This sequence of steps can be found, with some marginal variations, in the principal international guidelines for the implementation of disability management. For each step, some actions have been identified that should be performed to implement the disability management function. Finally, for each action to be performed, some alternative options are listed that have been found in the guidelines consulted for the study.

The complete grid with all the actions and the alternative implementation options is represented in the Figs. 1, 2 and 3 below.

DESIGN PHASE	
A.	**What motivates the need to implement a disability management function**
A.1	The need to comply with legislation
A.2	The opportunity of accessing funding by public or private organizations
A.3	The need to manage critical situations emerged within the organization (absence of personnel due to disability leave, deterioration of organizational climate, etc.)
A.4	The input from the top management
A.5	A line manager's autonomous initiative
A.6	The implementation of the organization's broader diversity management policy
B.	**Assessment of the initial conditions**
B.1	Assessment of disabilities within the workforce (known and emerging disabilities)
B.2	Assessment of the employment status of the employees with disabilities (tasks, wage status, skills, etc.)
B.3	Assessment of the potential barriers to the full employment of persons with disabilities (physical barriers, type of tasks, working hours, etc.)
B.4	Detection of stereotypes and preconceptions potentially affecting the full employment of persons with disabilities
B.5	Assessment of the diversity/disability management initiatives already implemented within the organization
B.6	Definition of a general organization's plan for the management of disability
C.	**Definition of the organizational arrangement**
C.1	Implementation of the disability management function as an autonomous organizational unit with a manager formally appointed as disability manager, possibly based on the appropriate certification (C.1a)
C.2	Appointment of a disability manager (without the establishment of as an autonomous disability management organizational unit), possibly with the appropriate certification (C.2a)
C.3	Hiring of external consultants to support the internal disability management organizational unit
C.4	Hiring of external consultants to support the organization's disability manager
C.5	Outsourcing of the disability management function to external consultants
C.6	Identification of non-managerial roles for supporting the integration of persons with disabilities at the operational level
D.	**Definition of the expected results**
D.1	Increased number of persons with disabilities employed in the organization
D.2	Improved the return-to-work conditions after disability leave periods (possibly also through appropriate workplace accommodations)
D.3	Improved conditions that help employees with disability stay at work (possibly also through appropriate workplace accommodations)
D.4	Make advancement opportunities available to employees with disabilities (guarantee to all the employees of the same training and career opportunities)

Fig. 1. The analysis grid: design phase

IMPLEMENTATION PHASE	
E.	**Implementation of disability management measures**
E.1	Design and implementation of training programs for managers devoted to specific aspects of the employment of persons with disabilities (recruitment, performance evaluation, career advancements, integration of persons with disabilities in teams, etc.)
E.2	Design and implementation of training programs specifically addressed to employees with disabilities to facilitate the acquisition of specific skills and operational capacities
E.3	Design and implementation of training programs addressed to all the employees on topics related to the integration of persons with disabilities
E.4	Managers' awareness raising interventions to sensitize the employees on topics related to the integration of persons with disabilities
E.5	Informational support provided by the HR function (or by other organizational units) to the employees with disabilities on their rights and obligations
E.6	Informational support provided by the HR function (or by other organizational units) to the line managers that must supervise the integration of persons with disabilities
E.7	Continuous involvement of the management in the development and implementation of the organization's disability management strategy
E.8	Design and implementation of measurement systems to assess the effectiveness of disability management interventions
E.9	Involvement of the 'competent doctor' in the design and implementation of the interventions for the integration of employees with disabilities
E.10	Collaboration with public and private organizations dealing with the employment of persons with disabilities both in the design and the implementation of the organization's disability management strategy
F.	**Structural interventions for the accommodation of the working conditions**
F.1	Interventions to remove physical barriers
F.2	Interventions to adapt the workplaces to different types of disabilities
F.3	Adoption of assistive technologies at the workplace
F.4	Accommodation of lighting, computer screens and communication devices
F.5	Interventions for easing the access to documents and files within the organization's information system
F.6	Adoption of a flexible working hours policy for the employees with disabilities
F.7	Adaptation of the tasks to the skills and abilities of the employees with disabilities

Fig. 2. The analysis grid: implementation phase

The cases to consider for the mapping have been identified starting from a report prepared for the DG Employment, Social Affairs and Equal Opportunities of the European Commission [31]. The report describes 24 company case studies of disability management across Europe. Each of the 24 cases has been considered and searched on the web to find further documentation for the aim of triangulation. The search involved both

EVALUATION PHASE	
G.	**Output evaluation of the disability management interventions**
G.1	Increased number of persons with disabilities employed (because of the disability management interventions)
G.2	Number of employees with disabilities involved in the disability management interventions implemented
G.3	Number of employees with disabilities who leave the work after the disability management interventions implemented
G.4	Improvement of the employees with disabilities' job positions and tasks because of the disability management interventions implemented
G.5	Improvement of the employees with disabilities' wage status because of the disability management interventions implemented
H.	**Outcome evaluation of the disability management interventions**
H.1	Detection of significant changes in the performances of the employees with disabilities
H.2	Detection of a significant reduction in the absence hours of the employees with disabilities
H.3	Detection of significant changes in the colleagues' perception of the performances of the employees with disabilities
H.4	Detection of a significant reduction of critical situations involving employees with disabilities
H.5	Detection of a positive impact on the general organizational climate
H.6	Detection of a positive impact on the organization's informal communication systems, especially with respect to the communication with the employees with disabilities

Fig. 3. The analysis grid: evaluation phase

secondary data sources and the companies' websites. At the end of the search, documentation useful for triangulation has been found only for 8 cases out of the 24 described in [31]. The selected cases are reported in Table 1.

Table 1. The selected cases

Case	Sector	Activity	Dimension (number of employees)	Employees with disabilities
1	Public	Local services	Large (>5000)	29% of the workforce
2	Private	Cosmetics	Large (>1800)	6% of the workforce
3	Private	Trade	Medium (110)	15% of the workforce
4	Private	Services	Large (>100000)	19% of the workforce
5	Private	Manufacturing	Small (40)	7% of the workforce
6	Private	Pharma	Large (>33000)	9% of the workforce
7	Private	ICT	Large (>350000)	12% of the workforce
8	Private	Bank	Large (>14000)	6% of the workforce

The 8 cases have been described by applying the grid developed in the first phase of the research to verify whether and how each element of the grid has been implemented in the specific case. This allowed to map different experiences of disability management with respect to the strategic vision behind the implementation, the contextual and organizational conditions that shaped the implementation, as well as the strengths and weaknesses of the implemented solution.

The steps of the research are summarized in Fig. 4.

Fig. 4. The steps of the research

4 Mapping the Selected Cases

4.1 Design Phase

In most of the cases considered in the study, the disability management function has been activated as part of the organization's broader diversity management function. In few cases the function has been activated because of an initiative directly promoted by the top management. Quite interestingly, in neither of the cases the need to comply with legislation or the opportunity to access funding - that are frequently mentioned among the reasons that can motivate firms to implement disability management - have played a role in the decision to implement the function. This can be considered as an indirect evidence that the more successful policies for disability management are those based on firms' autonomously designed strategies.

Concerning the organizational arrangement, the prevalent solution is the appointment of a disability manager (although only in one case based on the appropriate professional certification), possibly supported by external consultants. Only in three cases an autonomous unit has been created for disability management and, quite interestingly, one of them is a medium-size firm, meaning that the dimension of the organization does not necessarily represent an impeding condition for that solution.

Finally, for 7 of the 8 organizations considered, the expected results have been precisely defined already in the design phase. In most of the cases they concern the conditions that can help employees with disability to stay at work (possibly through appropriate workplace accommodations).

4.2 Implementation Phase

The implementation phase is the core of the firms' disability management strategies that, as observed above, in most of the cases have been designed to improve the conditions that can help employees with disabilities to stay at work. Hence, it is not surprising that most of the actions implemented by the firms amount to structural interventions for the accommodation of workplaces.

Quite interestingly, in almost all the cases considered in the study, measures have been implemented to adapt the job-tasks to the skills and abilities of the employees with disabilities. This, together with the design and implementation of intensive training programs specifically addressed to employees with disabilities, represents the core of the stay-to-work strategy implemented by the firms considered in the study.

In none of the cases, measures have been adopted to revise the working hours of the employees with disabilities, which means that the inclusion strategy implemented aims at introducing as few as possible differentiations between employees with disabilities and their colleagues. Interesting, although in somewhat negative terms, is also that in none of the cases the disability management strategy has been designed to make advancement opportunities available to employees with disabilities.

In most of the cases, measures have been implemented to assure the continuous involvement of the management in the development and implementation of the organization's disability management strategy. However, only in few cases specific information and training measures have been implemented to support the management in dealing with specific aspects of the employment and integration of PWDs. This helps explaining why only in two cases a role for managers has been envisaged to sensitize the employees on topics related to the integration of PWDs. Raising the employees' awareness on those topics has been considered relevant only in two of the cases. In these two cases specific training programs addressed to all the employees have been designed and implemented.

4.3 Evaluation Phase

In all the cases considered in the study, positive effects of the implementation of the disability management strategy are reported. These mainly concern significant changes in the performances of the employees with disabilities (6 cases), significant changes in the colleagues' perception of the performances of the employees with disabilities (5 cases) and a positive impact on the general organizational climate (4 cases). Interestingly, only in two cases an increase in the number of PWDs employed is reported, which confirms that for most of the organizations considered in the study, the implementation of the disability management function is intended more to retain employees with disabilities than to increase the employment of people with disabilities.

The mapping of the selected cases is summarized in the Figs. 5, 6 and 7 below.

DESIGN PHASE		
A.	**What motivates the need to implement a disability management function**	**Case**
A.1	The need to comply with legislation	
A.2	The opportunity of accessing funding by public or private organizations	
A.3	The need to manage critical situations emerged within the organization (absence of personnel due to disability leave, deterioration of organizational climate, etc.)	
A.4	The input from the top management	3,5,6
A.5	A line manager's autonomous initiative	
A.6	The implementation of the organization's broader diversity management policy	1,3,4,7,8
B.	**Assessment of the initial conditions**	
B.1	Assessment of disabilities within the workforce (known and emerging disabilities)	4
B.2	Assessment of the employment status of the employees with disabilities (tasks, wage status, skills, etc.)	
B.3	Assessment of the potential barriers to the full employment of persons with disabilities (physical barriers, type of tasks, working hours, etc.)	
B.4	Detection of stereotypes and preconceptions potentially affecting the full employment of persons with disabilities	3
B.5	Assessment of the diversity/disability management initiatives already implemented within the organization	4
B.6	Definition of a general organization's plan for the management of disability	1,2,3,4,6, 8
C.	**Definition of the organizational arrangement**	
C.1	Implementation of the disability management function as an autonomous organizational unit with a manager formally appointed as disability manager, possibly based on the appropriate certification (C.1a)	1,3,4
C.2	Appointment of a disability manager (without the establishment of as an autonomous disability management organizational unit), possibly with the appropriate certification (C.2a)	2,6,7,8
C.3	Hiring of external consultants to support the internal disability management organizational unit	
C.4	Hiring of external consultants to support the organization's disability manager	2,4
C.5	Outsourcing of the disability management function to external consultants	5
C.6	Identification of non-managerial roles for supporting the integration of persons with disabilities at the operational level	2,3,5
	Definition of the expected results	
D.1	Increased number of persons with disabilities employed in the organization	5,6,7
D.2	Improved the return-to-work conditions after disability leave periods (possibly also through appropriate workplace accommodations)	
D.3	Improved conditions that help employees with disability stay at work (possibly also through appropriate workplace accommodations)	1,2,3,4,6
D.4	Make advancement opportunities available to employees with disabilities (guarantee to all the employees of the same training and career opportunities)	

Fig. 5. Mapping of the design options

IMPLEMENTATION PHASE		
D.	**Definition of the expected results**	
D.1	Increased number of persons with disabilities employed in the organization	5,6,7
D.2	Improved the return-to-work conditions after disability leave periods (possibly also through appropriate workplace accommodations)	
D.3	Improved conditions that help employees with disability stay at work (possibly also through appropriate workplace accommodations)	1,2,3,4,6
D.4	Make advancement opportunities available to employees with disabilities (guarantee to all the employees of the same training and career opportunities)	
E.	**Implementation of disability management measures**	
E.1	Design and implementation of training programs for managers devoted to specific aspects of the employment of persons with disabilities (recruitment, performance evaluation, career advancements, integration of persons with disabilities in teams, etc.)	1,7
E.2	Design and implementation of training programs specifically addressed to employees with disabilities to facilitate the acquisition of specific skills and operational capacities	2,3,5,6,7, 8
E.3	Design and implementation of training programs addressed to all the employees on topics related to the integration of persons with disabilities	7,8
E.4	Managers' awareness raising interventions to sensitize the employees on topics related to the integration of persons with disabilities	3,4
E.5	Informational support provided by the HR function (or by other organizational units) to the employees with disabilities on their rights and obligations	4,6
E.6	Informational support provided by the HR function (or by other organizational units) to the line managers that must supervise the integration of persons with disabilities	4
E.7	Continuous involvement of the management in the development and implementation of the organization's disability management strategy	1,2,3,4,6
E.8	Design and implementation of measurement systems to assess the effectiveness of disability management interventions	1,4,6,8
E.9	Involvement of the 'competent doctor' in the design and implementation of the interventions for the integration of employees with disabilities	
E.10	Collaboration with public and private organizations dealing with the employment of persons with disabilities both in the design and the implementation of the organization's disability management strategy	1,2,7
F.	**Structural interventions for the accommodation of the working conditions**	
F.1	Interventions to remove physical barriers	2,6,8
F.2	Interventions to adapt the workplaces to different types of disabilities	2,4,6,8
F.3	Adoption of assistive technologies at the workplace	
F.4	Accommodation of lighting, computer screens and communication devices	6,7,8
F.5	Interventions for easing the access to documents and files within the organization's information system	6,7
F.6	Adoption of a flexible working hours policy for the employees with disabilities	
F.7	Adaptation of the tasks to the skills and abilities of the employees with disabilities	2,3,5,6,7, 8

Fig. 6. Mapping of the implementation options

EVALUATION PHASE		
G.	**Output evaluation of the disability management interventions**	
G.1	Increased number of persons with disabilities employed (because of the disability management interventions)	1,5
G.2	Number of employees with disabilities involved in the disability management interventions implemented	
G.3	Number of employees with disabilities who leave the work after the disability management interventions implemented	
G.4	Improvement of the employees with disabilities' job positions and tasks because of the disability management interventions implemented	
G.5	Improvement of the employees with disabilities' wage status because of the disability management interventions implemented	
H.	**Outcome evaluation of the disability management interventions**	
H.1	Detection of significant changes in the performances of the employees with disabilities	2,3,4,5,6,7
H.2	Detection of a significant reduction in the absence hours of the employees with disabilities	1,4
H.3	Detection of significant changes in the colleagues' perception of the performances of the employees with disabilities	1,2,3,5,7
H.4	Detection of a significant reduction of critical situations involving employees with disabilities	
H.5	Detection of a positive impact on the general organizational climate	1,2,3,6
H.6	Detection of a positive impact on the organization's informal communication systems, especially with respect to the communication with the employees with disabilities	

Fig. 7. Mapping of the evaluation options

5 Final Remarks, Limitations, and Further Research Directions

Corporate social innovation aims at the development of new and novel products, processes, and services to fulfil social needs and to improved quality and quantity of life. Work integration and work retention of PWDs are social issues that will involve more and more people in the forthcoming years because of population ageing and the emerging of new forms of disability and inability. From this point on view, the firms' implementation of disability management can actually be considered a corporate social innovation process, especially when disability management is implemented within a more general plan for the management of diversity at the workplace.

As a social innovation process, disability management answers to different general social needs. First, the employment needs of PWDs, which represents a powerful tool for social integration of disabled people [32]. Second, by favoring the adaptation of the tasks to the skills and abilities of the employees with disabilities and the creation of good jobs for them, disability management contributes to debunking stereotypes and preconceptions about the productivity of employees with disabilities. This is key to create positive identities for disabled employees, against the rhetoric of ableism at the workplace [33]. Third, the implementation of successful disability management measures can lead to significant changes in the colleagues' perception of the performances of the employees with disabilities, with a positive impact on the general organizational climate. This creates the conditions for the social integration of PWDs at the workplace [13, 14, 26]. However, once the development of a positive perception of PWDs has been achieved at the workplace, it does not stay confined there. It can contribute to the debunking of stereotypes and preconceptions also in everyday life, thus determining a more general positive social impact.

Firms also can benefit directly from disability management in many ways. First, as a means of promoting their social image and reputation [34]. Second, as a strategy to improve their employees' retention policies, especially in case of the emerging of new disabilities or inability conditions within the employed workforce [17, 35]. Third, as a way to increase PWDs' productivity at the workplace and contribute to the company's success and sustainable competitive advantage [16].

However, implementing disability management is not easy and the integration of disabled people at the workplace does not come for free. The mapping of the activities that should be performed to implement disability management presented in this exploratory study highlights the complexity of this endeavor.

Structural interventions for the accommodation of the working conditions are generally considered critical for the success of PWDs integration policies [36]. As expected, this is confirmed by the mapping of the firms considered in the paper. The accommodation of the working conditions requires investments in infrastructures and, even more importantly, more flexible working arrangements, which can impact on the firm's organization of work. However, important as they are, structural interventions are not the most critical aspect of disability management. Even more important are interventions aimed at creating a positive cultural environment, which requires a continuous involvement of the management in the development and implementation of the organization's disability management strategy [14, 16]. This point also has been confirmed by the mapping of the selected cases.

Disability management is not an isolated organizational function and neither one limited to a small fraction of the workforce. The implementation of successful disability management impacts, more or less directly, on the whole organization [16]. As such, it should be designed, implemented, and evaluated as an organizational innovation process. The grid defined in this study and the mapping of the successful cases considered in the paper can help organizations to manage this complex innovation process.

A word of caution is here necessary. The mapping of the selected cases should not be considered as the description of 'ideal models' that can be transferred to different organizational contexts, eventually with some adjustments. They are not 'on the shelf' solutions different organizations can adopt, as each case presents peculiarities that are quite difficult to replicate in different contexts. Rather, the aim of the mapping was to highlight some critical elements that should be considered by firms in developing their disability management programs, based on how the work integration and re-integration of PWDs has been managed in some successful cases. The analysis grid should thus be considered as a reference model and the elements included in it as some critical success factors for the development of corporate disability management policies.

From this point of view, besides providing a useful analytical tool to map examples of disability management (as it has been used in this exploratory study), the analysis grid can also have a practical utility as a guideline decision-makers and managers can resort to in the definition, establishment, development and evaluation of the firm's disability management function.

In the paper disability management has been discussed as an example of corporate social innovation. However, apart from those more strictly related to disability, the organizational aspects highlighted in the paper that should be considered to make the disability management function efficient and effective, are relevant for any corporate social innovation initiative. Those aspects mainly concern: the definition of a general plan to frame the CSI initiative; the clear definition (since the design phase) of the expected outputs and outcomes; the continuous involvement of the management to support the initiative; the creation of the appropriate organizational climate; and the willingness to adapt the working condition, as needed.

This exploratory study has been based on a small number of cases. This is the main limitation of the paper, which does not allow to draw more general conclusions. However, the aim of the study was not a systematic study of disability management and the analysis grid it has been based on was not intended to be a complete description of all the alternatives an organization can consider to implement disability management. Rather, the aim of the study was exploratory, and both the analysis grid and the results of the mapping should thus be considered as preliminary. Indeed, further research is needed to test the grid for completeness and explanatory power, and more cases should be mapped to confirm and extend the conclusions drawn in the paper.

References

1. UNIDO: The Role of the Social and Solidarity Economy in Reducing Social Exclusion - Budapest Conference Report. United Nations Industrial Development Organization, Vienna (2017)
2. Mulgan, G., et al.: In and out of sync: The challenge of growing social innovations (2007). http://www.socialinnovationexchange.org/node/238
3. Westley, F., et al.: Five configurations for scaling up social innovation: case examples of nonprofit organizations from Canada. J. Appl. Behav. Sci. 50(3), 234–260 (2014)
4. ILO: Financial Mechanisms for Innovative Social and Solidarity Economy Ecosystems. International Labour Organization (2019). https://www.ilo.org/wcmsp5/groups/public/---ed_emp/---emp_ent/---coop/documents/publication/wcms_728367.pdf
5. ISO: Guidance on social responsibility. ISO (International Organization for Standardization), Geneva (2010)
6. Mirvis, P.H., Googins, B., Kiser, C.: Corporate Social Innovatione. Lewis Institute Social Innovation Lab, Babson University, Wellesley, MA (2012)
7. Kanter, R.: From spare change to real change: the social sector as beta site for business innovation. Harv. Bus. Rev. 77(3), 122–132 (1999)
8. Jali Muhamad, N., Abas, Z., Ariffin Ahmad, S.: Corporate social responsibility and corporate social innovation: a conceptual understanding. In: SHS Web of Conferences, vol. 34, p. 01001 (2017)
9. EU: Financing Social Impact Funding social innovation in Europe – mapping. European Commission, Brussels (2012)
10. Altuna, N., et al.: Managing social innovation in for-profit organizations: the case of Intesa Sanpaolo. Eur. J. Innov. Manage. 18(2), 258–280 (2015)
11. Herrera, M.E.B.: Creating competitive advantage by institutionalizing corporate social innovation. J. Bus. Res. 68(7), 1468–1474 (2015)
12. Mirvis, P., et al.: Corporate social innovation: how firms learn to innovate for the greater good. J. Bus. Res. 69(11), 5014–5021 (2016)
13. Samant, D., et al.: Corporate culture and employment of people with disabilities: role of social workers and service provider organizations. J. Soc. Work Disabil. Rehabil. 8(3–4), 171–188 (2009)
14. Schur, L., Kruse, D., Blanck, P.: Corporate culture and the employment of persons with disabilities. Behav. Sci. Law 23(1), 3–20 (2005)
15. Miethlich, B., Šlahor, L.: Employment of persons with disabilities as a corporate social responsibility initiative: necessity and variants of implementation. In: CBU International Conference Proceedings, ISE Research Institute (2018)

16. Miethlich, B., Oldenburg, A.G.: Employment of persons with disabilities as competitive advantage: an analysis of the competitive implications. In: 33nd International Business Information Management Association Conference (IBIMA), Education Excellence and Innovation Management through Vision 2020. IBIMA Publishing, Granada, Spain (2019)
17. Csillag, S., Gyori, Z., Matolay, R.: Two worlds apart? Corporate social responsibility and employment of people with disabilities. In: Tench, R., Jones, B., Sun, W. (eds.) The Critical State of Corporate Social Responsibility in Europe, pp. 57–81. Emerald, Bingley (2018)
18. Kwan, C.K.: Socially responsible human resource practices to improve the employability of people with disabilities. Corp. Soc. Responsib. Environ. Manag. **27**(1), 1–8 (2020)
19. Khan, N., et al.: Diversity in the workplace: an overview of disability employment disclosures among UK firms. Corp. Soc. Responsib. Environ. Manag. **26**(1), 170–185 (2019)
20. Pérez Conesa, F.J., Romeo Delgado, M., Yepes I Baldó, M.: The corporate social responsibility policies for the inclusion of people with disabilities as predictors of employees' identification, commitment and absenteeism. Anales de Psicología, pp. 101–107 (2018)
21. Markel, K., Barclay, L.: Addressing the underemployment of persons with disabilities: recommendations for expanding organizational social responsibility. Empl. Responsib. Rights J. **21**(4), 305–318 (2009)
22. Gilbert, J., Stead, B., Ivancevich, J.: Diversity management: a new organizational paradigm. J. Bus. Ethics **21**(1), 61–76 (1999)
23. Böhm, S.A., Dwertmann, D.J.G., Baumgärtner, M.K.: How to deal with disability-related diversity: opportunities and pitfalls. In: Harder, H., Geisen, T. (eds.) Disability Management and Workplace Integration: International Research Findings, pp. 85–99. Gower Publishing Ltd, Furnham (2011)
24. Thomas, R.R.: From affirmative action to affirming diversity. Harv. Bus. Rev. **68**, 107–117 (1990)
25. Kopnina, H., Haafkens, J.: Disability management: organizational diversity and Dutch employment policy. J. Occup. Rehabil. **20**(2), 247–255 (2010)
26. Araten-Bergman, T.: Managers' hiring intentions and the actual hiring of qualified workers with disabilities. Int. J. Human Resour. Manage. **27**(14), 1510–1530 (2016)
27. Shrey, D., Lacertes, M.: Principles and Practices of Disability Management in Industry. GR Press, Winter Park, FL (1995)
28. Mor-Barak, M.: Managing Diversity. Towards a Globally Inclusive Workplace. Sage, Thousand Oaks (2005)
29. Beatty, J.E., Joffe, R.: An overlooked dimension of diversity: the career effects of chronic illness. Organ. Dyn. **35**(2), 182–195 (2006)
30. Lefever, M., et al.: The efficacy and efficiency of disability management in job-retention and job-reintegration. A systematic review. Work. Read. Mass. **59**(4), 501 (2018)
31. Heckl, E., Pecher, I.: Practices of Providing Reasonable Accommodation for Persons with Disabilities in the Workplace: 24 Company Case Studies across Europe. KMU FORSCHUNG Austria - Austrian Institute for SME Research, Vienna (2008)
32. Barnes, C., Mercer, G.: Disability, work, and welfare: challenging the social exclusion of disabled people. Work Employ Soc. **19**(3), 527–545 (2005)
33. Jammaers, E., Zanoni, P., Hardonk, S.: Constructing positive identities in ableist workplaces: disabled employees' discursive practices engaging with the discourse of lower productivity. Human Relations **69**(6), 1365–1386 (2016)
34. Bonaccio, S., Connelly, C.E., Gellatly, I.R., Jetha, A., Martin Ginis, K.A.: The participation of people with disabilities in the workplace across the employment cycle: employer concerns and research evidence. J. Bus. Psychol. **35**(2), 135–158 (2019). https://doi.org/10.1007/s10 869-018-9602-5

35. Houtenville, A., Kalargyrou, V.: Employers' perspectives about employing people with disabilities: a comparative study across industries. Cornell Hosp. Q. **56**(2), 168–179 (2015)
36. Nevala, N., Pehkonen, I., Koskela, I., Ruusuvuori, J., Anttila, H.: Workplace accommodation among persons with disabilities: a systematic review of its effectiveness and barriers or facilitators. J. Occup. Rehabil. **25**(2), 432–448 (2014). https://doi.org/10.1007/s10926-014-9548-z

Throw Money at ICD? The Effect of the Global Financial Crisis on the Link Between Intellectual Capital Disclosure and (Non-)audit Fees

Maria Chiara Demartini[1], Valentina Beretta[1], and Sara Trucco[2(✉)]

[1] University of Pavia, Pavia, Italy
[2] Università degli Studi Internazionali di Roma, Rome, Italy
sara.trucco@unint.eu

Abstract. This paper investigates the role of the Global Financial Crisis (GFC) in the relationship between Intellectual Capital Disclosure (ICD) on the one side, and non-audit fees (NAF) and audit fees (AF) on the other side, charged to UK listed companies. The prior literature confirmed mixed effects of ICD on the assessment of Audit Risk (AR) and AF charged to audited companies. By pertaining to the relationship between ICD and AF, many authors affirmed that the variation of the AF is primarily determined by auditor's effort. However, the relationship between AF and NAF is ambiguous, especially in conditions of instability. Therefore, to test the significance of ICD and NAF on the assessment of AF, an empirical analysis has been performed. The period of the GFC has been investigated in order to test whether the different economic conditions affect the relationships. Data from Thomson Reuter have been analyzed, by extracting data of UK listed firms for the years 2004, 2008, and 2011. Empirical findings show that ICD directly affects neither AF nor NAF, since its effect is mediated by AR. The mediated relationship between ICD on one side, and AF and NAF on the other, varies depending on different economic conditions. Considering the relationship between AF and NAF, a positive relationship has been found during the GFC.

Keywords: Audit fees · Audit risk · Non-audit fees · Global Financial Crisis · Intellectual capital disclosure

1 Introduction

Because of the increased complexity of business strategies, regulation, operations and mandatory disclosure, non-financial voluntary disclosure showed a constant increase in the last years (Beattie and Smith 2013). In fact, since the interpretation of financial statements is more and more complex (Treasury Committee 2009), the traditional financial reporting system is no more able to provide information that can satisfy all stakeholders' needs (Francis and Schipper 1999). Thus, in order to provide a clearer understanding of financial statements and to increase the long-term value of a company, more information should be disclosed (Watson et al. 2002). In particular, the spread of Intellectual Capital Disclosure (ICD) is the consequence of the need to supplement traditional financial performance measure with disclosure related to the non-financial value of the company and its possibilities and strategic opportunities for the future (FASB (Financial Accounting Standards Board) 2001; IASB (International Financial Reporting Standards) 2010). Since traditional accounting metrics do not provide a framework for the analysis of intangible assets, the ICD is considered quite challenging for governments, regulators and firms (Beattie, 2014; Mouritsen et al. 2001; O'Regan et al. 2001), despite it is considered strategic for companies (Giunta et al. 2015). The literature provides evidence for the relevance of the ICD on the assessment of the audit risk (AR) and audit fees (AF) (Simunic 1980; Hay et al. 2006; Hogan and Wilkins 2008; Chen et al. 2012a; Ball et al. 2012), however consensus on their relationship has not been achieved yet. In fact, lower AR and AF occur only if non-financial voluntary disclosure is valuable and reliable (Clarkson et al. 2003). However, as argued by Demartini and Trucco little empirical evidence is provided for the effect of ICD on AR and AF (Demartini and Trucco 2016).

In addition, firms can also purchase non-audit services from the same company responsible for their auditing, resulting in non-audit fees (NAF). Many studies in the literature analyzed whether the provision of non-audit services may compromise the auditors' independence (Wines 1994; Craswell 1999; DeFond et al. 2002; Kinney et al. 2004; Hay et al. 2006). In order to avoid that auditors may be willing to sacrifice their independence in order to retain clients ready to pay high amount of NAF (DeFond et al. 2002), the legislation in Europe imposes that NAF cannot exceed 70% of AF provided by the same auditor (Meuwissen 2014). Nevertheless, controversial results have been identified in the literature on the relationship between AF and NAF. The increase in the fees required by the auditors has been justified by Palmrose as the change of the organizational structure or control and accounting system (Palmrose, 1986). Even if the change in the economic conditions can be one of the determinants of the increase in the AF and NAF, the literature is lacking of studies of their relationship in the period of the Global Financial Crisis (herein GFC, (Pinnuck 2012; Xu et al., 2011); exceptions: (Sikka 2009, 2015; Xu et al. 2013; Krishnan and Zhang 2014; Doogar et al. 2015). Moreover, some studies predict that during the GFC audit fees increased due to the increased auditor's effort during a complex reporting period (Xu et al. 2013; Sikka 2009, 2015), whereas the opposite finding was reported by a different stream of literature (Krishnan and Zhang 2014). In order to shed some light on this research area, this paper seeks to investigate the effects of ICD on NAF and AF and it aims at replying to the following research questions. RQ1. Does ICD affect the assessment of audit and non-audit fees? RQ2. Is the relationship between ICD and (non-)audit fees affected by a change in the economic conditions?

The paper is organized as follow: in Sect. 2 the literature review is provided; Sect. 3 develops the research hypotheses; Sect. 4 introduces the research methodology; the results of the analysis are reported in Sect. 5; Sect. 6 discusses the empirical findings and summarizes the conclusions and suggestions for future research avenues.

2   Literature Review

2.1   Intellectual Capital Disclosure

The Intellectual Capital (IC) represents the long-lasting value embedded in the company's knowledge, capabilities, networks, operation processes, individual and organizational relations (Huang et al. 2010). The first publication of the term "Intellectual Capital" occurred in 1969 by John Kenneth Galbraith (Feiwel 1975). Over time, IC has been associated to the term "asset", despite the controversial definitions that have been provided in the literature. Intellectual capitalists provide a loose definition of asset, by comparing it to something that is able to transform the items - e.g. raw materials - into more valuable ones. According to this second definition, IC can be considered an asset only if it creates value. Therefore, IC represents an additional source for profit in the company, coming from the knowledge of the company's employees, structure and relations. In fact, IC is made up of three components (Stewart 1998; Bontis 2001): human capital, structural capital and relational capital. Human capital can be defined as "the knowledge embedded in people", whereas structural capital is "the knowledge embedded in the organization and its systems"; relational capital, instead, can be conceived of as "the knowledge embedded in customers and other relationships external to the organization" (Guthrie et al. 2012, p. 70). By reporting such valuable capital, firms aim at fulfilling a twofold need. First, ICD satisfy accountability needs (Nielsen and Madsen 2009). Second, the disclosure of IC enables decision-making activity (Sveiby 2001; Verrecchia 2001; Bozzolan et al. 2003).

2.2   Audit and Non-audit Fees

An AF is the amount of money a company has to pay to an external auditor in order to perform an audit, dependent upon the effort required (Dan A Simunic 1980; Chen et al. 2012b). Thus, AF are widely considered a proxy for the AR (Chan et al. 1993; Houston et al. 1999; Hay et al. 2006; Hogan and Wilkins 2008). NAF represent the amount of money that firms have to pay for non-audit services (DeFond et al. 2002).

   Companies have to sustain different amount of AF charges according to two variables: firm-specific factors and the AR acceptance level. First, firm-specific factors can vary the amount of the AF, according to the easiness with which information can be obtained by the management of the company. At this purpose, higher fees can be charged because additional efforts are required (Simunic 1980; Deis and Giroux 1996; Hay et al. 2006; Hogan and Wilkins 2008; Chen et al. 2012c). Even if this last factor can be considered as a proxy for the definition of AR, the relation between them is quite ambiguous. In fact, even if a stream of the literature did not find a significant relationship between the AF and the auditors' efforts (Mock and Wright 1993, 1999), the majority found evidence for this relationship (Chan et al. 1993; Houston et al. 1999; Hay et al. 2006; Hogan and Wilkins 2008). Thus, the literature is more and more investigating the AF residuals to understand whether they can be conceived of as either auditor rents (Abernathy et al. 2018) or unobserved audit costs (Doogar et al. 2015). Second, the level of AR that the auditor can accept influences the amount of AF the company has to pay, as well. This threshold is determined by the size of the auditor - if it is a Big4 accounting firm or not

-, the complexity of the client, the financial and inherent risk, the firm age and the audit tenure (Hay et al. 2006; Hogan and Wilkins 2008).

More and more studies are investigating the link between AF and NAF. The theoretical relationship between the provision of audit and non-audit services from the same provider is in fact unclear (Lennox 1999). In fact, while the provision of non-audit services may improve the audit quality, thanks to the deeper knowledge of the client, this may affect the auditor independence (Pany and Reckers 1983; Lennox 1999).

3 Background and Hypothesis Development

3.1 Effect of ICD on (N)AF

In the literature, many studies analyzed the association between ICD and AR and/or AF (Simunic 1980; Hay et al. 2006; Hogan and Wilkins 2008; Chen et al. 2012c; Ball et al. 2012).

The signaling theory has been used in the literature to explain the relationship between ICD and AR (Whiting and Miller 2008; An et al. 2015; Demartini and Trucco 2016). The theory underlines a negative relationship between ICD and AR, implying that lower AR is faced when companies start reporting more voluntary information. However, two conditions should be respected in order to obtain this desirable effect. In fact, the information disclosed, in order to be able to reduce the AR, should be both reliable (with low information asymmetries and, subsequently, information risk; Vergauwen and Alem 2005), and valuable (with low reputational risk; Bukh 2003).

Consequently, as for the relationship between ICD and AF, two trends have been observed in the literature. On the one hand, when the information disclosed is reliable and valuable, a negative relationship between them can be observed, since, in response to the additional information disclosed, lower AR is faced by companies and lower AF are charged to those firms (Simunic 1980). On the other hand, a positive relation between ICD and AF can be exploited in the case of internal control deficiencies. In fact, in this case, in order to control the reliability of voluntary disclosure, AF can be increased (Hogan and Wilkins 2008). For this purpose, auditors would put more effort in compensating these deficiencies, and, therefore, a higher amount of AF is charged to audited companies.

However, the relationship between ICD and AF is still under-developed with calls for further development of the field (Guthrie et al. 2012; Krishnan and Wang 2014; Demartini and Trucco 2017), given also that previous studies focussed primarily on the link between financial voluntary disclosure and AR (Ball et al. 2012). In order to contribute to the existent literature, the following hypothesis has been formulated.

H1: ICD is associated with AF.

To the best of our knowledge, no study has investigated the effect of ICD issued by the client firm on NAF charged by the auditor yet. However, previous research addressed that the amount of ICD issued by a client is dependent upon the size of the audit firm (Big4 vs non-Big4), with larger auditors associated with more disclosure of IC (Firth 1979; Lima Rodrigues et al. 2006). In this context, it can be argued that the auditor provides non-audit services to their client to support the preparation of high quality ICD, in order to avoid reputation risks, enhance their expertise (Mora and Rees 1998) and retain their client firm (Malone et al. 1993). To check for the association between ICD and the provision of non-audit services, the following hypothesis will be tested.

H2: ICD is associated with NAF.

3.2 Effect of Global Financial Crisis on the Link Between AF and NAF

In the literature, there is not a consensus on the relation between audit and non-audit fees. According to many scholars (Simunic 1984; Palmrose 1986; Ezzamel et al. 1996; Firth 2002; Thinggaard and Kiertzner 2008), there is a positive correlation between audit and non-audit services, while other streams of the literature did not find any correlation between them (ABDEL-KHALIK 1990; O'Keefe et al. 1994), and some authors found a negative one (Krishnan and Yu 2011). Krishnan and Yu (2011) argued that the differences in the results in the previous literature can be justified by the difference in the length of the time periods examined. In fact, when a longer time period is considered, fluctuations in the macroeconomic conditions can be captured. At this purpose, Alexeyeva and Svanström analysed the effects of the GFC on the assessment of audit and non-audit fees (Alexeyeva and Svanström 2015a, 2015b). Consistently with previous studies, a change in the macroeconomic conditions can affect client risks (Hill et al. 1994), demand for services (Cornett et al. 2011; Svanström and Sundgren 2012). According to Alexeyeva and Svanström, this is translated into an increase of AF and a decrease in NAF during GFC (Alexeyeva and Svanström 2015a, 2015b). However, different studies suggest that when an economic downturn occurs, there usually is a decrease in the demand for products, so a decrease of the liquidity of the company. In order to overcome this situation, organizational changes usually occur. As a consequence of the reorganization of the company, the demand for non-audit services can increase (Firth 2002). Thus, the auditors should put more effort in understanding the new organizational structure and, therefore, there could be a positive relationship between the AF and NAF. Given the fluctuations in the macroeconomic conditions associated with the GFC, and in order to contribute in understanding the link between AF and NAF, the following hypothesis has been formulated:

H3: In instability conditions, there is a positive relationship between NAF and AF.

Previous studies found that when a change in the external environment occurs, and the pricing models of AF and NAF are disturbed, both types of fees tend to change (Whisenant et al. 2003; Krishnan and Zhang 2014).

The GFC has provided a big change in the economic conditions. This was particularly challenging for both audit firms and their clients, since it influenced the price structure of both AF and NAF (Alexeyeva and Svanström 2015a, 2015b). Despite it is well known in the literature that AF and NAF change when a change in the economic conditions occurs, contradictory results on the impact of GFC on AF has been found in the literature (Krishnan and Zhang 2013; Xu et al. 2013; Zhang and Huang 2013), while it is largely unknown how the GFC impact NAF (Alexeyeva and Svanström 2015a, 2015b). In order to contribute in understanding the impacts that the fluctuations in the macroeconomic conditions may have on the relation between AF and NAF, the following hypothesis has been formulated:

H4: The change in the economic conditions affects the relationship between AF and NAF.

In order to increase their competitiveness, firms tend to focus on non-tangible assets, not embedded in financial statements (Bontis et al. 2000; Coy et al. 2001; Khalique et al. 2015). In particular, IC is one of the intangible assets that can increase the value of the company. However, it can be perceived as valuable from investors only if it can improve the performance of the firm (Abeysekera 2008). In fact, in making investment decisions, investors and stakeholders need relevant information, especially in the light of the recent scandals (Clarke 2007). At this purpose, since IC is considered a strategic resource, it has to be disclosed on a regular basis (Waterhouse and Svendsen 1998). However, in period of crisis, when the risk is spread everywhere, the benefits generated by intangible assets are scarcely perceived. However, prior studies found that the ICD is time-invariant, even in case of financial crisis (Rodrigues et al. 2017). In order to contribute in understanding the importance of ICD in assessing the amount of AF and NAF during periods of crisis, the following hypothesis has been formulated:

H5: ICD is not significant in the assessment of (N)AF during the Global Financial Crisis.

4 Research Methodology

4.1 Sample Definition and Data Collection

The analysis has been conducted by collecting data from ESG Asset4 database (Thomson Reuters Datastream). The firms selected are all industrial firms listed in the UK market. The final database has been obtained by excluding from the initial sample of UK listed firms the financial institutions - because of their different accounting treatment – and, consistent with prior research (Ghazali and Weetman 2006; Nelson 2014), two firms which were not audited by one of the Big4 accounting firms (Ernst & Young, Deloitte, PwC, KPMG). The final database is composed of 164 UK industrial listed firms. The firms are investigated during three periods of different economic conditions:

- 2004 represents the favorable period (pre GFC);
- 2008 represents the economic downturn (GFC);
- 2011 represents the post-crisis period (post GFC).

The data collected from ESG Asset4 encompasses the following variables:

- intellectual capital disclosure;
- audit risk;
- audit and non-audit fees;
- accruals.

While the QLAR, QNAR, AF and NAF represent the independent variables, accruals are used as control variable.

4.2 Variable Measurement

The dependent variable is intellectual capital disclosure (ICD), which has been developed following prior literature (Bozzolan et al. 2006; Demartini and Trucco 2016). In fact, according to Bozzolan et al. (2006) and Demartini and Trucco (2016), 20 items are useful in order to compute the amount of ICD, by splitting it into its three components:

- Relational Capital (RC Disclosure), defined as the value of the company's relationships - with customers, vendors and other external stakeholders;
- Human Capital (HC Disclosure), which is the value of the people in the company;
- Organizational Capital (OC Disclosure), which represents the value in all the infrastructures and processes that support the organization of the company.

The variable of the ICD has been obtained by creating a dummy variable for each of the item: each item has been assigned a value of 1 when the information related to a particular item is available, while 0 when the information is not available. The amount of ICD has been computed by summing up all the dummy variables of the 20 items.

In order to assess the Audit risk (AR), a differentiation between qualitative and quantitative AR has been made (Demartini and Trucco 2016):

- The qualitative audit risk (QLAR) encompasses the features and the ability of the top management and the audit committee, and the quality of the internal control of the firms (AICPA 1988; Johnstone 2000; Krishnan 2005). The higher is this ability, the lower is the possibility to obtain a qualified audit opinion, and therefore, the lower will be the AR. In order to build this variable, the following standardized ratios (ranging from 1 to 100), coming from ESG Asset4, have been summed up:
- Board Functions Audit Committee Independence - Percentage of independent board members on the audit committee as stipulated by the company;
- Board Structure/Strictly Independent Board Members – Percentage of strictly independent board members (not employed by the company; not served on the board for more than ten years; not a reference shareholder with more than 5% of holdings; no cross-board membership; no recent, immediate family ties to the corporation; not accepting any compensation other than compensation for board service);
- Corporate Governance Score - Does the company have a corporate governance committee?.
- The quantitative audit risk (QNAR) encompasses two different areas. First of all, it includes the size of the firm, which is considered a proxy for the assessment of the complexity of the firm, therefore auditors assessing the quality of the disclosure issued by bigger clients are expected to face higher AR (Contessotto and Moroney 2013). The second dimension of the quantitative AR is represented by the litigation expenses (Vergauwen and Alem 2005; Venkataraman et al. 2008). A positive relationship between the QNAR and the AR is expected: the higher is QNAR, the higher is

the AR. In order to build this variable, the log-values of the following ratios, coming from Eikon DFO Database (Datastream), have been summed:

- Net sales or revenues;
- Total asset;
- Total shareholder's equity;
- Litigation expenses.

The first three items are jointly considered a proxy for size (Simunic 1980; Contessotto and Moroney 2013), whereas the last directly captures litigation expensed as disclosed by the company.

The items of the QNAR and QLAR have been standardized and the logarithms of the components of the accruals have been computed (Dawson and Richter 2006).

Audit fees (AF) are the natural logarithm of the fees paid by the company to an external auditor to perform a mandatory audit (Simunic 1980; Chen et al. 2012a).

Non-audit fees (NAF) are the natural logarithm of the fees paid to auditors for services different from auditing one (Lennox 1999).

Accruals (ACC) have been computed in order to test the complexity of the firm (Francis and Krishnan 1999; Hogan and Wilkins 2008; Demartini and Trucco 2016; Maletta and Kida 1993; Pratt and Stice 1994; St. Pierre and Anderson 1984).

In this study, this variable has been conceived of as a control variable. In fact, they encompass the outstanding expenses which have to be added in the accounting results for the period. This variable has been obtained by summing the following:

- Log-values of inventories;
- Log-values of receivables.

4.3   Analytical Model

In order to test the research hypotheses, the Structural Equation Modelling (SEM) methodology has been applied. As argued by Kelley and Lai, SEM is widely used when the variables are measured with error and/or latent constructs are hypothesized to exist (Iacobucci 2009; Kelley and Lai 2011). Before running the SEM analysis, the natural log of AF and NAF has been normalized in order to avoid computational issues.

The robustness of the models has been tested with the following statistical tests:

- the Chi-square exact fit test of the model has been estimated in order to compare the model versus saturated test and the baseline versus saturated test (Barrett 2007);
- in order to assess the misfit/fit of the application of SEM, the root mean squared error of approximation (RMSEA) has been calculated (Browne and Cudeck 1992a; Taylor 2008; Jackson et al. 2009);
- in order to compare the fit of different models the Akaike information criterion (AIC) and Bayesian (or Schwarz) information criterion (BIC) have been adopted (Schwarz 1978; Akaike 1987; Raftery 1993);
- the goodness of fit of the model has been tested with the comparative fit index (CFI) and the Tucker–Lewis index (TLI), two indices such that a value close to 1 indicates a good fit (Bentler 1990);

- the standardized root mean squared residual (SRMR) has been calculated as an absolute measure of fit, which considers the standardized difference between the observed and the predicted correlation (Hu and Bentler 1999);
- last, the coefficient of determination (CD) has been adopted in order to measure the amount of variation accounted for in the endogenous constructs by the exogenous constructs (Netemeyer et al. 1990).

5   Empirical Findings

5.1   Principal Component Analysis

Before running the analysis, a principal component analysis has been performed in order to build up the variables related to the two components of audit risk (QLAR and QNAR) and accruals (Brown 2012) (Table 1). Then, after testing their reliability, all the items were summed in order to create QLAR, QNAR and accruals.

Results from the principal component analysis show that each retained factor includes only one item with an eigen-value above 1. Moreover, as suggested by Nunnally (1978), the internal consistency of the constructs is acceptable since the Cronbach's alpha of the constructs is above 0.8 in all cases, except for QLAR (alpha > 0.5). Despite to ensure reliability of the principal component analysis a Cronbach's alpha above 0.8 is preferred, results between 0.5 and 0.6, even if considered poor, are acceptable (George and Mallery 2003; Kline 2013). Additionally, following Oliver and Benet-Martinez (2000), since alpha coefficient is sensitive to the length of the test and the interrelatedness of items in a scale, parsimonious but informative constructs can show a Cronbach's alpha coefficient lower than 0.7 (Oliver and Benet-Martinez 2000).

5.2   Descriptive Statistics

Some descriptive statistics of the variables included in the model are provided in Table 2, whereas the correlation matrix is reported in Table 3. Descriptive statistics have been provided also for the different periods of analysis (2004, 2008, 2011).

Descriptive statistics highlight that ICD is higher in the periods of GFC and post-GFC, compared to the period of lower economic uncertainty. In particular, HC disclosure lived an enormous increase in 2008 compared to the previous analyzed period, which could be interpreted as a signal of the increased awareness of firms about the importance of voluntary disclosure of non-financial information (Abeysekera 2008).

Both the components of AR have been impacted by the GFC, since both QLAR and QNAR showed a stable increase from 2004 to 2011. More specifically, the improvement in the qualitative AR seemed to offset the worsening in the quantitative feature of AR.

Peculiar dynamics of (N)AF have been registered, as well. On average, the highest value of AF charged to audited companies was reached during the crisis. In the post-crisis period, instead, the amount of AF paid decreased, compared to 2004. These results are in line with the stream of the literature affirming that in periods of economic downturn, firms are facing higher risks, that can be translated into more extensive audit procedures and higher auditors' efforts (Choi et al. 2008; Francis and Wang 2008; Ghosh and Pawlewicz 2009; Zhang and Huang 2013).

Table 1. Principal component analysis of the research variables QLAR, QNAR and accruals

Variable	Loadings	Initial eigen value	% of variance	Cronbach's Alpha	Test KMO
Qualitative audit risk (QLAR)				0.512	0.612
Board structure/strictly independent board members	0.574	1.518	50.62		
Board functions audit committee independence	0.569	0.723	24.11		
Corporate governance score	0.590	0.758	25.27		
Quantitative audit risk (QNAR)				0.892	0.748
Net sales or revenues	0.541	2.902	72.54		
Total asset	0.573	0.863	21.58		
Total shareholder's equity	0.558	0.206	5.15		
Litigation expenses	0.261	0.029	0.72		
Accruals				0.8748	0.500
Inventories	0.707	1.777	88.87		
Receivables	0.707	0.223	11.13		
N of obs.	*492*				

The same path was followed by NAF. In fact, on average, the maximum amount of NAF was registered during the year of the crisis (2008). Three main aspects are usually influencing the demand for non-audit services: external support's need, ability to pay, and quality of services delivered (Svanström and Sundgren 2012). Results support the stream of the literature according to which, during a period of economic downturn, firms have to adapt to changing economic conditions, and, therefore, they are forced to restructure their operations (Alexeyeva and Svanström 2015b; Firth 2002; Alexeyeva and Svanström 2015a). In particular, results are in line with the findings of Firth, who argued that in instability conditions, the demand for non-audit services increases (Firth 2002).

Accruals slightly increased over time (Cohen et al. 2008).

Table 2. Descriptive statistics of the research variables

Variable	Overall					2004					2008					2011				
	Obs	Mean	Std. dev.	Min	Max	Obs	Mean	Std. dev.	Min	Max	Obs	Mean	Std. dev.	Min	Max	Obs	Mean	Std. dev.	Min	Max
HC	492	3.486	1.888	0	9	164	2.280	1.652	0	8	164	3.780	1.797	0	8	164	4.396	1.549	1	9
RC	492	2.031	0.960	0	5	164	1.537	1.059	0	4	164	2.116	0.854	0	4	164	2.439	0.711	1	5
SC	492	2.400	1.300	0	5	164	1.591	1.187	0	5	164	2.604	1.271	0	5	164	3.006	0.999	1	5
ICD	492	7.917	3.686	0	16	164	5.409	3.743	0	13	164	8.5	3.337	0	14	164	9.841	2.318	3	16
QLAR	492	217.170	31.206	7.960	274.030	164	207.477	35.009	7.960	271.560	164	211.409	27.473	69.58	265.55	164	232.623	24.184	120.21	274.03
QNAR	474	44.231	7.124	29.389	78.685	156	41.867	4.875	29.389	58.808	156	44.811	7.206	32.078	75.745	162	45.949	8.217	35.424	78.685
AF	404	14.186	1.491	10.597	21.985	109	13.861	1.508	10.597	18.02	147	14.327	1.384	11.503	18.179	162	14.276	1.550	11.670	21.985
NAF	418	13.611	1.503	8.517	22.312	105	13.524	1.451	10.275	16.455	144	13.762	1.472	11.035	18.486	155	13.530	1.565	8.517	22.312
ACCRUALS	448	23.973	3.757	10.960	34.450	151	23.255	3.802	12.336	32.697	149	24.208	3.701	11.160	34.192	148	24.470	3.680	10.960	34.450

Table 3. Correlation matrix

	HC	RC	SC	IC	QLAR	QNAR	AF	NAF	ACCRUALS
HC	1								
RC	0.628***	1							
SC	0.615***	0.610***	1						
ICD	0.914***	0.815***	0.845***	1					
QLAR	0.215***	0.104***	0.183***	0.206***	1				
QNAR	0.239***	0.309***	0.229***	0.291***	0.252***	1			
AF	0.157***	0.262***	0.152***	0.257***	0.256***	0.605***	1		
NAF	0.112***	0.241***	0.064**	0.179***	0.209***	0.479***	0.720***	1	
ACCRUALS	0.037	0.067**	0.042	0.052*	0.061**	0.073**	0.040	0.018	1

With regard to correlation analysis, it can be stated that all of the research variables are significantly correlated, but the size of the coefficient is not very high in all cases but two. Thus, any major concern of multicollinearity among the research variables is expected. The analysis of the variance inflation factor (VIF) also support this expectation, since all the research variables show a VIF value well below 10 (not tabulated; (Kline 2004).

5.3   Results of the Test of the Measurement and Structural Model

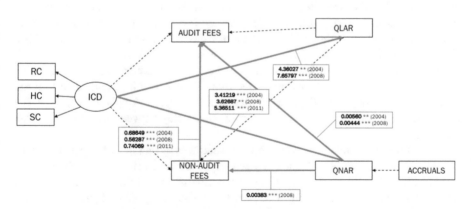

Fig. 1. Results of the path analysis

With regard to the structural model, the results are presented in Fig. 1 and discussed below.

First, the SEM results related to the direct relationship between ICD and AF are not statistically significant. Thus, H1 - ICD is associated with AF is not supported. However, ICD significantly affects the assessment of QNAR, which, in turn, is statistically significant for the determination of AF. Therefore, an indirect and significant effect is played by QNAR on the relationship between ICD and AF.

Second, with regard to H2 - ICD is associated with NAF – the empirical findings do not achieve a statistical significance level. Thus, H2 is not supported. However, as for H1, ICD is significant for the assessment of QNAR, which, in turn, is statistically significant for the determination of NAF.

Third, H3, stating that - In instability conditions, there is a positive relationship between NAF and AF – is confirmed. In 2008, identified as one of the years of the GFC, NAF positively and significantly affected AF. Furthermore, the change in the strength of the relationship between NAF and AF, contingent upon the change in economic conditions has been supported by empirical evidence. The sampled companies report a weaker impact of NAF on AF during GFC (beta$_{2008}$ = 0.56287, p-value < 0.001) compared to pre GFC (beta$_{2004}$ = 0.68649, p-value < 0.001) and post GFC (beta$_{2011}$ = 0.74069, p-value < 0.001).

In order to check whether there is a crisis effect on the auditor independence, prior literature has been followed (DeFond et al. 2002): first, we computed the ratios between NAF and AF and NAF on total fees (TF), that are represented by the sum of AF and NAF, in order to analyze how this ratios evolved over time; second, a t-test analysis has been performed in order to detect differences between the different periods of analysis in terms of NAF/AF and NAF/TF ratios (Table 5). By looking at NAF/AF ratios, a decreasing trend can be observed. Similarly, NAF/TF ratio shows a negative trend. According to the results of the t-test analysis, the mean difference in the two ratios is always significant when 2004 and 2011 values are included in the analysis, whereas the 2008 mean values are significantly different from either 2004 or 2011 only with reference to a specific ratio. In particular, the 2008 mean value of the ratio between NAF and total fees is significantly different from the 2004 one, whereas the 2011 mean value of the NAF on AF ratio is significantly different from the 2008 one. Therefore, by simultaneously looking at the NAF/AF ratios (Table 6) and the descriptive statistics of AF and NAF in the three analyzed periods (Table 3), we can assert that on average (a) higher (N)AF were charged to client firms during the period of crisis, compared to the periods of stable economic conditions, but (b) AF increased more during the GFC, compared to NAF, whereas they decreased in the post-crisis period, compared to NAF. Thus, H4 - The change in the economic conditions affects the relationship between AF and NAF – can be confirmed.

By analyzing the role of IC disclosure on audit fees during the crisis period, results show that this relationship does not achieve statistical significance (Table 4), enabling us to confirm H5 - ICD is not significant in the assessment of (N)AF during the period of the Global Financial Crisis. However, significant mediating effects in the relationship between ICD and (N)AF by means of QNAR can be observed. In fact, during the GFC, there is a positive relationship between ICD and QNAR, which, in turn, positively affect AF and NAF (Table 4). Results hold in the other analyzed reporting periods for the link between QNAR and AF, whereas QNAR does significantly affect NAF in neither 2004 nor 2011.

The measurement model of the ICD latent variable shows satisfactory results, since the path coefficients are positive and statistically significant (at the p < 0.05 level). The Chi2 exact-fit test of the model in the three analyzed years (2004 2008 and 2011; Table 5) provides support to the good fit of the model, since the significance level is above

Table 4. SEM results

	2004		2008		2011	
	Coefficient	SE	Coefficient	SE	Coefficient	SE
NAF → AF	**0.68649** **(0.000***)**	**0.00240**	**0.56287** **(0.000***)**	**0.04057**	**0.74069** **(0.000***)**	**0.01435**
QNAR → AF	**0.00560** **(0.027**)**	**0.00253**	**0.00444** **(0.000***)**	**0.00047**	0.00403 (0.369)	0.00449
QLAR → AF	0.00030 (0.917)	0.00291	0.00074 (0.610)	0.00145	0.010955 (0.501)	0.01628
ICD → AF	−0.02867 (0.386)	0.03306	−0.01302 (0.499)	0.01923	−0.05409 (0.566)	0.09415
Constant	**−0.00829** **(0.084*)**	**0.00480**	**−0.0181** **(0.000***)**	**0.00237**	0.00986 (0.601)	0.01886
QNAR → NAF	0.07709 (0.413)	0.09425	**0.00383** **(0.000***)**	**0.00092**	0.02449 (0.367)	0.02713
QLAR → NAF	0.08539 (0.428)	0.10772	0.00149 (0.615)	0.00296	0.01128 (0.908)	0.09728
ICD → NAF	−0.99362 (0.410)	1.20511	−0.01196 (0.765)	0.04007	−0.75560 (0.197)	0.58563
Constant	0.10291 (0.569)	0.18067	**−0.05052** **(0.000***)**	**0.00280**	0.045162 (0.689)	0.11269
ACCRUALS → QNAR	−0.02128 (0.833)	0.10074	−0.00623 (0.966)	0.14793	0.03285 (0.867)	0.19548
ICD → QNAR	**3.41219** **(0.000***)**	**0.85129**	**3.62687** **(0.042**)**	**1.77990**	**5.36511** **(0.006***)**	**1.97060**
Constant	−0.03449 (0.974)	1.04366	0.14619 (0.926)	1.56512	0.17168 (0.935)	2.09218
ICD → QLAR	**4.36027** **(0.000***)**	**1.17030**	**7.65797** **(0.007***)**	**2.83676**	0.71070 (0.109)	0.44283
Constant	**0.48481** **(0.032**)**	**0.22549**	−0.26219 (0.229)	0.21787	−0.05185 (0.603)	0.09976
ICD → RC	1(CONSTRAINED)		1(CONSTRAINED)		1 (CONSTRAINED)	
Constant	**2.22308** **(0.000***)**	**0.04387**	**2.301471** **(0.000***)**	**.0491272**	**2.43537** **(0.000***)**	**0.05857**
ICD → HC	**1.23763** **(0.012**)**	**0.48990**	**2.203766** **(0.011**)**	**.8678121**	**2.93579** **(0.013**)**	**1.18563**
Constant	**3.61539** **(0.000***)**	**0.10456**	**4.176471** **(0.000***)**	**.1138554**	**4.38095** **(0.000***)**	**0.12739**
ICD → SC	**1.03002** **(0.002***)**	**0.32828**	**1.616276** **(0.007***)**	**.6018704**	**0.84793** **(0.059*)**	**0.44973**
Constant	**2.54615** **(0.000***)**	**0.07225**	**2.852941** **(0.000***)**	**.0835324**	**3.01361** **(0.000***)**	**0.08275**
Var(RC)	0.13323	0.03322	0.2689894	.039842	0.39164	0.06518
Var(HC)	1.24208	0.17205	1.475254	.2062924	1.41418	0.42113
Var(SC)	0.55450	0.07895	.7941968	.1093699	0.92559	0.11758

(continued)

Table 4. (*continued*)

	2004		2008		2011	
	Coefficient	SE	Coefficient	SE	Coefficient	SE
Var(AF)	0.00269	0.00035	.0001939	.0000263	0.05115	0.00601
Var(NAF)	3.84062	0.48971	.0009805	.0001209	1.77332	0.21527
Var(QNAR)	4.88544	0.73586	11.46061	1.512641	21.24367	3.00440
Var(QLAR)	4.38572	0.79740	2.98105	1.179024	1.40613	0.16962
Var(ICD)	0.11701	0.03900	.0592437	.0323057	0.11269	0.05945
Goodness-of-fit statistics						
Chi2	21.85(0.112)		23.74 (0.0696)		13.80 (0.541)	
RMSEA	0.059		0.065		0.000	
AIC	2832.748		1694.710		3767.844	
BIC	2910.171		1773.352		3848.586	
CFI	0.992		0.970		1.000	
TLI	0.986		0.943		1.005	
SRMR	0.054		0.055		0.044	
CD	0.677		0.656		0.565	

the generally accepted 0.05 cut-off value. Root mean-square error of approximation (RMSEA) is acceptable, since it is below 0.08 threshold in the three years (Browne and Cudeck 1992b). Even though the standardized root mean square residual (SRMR) signals a discrete fit, since its value is not below 0.05 in all cases (Hu and Bentler 1999), the comparative fit index (CFI) achieves a satisfactory level of 0.99, 0.97 and 1, respectively (CFI values above 0.9 provide a satisfactory fit; (Bentler 1990). The same applies to TLI, whose value is always above 0.94 CFI. Furthermore, the CD achieves levels above 0.56 in all cases, mirroring an acceptable fit of the model.

Table 5. Non-audit fees ratios by year

5.1	Mean values			Mean difference (t-test)		
	2004	2008	2011	2004–2008	2004–2011	2008–2011
NAF/AF ratio	1.499	0.979	0.719	0.520 (1.577)	0.780 (2.622***)	0.260 (1.974**)
NAF/TF ratio	0.433	0.371	0.338	0.062 (2.206**)	0.095 (3.680***)	0.033 (1.453)

*NAF ratios are computed by dividing NAF by AF (or the sum of NAF and AF, that is TF) in the three analyzed years. t-test values are in brackets. Results of the t-test analysis are significant at the ** 0.05, and ***0.01 level.*

6   Discussion and Conclusions

This paper aimed at analyzing the relationship between ICD, AF and NAF, with a specific focus on their different correlations before, during and after the GFC. There is a paucity of studies investigating the impact of GFC on AF (Alexeyeva and Svanström 2015a, 2015b), which report controversial results. For this reason, it is important to deeply analyze the effect of GFC on AF, and to understand which are the determinants of AF. Previous studies defined the client size, the complexity, the risk and the auditor status as proxies for the assessment of AF (Roberts 1992). However, NAF can be considered one of the determinants of AF, as well. Despite, different studies underlined a positive association between NAF and AF, any evidence is provided for the impact of GFC on NAF (Alexeyeva and Svanström 2015a, 2015b).

Three main conclusions from empirical findings can be summarized and discussed as follows.

First, by considering the relationship between ICD and (N)AF, no significant direct effect can be stated. However, an indirect relationship mediated by QNAR exists. These findings are consistent with the extant literature on the costs of disclosing voluntary non-financial information. As Beattie and Smith declared, some costs, such as the costs the firm has to sustain in order to collect information, can disadvantage the firm in disclosing IC information (Beattie and Smith 2012). In fact, even if the ICD occurs with the aim of reducing the AR, this cannot be translated into lower AF. In fact, the variation of the (N)AF is primarily determined by the variation in the auditor's effort (Simunic 1980; Hay et al. 2006; Hogan and Wilkins 2008; Yu et al. 2012; Chen et al. 2012b). Therefore, the positive correlation between ICD and (N)AF can be due to higher efforts required to auditors for the services provided during the disclosure process and after that, in the assessment of the quality of voluntary information. As for the relationship between ICD and (N)AF during GFC, results confirm that ICD does not significantly impact the assessment of both AF and NAF during GFC, supporting the stream of the literature affirming that, when risk is spread everywhere, the benefits of ICD are rarely exploited (Lima Rodrigues et al. 2006). However, despite a direct effect of ICD on (N)AF cannot be detected, QNAR plays a mediating role between them. This result is in line with the stream of the literature arguing that, in instability conditions, firms with higher ICD show higher QNAR as well, compared to firms with lower ICD, since an economic turmoil makes the assessment of the validity and reliability of the disclosed information more and more difficult. This, in turn, can be translated into higher effort played by auditors, and, subsequently, higher AF. This relationship holds also for NAF, which tend to be higher when higher QNAR is associated with an increasing disclosure of non-financial information (Habib 2012). This can be justified by an increasing demand of non-audit services when a higher level of AR is faced by companies.

Second, the analysis proves evidence for the association between NAF and AF at times of distressed economic conditions. Therefore, if the provision of non-audit services increases, an increase in AF is expected, as well. Thus, this study also contributes to that part of the literature suggesting that a simultaneous analysis of AF and NAF should be conducted in order to control for the auditor independence (Whisenant et al. 2003; Antle et al. 2006). In particular, the analysis supports a positive relationship between NAF and AF. In all the three analyzed years, this positive correlation is confirmed, and, in all of them, the positive impact of NAF on AF is highly statistically significant. Thanks to the results obtained in this study, the American, Australian and European studies (Simunic 1984; Palmrose 1986; Barkess and Simnett 1994; Ezzamel et al. 1996; Thinggaard and Kiertzner 2008) can be confirmed and, therefore, there is an evidence of the positive relation between NAF and AF. The results of the models seem to support the prior literature (Palmrose 1986; Firth 2002) suggesting that changes in the organization are positively correlated to the link between AF and NAF. At this purpose, Palmrose (1986) suggested that more efforts are required for the auditing and, thus, higher AF are required.

Third, by analyzing the effect of the GFC on the change of the relationship between NAF and AF, it can be argued that the GFC significantly changed this relationship. In fact, the NAF coefficient remained significant in all the analyzed periods, but it was lower in 2004, compared to the other periods of analysis. This study also confirmed that stream of the literature suggesting that during distressed economic conditions there is a reduction in terms of NAF conditional to AF. In particular, compared to the pre-crisis period, we observed a lower mean value of the ratio between NAF and AF (or total fees), due to the fact that, during the GFC, AF increased much more compared to NAF. This result is in line with prior research arguing that AF increased during the GFC (Alexeyeva and Svanström 2015), instead it is in contrast with that part of the literature stating that at times of crisis the auditors cut their fees to retain their clients (Sikka 2009, 2015; Krishnan and Zhang 2014). The increase in AF could be due to different factors. First of all, the increase of the AF can be explained by the increase in the price of the audit services. However, the literature seems to not confirm this explanation because a large body of literature stated that the level of AF tends to decrease in periods of economic downturns (Abdel-Khalik 1990; Maher et al. 1992; Sikka 2009). Thus, the explanation of the increase of AF during and after the GFC could be different. In fact, this increase can be explained by the increased need for audit services, as well. As stated by Firth (2002), a change in the company's organization require more efforts to be audited, thus, higher AF can be requested. Third, since during the crisis the AR tends to increase, higher AF can be charged to audited companies to cover this risk. In fact, in order to provide a reliable audit service, audit firms would apply more extensive audit procedures, which cost more for the audited companies. Thus, one explanation could be associated to the fact that, during the GFC, the auditor perceived a higher audit risk in performing the auditing service and hence they decided to charge more the client (Alexeyeva and Svanström 2015). Moreover, the auditor's reputation risk increased during the GFC (Jin et al. 2011; Xu et al. 2013), thus more AF were charged to the client company.

Results from this study contribute to extend prior research in several ways. First, this analysis contributes to enrich the non-financial voluntary disclosure literature (Beattie and Smith Beattie and Smith 2012; Barth et al. 2017). In particular, the analysis is focused on the role of ICD on AF and NAF. In fact, since intellectual capital is considered as an intangible asset of the company – only in the case it produces additional value for the company -, its communication can increase the transparency of the company and it can reduce information asymmetries between stakeholders and managers (Chen et al. 2012). This contributes at enriching the signaling theory (Healy and Palepu 2001; Mahoney et al. 2013; An et al. 2015), according to which voluntary disclosure can reduce the knowledge gap between people inside and outside the company. In the study case, findings showed that the ICD and (N)AF link is mediated by the quantitative aspects of AR, and this effect increased during the period of crisis. Second, this analysis clearly figured out the auditors' effort as a determinant of the amount of AF. In fact, it supports the stream of the literature according to which higher AF are charged to audited companies in the case the audit firm has to put more efforts in analyzing the quality and the truthfulness of the IC information disclosed and, therefore, higher AF can be charged (Ball et al. 2012; Beattie and Smith 2012). Third, the findings underline that the audit firms usually retain the effect of knowledge spillover (Whisenant et al. 2003), since a positive relationship between AF and NAF has been discovered. This result contradicts prior studies addressing that the knowledge spillover flows from NAF to AF (Krishnan and Yu 2011). In particular, this study investigates the association between AF and NAF in different economic conditions. Therefore, since the fluctuation of the economic conditions is a complex phenomenon, this study aimed at improving its understanding. At this purpose, by considering the effect of the economic fluctuations, any change in the direction of the relationship between the two kinds of fees is underlined. This implies that the mediated effect of QNAR on the link between ICD and NAF remained significant during all the analyzed period, despite its fluctuations in terms of magnitude. Therefore, since there are not knowledge spillover effects, this implies that in the case of cost savings, they can be conceived as of auditor rents (Abernethy et al. 2016), even in the case of economic downturn. Fourth, this analysis contributes at defining the relevance of ICD in the period of economic downturn. As the signaling theory predicts, a negative relationship between ICD and the assessment of AR can be observed only in the case the information disclosed is valuable and reliable (Watson et al. 2002). The analysis supports the relevance of ICD in the indirect assessment of (N)AF, mediated by AR. On the one hand, empirical findings highlighted that in the period of crisis, voluntary non-financial disclosure is perceived as riskier by auditors, since it enhances the audit burden. On the other, during the GFC, ICD improved the qualitative feature of AR, which is a proxy for the quality of a firms' corporate governance (Demartini and Trucco 2016, 2017). However, this second AR feature did not significantly impact on (N)AF. This implies that the auditors are charging the client firm for the additional effort they have to provide in order to validate the quality of the non-financial voluntary disclosure, while not necessarily shifting the benefit to the client, through a reduction of (N)AF.

Moreover, the analysis does not support the evidence proved by a stream of literature, according to which, there is evidence of a negative relationship between voluntary disclosure and AR (Orlitzky and Benjamin 2001; Durand et al. 2012; Chen et al. 2012c). This analysis is instead supporting the positive relationship between non-financial voluntary disclosure and AR confirmed by other scholars (Hogan and Wilkins 2008). This result can be motivated by the additional efforts that auditors put in order to control the reliability of voluntary disclosure or the lack of suitable tools to effectively audit voluntary non-financial information (Earley 2015).

The implications for practitioners that emerge from this analysis are related to the importance of the ICD on the assessment of (N)AF, especially in distressed economic conditions. At this purpose, the results found that benefits can be perceived by managers, audit firms and stakeholders. First, managers can use the ICD to manage the assessment of AR and (N)AF. In fact, by providing valuable and reliable intellectual capital information, lower efforts are required to audit firms and, therefore, lower (N)AF can be charged to audited companies. Moreover, it can be used also for perceiving non-economic benefits. In fact, an increase in the ICD can be correlated to a strengthening of the competitive position of the company and an improvement of its credibility. Second, audit firms can perform an audit with higher quality, by jointly analyzing both the mandatory and the voluntary disclosure. In this way, in the case of valuable and reliable disclosure, lower efforts are required. Last, stakeholders can benefit from the ICD in several ways. First of all, they can have a holistic view of the company and, therefore, they can better manage their investment decision process. At this purpose, they can have a better understanding of the financial statements by analyzing the voluntary disclosure (Barth et al. 2017). Moreover, by pertaining to the agency theory, the agency costs can be reduced by increasing voluntary disclosure. This implies that interests of the two parties – stakeholders and managers – can be aligned and promptly communicated through ICD (Beattie and Smith 2012).

Additional implications emerge for the period of crisis. Audit firms can benefit from the joint provision of audit and non-audit services. Since the knowledge spillover effects are not visible, and the NAF remain statistically significant for the assessment of AR, this implies that potential cost savings, deriving from the joint provision of both services, are retained by audit companies (Abernethy et al. 2016).

This study is not without its limitations. First, the analysis is conducted on a single country. Therefore, more research in different geographical, legal, cultural contexts could corroborate these preliminary findings. Furthermore, this study ran a set of path analyses on different time periods. However, a panel data analysis could provide more robust results. Moreover, the research model did not include some controls which could add further valuable knowledge. For instance, the analysis could also compare the size of the auditor (Big 4 vs non-Big4), and control for the rotation of the auditor during the GFC, the complexity of the client firm in terms of internationalization, sector, crucial events occurred during the GFC (e.g. M&A) and size. Concerning the analysis of NAF on AF ratio, this study underlines that it decreased during the period of economic downturn. However, the quantitative analysis of this path is not able to explain the real reason of this trend. Thus, further research could fill this gap. Finally, future research on this topic could include smart technologies applied to non-audit service or to intellectual capital.

References

Abdel-Khalik, A.R.: The jointness of audit fees and demand for MAS: a self-selection analysis. Contemp. Account. Res. **6**, 295–322 (1990)

Abernathy, J.L., Kang, T., Krishnan, G.V., Wang, C.: Is There a relation between residual audit fees and analysts' forecasts? J. Account. Audit. Finance **33**, 299–323 (2018). https://doi.org/10.1177/0148558X16637963

Abeysekera, I.: Intellectual capital disclosure trends: Singapore and Sri Lanka. J. Intellect. Cap. **9**, 723–737 (2008)

Acemoglu, D., Gietzmann, M.B.: Auditor independence, incomplete contracts and the role of legal liability. Eur. Account. Rev. **6**, 355–375 (1997)

Akaike, H.: Factor analysis and AIC. Psychometrika **52**, 317–332 (1987). https://doi.org/10.1007/BF02294359

Alexeyeva, I., Svanström, T.: The impact of the global financial crisis on audit and non-audit fees: evidence from Sweden. Manag. Audit. J. **30**, 302–323 (2015). https://doi.org/10.1108/MAJ-04-2014-1025

Antle, R.: Auditor independence. J. Account. Res. 1–20 (1984)

Antle, R., Gordon, E., Narayanamoorthy, G., Zhou, L.: The joint determination of audit fees, non-audit fees, and abnormal accruals. Rev. Quant. Finance Account. **27**, 235–266 (2006). https://doi.org/10.1007/s11156-006-9430-y

An, Y., Davey, H., Eggleton, I.R.C., Wang, Z.: Intellectual capital disclosure and the information gap: evidence from China. Adv. Account. **31**, 179–187 (2015). https://doi.org/10.1016/j.adiac.2015.09.001

Armitage, S., Marston, C.: Corporate disclosure, cost of capital and reputation: evidence from finance directors. Br. Account. Rev. **40**, 314–336 (2008). https://doi.org/10.1016/j.bar.2008.06.003

Ball, R., Jayaraman, S., Shivakumar, L.: Audited financial reporting and voluntary disclosure as complements: a test of the confirmation hypothesis. J. Account. Econ. **53**, 136–166 (2012)

Bamber, L.S., Jiang (Xuefeng), J., Wang, I.Y.: What's my style? The influence of top managers on voluntary corporate financial disclosure. Account. Rev. **85**, 1131–1162 (2010). https://doi.org/10.2308/accr.2010.85.4.1131

Baron, R.: The evolution of corporate reporting for integrated performance. In: Background Paper for the 30th Round Table Sustainable Development. OECD (2014)

Barrett, P.: Structural equation modelling: adjudging model fit. Personal. Individ. Differ. **42**, 815–824 (2007)

Barth, M.E., Cahan, S.F., Chen, L., Venter, E.R.: The economic consequences associated with integrated report quality: capital market and real effects. Account. Organ. Soc. **62**, 43–64 (2017). https://doi.org/10.1016/j.aos.2017.08.005

Beattie, V.: Accounting narratives and the narrative turn in accounting research: issues, theory, methodology, methods and a research framework. Br. Account. Rev. **46**, 111–134 (2014). https://doi.org/10.1016/j.bar.2014.05.001

Beattie, V., McInnes, B., Fearnley, S.: A methodology for analysing and evaluating narratives in annual reports: a comprehensive descriptive profile and metrics for disclosure quality attributes. Account. Forum Corp. Financ. Commun. Volunt. Disclos. **28**, 205–236 (2004). https://doi.org/10.1016/j.accfor.2004.07.001

Beattie, V., Smith, S.J.: Value creation and business models: refocusing the intellectual capital debate. Br. Account. Rev. **45**, 243–254 (2013). https://doi.org/10.1016/j.bar.2013.06.001

Beattie, V., Smith, S.J.: Evaluating disclosure theory using the views of UK finance directors in the intellectual capital context. Account. Bus. Res. **42**, 471–494 (2012). https://doi.org/10.1080/00014788.2012.668468

Bentler, P.M.: Comparative fit indexes in structural models. Psychol. Bull. **107**, 238–246 (1990a). https://doi.org/10.1037/0033-2909.107.2.238

Bentler, P.M.: Comparative fit indexes in structural models. Psychol. Bull. **107**, 238–246 (1990b)

Boesso, G., Kumar, K.: Drivers of corporate voluntary disclosure: a framework and empirical evidence from Italy and the United States. Account. Audit. Account. J. **20**, 269–296 (2007)

Bontis, N.: Assessing knowledge assets: a review of the models used to measure intellectual capital. Int. J. Manag. Rev. **3**, 41–60 (2001). https://doi.org/10.1111/1468-2370.00053

Bontis, N., Keow, W.C.C., Richardson, S.: Intellectual capital and business performance in Malaysian industries. J. Intellect. Cap. **1**, 85–100 (2000)

Bozzolan, S., Favotto, F., Ricceri, F.: Italian annual intellectual capital disclosure: an empirical analysis. J. Intellect. Cap. **4**, 543–558 (2003). https://doi.org/10.1108/14691930310504554

Browne, M.W., Cudeck, R.: Alternative ways of assessing model fit. Sociol. Methods Res. **21**, 230–258 (1992). https://doi.org/10.1177/0049124192021002005

Brown, T.A.: Confirmatory Factor Analysis for Applied Research. Guilford Press, New York (2012)

Brüggen, A., Vergauwen, P., Dao, M.: Determinants of intellectual capital disclosure: evidence from Australia. Manag. Decis. **47**, 233–245 (2009). https://doi.org/10.1108/002517409109 38894

Bukh, P.N.: The relevance of intellectual capital disclosure: a paradox? Account. Audit. Account. J. **16**, 49–56 (2003). https://doi.org/10.1108/09513570310464273

Chan, P., Ezzamel, M., Gwilliam, D.: Determinants of audit fees for quoted UK companies. J. Bus. Finance Account. **20**, 765–786 (1993)

Chen, C.X., Lu, H., Sougiannis, T.: The agency problem, corporate governance, and the asymmetrical behavior of selling, general, and administrative costs. Contemp. Account. Res. **29**, 252–282 (2012a)

Chen, L., Srinidhi, B., Tsang, A., Yu, W.: Corporate social responsibility, audit fees, and audit opinions. Audit Fees Audit Opin. (2012b)

Chen, M.Y., Wang, Y.S., Sun, V.: Intellectual capital and organizational commitment: evidence from cultural creative industries in Taiwan. Pers. Rev. **41**, 321–339 (2012c). https://doi.org/10. 1108/00483481211212968

Chen, Y.-C., Hung, M., Wang, Y.: The effect of mandatory CSR disclosure on firm profitability and social externalities: evidence from China. J. Account. Econ. **65**, 169–190 (2018). https:// doi.org/10.1016/j.jacceco.2017.11.009

Clarke, F.: Indecent Disclosure: Gilding the Corporate Lily. Cambridge University Press, Cambridge (2007)

Clarkson, P.M., Ferguson, C., Hall, J.: Auditor conservatism and voluntary disclosure: evidence from the Year 2000 systems issue. Account. Finance **43**, 21–40 (n.d.). https://doi.org/10.1111/ 1467-629X.00081

Conaboy, R.P.: Corporate Crime in America: Strengthening the Good Citizen Corporation Proceedings. DIANE Publishing, Darby (1998)

Coy, D., Fischer, M., Gordon, T.: Public accountability: a new paradigm for college and university annual reports. Crit. Perspect. Account. 12, 1–31 (2001)

Cuozzo, B., Dumay, J., Palmaccio, M., Lombardi, R.: Intellectual capital disclosure: a structured literature review. J. Intellect. Cap. **18**, 9–28 (2017). https://doi.org/10.1108/JIC-10-2016-0104

Darrell, W., Schwartz, B.N.: Environmental disclosures and public policy pressure. J. Account. Publ. Policy **16**(2), 125–154 (1997)

Dawson, J.F., Richter, A.W.: Probing three-way interactions in moderated multiple regression: development and application of a slope difference test. J. Appl. Psychol. **91**, 917–926 (2006). https://doi.org/10.1037/0021-9010.91.4.917

DeAngelo, L.E.: Auditor size and audit quality. J. Account. Econ. **3**, 183–199 (1981)

Deegan, C., Samkin, G.: New Zealand Financial Accounting. McGraw-Hill, North Ryde (2009)

DeFond, M.L., Raghunandan, K., Subramanyam, K.R.: Do non-audit service fees impair auditor independence? Evidence from going concern audit opinions. J. Account. Res. **40**, 1247–1274 (2002). https://doi.org/10.1111/1475-679X.00088

Deis, D.R., Jr., Giroux, G.: The effect of auditor changes on audit fees, audit hours, and audit quality. J. Account. Publ. Policy **15**(1), 55–76 (1996)

Demartini, C., Trucco, S.: Integrated Reporting and Audit Quality: An Empirical Analysis in the European Setting. Contributions to Management Science, Springer, Heidelberg (2017). https:// doi.org/10.1007/978-3-319-48826-4

Demartini, C., Trucco, S.: Does intellectual capital disclosure matter for audit risk? Evidence from the UK and Italy. Sustainability **8**, 867 (2016). https://doi.org/10.3390/su8090867

Doogar, R., Sivadasan, P., Solomon, I.: Audit fee residuals: costs or rents? Rev. Acc. Stud. **20**(4), 1247–1286 (2015). https://doi.org/10.1007/s11142-015-9322-2

Dumay, J., Garanina, T.: Intellectual capital research: a critical examination of the third stage. J. Intellect. Cap. **14**, 10–25 (2013). https://doi.org/10.1108/14691931311288995

Dumay, J., Guthrie, J.: Involuntary disclosure of intellectual capital: is it relevant? J. Intellect. Cap. **18**, 29–44 (2017). https://doi.org/10.1108/JIC-10-2016-0102

Earley, C.E.: Data analytics in auditing: opportunities and challenges. Bus. Horiz. **58**, 493–500 (2015). https://doi.org/10.1016/j.bushor.2015.05.002

Eng, L.L., Mak, Y.T.: Corporate governance and voluntary disclosure. J. Account. Publ. Policy **22**, 325–345 (2003). https://doi.org/10.1016/S0278-4254(03)00037-1

Ezzamel, M., Gwilliam, D.R., Holland, K.M.: Some empirical evidence from publicly quoted UK companies on the relationship between the pricing of audit and non-audit services. Account. Bus. Res. **27**, 3–16 (1996)

FASB (Financial Accounting Standards Board): Improving Business Reporting: Insights into Enhancing Voluntary Disclosure, The Financial Accounting Standards Board (2001)

Feiwel, G.R.: The Intellectual Capital of Michał Kalecki: A Study in Economic Theory and Policy. University of Tennessee Press, Knoxville (1975)

Firth, M.: Auditor–provided consultancy services and their associations with audit fees and audit opinions. J. Bus. Finance Account. **29**, 661–693 (2002)

Firth, M.: The impact of size, stock market listing, and auditors on voluntary disclosure in corporate annual reports. Account. Bus. Res. **9**, 273–280 (1979). https://doi.org/10.1080/00014788.1979.9729168

Francis, J., Schipper, K.: Have financial statements lost their relevance? J. Account. Res. **37**, 319–352 (1999)

Giunta, F., Bini, L., Dainelli, F.: Business model disclosure in the strategic report: entangling intellectual capital in value creation process. J. Intellect. Cap. **17**, 83–102 (2015). https://doi.org/10.1108/JIC-09-2015-0076

Goldman, A., Barlev, B.: The auditor-firm conflict of interests: its implications for independence. Account. Rev. **49**, 707–718 (1974)

Guthrie, J., Ricceri, F., Dumay, J.: Reflections and projections: a decade of intellectual capital accounting research. Br. Account. Rev. **44**, 68–82 (2012). https://doi.org/10.1016/j.bar.2012.03.004

Hay, D.: Further evidence from meta-analysis of audit fee research. Int. J. Audit. **17**, 162–176 (2013). https://doi.org/10.1111/j.1099-1123.2012.00462.x

Hay, D.C., Knechel, W.R., Wong, N.: Audit fees: a meta-analysis of the effect of supply and demand attributes. Contemp. Account. Res. **23**, 141–191 (2006)

Healy, P.M., Palepu, K.G.: Information asymmetry, corporate disclosure, and the capital markets: a review of the empirical disclosure literature. J. Account. Econ. **31**, 405–440 (2001). https://doi.org/10.1016/S0165-4101(01)00018-0

Hogan, C.E., Wilkins, M.S.: Evidence on the audit risk model: do auditors increase audit fees in the presence of internal control deficiencies? Contemp. Account. Res. **25**, 219–242 (2008). https://doi.org/10.1506/car.25.1.9

Ho, S.S.M., Wong, K.S.: A study of corporate disclosure practice and effectiveness in Hong Kong. J. Int. Financ. Manag. Account. **12**, 75–102 (n.d.). https://doi.org/10.1111/1467-646X.00067

Houston, R.W., Peters, M.F., Pratt, J.H.: The audit risk model, business risk and audit-planning decisions. Account. Rev. **74**, 281–298 (1999)

Huang, Y.-C., Wu, Y.C.J.: Intellectual capital and knowledge productivity: the Taiwan biotech industry. Manag. Decis. **48**, 580–599 (2010)

Hu, L., Bentler, P.M.: Cutoff criteria for fit indexes in covariance structure analysis: conventional criteria versus new alternatives. Struct. Equ. Model. Multidiscip. J. **6**, 1–55 (1999). https://doi.org/10.1080/10705519909540118

Iacobucci, D.: Everything you always wanted to know about SEM (structural equations modeling) but were afraid to ask. J. Consum. Psychol. **19**(4), 673–680 (2009)

IASB (International Financial Reporting Standards): IFRS Practice Statement. Management Commentary. A Framework for Presentation. IFRS Foundation, London (2010)

IFRS: Conceptual Framework Round-Table Meeting, Staff Paper (2013)

IIRC Newsletter - Highlights from 2016 [WWW Document] (n.d.). https://us4.campaign-archive.com/?u=b36f6aeef75cea67e62812844&id=ce981ad463&e=ee7e66415f. Accessed 27 July 2018

Jackson, D.L., Gillaspy, J.A., Purc-Stephenson, R.: Reporting practices in confirmatory factor analysis: an overview and some recommendations. Psychol. Methods **14**, 6–23 (2009). https://doi.org/10.1037/a0014694

Jin, J.Y., Kanagaretnam, K., Lobo, G.J.: Ability of accounting and audit quality variables to predict bank failure during the financial crisis. J. Bank. Finance **35**, 2811–2819 (2011). https://doi.org/10.1016/j.jbankfin.2011.03.005

Kelley, K., Lai, K.: Accuracy in parameter estimation for the root mean square error of approximation: sample size planning for narrow confidence intervals. Multivar. Behav. Res. **46**, 1–32 (2011). https://doi.org/10.1080/00273171.2011.543027

Khalique, M., Bontis, N., Shaari, J.A.N., Isa, A.H.M.: Intellectual capital in small and medium enterprises in Pakistan. J. Intellect. Cap. **16**, 224–238 (2015). https://doi.org/10.1108/JIC-01-2014-0014

Kline, R.B.: Principles and Practice of Structural Equation Modeling, 2nd edn. The Guilford Press, New York (2004)

Kramer, M., Kania, J.: Game changing CSR. In: Corporate Social Responsibility Initiative Working Paper, vol. 18 (2006)

Krishnan, G.V., Wang, C.: The relation between managerial ability and audit fees and going concern opinions. Audit. J. Pract. Theory **34**, 139–160 (2014). https://doi.org/10.2308/ajpt-50985

Krishnan, G.V., Zhang, Y.: Is there a relation between audit fee cuts during the global financial crisis and banks' financial reporting quality? J. Account. Publ. Policy Spec. Issue Account. World Econ. Cris. **33**, 279–300 (2014). https://doi.org/10.1016/j.jaccpubpol.2014.02.004

Krishnan, G.V., Yu, W.: Further evidence on knowledge spillover and the joint determination of audit and non-audit fees. Manag. Audit. J. **26**, 230–247 (2011)

Kumar, K., Boesso, G.: Drivers of corporate voluntary disclosure: a framework and empirical evidence from Italy and the United States. Account. Audit. Account. J. **20**, 269–296 (2007). https://doi.org/10.1108/09513570710741028

Lennox, C.S.: Non-audit fees, disclosure and audit quality. Eur. Account. Rev. **8**, 239–252 (1999)

Li, J., Pike, R., Haniffa, R.: Intellectual capital disclosure and corporate governance structure in UK firms. Account. Bus. Res. **38**, 137–159 (2008). https://doi.org/10.1080/00014788.2008.9663326

Lima Rodrigues, L., Oliveira, L., Craig, R.: Firm-specific determinants of intangibles reporting: evidence from the Portuguese stock market. J. Hum. Resour. Cost. Account. **10**, 11–33 (2006). https://doi.org/10.1108/14013380610672657

Lydenberg, S.: Emerging trends in environmental, social, and governance data and disclosure: opportunities and challenges. In: Global Corporate Governance Forum: Issue Number (2014)

Maher, M.W., Tiessen, P., Colson, R., Broman, A.J.: Competition and audit fees. Account. Rev. **67**, 199–211 (1992)

Mahoney, L.S., Thorne, L., Cecil, L., LaGore, W.: A research note on standalone corporate social responsibility reports: signaling or greenwashing? Crit. Perspect. Account. **24**, 350–359 (2013). https://doi.org/10.1016/j.cpa.2012.09.008

Malone, D., Fries, C., Jones, T.: An empirical investigation of the extent of corporate financial disclosure in the oil and gas industry, an empirical investigation of the extent of corporate financial disclosure in the oil and gas industry. J. Account. Audit. Finance **8**, 249–273 (1993). https://doi.org/10.1177/0148558X9300800306

Mangena, M., Pike, R., Li, J.: Intellectual Capital Disclosure Practices and Effects on the Cost of Equity Capital: UK Evidence. Institute of Chartered Accountants of Scotland, Edinburgh (2010)

Meek, G.K., Gray, S.J.: Globalization of stock markets and foreign listing requirements: voluntary disclosures by continental European companies listed on the London stock exchange. J. Int. Bus. Stud. 20, 315–336 (1989). https://doi.org/10.1057/palgrave.jibs.8490854

Meek, G.K., Roberts, C.B., Gray, S.J.: Factors influencing voluntary annual report disclosures by U.S., U.K. and continental European multinational corporations. J. Int. Bus. Stud. 26, 555–572 (1995)

Mock, T.J., Wright, A.: An exploratory study of auditors' evidential planning judgments. Auditing 12, 39 (1993)

Mock, T.J., Wright, A.M.: Are audit program plans risk-adjusted? Audit. J. Pract. Theory 18, 55–74 (1999)

Mora, A., Rees, W.: The early adoption of consolidated accounting in Spain. Eur. Account. Rev. 7, 675–696 (1998). https://doi.org/10.1080/096381898336259

Mouritsen, J., Larsen, H.T., Bukh, P.N.D.: Intellectual capital and the "capable firm": narrating, visualising and numbering for managing knowledge. Account. Organ. Soc. 26, 735–762 (2001)

Murthy, V., Mouritsen, J.: The performance of intellectual capital: mobilising relationships between intellectual and financial capital in a bank. Account. Audit. Account. J. 24, 622–646 (2011). https://doi.org/10.1108/09513571111139120

Netemeyer, R.G., Johnston, M.W., Burton, S.: Analysis of role conflict and role ambiguity in a structural equations framework. J. Appl. Psychol. 75, 148–157 (1990). https://doi.org/10.1037/0021-9010.75.2.148

Nielsen, C., Madsen, M.T.: Discourses of transparency in the intellectual capital reporting debate: moving from generic reporting models to management defined information. Crit. Perspect. Account. Crit. Perspect. Intellect. Cap. 20, 847–854 (2009). https://doi.org/10.1016/j.cpa.2008.09.007

O'Keefe, T.B., Simunic, D.A., Stein, M.T.: The production of audit services: evidence from a major public accounting firm. J. Account. Res. 241–261 (1994)

O'Regan, P., O'Donnell, D., Kennedy, T., Bontis, N., Cleary, P.: Perceptions of intellectual capital: Irish evidence. J. Hum. Resour. Cost. Account. 6, 29–38 (2001)

Palmrose, Z.-V.: Audit fees and auditor size: further evidence. J. Account. Res. 97–110 (1986)

Pany, K., Reckers, P.M.: Auditor independence and nonaudit services: director views and their policy implications. J. Account. Publ. Policy 2(1), 43–62 (1983)

Pinnuck, M.: A review of the role of financial reporting in the global financial crisis. Aust. Account. Rev. 22, 1–14 (n.d.). https://doi.org/10.1111/j.1835-2561.2011.00155.x

Raftery, A.E.: Bayesian model selection in structural equation models. Test. Struct. Equ. Models 163–180 (1993)

Richard Howitt talks about the importance of Integrated Reporting for India [WWW Document].. Econ. Times Blog (2017). https://blogs.economictimes.indiatimes.com/et-commentary/richard-howitt-talks-about-the-importance-of-integrated-reporting-for-india/. Accessed 27 July 2018

Riley Jr., R.A., Pearson, T.A., Trompeter, G.: The value relevance of non-financial performance variables and accounting information: the case of the airline industry. J. Account. Publ. Policy 22(3), 231–254 (2003)

Rodrigues, L.L., Tejedo-Romero, F., Craig, R.: Corporate governance and intellectual capital reporting in a period of financial crisis: evidence from Portugal. Int. J. Discl. Gov. 14, 1–29 (2017). https://doi.org/10.1057/jdg.2015.20

Schaper, S., Nielsen, C., Roslender, R.: Moving from irrelevant intellectual capital (IC) reporting to value-relevant IC disclosures: key learning points from the Danish experience. J. Intellect. Cap. 18, 81–101 (2017). https://doi.org/10.1108/JIC-07-2016-0071

Schwarz, G.: Estimating the dimension of a model. Ann. Stat. **6**, 461–464 (1978). https://doi.org/10.1214/aos/1176344136

SEC: Business and Financial Disclosure Required by Regulation S-K (2016)

Sikka, P.: The hand of accounting and accountancy firms in deepening income and wealth inequalities and the economic crisis: some evidence. Crit. Perspect. Account. Glob. Financ. Cris. **30**, 46–62 (2015). https://doi.org/10.1016/j.cpa.2013.02.003

Sikka, P.: Financial crisis and the silence of the auditors. Account. Organ. Soc. **34**, 868–873 (2009). https://doi.org/10.1016/j.aos.2009.01.004

Simon, D.T.: The audit services market-additional empirical-evidence. Audit.- J. Pract. Theory (1985)

Simunic, D.A.: Auditing, consulting, and auditor independence. J. Account. Res. 679–702 (1984)

Simunic, D.A.: The pricing of audit services: theory and evidence. J. Account. Res. 161–190 (1980)

Stewart, T.A.: Intellectual Capital: The New Wealth of Organization, 1st edn. Crown Business, New York (1998)

Sveiby, K.-E.: A knowledge-based theory of the firm to guide in strategy formulation. J. Intellect. Cap. **2**, 344–358 (2001). https://doi.org/10.1108/14691930110409651

Taylor, A.B.: Two new methods of studying the performance of SEM fit indexes. Diss. Abstr. Int. Sect. B Sci. Eng. (2008)

Thinggaard, F., Kiertzner, L.: Determinants of audit fees: evidence from a small capital market with a joint audit requirement. Int. J. Audit. **12**, 141–158 (2008)

Treasury Committee: Banking crisis: reforming corporate governance and pay in the City. In: Ninth Report of the Session 2008/9. HC 519 (2009)

Tull, J.A., Dumay, J.C.: Intellectual capital disclosure and price-sensitive Australian stock exchange announcements. J. Intellect. Cap. **8**, 236–255 (2007). https://doi.org/10.1108/14691930710742826

Turpen, R.A.: Differential pricing on auditors initial engagements-further evidence. Audit. J. Pract. Theory **9**, 60–76 (1990)

Vafaei, A., Taylor, D., Ahmed, K.: The value relevance of intellectual capital disclosures. J. Intellect. Cap. **12**, 407–429 (2011). https://doi.org/10.1108/14691931111154715

Vergauwen, P.G.M.C., van Alem, F.J.C.: Annual report IC disclosures in The Netherlands, France and Germany. J. Intellect. Cap. **6**, 89–104 (2005). https://doi.org/10.1108/14691930510574681

Verrecchia, R.E.: Essays on disclosure. J. Account. Econ. **32**, 97–180 (2001). https://doi.org/10.1016/S0165-4101(01)00025-8

Waterhouse, J.H., Svendsen, A.: Strategic performance monitoring and management: using non-financial measures to improve corporate governance. Can. Inst. Charter. Account. (1998)

Watson, A., Shrives, P., Marston, C.: Voluntary disclosure of accounting ratios in the UK. Br. Account. Rev. **34**, 289–313 (2002)

Whisenant, S., Sankaraguruswamy, S., Raghunandan, K.: Evidence on the joint determination of audit and non-audit fees. J. Account. Res. **41**, 721–744 (n.d.). https://doi.org/10.1111/1475-679X.00121

Whiting, R.H., Miller, J.C.: Voluntary disclosure of intellectual capital in New Zealand annual reports and the "hidden value." J. Hum. Resour. Cost. Account. **12**, 26–50 (2008). https://doi.org/10.1108/14013380810872725

Xu, Y., Carson, E., Fargher, N., Jiang, L.: Responses by Australian auditors to the global financial crisis. Account. Finance **53**, 301–338 (2013). https://doi.org/10.1111/j.1467-629X.2011.00459.x

Xu, Y., Jiang, A.L., Fargher, N., Carson, E.: Audit reports in Australia during the global financial crisis. Aust. Account. Rev. **21**, 22–31 (2011). https://doi.org/10.1111/j.1835-2561.2010.00118.x

Why More CSR Disclosure Does Not Mean More Favourable CSR Perception? Insights from Fast Fashion Industry of Italy

Manuel De Nicola[1(✉)] and Umair Anees[2]

[1] Faculty of Communication Studies, University of Teramo, Teramo, Italy
mdenicola@unite.it
[2] Department of Economia Aziendale, University "G. d'Annunzio"
of Chieti-Pescara, Pescara, Italy

Abstract. Corporate reputation (CR) is one of the most important intangible assets for a firm. Even though the role of corporate social responsibility (CSR) has long been examined in building or destroying CR, findings from these studies are usually inconclusive. When it comes to studies related to the positive impacts of CSR disclosure on CR, more decisive results can be drawn if CSR disclosure is actually leading to a good perception of CSR among different stakeholder groups. This study argues that CSR disclosure alone does not guarantee positive sentiments from different stakeholders, so it is required to investigate how CSR is perceived and which levers can be used to stimulate value co-creation behaviours in the stakeholders. Hence, the present work aims at investigating the mediating role of CR on the relationship between CSR perception and customer citizenship behaviour (CCB) in the context of social identity theory. This study uses structural equation modelling to investigate these relationships in a sample of 278 fast fashion customers of Italy and found that CSR perception has direct positive effect on CCB and CR acts as mediator in the relationship between CSR and CCB.

Keywords: Corporate social responsibility · Corporate reputation · Customer citizenship behaviour · Social identity theory · Tolerance · Helping others · Feedback

1 Introduction

Fombrun [1: 72] defined corporate reputation as "a perceptual representation of a company's past actions and future prospects that describes the firm's overall appeal to all of its key constituents when compared with other leading rivals". Corporate reputation (CR) is considered one of the most important, if not the most important, intangible assets that a firm can have [2]. Researches have shown that a strong corporate reputation: helps a firm charge premium price [3–6], enhances consumer trust [7, 8], increases consumer loyalty [9–11] and consumer satisfaction [10, 12, 13], improves investors' access to better financing [14]. A good corporate reputation takes time to develop [15], is hard to imitate [16] and thus provides a sustainable strategic advantage to a firm [17, 18].

S. Za et al. (Eds.): ItAIS 2020, LNISO 50, pp. 129–142, 2022.
https://doi.org/10.1007/978-3-030-86858-1_8

Given the strategic importance of corporate reputation, many researchers have tried to identify its determinants [19, 20]. Among these determinants, corporate social responsibility (CSR) has received increasing attention. Sheehay [21: 639] defined CSR as "a socio-political movement which generates private self-regulatory initiatives, incorporating public and private international law norms seeking to ameliorate and mitigate the social harms of and to promote public good by industrial organisations". Importance of being socially and environmentally responsible to get stakeholders' approval cannot be overstated in today's world.

Even though the role of corporate social responsibility has long been examined in building or destroying corporate reputation, findings from these studies are usually inconclusive [22]. Pérez [22] observed that most of these researches are descriptive, with very few works emphasizing on empirical evidences to validate the respective frameworks and to reach a conclusion or a consensus. Moreover, CSR and CR relationship is mostly examined using published ratings or CSR reporting [23–25] rather than measuring them directly from the stakeholders i.e., customers. Our study attempts to provide empirical evidences about the relationship between CSR perception and CR for one stakeholder group represented by the customers of the firms.

Being socially responsible can bring many benefits to a firm [26, 27], even though researchers have pointed out the lack of practical approaches to measure these benefits [28]. Moreover, the relationship between CSR and customer citizenship behaviour (CCB) has hardly been discussed theoretically or tested empirically. Groth [29: 11] referred to customer citizenship behaviour as "voluntary and discretionary behaviours that are not required for the successful production and delivery of the service but that, in the aggregate, help the service organization overall". This study shall look into the relationship between CSR, CR and CCB to further our understanding of the interactions between these important concepts. This study shall use the lens of social identity theory to explain when and how CSR disclosure and practices lead to CSR perception and positive customer outcomes such as CCB.

2 Theoretical Background and Hypotheses Development

2.1 CSR Perception and CSR Disclosure

Omran and Ramdhony [30] provided an extensive review of the theoretical pillars on which CSR disclosure literature was based on and discussed four of the most widely used theories in this field, i.e., legitimacy theory, stakeholder theory, social contract theory and signaling theory. They also assert that none of these theories alone provides a satisfactory framework to explain diverse and often conflicting assertions of CSR disclosure literature.

Given this, it is unsurprising that many of the past studies related to positive implications of CSR disclosure have failed to provide proper theoretical justifications of their conflicting results [31]. Therefore, we propose that social identity theory can provide a new approach to explain such diverse findings. Social identity theory proposed by Henri Tajfel and John Turner in the 1970s [32] entails that the groups (e.g., social class, family, sport team etc.) which people belong to are an important source of pride and self-esteem for them. These groups give people a sense of belonging to the society: a sense of social identity. These associations with the groups help people develop, protect and promote a sense of self (who am/are I/we?). Scholars have since utilized social identity theory's rationales in organizational settings to better explain stakeholder behaviours [33–35]. Researchers have proposed that people identify with organizations (or firms) just as if they would identify with any other social group when they perceive an overlap between organizational attributes and their individual attributes [36]. When such overlap exists, stakeholders tend to develop a sense of association and emotional attachment with the firms and exhibit constructive in-role and extra-role behaviours [37]. Thus, CSR practices and subsequent disclosure can lead to stakeholders identifying themselves with the firm and develop a strong feeling of attachment and dedication for the firm.

However, previous researches showed that not all types of CSR practices and disclosures are seen positively by stakeholders. Researches pointed out that, to better reap the benefits of CSR disclosure, firms must provide relevant, understandable and timely social information [38], exhibit the level of managerial commitment that is required by different stakeholder groups [39, 40] and tailor the contents of the social reports according to the needs of different stakeholder groups [19, 24]. Only then CSR practices and disclosure are seen as trustworthy and admired by stakeholders, leading to strong firm-stakeholder identification. Hence firms need to start relying more on channels other than their websites and on disclosure tools other than annual reports, to learn and cater to diverse social concerns of different stakeholders.

Many studies in the past have shown that CSR disclosure in itself does not necessarily lead to positive firm outcomes (as it was expected) until such CSR actions are perceived as substantial, relevant and genuine. Pérez and López [24] highlighted that reporting intensity to stakeholders does not necessarily mean a better CSR reporting outcome such as reputation. Role of different communication channels cannot be overstated either. CSR actions, if not noticed and acknowledged by different stakeholders, can hardly bring anything to the firm.

What is needed is to understand that CSR practices and communications do not guarantee high CSR perception among different stakeholders. CSR practices and disclosures are most relevant for positive firm outcomes when these actions lead to strong company-stakeholders identification. Firms also need to look past the traditional approaches in reporting and disclosing about their social performance and utilize other channels such as social networks, online apps and other electronic media to reach diverse stakeholders. As more and more people have started to rely on social and online media for information and communication, firms must utilize these channels to improve the stakeholder engagement, to better learn contemporary social concerns and to foster strong firm-stakeholder identifications.

Most of the studies that have tried to investigate the link between CSR disclosure practices and their positive outcomes have either relied on published CSR ratings [23, 25] or on CSR disclosure practices as a proxy for CSR perception [23, 39]. However, a company's CSR initiatives are only as good as they are learnt and acknowledged to be genuine by different stakeholder groups and lead to positive identification with the firm by different stakeholders. This study, therefore, measures the CSR perception directly from the specific category of stakeholders represented by the customers, instead of relying on published ratings or reports.

2.2 CSR and CCB

In recent times, CSR has received increasing attention and firms are under constant pressure to act in socially and environmentally responsible manners [41]. The effect of CSR on CCB can be better understood by first looking into the literature of organizational citizenship behaviour (OCB) and organizational identification theory. Organizational identification theory, building on social identity theory, refers to the degree to which employees define themselves as members of an organization and to what extent they experience a sense of association with it [36]. When employees perceive that key organizational features are in congruence with their self-identity, they are more likely to identify and associate themselves with the organization that may bring many benefits to firms such as: enhanced employee motivation and loyalty [42], higher employee commitment [43], job satisfaction [44] and extra-role performance [45]. Organ [46: 4] defined extra-role performance or organizational citizenship behaviour (OCB) as "individual behaviour that is discretionary, not explicitly recognized by the formal reward system and that in the aggregate promotes the effective functioning of the organization". In context of organizational identification theory, the motivations for such extra-role behaviours may stem from a strong sense of associations and emotional attachment of employees to the organization [37]. Since a socially and environmentally responsible firm is always seen in a positive light, we can expect employees to identify more strongly with such firms and support them more with extra-role activities i.e., organizational citizenship behaviour.

Scott and Lane [47] argued that the concept of social identification apply to all stakeholders (i.e., customers, investors, suppliers etc.) and not just only to employees. Even though employees were regarded as the key players in creating value through OCB in the past [48], customers' extra-role behaviour or customer citizenship behaviour (CCB) is increasingly considered to be an influential factor in value co-creation [29]. Yi and Gong [49] identified four dimensions of CCB i.e., "helping others", "feedback", "tolerance" and "advocacy". Where helping others refers to customer behaviour aimed at assisting other customers in the acquisition or utilization of a service; feedback refers to solicited and unsolicited information that customers provide voluntarily to the employees, which helps employees and the firm improve the service creation process in the long run; tolerance refers to customer willingness to be patient when the service delivery does not meet the customer's expectations, as in the case of delays or mistakes made by the employees of the firm; advocacy refers to recommending the firm to others [49]. This study focuses on three dimensions of customer citizenship behaviour identified by Yi and Gong [49] that is helping others, feedback and tolerance as they have received the least attention, if any, in the past.

Drawing on theories of social identity and organizational identification, Bhattacharya and Sen [50] proposed that strong consumer-company relationships often result from consumers' identification with certain companies (i.e., firms which are more socially responsible) resulting into consumer-company identifications which prompt the customers to become 'champions' of these companies and their products.

Thus, we argue that the positive perception of CSR leads to stronger customers' identification with the firm and these associations are likely to increase extra-role behavior that is CCB. In light of this argument, we propose the following hypotheses.

H1a: CSR perception has a positive direct effect on "helping others" dimension of CCB.
H1b: CSR perception has a positive direct effect on "feedback" dimension of CCB.
H1c: CSR perception has a positive direct effect on "tolerance" dimension of CCB.

2.3 Mediating Effect

When it comes to the relationship between CSR disclosure and CR, scholars have observed that findings are inconclusive. This limitation derives from the fact that the literature on this issue is mostly theoretical in nature [51], with scholars having developed very few empirical papers to discuss the validity of their theoretical reasoning [52]. Though, studies that have focused on CSR perception instead of CSR disclosure as an antecedent of corporate reputation have, in fact, found more consistent results. Javed et al. [53], for example, found that diverse CSR initiatives lead to a higher perception of CR. Bianchi et al. [54] also showed that a good CSR perception leads to a good perception of CR among customers. Thus, being socially responsible can help a firm in building and maintaining its reputation over time [39, 55]. The findings of these studies imply that CSR perception, rather than CSR disclosure or CSR initiatives alone, is a more consistent antecedent to corporate reputation.

Past studies that have tried to examine the link between CSR disclosure and CR have frequently relied on the legitimization concerns in response to the pressures by stakeholders [56–58]. This legitimation process, in turn, helps the firm build up reputation capital [59]. Besides legitimacy theory, scholars have also utilized stakeholder theory, agency theory, impression management theory, social contract theory and signaling theory to explain why a firm might be involved in CSR practices and how these practices can benefit the firm [22, 30].

In the context of social identity theory, we propose that strong consumer-company identification results when a firm's CSR practices and disclosures are consistently acknowledged and appreciated by customers over a period of time. These continuous positive evaluations then lead to strong customer-company identification resulting into feelings of admiration, respect and trust embodied in a strong reputation for the firm. Therefore, we propose that CSR perception is antecedent of corporate reputation. This is an intangible asset created and sustained after the accumulation of stakeholders' evaluations of the firm's social performance in successive periods [60]. Therefore, to prepare and disclose social reporting at any given time does not necessarily lead to a good overall reputation, as building reputation requires time and consistency.

Corporate reputation in turn has been found to be the antecedent of CCB. We propose that customers identify strongly with the firm they perceive of high reputation and enhance their self-concept by supporting that firm. Thus, it can be argued that the effect of CSR onto CCB is mediated through CR. Some of the previous studies do highlight the positive effect of CR on CCB. Jinfeng et al. [61] demonstrated that CR significantly affects CCB. Bartikowski and Walsh [62] found that customer-based corporate reputation positively affects the 'helping others' dimension of corporate citizenship behaviour. Lii and Lee [63] found that employees' perception of a firm's reputation leads to higher levels of corporate citizenship behaviour. Walsh et al. [64] highlighted the positive influence corporate reputation has on customer feedback. Hong and Yang [65] found a positive relationship between corporate reputation and word-of-mouth. Thus, we propose that CR mediates the effect of CSR on CCB, formulating the following hypotheses.

H2a: CR mediates the effect of CSR on "helping others" dimension of CCB.
H2b: CR mediates the effect of CSR on "feedback" dimension of CCB.
H2c: CR mediates the effect of CSR on "tolerance" dimension of CCB.

3   Methodology: Measures, Sample and Data Collection

Lange et al. [66] identified three conceptualizations of corporate reputation i.e., being known, being known for something and generalized favorability. This study uses Rep-Trak pulse developed by Ponzi et al. [67] to measure corporate reputation in term of generalized favorability of a firm. The dimensions of customer citizenship behaviour "helping others", "feedback" and "tolerance" are measured by adapting the scale developed by Yi and Gong [49].

Perception of CSR was measured from a three-item scale adapted from Walsh and Beatty [68]. Items used to measure these concepts can be found in Table 2. This study used five-point Likert scales (1 = strongly disagree, 5 = strongly agree). Responses were collected online from customers of fast-fashion retailers in Italy with a useable sample size of 278 customers. Collected data underwent the standard checks for normality, missing values and outliers in SPSS [69].

4   Measurement Model

After initial data screening, an exploratory factor analysis (EFA) was run initially using maximum likelihood method and oblique promax rotation [70, 71]. All items loaded in their respective factors with loadings having a range of .67 to .91 as shown in Table 1.

Table 1. Exploratory factor analysis of the variables: Csr refers to the perception of corporate social responsibility; Crp refers to the perception of corporate reputation; Fee refers to feedback; Hel refers to helping other customers; Tol refers to tolerance.

Items	Factors				
	1	2	3	4	5
Csr1					.688
Csr2					.827
Csr3					.700
Crp1	.866				
Crp2	.844				
Crp3	.633				
Crp4	.848				
Fee1		.916			
Fee2		.917			
Fee3		.798			

(*continued*)

Table 1. (*continued*)

Items	Factors				
	1	2	3	4	5
Hel1			.727		
Hel2			.932		
Hel3			.789		
Tol1				.671	
Tol2				.866	
Tol3				.792	

The variance explained by the model was 64.8% thus exhibiting reasonable factor structure. Harman's single factor test had been run to test for the common method bias [72]. The single factor accounted for 23.5% variance which is well below the threshold of 50%.

Next, confirmatory factor analysis (CFA) was performed. The CFA indicated excellent model fit with comparative fit index (CFI) of .978, goodness of fit index (GFI) of .938, root mean squared error of approximation (RMSEA) of .046, χ^2/df of 1.574 and standardized root mean squared residual (SRMR) of .0374. All the items loaded substantially on their respective factors as can be seen from Table 2.

Table 2. Standardized regression weights of confirmatory factor analysis: Csr refers to the perception of corporate social responsibility; Crp refers to the perception of corporate reputation; Fee refers to feedback; Hel refers to helping other customers; Tol refers to tolerance.

Items of the scales		Estimate	
This company seems to make an effort to create new jobs	←	Csr	.720
This company would reduce its profits to ensure a clean environment	←	Csr	.781
This company seems to be environmentally responsible	←	Csr	.803
This company has a good overall reputation	←	Crp	.808
This is a company that I admire and respect	←	Crp	.748
This is a company that I trust	←	Crp	.860
This is a company I have a good feeling about	←	Crp	.839
I would Provide information when surveyed by this company	←	Fee	.899
I would Provide helpful feedback to customer service	←	Fee	.905

(*continued*)

Table 2. (*continued*)

Items of the scales		Estimate	
When I receive good service from the employees of this firm, I comment about it	←	Fee	.827
I would assist other customers in finding products for this company	←	Hel	.838
I would help others with their shopping in this company	←	Hel	.863
I would explain to other customers how to use different services correctly	←	Hel	.772
If a product or service from this firm does not meet my expectation, I would be willing to put up with it	←	Tol	.648
If the employee makes a mistake during product delivery, I would be willing to be patient	←	Tol	.832
I would be willing to adapt if I have to wait longer than normally expected to receive the products or service	←	Tol	.842

Thereafter, we tested for reliability and discriminant and convergent validity of the scales. The tests showed no reliability and validity concerns as composite reliability (CoR) for all factors was found to be greater than .70, average variance extracted (AVE) greater than .50 and maximum shared variance (MSV), and square root of AVE greater than inter-factor correlations [73], as can be seen in Table 3. To test the presence of common method bias at factor level we ran two different models, one with unmeasured common latent factor and one without it [72]. The difference between standardized regression weights of the two models did not increase the recommended threshold of .20 [74]. Hence common method bias did not appear to be a significant concern in the study.

Table 3. Validity and reliability test: Hel refers to helping other customers; Csr refers to the perception of corporate social responsibility; Crp refers to the perception of corporate reputation; Fee refers to feedback; Tol refers to tolerance; CoR refers to composite reliability; AVE refers to average variance extracted; MSV refers to maximum shared variance.

	CoR	AVE	MSV	Hel	Csr	Crp	Fee	Tol
Hel	0.865	0.681	0.289	0.825				
Csr	0.812	0.591	0.428	0.241	0.769			
Crp	0.887	0.664	0.428	0.322	0.654	0.815		
Fee	0.909	0.770	0.289	0.538	0.239	0.342	0.878	
Tol	0.821	0.607	0.086	0.294	0.037	0.147	0.254	0.779

5 Test of the Hypotheses

Structural equation modeling was performed in AMOS to test the hypothesis while boot-strapping on 1000 samples was used to estimate the mediating effects at 95% confidence interval. Hypotheses H1a, H1b and H1c predict a positive relationship between CSR and "helping others", "feedback" and "tolerance" respectively. When three dimensions of CCB were regressed on CSR, the results supported the hypothesis H1a and H1b with significant standardized regression weights of .244 and .247 respectively, supporting these hypotheses. While hypotheses H1c was rejected in favor of null as no significant relationship between CSR and tolerance could be found. The model showed good fit indices with GFI of .951, CFI of .977, RMSEA .052 and SRMR of .085. These result, therefore, indicates a strong positive correlation between CSR and helping others and feedback dimension of CCB.

Next, corporate reputation was introduced as mediator and both direct and indirect effects were estimated again. A good model fit was attained with CFI of .974, GFI of .934, RMSEA of .049 and SRMR of .0516. The introduction of CR turned all direct paths from CSR to CCB insignificant, indicating perfect mediation to all three dimensions of CCB, as shown in Table 4. Significance of the mediating effect of corporate reputation was estimated using bootstrapping. Results showed that CR significantly mediates the relationship between CSR and CCB dimensions at 95% confidence interval as 0 does not fall between low and high confidence level, rejecting null hypothesis (no mediation) as shown in Table 5. Such finding suggests that CSR probably does not lead directly to customer citizenship behaviour, but it does so through creating a high corporate reputation.

Table 4. Regression weights for mediating model: DV refers to dependent variable; IV refers to independent variable; Csr refers to the perception of corporate social responsibility; Crp refers to the perception of corporate reputation; Fee refers to feedback; Hel refers to helping other customers; Tol refers to tolerance; *** refers to p-value less than 0.001.

DV		IV	Unstandardized	Standardized	P
Crp	←	Csr	.694	.654	***
Tol	←	Csr	.024	−.106	.314
Hel	←	Csr	.068	.047	.639
Fee	←	Csr	−.008	.013	.891
Tol	←	Crp	.238	.223	.002
Hel	←	Crp	.413	.299	***
Fee	←	Crp	.590	.339	***

Table 5. Significance of indirect effects: Tol refers to tolerance; Hel refers to helping other; Fee refers to feedback; CL low refers to lower bound of confidence level; CL high refers to higher bound of confidence level.

	CSR	CL low	CL high	Hypotheses	Support
Tol	.165	.005	.339	H2c	Yes
Hel	.287	.090	.562	H2b	Yes
Fee	.410	.168	.765	H2a	Yes

6   Implications and Discussions

When it comes to CSR reporting, many studies [31] have pointed out that the adoption of CSR reporting and CSR disclosing does not necessarily lead the stakeholders to develop a better perception of the company's actions over social, ethical and environmental dimensions of CSR. Consequently, studies that explore the direct effect of CSR disclosure alone onto positive stakeholder outcomes (i.e., CCB), ignoring the fact that this reporting might not represent or lead to high CSR perception, might fail to see the benefits that a good CSR perception can bring to the firm. CSR reporting and disclosing is considered more effective in generating positive stakeholder outcomes when corporate transparency, information quantity and information quality are high [22]. Only then such reporting can be appreciated by stakeholders and lead to firm-stakeholder identifications, which in turn can lead to positive customer outcomes i.e., CCB.

This study, unlike most previous studies, uses the lens of social identity theory to explain how CSR initiative and disclosure can lead to positive customer outcomes and asserts that firms need to be consistent, relevant and honest about their CSR commitments. The present research also finds that CSR perceptions alone do not necessarily determine positive customer outcomes, but it does so by some stable mediator i.e., reputation. CSR disclosure and initiatives that fail to lead to such stable emotional outcomes probably would not gain much in term of positive customer outcomes i.e., retention, CCB, willingness to pay premium prices. This is the reason why this work investigated the relationship between CSR perception-CCB in place of CSR disclosure-CCB in the first stage. Instead of relying on existing CSR ratings and instead of assuming that these ratings represent the true perception of CSR standings among customers, this study has directly asked the customers about their perceptions of CSR about the fast fashion industry in Italy.

This research also investigated the mediating role of CR on the relationship CSR perception-CCB. Managers and researchers thus are invited to look in-depth the role different CSR initiative plays into building company-stakeholders identification and explore new ways to make stakeholders feel more involved in CSR initiatives.

When it comes to direct effects of CSR on three dimensions of CCB as proposed in hypotheses H1a, H1b and H1c, there are enough evidences to prove that CSR directly affects helping others and feedback dimensions of CCB thus supporting hypotheses H1a and H2b. When these direct relationships were tested along with the mediating role

CR, CR proved to completely mediate the effects of CSR onto feedback, tolerance and helping others, thus supporting hypotheses H2a, H2b and H2c.

7 Limitations and Recommendations for Future Study

Like any study, this study has limitations. First, the mediating role of only corporate reputation was considered. Future research can include other mediators, along with reputation such as commitment, organizational identifications for different stakeholders, loyalty to better explain the ways CSR leads to discretionary behavior.

Second, the study only focused on one stakeholder group i.e., customers. Future studies can explore these relationships for different stakeholder groups and incorporate multiple group analysis with a big enough sample size to draw finer results for each group of stakeholders.

Third, this study did not discuss or look into the possibility of bidirectional nature (non-recursive model, simultaneous causality) of the relationship between CSR perception and corporate reputation. Future researches can look deeper into it and see how it affects the model and outcomes.

References

1. Fombrun, C.J.: Reputation: Realizing Value from the Corporate Image. Harvard Business School Press, Boston (1996)
2. Hall, R.: The strategic analysis of intangible resources. Strateg. Manag. J. 13(2), 135–144 (1992)
3. Rindova, V.P., Williamson, I.O., Petkova, A.P., Sever, J.M.: Being good or being known: an empirical examination of the dimensions, antecedents, and consequences of organizational reputation. Acad. Manag. J. 48(6), 1033–1049 (2005)
4. Graham, M.E., Bansal, P.: Consumers' willingness to pay for corporate reputation: the context of airline companies. Corp. Reput. Rev. 10(3), 189–200 (2007)
5. Benjamin, B.A., Podolny, J.M.: Status, quality, and social order in the California wine industry. Adm. Sci. Q. 44(3), 563–589 (1999)
6. Boyd, B.K., Bergh, D.D., Ketchen, D.J., Jr.: Reconsidering the reputation—performance relationship: a resource-based view. J. Manag. 36(3), 588–609 (2010)
7. Keh, H.T., Xie, Y.: Corporate reputation and customer behavioral intentions: the roles of trust, identification and commitment. Ind. Mark. Manag. 38(7), 732–742 (2009)
8. Walsh, G., Schaarschmidt, M., Ivens, S.: Effects of customer-based corporate reputation on perceived risk and relational outcomes: empirical evidence from gender moderation in fashion retailing. J. Prod. Brand Manag. 26(3), 227–238 (2017)
9. Helm, S.: Exploring the impact of corporate reputation on consumer satisfaction and loyalty. J. Cust. Behav. 5(1), 59–80 (2006)
10. Helm, S., Eggert, A., Garnefeld, I.: Modeling the impact of corporate reputation on customer satisfaction and loyalty using partial least squares. In: Esposito, Vinzi V., Chin, W., Henseler, J., Wang, H. (eds.) Handbook of Partial Least Squares. Springer Handbooks of Computational Statistics. Springer, Berlin, Heidelberg (2010). https://doi.org/10.1007/978-3-540-32827-8_23
11. Walsh, G., Beatty, S.E., Shiu, E.M.: The customer-based corporate reputation scale: replication and short form. J. Bus. Res. 62(10), 924–930 (2009)

12. Chun, R., Davies, G.: The effect of merger on employee views of corporate reputation: time and space dependent theory. Ind. Mark. Manag. **39**(5), 721–727 (2010)
13. Helm, S.: The role of corporate reputation in determining investor satisfaction and loyalty. Corp. Reput. Rev. **10**(1), 22–37 (2007)
14. Dowling, G.R.: Corporate reputations: should you compete on yours? Calif. Manag. Rev. **46**(3), 19–36 (2004)
15. Fombrun, C.J., Gardberg, N.A., Sever, J.M.: The reputation quotient SM: a multi-stakeholder measure of corporate reputation. J. Brand Manag. **7**(4), 241–255 (2000)
16. Melo, T., Garrido-Morgado, A.: Corporate reputation: a combination of social responsibility and industry. Corp. Soc. Responsib. Environ. Manag. **19**(1), 11–31 (2012)
17. Bergh, D.D., Ketchen, D.J., Jr., Boyd, B.K., Bergh, J.: New frontiers of the reputation—performance relationship: Insights from multiple theories. J. Manag. **36**(3), 620–632 (2010)
18. Roberts, P.W., Dowling, G.R.: Corporate reputation and sustained superior financial performance. Strateg. Manag. J. **23**(12), 1077–1093 (2002)
19. Brammer, S.J., Pavelin, S.: Corporate reputation and social performance: the importance of fit. J. Manag. Stud. **43**(3), 435–455 (2006)
20. Delgado-García, J.B., De Quevedo-Puente, E., De La Fuente-Sabaté, J.M.: The impact of ownership structure on corporate reputation: evidence from Spain. Corp. Gov. Int. Rev. **18**(6), 540–556 (2010)
21. Sheehy, B.: Defining CSR: problems and solutions. J. Bus. Ethics **131**(3), 625–648 (2015)
22. Pérez, A.: Corporate reputation and CSR reporting to stakeholders: gaps in the literature and future lines of research. Corp. Commun. Int. J. **20**(1), 11–29 (2015)
23. Pérez-Cornejo, C., de Quevedo-Puente, E., Delgado-García, J.B.: Reporting as a booster of the corporate social performance effect on corporate reputation. Corp. Soc. Responsib. Environ. Manag. **27**(3), 1252–1263 (2020)
24. Pérez, A., López, C., Salmones, M.D.: An empirical exploration of the link between reporting to stakeholders and corporate social responsibility reputation in the Spanish context. Account. Audit. Account. J. **30**, 668–698 (2017)
25. Pradhan, S.: Impact of corporate social responsibility intensity on corporate reputation and financial performance of Indian firms. Verslas: teorija ir praktika **17**(4), 371–380 (2016)
26. Radhakrishnan, M.S., Chitrao, P., Nagendra, A.: Corporate social responsibility (CSR) in market driven environment. Procedia Econ. Financ. **11**, 68–75 (2014)
27. Sprinkle, G.B., Maines, L.A.: The benefits and costs of corporate social responsibility. Bus. Horiz. **53**(5), 445–453 (2010)
28. Levy, S.E., Park, S.Y.: An analysis of CSR activities in the lodging industry. J. Hosp. Tour. Manag. **18**(1), 147–154 (2011)
29. Groth, M.: Customers as good soldiers: examining citizenship behaviors in internet service deliveries. J. Manag. **31**(1), 7–27 (2005)
30. Omran, M.A., Ramdhony, D.: Theoretical perspectives on corporate social responsibility disclosure: a critical review. Int. J. Account. Financ. Rep. **5**(2), 38–55 (2015)
31. Aksak, E.O., Ferguson, M.A., Duman, S.A.: Corporate social responsibility and CSR fit as predictors of corporate reputation: a global perspective. Publ. Relat. Rev. **42**(1), 79–81 (2016)
32. Tajfel, H., Turner, J.C.: An integrative theory of inter-group conflict. In: Austin, W.G., Worchel, S. (eds.) The Social Psychology of Inter-group Relations, pp. 33–47. Brooks/Cole, Monterey (1979)
33. Abrams, D., Ando, K., Hinkle, S.: Psychological attachment to the group: cross-cultural differences in organizational identification and subjective norms as predictors of workers' turnover intentions. Pers. Soc. Psychol. Bull. **24**(10), 1027–1039 (1998)
34. Turner, J.C., Haslam, S.A.: Social identity, organizations, and leadership. In: Groups at Work: Theory and Research, pp. 25–65 (2001)

35. Van Knippenberg, D., Van Schie, E.C.: Foci and correlates of organizational identification. J. Occup. Organ. Psychol. **73**(2), 137–147 (2000)
36. Ashforth, B.E., Mael, F.: Social identity theory and the organization. Acad. Manag. Rev. **14**(1), 20–39 (1989)
37. Van Knippenberg, D.: Work motivation and performance: a social identity perspective. Appl. Psychol. **49**(3), 357–371 (2000)
38. Baraibar Díez, E.P., Luna Sotorrio, L.: The mediating effect of transparency in the relationship between corporate social responsibility and corporate reputation. Revista Brasileira de Gestão de Negócios **20**(1), 5–21 (2018)
39. Calabrese, A., Costa, R., Menichini, T., Rosati, F., Sanfelice, G.: Turning corporate social responsibility-driven opportunities in competitive advantages: a two-dimensional model. Knowl. Process. Manag. **20**(1), 50–58 (2013)
40. Chao, P., Polonsky, M., Jevons, C.: Global branding and strategic CSR: an overview of three types of complexity. Int. Mark. Rev. **26**(3), 327–347 (2009)
41. Šontaitė-Petkevičienė, M.: CSR reasons, practices and impact to corporate reputation. Procedia Soc. Behav. Sci. **213**, 503–508 (2015)
42. Heikkurinen, P.: Image differentiation with corporate environmental responsibility. Corp. Soc. Responsib. Environ. Manag. **17**(3), 142–152 (2010)
43. Maignan, I., Ferrell, O.C., Hult, G.T.M.: Corporate citizenship: cultural antecedents and business benefits. J. Acad. Mark. Sci. **27**(4), 455–469 (1999)
44. Van Dick, R., et al.: Should I stay or should I go? Explaining turnover intentions with organizational identification and job satisfaction. Br. J. Manag. **15**(4), 351–360 (2004)
45. Riketta, M.: Organizational identification: a meta-analysis. J. Vocat. Behav. **66**(2), 358–384 (2005)
46. Organ, D.W.: Organizational Citizenship Behavior: The Good Soldier Syndrome. Lexington Books/D. C. Heath and Company, Lexington (1988)
47. Scott, S.G., Lane, V.R.: A stakeholder approach to organizational identity. Acad. Manag. Rev. **25**(1), 43–62 (2000)
48. Grönroos, C., Gummerus, J.: The service revolution and its marketing implications: service logic vs service-dominant logic. Manag. Serv. Qual. Int. J. **24**(3), 206–229 (2014)
49. Yi, Y., Gong, T.: Customer value co-creation behavior: scale development and validation. J. Bus. Res. **66**(9), 1279–1284 (2013)
50. Bhattacharya, C.B., Sen, S.: Consumer–company identification: a framework for understanding consumers' relationships with companies. J. Mark. **67**(2), 76–88 (2003)
51. Bebbington, J., Larrinaga, C., Moneva, J.M.: Corporate social reporting and reputation risk management. Account. Audit. Account. J. **21**(3), 337–361 (2008)
52. Toms, J.S.: Firm resources, quality signals and the determinants of corporate environmental reputation: some UK evidence. Br. Account. Rev. **34**(3), 257–282 (2002)
53. Javed, M., Rashid, M.A., Hussain, G., Ali, H.Y.: The effects of corporate social responsibility on corporate reputation and firm financial performance: moderating role of responsible leadership. Corp. Soc. Responsib. Environ. Manag. **27**(3), 1395–1409 (2020)
54. Bianchi, E., Bruno, J.M., Sarabia-Sanchez, F.J.: The impact of perceived CSR on corporate reputation and purchase intention. Eur. J. Manag. Bus. Econ. **28**(3), 206–221 (2019)
55. Khojastehpour, M., Johns, R.: The effect of environmental CSR issues on corporate/brand reputation and corporate profitability. Eur. Bus. Rev. **26**(4), 330–339 (2014)
56. Deegan, C.: The legitimising effect of social and environmental disclosures–a theoretical foundation. Account. Audit. Account. J. **15**(3), 282–311 (2002)
57. King, B.G., Whetten, D.A.: Rethinking the relationship between reputation and legitimacy: a social actor conceptualization. Corp. Reput. Rev. **11**(3), 192–207 (2008)

58. Nikolaeva, R., Bicho, M.: The role of institutional and reputational factors in the voluntary adoption of corporate social responsibility reporting standards. J. Acad. Mark. Sci. **39**(1), 136–157 (2011)
59. Rao, H.: The social construction of reputation: certification contests, legitimation, and the survival of organizations in the American automobile industry: 1895–1912. Strateg. Manag. J. **15**(S1), 29–44 (1994)
60. Logsdon, J.M., Wood, D.J.: Reputation as an emerging construct in the business and society field: an introduction. Bus. Soc. **41**(4), 365–370 (2002)
61. Jinfeng, L.V., Runtian, J.I.N.G., Qian, C.A.O.: Antecedents of corporate reputation and customer citizenship behavior: evidence from China. Int. Bus. Manag. **9**(1), 128–132 (2014)
62. Bartikowski, B., Walsh, G.: Investigating mediators between corporate reputation and customer citizenship behaviors. J. Bus. Res. **64**(1), 39–44 (2011)
63. Lii, Y.S., Lee, M.: Doing right leads to doing well: when the type of CSR and reputation interact to affect consumer evaluations of the firm. J. Bus. Ethics **105**(1), 69–81 (2012)
64. Walsh, G., Bartikowski, B., Beatty, S.E.: Impact of customer-based corporate reputation on non-monetary and monetary outcomes: the roles of commitment and service context risk. Br. J. Manag. **25**(2), 166–185 (2014)
65. Hong, S.Y., Yang, S.U.: Effects of reputation, relational satisfaction, and customer–company identification on positive word-of-mouth intentions. J. Publ. Relat. Res. **21**(4), 381–403 (2009)
66. Lange, D., Lee, P.M., Dai, Y.: Organizational reputation: a review. J. Manag. **37**(1), 153–184 (2011)
67. Ponzi, L.J., Fombrun, C.J., Gardberg, N.A.: RepTrak^{TM} pulse: conceptualizing and validating a short-form measure of corporate reputation. Corp. Reput. Rev. **14**(1), 15–35 (2011)
68. Walsh, G., Beatty, S.E.: Customer-based corporate reputation of a service firm: scale development and validation. J. Acad. Mark. Sci. **35**(1), 127–143 (2007)
69. Hair, J.F., Black, W.C., Babin, B.J., Anderson, R.E., Tatham, R.L.: Multivariate Data Analysis. Prentice Hall, Upper Saddle River (1998)
70. Anderson, J.C., Gerbing, D.W.: Structural equation modeling in practice: a review and recommended two-step approach. Psychol. Bull. **103**(3), 411–423 (1988)
71. Matsunaga, M.: How to factor-analyze your data right: do's, don'ts, and how-to's. Int. J. Psychol. Res. **3**(1), 97–110 (2010)
72. Podsakoff, P.M., MacKenzie, S.B., Lee, J.Y., Podsakoff, N.P.: Common method biases in behavioral research: a critical review of the literature and recommended remedies. J. Appl. Psychol. **88**(5), 879–903 (2003)
73. Bagozzi, R.P., Yi, Y.: Specification, evaluation, and interpretation of structural equation models. J. Acad. Mark. Sci. **40**(1), 8–34 (2012)
74. Chin, W.W., Thatcher, J.B., Wright, R.T.: Assessing common method bias: problems with the ULMC technique. MIS Q. **36**(3), 1003–1019 (2012)

Exploring Sustainability Discourse in Accounting: A Literature Analysis

Kashif Nadeem$^{(\boxtimes)}$, Stefano Za, Michelina Venditti, and Ida Verna

Department of Management and Business Economics,
University of Chieti-Pescara, Pescara, Italy
{kashif.nadeem,stefano.za,michelina.venditti,ida.verna}@unich.it

Abstract. The relationship between sustainability and accounting has been continuously discussed in the academic literature over the last three decades. From a sustainability perspective, the accounting discipline must play a major role in the measurement, reporting, and auditing of sustainability performance. The aim of this study is to explore the discourse on sustainability and its performance in the accounting field. For this purpose, we selected articles from 3, 4, and 4* accounting journals and analysed the sustainability trend with each sustainability dimension, both separately and jointly. Based on our analysis, findings suggest that environmental sustainability is more discussed than economic and social sustainability in the accounting field. By examining sustainability performance management, we found that accounting and auditing have been highly emphasized in top accounting journals as compared to auditing. The aspect of reporting covers social, economic, and environmental sustainability equally. As regards accounting, on the other hand, higher attention is given to environmental sustainability compared to social and economic sustainability. Assurance has been found to be an emerging topic in the accounting field. With the limitations of the current study, we proposed a bibliometric analysis in order to capture the large dataset and generalization of the discourse on accounting and sustainability in the accounting field.

Keywords: Sustainability · Accounting · Sustainability performance management · Taxonomy

1 Introduction

The idea of sustainable development originated from the Declaration of the United Nations Conference on the Human Environment of 1972 [1] and was further promoted by The World Conservation Strategy of 1980 [2]. Afterwards, the United Nation's Brundtland Commission report "Our Common Future, From One Earth to One World" in 1987 defined Sustainable development as the "development that meets the needs of the present without compromising the ability of future generations to meet their own needs." [3]. It has been widely accepted that sustainable development has three dimensions: environmental, economic and social [4, 5]. Based on this assumption, the world is moving towards the implementation of sustainable development in every sector, and

S. Za et al. (Eds.): ItAIS 2020, LNISO 50, pp. 143–175, 2022.
https://doi.org/10.1007/978-3-030-86858-1_9

it has become a very attractive research field for business, academics and regulators [6]. Nowadays, sustainable development covering the economic, social and environmental aspects has emerged as the vital challenge for society and organizations [7].

In order to measure economic efforts concerning sustainable practices at the organizational level, the concept of sustainability accounting first appeared in the early 1990s [8, 9]. Based on the concept of Triple Bottom Line [10], the Global Reporting Initiative (GRI) sustainability reporting guidelines were introduced to assist organization and stakeholders in reporting economic, social and environmental performance and accountability [11]. In the past, a stream of research has attempted to link sustainability and sustainability performance (measurement, accounting and reporting) separately [12–15], but no prior study has examined this one-to-one relationship, especially in the accounting domain.

Sustainability accounting has captured the central position in the overall development of sustainability practices, measurement and governance at the organizational level [16]. Schaltegger and Burritt (2010) defined sustainability accounting as follows: "Sustainability accounting describes a subset of accounting that deals with activities, methods and systems to record, analyse and report: First, environmentally and socially induced financial impacts, Second, ecological and social impacts of a defined economic system (e.g., the company, production site, nation, etc.), and Third, the interactions and linkages between social, environmental and economic issues constituting the three dimensions of sustainability."

The aim of this research study is to explore the discourse on sustainability in the accounting research domain. Through literature review in top-ranked accounting journals, we attempted to classify a number of papers dealing with aspects of sustainability performance management, such as accounting, reporting and auditing. We classified the selected papers into a new specific framework and tried to provide some preliminary trends and significant insights for future research.

The flow of the paper is as follows: first, we defined the research methodology, including the search protocol and literature taxonomy with definitions. Second, we presented the results, including research trends and key data descriptions. Finally, we presented the discussion, future research directions, limitations and concluding remarks.

2 Methodology

This section explains the method of data selection, refinement, classification and analysis strategy. This approach is well established in the literature and has been employed by Seuring and Muller [18]. To align with the objective of this study, we focused on mean systematicity as suggested by Rowe [19]. Rowe [19] argued that this type of review is legitimate when the aim of the study is to highlight the theoretical understanding of the domain as opposed to the broader coverage of the topic. We categorise our research methodology into four parts: dataset setting, data refinement, taxonomy development for classifying the selected literature, and data analysis. First, we defined the dataset that collects the literature on sustainability we want to analyse. As we focused on sustainability and accounting perspectives, we selected ABS journals falling into the category of 3, 4 and 4* ranking. In this phase, we first defined the scope and search criteria to create a preliminary dataset. Secondly, we refined the dataset by carefully reading the content of each research article. In the third step, we analysed the selected article for the development of the taxonomy based on the theoretical dimensions of sustainability and sustainability accounting, specifically sustainable performance management. Finally, we presented the results of our analysis. The following sections provide further details on each step.

2.1 Dataset Selection

In order to create a first version of our dataset, we select SCOPUS as an appropriate source of information where to perform our search. The main reason for selecting this database was that it fully accessed the top 20000 journals covering almost 70000 traceable records and has been recognized as reliable source for peer-reviewed journals in the social sciences [20]. We selected articles from ABS journals related to the accounting field only. For this purpose, we used the keyword "Sustainability" along with the ISSN of ABS journals ranked 3, 4 and 4*. Then, we performed the following query to create the dataset.

```
( TITLE-ABS-KEY ( sustainability ) AND ISSN ( "0001-4826" OR "0361-
3682" OR "0165-4101" OR "0021-8456" OR "0823-9150" OR "1380-6653"
OR "0001-3072" OR "0001-4788" OR "0155-9982" OR "0888-7993" OR
"0951-3574" OR "0278-0380" OR "1050-4753" OR "0890-8389" OR "0007-
1870" OR "1045-2354" OR "0963-8180" OR "0267-4424" OR "1554-0642"
OR "1094-4060" OR "0278-4254" OR "0737-4607" OR "0148-558X" OR
"0306-686X" OR "1061-9518" OR "0198-9073" OR "1044-5005" ) )
```

By running the above query, we identified 278 research papers for our initial dataset. The above query was not limited to any language specification because these journals only published articles in English.

2.2 Data Refining

After carefully reading the content (mainly title and abstract) of the 278 articles, we identified 129 papers as being totally out of topic, while 67 research articles were excluded since they were too far from the scope of this paper. Finally, we identified 82 articles relevant to the topic of sustainability and accounting. During further refinement, we removed one additional article since it was a duplicate. The final dataset on which we performed our analysis was composed by 81 articles published in 3, 4 and 4* journals (see the list of articles as Appendix A).

2.3 Selection of Dimensions and Taxonomy Development

To create a taxonomy of the papers included in the dataset, the researcher should focus on past theoretical considerations [21]. For this purpose, we reviewed the past literature for conceptual clarity and classification of the dimensions of sustainability and sustainability performance management. In the following section, we explained the two dimensions used to develop our taxonomy, specifically *sustainability* and *sustainability performance management*. For the development of the taxonomy, we adopted the well-established criteria by [22]. Nickerson et al. [22] presented the methodology of taxonomy development. Following this method, we first identified the *meta-characteristics* and *subjective and objective ending conditions*. During our 1st iteration (conceptual to empirical), we reviewed past literature regarding *sustainability* and *sustainability performance management*. For each dimension we identified a set of values to assign to each paper to create our taxonomy. Environmental, social and economic are the possible values for the sustainability dimension. For the sustainability performance management dimension, on the other hand, we identified the following four key concepts in the accounting domain: accounting, reporting, auditing and assurance. During our *2nd iteration (empirical to conceptual)*, we performed an in-depth analysis of title, abstract, keywords and assigned a value to each article until robustness was achieved. In this process, we also observed the different combinations of the already identified dimensions of sustainability (social, environmental, economic) and sustainability performance management (accounting, auditing, assurance, reporting) in *iteration 1 (conceptual to empirical)*. For the sustainability dimension, we also found two more categories covering the combination of 1) social, economic and environmental sustainability and 2) social and environmental sustainability separately. Thus, we obtained a total of 5 categories of sustainability. Similarly, we included sustainability assurance in the sustainability auditing due to the same nature of both values. In this *iteration 2*, we also identified the new category of *sustainability performance management* with the combination of both accounting and reporting. These two iterations were performed by two independent researchers. After meeting the ending conditions according to the meta-characteristics, we classified the taxonomy for further analysis. Moreover, as we addressed the small set of studies in accounting field, we only focused on the conceptual insights from the previous body of literature in this specific domain *(meta-characteristic)*. Further details concerning the definition of each of the *sustainability* and *sustainability performance management* values are presented in the following sections.

Sustainability Dimension

At the corporate level, multiple sources, including corporate objectives, stakeholder demand, company reputation, regulations, are pressing for sustainability management [23]. There is a debate about the dimensionality of sustainability. Most researchers agree that sustainability consists of three dimensions, including social, economic and environmental [24]. Based on these arguments, Inayatullah [25] suggested that spirituality should be the fourth domain of sustainability. Similarly, Seghezzo [26] presented the five dimensions of the sustainability framework by including people and permanence in the sustainability domain. Bansal [27] described the nested nature of sustainability based on the argument that economy is a primary aspect of society, which is based on the ecological system. Similarly, Sheth et al. [28] contended that the dimensions of sustainability, such as social, economic and environmental, are interconnected. The concept of Triple Bottom Line (TPL) has further strengthened the three dimensions of sustainability by measuring them separately.

At the universal level, sustainability has become much popular with the launch of the 2030 agenda of Sustainable Development Goals (SDGs) by the United Nations.

It involved international cooperation through global indicators and the cooperation of governments, civil society, the private sector and institutions [29]. The SD framework identifies the 17 SDGs that are based on social, economic and environmental challenges [30].

Apart from above conceptual insights, the three-dimensionality of sustainability has been widely acknowledged by international communities [29] and guidelines for the three dimensions of sustainability have been published [11]. Based on the above discussion, we believe that the social, economic and environmental dimensions are major aspects of sustainability. Table 1 presents the definition of each value of the sustainability dimension used to create our taxonomy.

Table 1. Sustainability dimension

Value	Description
Environmental	Meeting human needs without compromising the health of ecosystems [31] Maintaining natural resources and nature's services at a 'suitable level' [32] The ability to maintain things or qualities that are valued in the physical environment [33]
Social	Social sustainability is a quality of society that encourages durable circumstances for human well-being, particularly for susceptible people or groups. [34] Development that can take place by balancing the evolution of civil society, and this development will result in a more prosperous environment [35]
Economic	"Maintenance of capital", or keeping capital intact [36] Economic sustainability is the ability of an economy to support a defined level of economic production indefinitely [37] "The widely accepted definition of economic sustainability is maintenance of capital, or keeping capital intact. Thus Hicks's definition of income - the amount one can consume during a period and still be as well off at the end of the period - can define economic sustainability, as it devolves on consuming value-added (interest), rather than capital." [38]

Sustainability Performance Management Dimension

Due to increasing unsustainable practices, sustainability performance management has become a challenge for organizations. Büyüközkan and Karabulut [6] defined sustainability performance as "the aggregate negative or positive bottom line of economic, environmental and social impacts of an entity against a defined baseline". Accounting and reporting have been considered the main aspects of sustainability performance management [17, 39]. Accounting deals with identifying information for defined indicators and measure them in precise manner, while reporting includes the communication and utilization of reports for decision making [15].

Adams and Whelan [40] found that sustainability reporting leads to increased transparency and accountability among corporations. Sustainability reporting plays a vital role in the development of company reputation. Previous literature indicates that there are many compelling factors behind sustainability reporting, including institutional, societal and stakeholder factors (e.g. [41, 42]).

Sustainability assurance has become the emerging stream of research in the accounting literature [13]. Manetti and Becatti [43] defined sustainability assurance as "assurance services for sustainability-related information in corporate reports". A recent survey conducted by KPMG found a tremendous increase in organizations for the assurance of sustainability reports [44]. The International Audit and Assurance Standards Board (IAASB) defines assurance as "an engagement in which a practitioner aims to obtain sufficient appropriate evidence in order to express a conclusion designed to enhance the degree of confidence of the intended users other than the responsible party about the subject matter information" [45]. Gray [14] reported that sustainability reporting lacks balanced and reliable information on sustainability performance. To increase the credibility of the report, third-party assurance was initiated on voluntarily basis [46].

It has been observed that 93% out of 250 large companies are disclosing sustainability reports [47]. This upward trend has been further supported by the issuance of the Global Reporting Initiatives (GRI) indicators. In order to address at corporate level, sustainability auditing has emerged as a relevant field [48]. Auditing plays an important role in authenticating accounts, specifically with respect to sustainability and subsequent disclosure. In contrast to this fact, past literature has widely questioned the reliability and quality of sustainability reports [49, 50].

Nitkin and Brooks [48] defined sustainability auditing as "involving three essential characteristics: (a) measurable standards are employed to assess environmental management and performance and link them to other standards or factors; (b) use of a trained audit team; and (c) the organization releases a progress report, either internally to the Board of Directors, externally to the public, or both".

Past researchers have contended that there is a credibility gap between the measurement and disclosure of sustainability reports [43, 51]. To overcome this gap and enhance the reliability of sustainability disclosure, reports have been observed to be assured by auditors [52, 53].

Auditing is the pre-requisite step for reporting and it has been commonly recognised that there is a negative relationship between financial reporting restatement and audit quality [54]. Despite its significant role in the organization, auditing has been criticized for its role. Detailed definitions of the possible values of the Sustainability Performance Management (SPM) dimension are presented in Table 2.

Table 2. Sustainability performance management

Value	Description
Accounting	"Sustainability accounting describes a subset of accounting that deals with activities, methods and systems to record, analyse and report: first, environmentally and socially induced financial impacts, Second, ecological and social impacts of a defined economic system (e.g., the company, production site, nation, etc.), and Third, the interactions and linkages between social, environmental and economic issues constituting the three dimensions of sustainability." [17]
Reporting	"Practice of measuring, disclosing, and being accountable to internal and external stakeholders for organizational performance towards the goal of sustainable development" [11]
Auditing	"Involving three essential characteristics: (a) measurable standards are employed to assess environmental management and performance and link them to other standards or factors; (b) use of a trained audit team; and (c) the organization releases a progress report, either internally to the Board of Directors, externally to the public, or both" [48]
Assurance	"An engagement in which an external third-party assurance provider (i.e. an SAP) is appointed to provide assurance over a sustainability report" [55]

Features of the Dimensions. As clarified by the above explanation, we classified the dimensions of sustainability and sustainability performance management by using the deductive approach. We categorized each dimension based on the literature review and conceptualization of accounting scholars. During coding, we segregated each dimension both separately and with the combination of two or more, after a careful content analysis of each paper.

3   Data Description and Analysis

In order to explore the dimensions of sustainability and sustainability performance management in our dataset, we initially described the entire dataset considering the publication trend and the most productive journals. Afterwards, we first focus on each specific dimension and then analysed the dataset combining both dimensions.

Based on our literature review, for the *sustainability* dimension we labelled the 81 papers using the three values identified for this specific dimension, also employing two additional labels resulting by the combination of these values, based on which aspects of sustainability are discussed in each paper. The resulting labels are: 1) social 2) environmental 3) economic 4) social, environmental and 5) social, environmental, economic.

Similarly, for the sustainability performance management dimension we identified four labels, where auditing and assurance were merged together, namely: 1) accounting 2) reporting 3) auditing (including assurance) and 4) accounting and reporting (for the paper discussing both aspects). This classification was performed based on our critical analysis of the 81 articles. Assurance was included in the category of auditing since it was conceived from the definition that both concepts are somehow interconnected. Further details are provided in the following sections.

3.1 Publication Trend

Figure 1 shows the publication trend of papers discussing sustainability issues in the leading journals in the accounting fields, covering 28 years, with the first publication in 1992 [8]. From 1992, the publication trend remains stagnant until 2011 (no more than 2 publication every year). From 2012 to 2015, a slight increase in publications in this field is observed. Afterwards, from 2015 to 2017, a decline is witnessed in the sustainability and accounting field. From 2017 to 2019, the number of publications sharply increases to 19. Only two studies are published in 2020, this low number being related to the fact that the query was performed on 25th May 2020, therefore this number is still incomplete.

PUBLICATIONS TREND

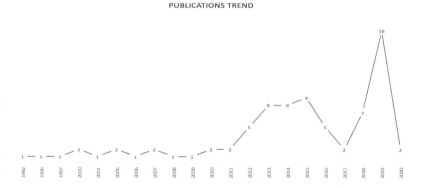

Fig. 1. Number of publications per year in sustainability accounting research since 1992

Figure 2 provides further information on the publication trend, complementing information on the most productive journals. It shows that *Accounting, Auditing and Accountability Journal* is the leading journal with 28 publication, and most of the studies (10) were published during the year 2019. The second highest ranked journal is *Critical Perspectives on Accounting* with 16 publications, and most of the studies (06) were published during the year 2016. Similarly, the third highest ranked journal is *Accounting Forum* which published 11 studies out of the total 81. The rest of the journals published articles on sustainability and accounting ranging from 1 to 4 in different years.

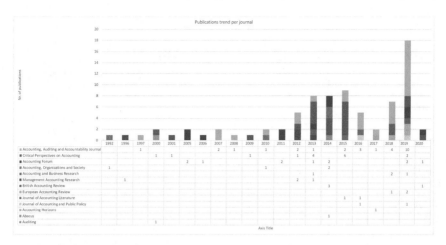

Fig. 2. Number of publications per year in accounting journals since 1992

3.2 Sustainability Dimension vs Journals

Table 3 below presents the sustainability aspects addressed in the accounting journals in categories 3, 4 and 4*. It describes that 54 publications cover all three aspects of sustainability (social, environmental and economic) and that *Accounting, Auditing and Accountability Journal* is the leading one with 19 studies. At the same time, 14 papers address both social and environment aspects of sustainability, with the most productive journals in this subset being *Critical Perspectives on Accounting* and A*ccounting, Auditing and Accountability Journal*. Finally, the remaining papers discuss one of the three main aspects of sustainability individually. Environmental sustainability is addressed by 10 papers, 4 of them being published on *Critical Perspectives on Accounting*, while the articles discussing only the social (2 papers) or the economic (1 paper) aspects are published on *Accounting, Auditing and Accountability Journal*. According to the table, economic and social aspects are rarely discussed individually.

Table 3. Sustainability dimension vs Journals

Journals	Social	Environmental	Economic	Social, environmental	Social, environmental, economic	Total
Abacus					1	**1**
Accounting and Business Research				1	3	**4**
Accounting Forum		1		2	8	**11**

(continued)

Table 3. (*continued*)

Journals	Social	Environmental	Economic	Social, environmental	Social, environmental, economic	Total
Accounting Horizons					1	**1**
Accounting, Auditing and Accountability Journal	2	2	1	4	19	**28**
Accounting, Organizations and Society		1			3	**4**
Auditing					1	**1**
British Accounting Review		1		1	2	**4**
Critical Perspectives on Accounting		4		4	8	**16**
European Accounting Review					3	**3**
Journal of Accounting and Public Policy				1	1	**2**
Journal of Accounting Literature					2	**2**
Management Accounting Research		1		1	2	**4**
Total	**2**	**10**	**1**	**14**	**54**	**81**

3.3 Sustainability Performance Management vs Journals

Table 4 describes the distribution of papers discussing the dimension of sustainability performance management among the top accounting journals. *Accounting* is the main aspect addressed in 33 research articles, followed by *reporting* with 30 articles. *Auditing* including *assurance* is only discussed in 13 articles, while 5 papers deal with *accounting and reporting* together. *Auditing, Accounting and Accountability Journal* mostly addresses the aspects of *reporting* (12 out of 28 publications) and *accounting* (08), while *Critical Perspectives on Accounting* addresses the *accounting* (09) and *reporting* (05) aspects, covering 87.5% of its articles. The third most productive journal, *Accounting Forum* is much focused on *reporting* (07 papers) as compared to *accounting* (03) and *auditing including assurance* (01) in its articles.

Table 4. Sustainability performance management vs Journals

Journals	Accounting	Reporting	Auditing (assurance)	Accounting, reporting	Total
Abacus		1			**1**
Accounting and Business Research	1	1	1	1	**4**
Accounting Forum	3	7	1		**11**
Accounting Horizons		1			**1**
Accounting, Auditing and Accountability Journal	8	12	5	3	**28**
Accounting, Organizations and Society	4				**4**
Auditing		1			**1**
British Accounting Review	3		1		**4**
Critical Perspectives on Accounting	9	5	1	1	**16**
European Accounting Review			3		**3**
Journal of Accounting and Public Policy		1	1		**2**
Journal of Accounting Literature	1	1			**2**

(*continued*)

Table 4. (*continued*)

Journals	Accounting	Reporting	Auditing (assurance)	Accounting, reporting	Total
Management Accounting Research	4				**4**
Total	**33**	**30**	**13**	**5**	**81**

3.4 Sustainability vs Sustainability Performance Management

Figure 3 describes the comparison between the dimensions of sustainability and sustainability performance management. Among the 54 research articles addressing all three aspects of sustainability, 24 papers focused on the reporting (disclosure) side of sustainability, 15 on accounting, 13 on auditing (including assurance) and 2 articles focused on the *accounting and reporting* issues. Similarly, the 2nd largest category (14 publications) is *social and environmental* sustainability. Among the 14 papers, accounting (6) and reporting (05) are the main aspects discussed, with only three of these papers debating issues concerning *accounting and reporting* (03). The 3rd most populous category is environmental sustainability (10), with all publications focusing on *accounting* issues as well as the two papers discussing the social aspect of sustainability.

Fig. 3. Sustainability vs Sustainability performance management dimensions

Figure 4 describes the comparison between the dimensions of sustainability performance management and sustainability. A*ccounting* is the most populous category (33 publications), with 15 papers debating the three aspects of sustainability, while 10 discuss only environmental issues, 2 cover social issues while none addresses economic issues individually. Similarly, the reporting category contains 30 articles mainly addressing all three aspects of sustainability (24) together, while 5 papers concern both social and environment aspects and only one focuses on the economic aspect. All 13 papers in the auditing (including assurance) category address all three aspects of sustainability. Finally, out of 5 articles in the *accounting and reporting* category two focus on all three aspects of sustainability while three cover the *social* and *environmental* aspects. Looking at Fig. 4, the categories of sustainability performance management seem to ignore the economic aspect of sustainability (individually) as well as the social one, while they usually consider all three aspects together.

Fig. 4. Sustainability performance management vs Sustainability dimensions

4 Discussion

Based on our analysis, it has been revealed that most studies focus on all three aspects of sustainability including social, economic and environmental in the accounting field. At the individual level, environmental sustainability is more debated as compared to social and economic sustainability in the accounting field. Social and economic sustainability are less debated in the accounting journals individually, while the former is quite discussed in combination with environmental aspects. This is consistent with the arguments made by Büyüközkan and Karabulut [6] that social and economic sustainability is ignored in the sustainability literature. In the context of sustainability performance management, we found that accounting and reporting (disclosure) are mostly addressed in the top ranked accounting journals. A large number of research articles discuss reporting (disclosure) and cover all dimensions of sustainability (social, economic and environmental). A similar trend was observed in the case of the accounting side in the top accounting journals. In the accounting field, most of the papers address environmental sustainability as compared to social and economic. The accounting aspect is less debated in sustainability accounting. Similarly, the reporting side is heavily focused on all dimensions of sustainability, while ignoring the combination of social and economic.

Papers in the auditing (assurance) category cover all dimensions of sustainability. At the individual level, it has been observed that scant research is available on sustainability auditing in the accounting domain. While comparing the different methods of sustainability performance evaluation, similar arguments have also been highlighted by Büyüközkan and Karabulut [6]. They argued that lack of auditing is the major limitation of the GRI framework. In combining accounting and reporting, most of the studies focused on all aspects of sustainability, while ignoring the individual ones.

Based on the above findings, we hereby argue that all dimensions of sustainability including environmental, economic and social, are being addressed in a fragmented way. Although more studies are focusing on environmental sustainability, the overall research in the accounting field should try to focus on integrating all three dimensions of sustainability. Similarly, we did not find any study discussing all aspects of sustainability performance management in the accounting field under one umbrella. Our analysis shows that there is little research for sustainability related personnel including decision makers, policy makers, sustainability mangers, accountants etc. We hereby argue that the training and development aspects of sustainability related personnel in accounting, reporting, auditing and assurance should be addressed in the accounting fields.

Accounting, Auditing and Accountability Journal is the leading journal publishing articles on sustainability performance management. The second most influential journal in this field is *Critical Perspective in Accounting*, followed by *Accounting Forum*. Finally, our analysis revealed that the emerging topic in sustainability performance is sustainability assurance which has gained momentum since 2018.

5   Conclusions

The aim of this study is to explore the link between sustainability discourse and sustainability performance management debate in the accounting field, considering top accounting journals.

This study presents a preliminary analysis of 28 years of literature encompassing sustainability and its performance management in the accounting research domain published in ABS 3, 4 and 4* journals. Based on the analysis of 81 articles, we can conclude that sustainability dimensions (social, economic and environmental) have a strong connection with the sustainability performance management dimension, specifically the aspects of *accounting*, *reporting* and *auditing* (assurance) in the accounting field. Social and economic sustainability is being ignored, while the discourse in top accounting journals is highly focused on environmental sustainability. The accounting and reporting (disclosure) aspects of sustainability performance, on the other hand, are widely addressed in top accounting journals.

This study presents the preliminary results of our research journey in exploring sustainability performance management in the sustainability discourse. Despite some interesting findings, we present some future research directions for researchers in the accounting field. First, we performed our analysis with a limited dataset from 3, 4 and 4* journals in the accounting field. An analysis with a large dataset is required to explore the discourse on sustainability and performance in the accounting field. Second, we also recommend a bibliometric analysis, which might be useful to further investigate the debate on sustainability and its performance management. Third, as we have presented a preliminary analysis of the papers in a specific dataset, future research might perform a deeper content analysis of these contributions in order to develop a conceptual framework describing the relationships between the two dimensions, which could be useful for policy makers, sustainability managers and decision makers. Fourth, future research should study the research characteristics of the sustainability discourse in the accounting field and try to build the taxonomy based on the aspects related to sustainability and sustainability performance management. Fifth, a new research stream has emerged with special focus on smart technologies and sustainability [56], so we propose that the role of smart technologies should be further explored in this context, investigating their impact on the issues concerning sustainability and sustainability performance management. Finally, recent literature has started to discuss the methods of sustainability accounting and reporting in Industry 4.0 [57], we hereby suggest that further research should empirically address sustainability and its performance management issues with a special consideration of Industry 4.0.

Appendix A. List of Final Articles

Sr. no.	Paper	Sustainability	Sustainability performance management
1	Gray, R. (1992). Accounting and environmentalism: an exploration of the challenge of gently accounting for accountability, transparency and sustainability. *Accounting, organizations and society, 17*(5), 399–425	Environmental	Accounting
2	Milne, M. J. (1996). On sustainability; the environment and management accounting. *Management Accounting Research, 7*(1), 135–161	Environmental	Accounting
3	Bebbington, J. (1997). Engagement, education and sustainability. *Accounting, Auditing & Accountability Journal*	Environmental	Accounting
4	Wallage, P. (2000). Assurance on sustainability reporting: An auditor's view. *Auditing: A Journal of Practice & Theory, 19*(s-1), 53–65	Social, environmental, economic	Reporting

(*continued*)

(*continued*)

Sr. no.	Paper	Sustainability	Sustainability performance management
5	Lamberton, G. (2000). Accounting for sustainable development—A case study of city farm. *Critical Perspectives on Accounting*, *11*(5), 583–605	Social, environmental, economic	Accounting
6	Bebbington, J., & Gray, R. (2001). An account of sustainability: failure, success and a reconceptualization. *Critical perspectives on accounting*, *12*(5), 557–587	Environmental	Accounting
7	Lamberton, G. (2005, March). Sustainability accounting—a brief history and conceptual framework. In *Accounting forum* (Vol. 29, No. 1, pp. 7–26). No longer published by Elsevier	Social, environmental, economic	Accounting
8	Dillard, J., Brown, D., & Marshall, R. S. (2005, March). An environmentally enlightened accounting. In *Accounting Forum* (Vol. 29, No. 1, pp. 77–101). No longer published by Elsevier	Environmental	Accounting
9	Moneva, J. M., Archel, P., & Correa, C. (2006, June). GRI and the camouflaging of corporate unsustainability. In *Accounting forum* (Vol. 30, No. 2, pp. 121–137). No longer published by Elsevier	Social, environmental, economic	Reporting

(*continued*)

(*continued*)

Sr. no.	Paper	Sustainability	Sustainability performance management
10	Adam, C. A., & McNicholas, P. (2007). Making a difference: Sustainability reporting, accountability and organizational change. *Accounting, Auditing & Accountability Journal*, *20*(3), 382–402	Social, environmental, economic	Reporting
11	Adams, C. A., & Larrinaga-González, C. (2007). Engaging with organisations in pursuit of improved sustainability accounting and performance. *Accounting, Auditing & Accountability Journal*	Social, environmental, economic	Reporting
12	Adams, C. A. (2008). A commentary on: corporate social responsibility reporting and reputation risk management. *Accounting, Auditing & Accountability Journal*	Economic	Reporting
13	Brown, J. (2009). Democracy, sustainability and dialogic accounting technologies: Taking pluralism seriously. *Critical Perspectives on Accounting*, *20*(3), 313–342	Environmental	Accounting
14	Gray, R. (2010). Is accounting for sustainability actually accounting for sustainability… and how would we know? An exploration of narratives of organisations and the planet. *Accounting, organizations and society*, *35*(1), 47–62	Social, environmental, economic	Accounting

(*continued*)

(*continued*)

Sr. no.	Paper	Sustainability	Sustainability performance management
15	Burritt, R. L., & Schaltegger, S. (2010). Sustainability accounting and reporting: fad or trend?. *Accounting, Auditing & Accountability Journal*	Social, environmental, economic	Accounting, reporting
16	Williams, B., Wilmshurst, T., & Clift, R. (2011, September). Sustainability reporting by local government in Australia: Current and future prospects. In *Accounting Forum* (Vol. 35, No. 3, pp. 176–186). No longer published by Elsevier	Social, environmental, economic	Reporting
17	Joseph, C., & Taplin, R. (2011, March). The measurement of sustainability disclosure: Abundance versus occurrence. In *Accounting forum* (Vol. 35, No. 1, pp. 19–31). No longer published by Elsevier	Social, environmental, economic	Reporting
18	Songini, L., & Pistoni, A. I. (2012). Accounting, auditing and control for sustainability	Social, environmental, economic	Accounting
19	Gond, J. P., Grubnic, S., Herzig, C., & Moon, J. (2012). Configuring management control systems: Theorizing the integration of strategy and sustainability. *Management Accounting Research, 23*(3), 205–223	Social, environmental	Accounting

(*continued*)

(*continued*)

Sr. no.	Paper	Sustainability	Sustainability performance management
20	Joseph, G. (2012). Ambiguous but tethered: An accounting basis for sustainability reporting. *Critical perspectives on Accounting, 23*(2), 93–106	Social, environmental, economic	Reporting
21	Fraser, M. (2012). "Fleshing out" an engagement with a social accounting technology. *Accounting, Auditing & Accountability Journal*	Social	Accounting
22	Gray, R., & Laughlin, R. (2012). It was 20 years ago today: Sgt Pepper, accounting, auditing & accountability journal, green accounting and the blue meanies. *Accounting, Auditing & Accountability Journal, 25*(2), 228–255	Social, environmental, economic	Accounting
23	Gray, R. (2013). Back to basics: What do we mean by environmental (and social) accounting and what is it for?—A reaction to Thornton. *Critical Perspectives on Accounting, 24*(6), 459–468	Social, environmental, economic	Reporting
24	Cho, C. H., & Patten, D. M. (2013). Green accounting: Reflections from a CSR and environmental disclosure perspective. *Critical Perspectives on Accounting, 24*(6), 443–447	Social, environmental	Accounting

(*continued*)

(continued)

Sr. no.	Paper	Sustainability	Sustainability performance management
25	Deegan, C. (2013). The accountant will have a central role in saving the planet… really? A reflection on 'green accounting and green eyeshades twenty years later'. *Critical Perspectives on Accounting*, *24*(6), 448–458	Environmental	Accounting
26	Cooper, D. J., & Morgan, W. (2013). Meeting the evolving corporate reporting needs of government and society: arguments for a deliberative approach to accounting rule making. *Accounting and Business Research*, *43*(4), 418–441	Social, environmental, economic	Accounting
27	Contrafatto, M., & Burns, J. (2013). Social and environmental accounting, organisational change and management accounting: A processual view. *Management Accounting Research*, *24*(4), 349–365	Social, environmental	Accounting
28	Comyns, B., Figge, F., Hahn, T., & Barkemeyer, R. (2013, September). Sustainability reporting: The role of "Search", "Experience" and "Credence" information. In *Accounting Forum* (Vol. 37, No. 3, pp. 231–243). No longer published by Elsevier	Social, environmental	Accounting, reporting
29	Boiral, O. (2013). Sustainability reports as simulacra? A counter-account of A and A + GRI reports. *Accounting, Auditing & Accountability Journal*	Social, environmental, economic	Reporting

(continued)

(*continued*)

Sr. no.	Paper	Sustainability	Sustainability performance management
30	Spence, C., Chabrak, N., & Pucci, R. (2013). Doxic sunglasses: A response to "Green accounting and Green Eyeshades: Twenty years later". *Critical Perspectives on Accounting*, *24*(6), 469–473	Environmental	Accounting
31	Lee, K. H., & Wu, Y. (2014). Integrating sustainability performance measurement into logistics and supply networks: A multi-methodological approach. *The British Accounting Review*, *46*(4), 361–378	Social, environmental, economic	Accounting
32	Barkemeyer, R., Comyns, B., Figge, F., & Napolitano, G. (2014, December). CEO statements in sustainability reports: Substantive information or background noise?. In *Accounting Forum* (Vol. 38, No. 4, pp. 241–257). No longer published by Elsevier	Social, environmental, economic	Accounting
33	Spence, L. J., & Rinaldi, L. (2014). Governmentality in accounting and accountability: A case study of embedding sustainability in a supply chain. *Accounting, Organizations and Society*, *39*(6), 433–452	Environmental	Accounting
34	Herbohn, K., Walker, J., & Loo, H. Y. M. (2014). Corporate social responsibility: The link between sustainability disclosure and sustainability performance. *Abacus*, *50*(4), 422–459	Social, environmental, economic	Reporting

(*continued*)

(*continued*)

Sr. no.	Paper	Sustainability	Sustainability performance management
35	Bebbington, J., & Larrinaga, C. (2014). Accounting and sustainable development: An exploration. *Accounting, organizations and society*, *39*(6), 395–413	Social, environmental, economic	Accounting
36	Passetti, E., Cinquini, L., Marelli, A., & Tenucci, A. (2014). Sustainability accounting in action: Lights and shadows in the Italian context. *The British Accounting Review*, *46*(3), 295–308	Social, environmental, economic	Reporting
37	Allen, B. G. (2014, December). What's new about New accounts? Assessing change proposals for social and environmental accounting. In *Accounting forum* (Vol. 38, No. 4, pp. 278–287). No longer published by Elsevier	Social, environmental	Accounting
38	Burritt, R., & Schaltegger, S. (2014). Accounting towards sustainability in production and supply chains. *The British Accounting Review*, *46*(4), 327–343	Social, environmental	Accounting
39	Brown, J., Dillard, J., Hopper, T., Atkins, J., Atkins, B. C., Thomson, I., & Maroun, W. (2015). "Good" news from nowhere: imagining utopian sustainable accounting. *Accounting, Auditing & Accountability Journal*	Social, environmental, economic	Reporting

(*continued*)

(*continued*)

Sr. no.	Paper	Sustainability	Sustainability performance management
40	Roberts, R. W., & Wallace, D. M. (2015). Sustaining diversity in social and environmental accounting research. *Critical Perspectives on Accounting, 32*, 78–87	Social, environmental	Reporting
41	Thoradeniya, P., Lee, J., Tan, R., & Ferreira, A. (2015). Sustainability reporting and the theory of planned behaviour. *Accounting, Auditing & Accountability Journal*	Social, environmental, economic	Accounting
42	Watson, L. (2015). Corporate social responsibility research in accounting. *Journal of Accounting Literature, 34,* 1–16	Social, environmental, economic	Reporting
43	Flower, J. (2015). The international integrated reporting council: a story of failure. *Critical Perspectives on Accounting, 27*, 1–17	Social, environmental, economic	Accounting
44	Thomson, I. (2015). 'But does sustainability need capitalism or an integrated report' a commentary on 'The International Integrated Reporting Council: A story of failure' by Flower, J. *Critical Perspectives on Accounting, 27*, 18–22	Social, environmental, economic	Accounting
45	Adams, C. A. (2015). The international integrated reporting council: a call to action. *Critical Perspectives on Accounting, 27*, 23–28	Social, environmental, economic	Reporting

(*continued*)

(continued)

Sr. no.	Paper	Sustainability	Sustainability performance management
46	Humphrey, C., & Gendron, Y. (2015). What is going on? The sustainability of accounting academia. *Critical Perspectives on Accounting, 26*(C), 47–66	Social, environmental	Accounting
47	Saravanamuthu, K. (2015). Instilling a sustainability ethos in accounting education through the Transformative Learning pedagogy: A case-study. *Critical Perspectives on Accounting, 32*, 1–36	Social, environmental, economic	Accounting
48	O'Dwyer, B., & Unerman, J. (2016). Fostering rigour in accounting for social sustainability. *Accounting, Organizations and Society, 49*, 32–40	Social, environmental	Reporting
49	Hummel, K., & Schlick, C. (2016). The relationship between sustainability performance and sustainability disclosure–Reconciling voluntary disclosure theory and legitimacy theory. *Journal of Accounting and Public Policy, 35*(5), 455–476	Social, environmental, economic	Reporting
50	Manetti, G., & Bellucci, M. (2016). The use of social media for engaging stakeholders in sustainability reporting. *Accounting, Auditing & Accountability Journal*	Social, environmental, economic	Reporting

(continued)

(*continued*)

Sr. no.	Paper	Sustainability	Sustainability performance management
51	Chatelain-Ponroy, S., & Morin-Delerm, S. (2016). Adoption of sustainable development reporting by universities. *Accounting, Auditing & Accountability Journal*	Social	Accounting
52	Rezaee, Z. (2016). Business sustainability research: A theoretical and integrated perspective. *Journal of Accounting literature, 36,* 48–64	Social, environmental, economic	Reporting
53	Bradford, M., Earp, J. B., Showalter, D. S., & Williams, P. F. (2017). Corporate sustainability reporting and stakeholder concerns: Is there a disconnect?. *Accounting Horizons, 31*(1), 83–102	Social, environmental, economic	Reporting
54	Diouf, D., & Boiral, O. (2017). The quality of sustainability reports and impression management. *Accounting, Auditing & Accountability Journal*	Social, environmental, economic	Reporting
55	Kaur, A., & Lodhia, S. (2018). Stakeholder engagement in sustainability accounting and reporting. *Accounting, Auditing & Accountability Journal*	Social, environmental, economic	Accounting
56	Bebbington, J., & Unerman, J. (2018). Achieving the United Nations sustainable development goals. *Accounting, Auditing & Accountability Journal*	Social, environmental, economic	Auditing (assurance)

(*continued*)

(continued)

Sr. no.	Paper	Sustainability	Sustainability performance management
57	Stolowy, H., & Paugam, L. (2018). The expansion of non-financial reporting: an exploratory study. *Accounting and Business Research*, *48*(5), 525–548	Social, environmental, economic	Accounting, reporting
58	Unerman, J., Bebbington, J., & O'dwyer, B. (2018). Corporate reporting and accounting for externalities. *Accounting and business research*, *48*(5), 497–522	Social, environmental	Accounting, reporting
59	Reimsbach, D., Hahn, R., & Gürtürk, A. (2018). Integrated reporting and assurance of sustainability information: An experimental study on professional investors' information processing. *European Accounting Review*, *27*(3), 559–581	Social, environmental, economic	Reporting
60	Busco, C., Giovannoni, E., Granà, F., & Izzo, M. F. (2018). Making sustainability meaningful: Aspirations, discourses and reporting practices. *Accounting, Auditing & Accountability Journal*	Social, environmental, economic	Accounting
61	Egan, M., & Tweedie, D. (2018). A "green" accountant is difficult to find: Can accountants contribute to sustainability management initiatives?. *Accounting, Auditing & Accountability Journal*, *31*(6), 1749–1773	Social, environmental	Reporting

(continued)

(continued)

Sr. no.	Paper	Sustainability	Sustainability performance management
62	Dillard, J., & Vinnari, E. (2019). Critical dialogical accountability: From accounting-based accountability to accountability-based accounting. *Critical Perspectives on Accounting, 62*, 16–38	Social, environmental, economic	Auditing (assurance)
63	Ferdous, M. I., Adams, C. A., & Boyce, G. (2019). Institutional drivers of environmental management accounting adoption in public sector water organisations. *Accounting, Auditing & Accountability Journal*	Social, environmental, economic	Auditing (assurance)
64	Farooq, M. B., & De Villiers, C. (2019). Understanding how managers institutionalise sustainability reporting. *Accounting, Auditing & Accountability Journal*	Social, environmental, economic	Auditing (assurance)
65	Bellucci, M., Simoni, L., Acuti, D., & Manetti, G. (2019). Stakeholder engagement and dialogic accounting. *Accounting, Auditing & Accountability Journal*	Social, environmental, economic	Reporting
66	Leong, S., & Hazelton, J. (2019). Under what conditions is mandatory disclosure most likely to cause organisational change?. *Accounting, Auditing & Accountability Journal*	Social, environmental, economic	Auditing (assurance)

(continued)

(continued)

Sr. no.	Paper	Sustainability	Sustainability performance management
67	Moggi, S. (2019, July). Social and environmental reports at universities: a Habermasian view on their evolution. In *Accounting Forum* (Vol. 43, No. 3, pp. 283–326). Routledge	Social, environmental, economic	Auditing (assurance)
68	Maroun, W. (2019). Does external assurance contribute to higher quality integrated reports?. *Journal of Accounting and Public Policy*, *38*(4), 106670	Social, environmental	Reporting
69	Farooq, M. B., & De Villiers, C. (2019). How sustainability assurance engagement scopes are determined, and its impact on capture and credibility enhancement. *Accounting, Auditing & Accountability Journal*	Social, environmental	Accounting, reporting
70	Boiral, O., Heras-Saizarbitoria, I., & Brotherton, M. C. (2019). Professionalizing the assurance of sustainability reports: the auditors' perspective. *Accounting, Auditing & Accountability Journal*	Social, environmental, economic	Auditing (assurance)
71	Adams, C. A., & Larrinaga, C. (2019). Progress: engaging with organisations in pursuit of improved sustainability accounting and performance.*Accounting, Auditing & Accountability Journal*	Social, environmental, economic	Auditing (assurance)

(continued)

(*continued*)

Sr. no.	Paper	Sustainability	Sustainability performance management
72	Maroun, W. (2019). Exploring the rationale for integrated report assurance. *Accounting, Auditing & Accountability Journal*	Environmental	Accounting
73	Gazzola, P., Amelio, S., Papagiannis, F., & Michaelides, Z. (2019). Sustainability reporting practices and their social impact to NGO funding in Italy. *Critical Perspectives on Accounting*, 102085	Social, environmental, economic	Auditing (assurance)
74	Steinmeier, M., & Stich, M. (2019). Does sustainability assurance improve managerial investment decisions?. *European Accounting Review*, 28(1), 177–209	Social, environmental, economic	Reporting
75	Michelon, G., Patten, D. M., & Romi, A. M. (2019). Creating legitimacy for sustainability assurance practices: Evidence from sustainability restatements. *European Accounting Review*, 28(2), 395–422	Social, environmental	Reporting
76	Channuntapipat, C., Samsonova-Taddei, A., & Turley, S. (2019). Exploring diversity in sustainability assurance practice. *Accounting, Auditing & Accountability Journal*	Social, environmental, economic	Auditing (assurance)
77	Canning, M., O'Dwyer, B., & Georgakopoulos, G. (2019). Processes of auditability in sustainability assurance–the case of materiality construction. *Accounting and Business Research*, 49(1), 1–27	Social, environmental, economic	Auditing (assurance)

(*continued*)

(continued)

Sr. no.	Paper	Sustainability	Sustainability performance management
78	Farooq, M. B., & De Villiers, C. (2019). The shaping of sustainability assurance through the competition between accounting and non-accounting providers. *Accounting, Auditing & Accountability Journal*	Social, environmental, economic	Reporting
79	Margerison, J., Fan, M., & Birkin, F. (2019, July). The prospects for environmental accounting and accountability in China. In *Accounting Forum* (Vol. 43, No. 3, pp. 327–347). Routledge	Social, environmental, economic	Auditing (assurance)
80	Channuntapipat, C., Samsonova-Taddei, A., & Turley, S. (2020). Variation in sustainability assurance practice: An analysis of accounting versus non-accounting providers. *The British Accounting Review*, 52(2), 100843	Social, environmental, economic	Auditing (assurance)
81	Safari, M., & Areeb, A. (2020, March). A qualitative analysis of GRI principles for defining sustainability report quality: an Australian case from the preparers' perspective. In *Accounting Forum* (pp. 1–32). Routledge	Social, environmental, economic	Reporting

References

1. Handl, G.: Declaration of the United Nations conference on the human environment, 1972. Indian J. Publ. Adm. **35**, 680–684 (1989). https://doi.org/10.1177/0019556119890340
2. IUCN–UNEP–WWF: World conservation living resource conservation for sustainable development (1980)
3. UNWECD: World commission on environment and development: our common future (1987)

4. Elkington, J.: Partnerships fromcannibals with forks: the triple bottom line of 21st-century business. Environ. Qual. Manag. **8**, 37–51 (1998). https://doi.org/10.1002/tqem.3310080106
5. Lamberton, G.: Sustainability accounting - a brief history and conceptual framework. Account. Forum. **29**, 7–26 (2005). https://doi.org/10.1016/j.accfor.2004.11.001
6. Büyüközkan, G., Karabulut, Y.: Sustainability performance evaluation: literature review and future directions. J. Environ. Manag. (2018). https://doi.org/10.1016/j.jenvman.2018.03.064
7. Lodhia, S.K.: Mining and Sustainable Development: Current Issues. Routledge, London (2018)
8. Gray, R.: Accounting and environmentalism: an exploration of the challenge of gently accounting for accountability, transparency and sustainability. Account. Organ. Soc. **17**, 399–425 (1992). https://doi.org/10.1016/0361-3682(92)90038-T
9. Elkington, J.: Coming clean: the rise and rise of the corporate environment report. Bus. Strateg. Environ. **2**, 42–44 (1993). https://doi.org/10.1002/bse.3280020204
10. Elkington, J.: Triple bottom-line reporting: looking for balance. Aust. CPA. **69**, 18–21 (1999)
11. GRI: Sustainability reporting guidelines (2002)
12. Bebbington, J., Larrinaga, C.: Accounting and sustainable development: an exploration. Account. Organ. Soc. (2014). https://doi.org/10.1016/j.aos.2014.01.003
13. Channuntapipat, C., Samsonova-Taddei, A., Turley, S.: Variation in sustainability assurance practice: an analysis of accounting versus non-accounting providers. Br. Account. Rev. (2020). https://doi.org/10.1016/j.bar.2019.100843
14. Gray, R.: Is accounting for sustainability actually accounting for sustainability…and how would we know? An exploration of narratives of organisations and the planet. Account. Organ. Soc. (2010). https://doi.org/10.1016/j.aos.2009.04.006
15. Maas, K., Schaltegger, S., Crutzen, N.: Advancing the integration of corporate sustainability measurement, management and reporting. J. Clean. Prod. (2016). https://doi.org/10.1016/j.jclepro.2016.06.006
16. Rinaldi, L.: Accounting for sustainability governance: the enabling role of social and environmental accountability research (2019). https://doi.org/10.1080/0969160X.2019.1578675
17. Schaltegger, S., Burritt, R.L.: Sustainability accounting for companies: catchphrase or decision support for business leaders? J. World Bus. **45**, 375–384 (2010). https://doi.org/10.1016/j.jwb.2009.08.002
18. Seuring, S., Muller, M.: From a literature review to a conceptual framework for sustainable supply chain management. J. Clean. Prod. **16**, 1699–1710 (2008)
19. Rowe, F.: What literature review is not: diversity, boundaries and recommendations. Eur. J. Inf. Syst. **23**, 241–255 (2014). https://doi.org/10.1057/ejis.2014.7
20. Donthu, N., Kumar, S., Pattnaik, D.: Forty-five years of Journal of Business Research: a bibliometric analysis. J. Bus. Res. **109**, 1–14 (2020). https://doi.org/10.1016/j.jbusres.2019.10.039
21. Kappos, B.A., Rivard, S.: A three-perspective model of culture, information systems, and their development and use. MIS Q. **32**, 601–634 (2008)
22. Nickerson, R.C., Varshney, U., Muntermann, J., Varshney, U., Muntermann, J.: A method for taxonomy development and its application in information systems. Eur. J. Inf. Syst. **22**, 336–359 (2013). https://doi.org/10.1057/ejis.2012.26
23. Siegel, D.S.: Green management matters only if it yields more green: an economic/strategic perspective. Acad. Manag. Perspect. (2009)
24. Giddings, B., Hopwood, B., O'Brien, G.: Environment, economy and society: fitting them together into sustainable development. Sustain. Dev. (2002). https://doi.org/10.1002/sd.199
25. Inayatullah, S.: Spirituality as the fourth bottom line? Futures (2005). https://doi.org/10.1016/j.futures.2004.10.015

26. Seghezzo, L.: The five dimensions of sustainability. Env. Polit. (2009). https://doi.org/10.1080/09644010903063669
27. Bansal, P.: Evolving sustainably: a longitudinal study of corporate sustainable development. Strateg. Manag. J. (2005). https://doi.org/10.1002/smj.441
28. Sheth, J.N., Sethia, N.K., Srinivas, S.: Mindful consumption: a customer-centric approach to sustainability. J. Acad. Mark. Sci. (2011). https://doi.org/10.1007/s11747-010-0216-3
29. United Nations: Transforming Our World: The 2030 Agenda for Sustainable Development. Springer Publishing Company, New York (2015)
30. Gupta, J., Vegelin, C.: Sustainable development goals and inclusive development. Int. Environ. Agreements: Polit. Law Econ. **16**(3), 433–448 (2016). https://doi.org/10.1007/s10784-016-9323-z
31. Callicott, J.B., Mumfordf, K.: Ecological sustainability as a conservation concept. Sustainability (2017). https://doi.org/10.4324/9781315241951-21
32. Moldan, B., Janoušková, S., Hák, T.: How to understand and measure environmental sustainability: indicators and targets. Ecol. Indic. (2012). https://doi.org/10.1016/j.ecolind.2011.04.033
33. Sutton, P.: A perspective on environmental sustainability. Paper on the Victorian Commissioner for Environmental Sustainability (2004)
34. Hollander, R., et al.: Network priorities for social sustainability research and education: memorandum of the integrated network on social sustainability research group. Sustain. Sci. Pract. Policy (2016). https://doi.org/10.1080/15487733.2016.11908150
35. Caulfield, J., Polèse, M., Stren, R., Polese, M.: The social sustainability of cities: diversity and the management of change. Can. Public Policy/Anal. Polit. (2001). https://doi.org/10.2307/3552480
36. Hicks, J.R.: Value and Capital. Clarendon Press, Oxford (1939)
37. Park, Y.S., Lek, S.: Introduction: global changes and sustainable ecosystem management. Elsevier B.V. (2015). https://doi.org/10.1016/B978-0-444-63536-5.00001-6
38. Goodland, R.: The concept of environmental sustainability. Annu. Rev. Ecol. Syst. **26**, 1–24 (1995). https://doi.org/10.1146/annurev.es.26.110195.000245
39. Kaur, A., Lodhia, S.: Stakeholder engagement in sustainability accounting and reporting. Account. Audit. Account. J. **31**, 338–368 (2018). https://doi.org/10.1108/AAAJ-12-2014-1901
40. Adams, C.A., Whelan, G.: Conceptualising future change in corporate sustainability reporting. Account. Audit. Account. J. **22**, 118–143 (2009). https://doi.org/10.1108/09513570910923033
41. Deegan, C., Gordon, B.: A study of the environmental disclosure practices of Australian corporations. Account. Bus. Res. (1996). https://doi.org/10.1080/00014788.1996.9729510
42. Freedman, M., Jaggi, B.: Global warming and corporate disclosures: a comparative analysis of companies from the European Union, Japan and Canada (2009). https://doi.org/10.1108/s1479-3598(2010)0000004009
43. Manetti, G., Becatti, L.: Assurance services for sustainability reports: standards and empirical evidence. J. Bus. Ethics (2009). https://doi.org/10.1007/s10551-008-9809-x
44. KPMG International: Currents of Change - The KPMG Survey of Corporate Responsibility Reporting 2015. KPMG Corp. Responsib. Report. (2015). www.kpmg.com/sustainability
45. IAASB: International Standard on Assurance Engagements (ISAE) 3000 Revised, Assurance Engagements Other than Audits or Reviews of Historical Financial Information—IFAC (2013)
46. O'dwyer, B.: The case of sustainability assurance: constructing a new assurance service. Contemp. Account. Res. (2011). https://doi.org/10.1111/j.1911-3846.2011.01108.x
47. KPMG: International survey of corporate responsibility reporting 2013 (2013)

48. Nitkin, D., Brooks, L.J.: Sustainability auditing and reporting: the Canadian experience. J. Bus. Ethics. **17**, 1499–1507 (1998). https://doi.org/10.1023/A:1006044130990

49. Cho, C.H., Michelon, G., Patten, D.M.: Impression management in sustainability reports: an empirical investigation of the use of graphs. Account. Publ. Interes. **12**, 16–37 (2012). https://doi.org/10.2308/apin-10249

50. Milne, M.J., Gray, R.: Future prospects for corporate sustainability reporting. In: O'Dwyer, B., Bebbington, J., Unerman, J. (eds.) Sustainability Accounting and Accountability, pp. 184–207. Routledge, London (2007). https://doi.org/10.4324/NOE0415384889.ch10

51. Gray, R.: Thirty years of social accounting, reporting and auditing: what (if anything) have we learnt? Bus. Ethics A Eur. Rev. **10**, 9–15 (2001). https://doi.org/10.1111/1467-8608.00207

52. King, A., Bartels, W.: KPMG international survey of corporate responsibility reporting 2015. KPMG Corp. Responsib. Report. (2015)

53. Maroun, W.: Modifying assurance practices to meet the needs of integrated reporting: the case for "interpretive assurance." Account. Audit. Account. J. (2018). https://doi.org/10.1108/AAAJ-10-2016-2732

54. Pomeroy, B., Thornton, D.B.: Meta-analysis and the accounting literature: the case of audit committee independence and financial reporting quality. Eur. Account. Rev. (2008). https://doi.org/10.1080/09638180701819832

55. Farooq, M.B., de Villiers, C.: The market for sustainability assurance services: a comprehensive literature review and future avenues for research. Pac. Account. Rev. (2017). https://doi.org/10.1108/PAR-10-2016-0093

56. Saunila, M., Nasiri, M., Ukko, J., Rantala, T.: Smart technologies and corporate sustainability: the mediation effect of corporate sustainability strategy. Comput. Ind. **108**, 178–185 (2019). https://doi.org/10.1016/j.compind.2019.03.003

57. Tiwari, K., Khan, M.S.: Sustainability accounting and reporting in the industry 4.0. J. Clean. Prod. **258**, 1–14 (2020). https://doi.org/10.1016/j.jclepro.2020.120783

An Analysis of United Kingdom Schools' Information Security Policies: A Socio-Technical Approach

Martin Sparrius$^{(\boxtimes)}$ ⓘ and Moufida Sadok ⓘ

University of Portsmouth, Portsmouth, UK
`martin.sparrius@port.ac.uk`

Abstract. UK schools collect and store large amounts of data on their students, parents, and staff. This makes them attractive targets for both external and internal attackers. To respond to and manage security risks, many schools have developed and implemented Information Security policies. This paper explores and analyses the content of 100 UK schools' security policies with an aim to examine the extent to which these policies address security risks faced by schools. Such exploration has the potential to assess the effectiveness and the relevance of security policies. The key findings show that many security policies are primarily centered on traditional technology-focused solutions and not on threats targeting the human elements in their organisations. In addition, it could be argued that between poor readability scores and large word counts, these policies are not very accessible to staff. This paper proposes that a socio-technical approach to information security would potentially result in better understanding of the role and application of security policies in schools and, therefore, improved information security.

Keywords: Cyber security · UK schools · Information security policies · Socio-technical approach

1 Introduction

Schools within the United Kingdom (UK) collect and store large amounts of data on their students, parents and staff. This makes them an attractive target for cyber-attacks, and it has been noted by previous researchers that data breaches and cyber-attacks targeting educational organisations have been on the rise [1, 2]. In their Data Breaches Investigation from 2019, Verizon found that 79% of the cyber-attacks involving educational organisations were financially motivated and that they specifically targeted personal data held by these organisations [3]. The report further notes that internal threat actors are still a major threat to educational organisations, accounting for 45% of the total breaches, with unintentional actions that led to a security incident comprising 35% of the incidents reported by these organisations.

In response to the general rise in cyber-attacks, the UK implemented the General Data Protection Regulation (GDPR) and the Data Protection Act 2018 in May 2018 to encourage improved Information Security (IS) within UK organisations. Since then,

S. Za et al. (Eds.): ItAIS 2020, LNISO 50, pp. 176–189, 2022.
https://doi.org/10.1007/978-3-030-86858-1_10

30% of UK business and educational organisations are reported to have made changes to their cyber security and of these changes, 60% focused on the creation of new policies [4]. Additionally, it became a statutory obligation for UK schools to create and annually review a Data Protection policy [5].

This focus on policy creation meshes with research that has identified that the 'construction and implementation of strong technology and information policies' forms a key component in the improvement of an organisation's IS [6]. Subsequent to the implementation of the GDPR, it was found that the UK education sector was more likely than average to have an IS policy in place (57%) [4] and while self-reported data identified a general increase in IS content [4], there has been no independent academic research into the nature and quality of this content or how staff interact with school IS policies. This research plans to use a series of qualitative and quantitative analysis to answer the following research questions:

- RQ1: What organisational and technical content is contained within school policies?
- RQ2: How accessible are these policies to the teaching staff?
- RQ3: To what extent does the IS policy content address the current threat landscape faced by schools?

2   Background

This literature review focuses on three themes: the use of the socio-technical approach within Information Security, the use of policies within IS and research involving Information Security within educational organisations for students aged 5–16.

2.1   The Use of the Socio-Technical Approach Within IS

The interplay between the technical and human elements within an organisation performs an important role in the effectiveness of security measures within the organisation. Research has been undertaken within each of these elements and their combinations, with Siponen observing that each field has developed its own research community [7]. While the positivist orientation within computer science is more common within the UK, there is an increasing realisation that a more interpretivist orientation within Information Security has an important role to play in the development of security practices [7]. Coles-Kemp described the need for more research to be undertaken into how the human, organisational and technical elements relate to each other and how these elements impact on IS [8].

In their investigation of the human aspects of security, Furnell and Clarke and found that investment was targeted at technological solutions and different forms of security control, such as awareness, was lagging behind [9]. Researchers have even detailed how failing to consider the ways in which caseworkers operate in an organisation led to the IS procedures of that organisation proving to be a hinderance to legitimate work. This resulted in employees actively circumnavigating security controls to effectively perform their required duties [10, 11]. In a following paper, Coles-Kemp and Hansen discussed how real-world security problems developed from the consequences of human interactions with the technology within an organisation and that separating out the social and technical elements was unadvisable; however, they noted this was still a dominant theme in IS policy creation [12].

2.2 The Use of Policies Within IS

As discussed by Weidman and Grossklags, a policy is "designed to set the strategic direction, scope and tone for an entire organisation regarding a particular topic" [1]. In terms of the content of an IS policy, this would include a description, important dates for the policy, describe IT procedures and key personnel who are critical to IS within the organisation. It is also expected that an organisational security policy addresses specific areas such complying as with regulatory frameworks and using of new technologies. There is a widespread belief in IS literature that enforcing compliance with the IS policy is a solution for security effectiveness [13]; however, this this can be counterproductive [14]. This focus on employee compliance in policy research has been due to many researchers considering employees the 'weak link' within an organisation [15, 16]. However, it is also recognised that with proper motivation, these self-same employees can, instead, be a vital part of an organisation's IS and this motivation can come in the form of feeling that they are part of the IS solution by building in value congruence [17, 18].

As Weidman and Grossklags note, an effective IS policy needs to recognise the internal threat posed by employees by including suitable technical and organisational controls while not making the employees feel like an enemy of their own organisation [1]. This realisation is missing from many organisations, though, and as Albrechtsen and Hovden observed, there is a "digital divide" between the security managers who are designing these policies and the users to whom the policies apply [19]. This, in turn, leads to development of security policies that are independent of the needs of users within the organisation who then, ironically, breach the system security to perform their job to a satisfactory standard [20, 21] or become distrustful and resentful towards the organisation [14]. The impact of these policy creation decisions and how organisations are adapting their policies in an evolving environment is, however, still insufficiently researched [22].

2.3 The Analysis of Information Security and IS Policies Within Educational Organisations

IS within primary and secondary schools, organisations which serve students aged 5–16, appears to be an under-researched topic. A few authors around the world have studied different aspects of IS. Chou and Chou investigated Taiwanese teachers' perceptions of their own IS behaviour and found the perceived inconvenience of taking preventative measures resulted in poor IS behaviour amongst primary and secondary teachers [23]. Moyo et al. looked at how an optimised risk assessment exercise in two South African secondary schools could lead to improved appreciation of IS amongst the staff of these schools [24]. In the United States of America (USA), Pusey and Sadera investigated whether trainee teachers felt comfortable with cybersecurity and found that most of their respondents did not feel prepared to model or teach this topic [25]. Shen et al., in their study of data breaches within USA schools, found that data security still focused on basic measures, such as password use, and that staff lacked an understanding of cybersecurity [26].

The consensus amongst these researchers is that there is a lack of effective IS within educational organisations and there is a persistent and increasing threat of IS breaches involving these organisations. An understanding of IS work done in other fields is being used to jump start research into the IS of educational organisations, but at this stage it appears fragmented and localised to specific countries.

In 2020, the UK government conducted its first Data Breach Survey of UK schools, where schools were asked to respond to a series of questions relating to IS and data breaches. It found that approximately 87% of schools possessed an IS policy. 52% of the surveyed schools reported multiple security breaches, with 92% of these schools suffering at least one breach due to fraudulent emails or website redirects, 24% reporting successful phishing or malware attacks and 10% suffering at least one breach a week [12]. These findings support the concerns raised by researchers investigating IS in schools and present an increasingly threatening security landscape for these schools.

3   The Study

3.1   Data Selection and Collection

Researchers in the field have found that collecting policies for analysis is incredibly difficult [19], with many organisations regarding the analysis of this documentation as very intrusive [1]. To find a more accessible source of IS policies, some researchers chose to focus on educational organisations, in particular universities, as they appear to be more likely to host IS policies on their websites to guide their staff and students [1, 20]. In this study on schools, initial Information Security policy collection was also attempted in this manner. The online policy section of the top 100 schools within the researchers' local county was searched. This involved both checking each relevant policy webpage or performing a search using the website's search tool. E-Safety and Safe Internet use policies were disregarded as having a focus on students, rather than the staff. Additionally, policies which were too specific in nature (BYOD, GDPR, Use of Mobile Phones) were also disregarded because, as Weidman and Grossklags noted, while smaller, issue-specific policies are useful for an organisation, it is important to have a consolidated high-level policy to provide a foundation for an organisation's IS [1]. Only one school in the first 50 listed an Information Security policy and the search was adjusted to instead make use of popular internet search engines to search for IS policies hosted by schools within the whole of England.

This search used two different search engines (Google and Duck Duck Go) to make use of different searching algorithms to produce different search results. The core terms used in this search were "Information Security", "Policy" and "UK School", with other variations and additions as the search progressed. The search was concluded once 100 policies were found, which met the criteria used for the initial school-by-school search. Next, the UK Government database was used to collect data on each school, such as school capacity and organisation type. The policies where then loaded into an NVivo database and relevant data for each school added as attributes prior to the initial coding.

3.2 Qualitative Coding and Readability Analysis

Initial coding used the 4 item categories that were based on Weidman and Grossklags' analysis of university IS policies, as well as iterative analysis of a sample of 10 policies. This coding was binary in nature and only focused on the presence of the stipulated code within the policy. Once the coding criteria had been identified, the whole set of policies was coded, checked for coding errors, and then was rechecked using keywords identified in the initial coding run. To differentiate policies which contained detailed technical instruction, the code of "has detailed technical terms" was allocated to relevant policies. Each policy was then entered into a website readability calculator, Readable, and the word count, Flesch Reading Ease and Simple Measure of Gobbledygook (SMOG) scores added to the attribute date for each policy.

4 Data Analysis of Selected Components from the IS Policies

4.1 School Characteristics

State-funded English schools are generally split into age groups that correspond to 5–11 years (Primary) and 11–16 (Secondary). This distinction is important as funding for these schools is on a per pupil basis and differs based on the age focus of the school [27]. Official government data was obtained by accessing the Department of Education website [28].

Table 1. Relative age focus proportions of UK schools

Age focus	Proportion of sample	UK Government data
Primary schools	75%	83%
Secondary schools	25%	17%

Table 2. Mean school capacities of UK schools

School capacity	Number of students (mean)	Standard deviation	UK Government data (mean)
Primary schools	318	231	282
Secondary schools	991	135	965

4.2 Content of IS Policies

As previously stated, coding only notes the presence of content that corresponds to the relevant code. All 100 policies had some relevant text; however, no single policy had all the searched-for content. For each age focus, the sum of policies which contained the specific content code was divided into the total number of policies for that age focus and presented in Tables 3 and 4.

Table 3. Relative age focus proportions of coded organisational content in school IS policies

Content code	Primary schools	Secondary schools
Clearly states who issued policy	59%	88%
Has a next review date	57%	68%
Has an effective date	78%	92%
Explicitly provides motivation or justification for policy	93%	88%
Clearly states who is affected by the policy	93%	88%
Defines responsibilities for standard roles	42%	32%
Defines responsibilities for specific roles	70%	52%
Mentions methods of enforcement	54%	68%
Mentions nature of sanctions	70%	72%
Has detailed technical items	55%	48%
Has information security definitions	16%	28%
References computer misuse act	35%	48%
References GDPR or data protection	82%	80%
Refers to other school policy documents	86%	88%

Table 4. Relative age focus proportions for coded technical content in school IS policies

Use of:	Primary schools	Secondary schools
Account control	54%	48%
Anti-virus or malware	64%	56%
Awareness campaign	42%	28%
Backups	53%	44%
BYOD conditions	64%	60%
Encryption	69%	76%
Firewalls	42%	44%
Locking stations	62%	72%
Multi-Factor Authentication	4%	8%
Passwords	85%	88%
Patching schedule	24%	40%
Physical security procedures	73%	80%
Public Wi-Fi usage restrictions	14%	8%
Definitions for security breaches	22%	44%
IS incident response guidelines	80%	88%
Software licensing and software restrictions	66%	60%
Spam or Phishing emails guidance	22%	32%

4.3 Accessibility

Two measures of readability were investigated. Flesch Reading Ease, due to its popularity in research [29], and Simple Measure of Gobbledygook (SMOG) due to its recommended use by the UK's National Health Service [30]. Flesch Reading Ease bases its results on word/sentence length ratios and syllables/word ratios. The scoring ranges from 0–100, with a higher value representing text which is easier to read. Flesch has a recommended target of 30–50 [1]. SMOG examines the number of polysyllabic words, perceived as being difficult words, compared to the number of sentences in the text. SMOG ranges from 1 to 20, with a higher score being harder to read, and a recommended target of 12–13. The NHS suggests that a score of 14 or higher would result in most adults battling to read the text [30]. For the SMOG results, a standard deviation of 1.43 places nearly 15% of the policies over this recommended threshold (Table 5).

Table 5. Readability analysis of school IS policies

	Mean	Standard deviation	Minimum	Maximum
Flesch reading ease	42.7	7.9	18.1	65.2
SMOG	12.9	1.43	10.1	15.5
Word count	3962	3327	424	20352

5   Key Findings and Discussion

5.1 Demographic Characteristics of Schools and Their Impact on Their Information Security

Despite using an internet search to obtain the IS policies, school characteristics for English schools compare favourably with the UK government's statistics in Table 1. These characteristics are important as state funding for English schools is on a per-pupil basis and depends on the age focus of the school. As shown in Table 2, primary schools tend to be substantially smaller than secondary schools and this is likely to have a knock-on effect in terms of their financial resources and staffing resources. This difference in resources will lead to a split in how primary and secondary schools approach their Information Security, with secondary schools more likely to have the resources to develop a dedicated IT team and assign a senior manager to deal with Information Security. Primary schools, with their smaller number of employees, are likely to have staff assume numerous roles with a wider set of responsibilities and may not be as focused on their Information Security policy.

To test this assumption, analysis of the coding with a primary and secondary division was conducted and it found that there was a distinct difference in their respective policies. Some of the key differences were:

- Primary schools were more likely to try to persuade staff with justifications (93% versus 88%) and explain what specific roles involved (70% versus 52%)
- Administration of policies was less consistent in primary schools:

  - Review date present (57% versus 68%)
  - Effective from date present (78% versus 92%)
  - Stating who was responsible for the policy (59% versus 88%)

- Primary schools are less likely to focus on monitoring staff IT usage (54% versus 68%).

These findings indicate that primary schools rely more on informal measures which consist mainly of persuading their staff of the importance and role of IS, while secondary schools are more focused on administrative details and the monitoring of staff members.

5.2 Technical Content

Analysis of the technical controls found that controls regarding passwords, physical security, encryption, locking workstations and IS incident response guidelines are the most encountered items within the policies. This is in line with the requirements for GDPR compliance and is a legal obligation for UK schools to avoid financial penalties in the event of a data breach [5]. Additional technical items referring to account control, anti-virus, backups, patching and firewalls occur inconsistently, with several policies implying their presence but not providing any detail. The tone of this content consists largely of admonishments to not interfere with the technology.

The least common items deal with security issues that involve staff interactions with the broader IT world: spam/phishing attacks, public Wi-Fi usage and awareness of IS threats. There is little indication within the policies of why these are under-represented, but considering that Multi-Factor Authentication is effectively non-existent in the surveyed policies, it is possible that the policies are focusing on aspects which are deemed to be of a higher priority or are more easily managed. This is consistent with the findings in previous research where Furnell and Clarke observed that the selection of controls in an IS policy were based on the criteria that "they target a defined threat and deliver a more easily measurable return" [9].

This skewed focus in the studied policies is concerning, particularly in regards to raising awareness (35% across all schools) and defining what exactly a security breach is (33% across all schools), as it leaves the staff unprepared and guessing about the nature of cyber-attacks. This, in turn, leaves the schools unprepared to face evolving security threats. It is likely that this will be seen in the breach data from the period where UK schools had to shift to working from home during the Covid-19 outbreak as staff and schools had to suddenly make use of programs, like Microsoft Team/Google Meet, with which they had relatively little or no training.

5.3 Accessibility

Analysis of the school IS policies found that there was substantial variation in the accessibility of the policies, representing a wide range of writing styles. With a mean Flesch reading ease of 42.7 and a SMOG score of 12.9, the policies can be considered to have an average or higher readability difficulty. For these figures, the average policy would require 11 years of education to access reliably and exclude approximately 50% of the UK population [30]. While UK teachers must all possess an undergraduate degree, this still presents a substantial barrier to interacting with the policy on anything besides a superficial level.

During the analysis, it was also noted that there was a large variation in word count for the policies. In their analysis of policy accessibility, McDonald and Cranor used a value of 250 words per minute to find the time spent reading a policy [31]. Using that same value, it was calculated that an IS policy with the mean wordcount of just under 4000 words would take 16 min to read. Though most of the policies cluster on the short side, there are 6 policies that would take an hour or more to read.

Based on the results from Weidman and Grossklags' study, further analysis was conducted to see if there was a correlation between readability and either wordcount or technical content [1]. Bivariate analysis of the word count and reading difficulty revealed that there was a significant positive correlation between the word count of the policies and improved readability. This confirmed Weidman and Grossklags' findings that an increased word count resulted in improved readability [1] (Table 6).

Table 6. Bivariate analysis of word count against readability scores (Note *$p < 0.01$; **$p < 0.001$)

	Flesch reading ease	SMOG score
Word count of IS policy	.386**	−.202*

Bivariate analysis of the coded content and the readability scores was also conducted to see if the presence of technical content significantly decreased accessibility. Selected results with significant correlations are reported in Table 7 and confirm, particularly for the Flesch Reading Ease score, that the presence of a coded technical control increased with readability. While there are only a few contrary correlations in the SMOG results, this analysis still appears to indicate that the presence of the content does not in itself make the text harder to access. This result contrasts with Weidman and Grossklags' result and suggests that other factors are decreasing the readability [1]. It was noted during coding that many of the policies use very precise language for the technical content, as demonstrated by this example, "Do not click on links in emails unless you know they are from a trusted source and never provide passwords in response to email requests". To confirm this further research would need to be conducted into the impact of the writing style of the policies.

Table 7. Bivariate analysis of the presence of technical content against Readability Scores (Note *p < 0.01; **p < 0.001)

	Flesch reading ease score	SMOG score
Has detailed technical items	.294**	.211*
Mentions account control		.293**
Mentions anti-virus or malware	.296**	.
Mentions BYOD conditions	.280**	.243*
Mentions locking stations	.249*	
Mentions passwords	.553**	
Mentions physical security	.274**	
Mentions security breaches or incidents	.244*	

5.4 Content versus Breach Data

In 2020 the UK government conducted a survey encouraging educational organisations to report on the state of Information Security within their organisation and the incidence of security breaches over the last year. This data has proved incredibly useful as prior to this survey the only breach data benchmarks in the UK were based around UK businesses [32].

It should be noted that the UK government survey is focused on technological controls in its questioning and it uses self-reported data submitted that is likely to have been reported by the school's IT manager. A case could be made that these are the schools which feel confident in reporting their breaches and represent a best-case scenario.

Key points from this report are that:

- 11% of Primary and 13% of Secondary schools have an attack at least once a week
- 23% of Primary and 32% of Secondary schools reported material losses
- 41% of Primary and 65% of Secondary schools had to devote time or delay work to deal with these breaches
- 80% of Primary and 92% of Secondary schools have an IS policy

The report highlights that secondary schools are substantially more proactive than the average UK business (46% versus 76%) about identifying breaches due to GDPR; however, it should be noted that these breaches can range from an email redirect to a ransomware attack. The increased number of attacks reported by secondary schools in Table 8 is likely to be because secondary schools have a different threat profile from primary schools. Secondary schools have an increased internal threat from students, hold more financial and personal data due their larger size and have the funding for IT resources to detect security incidents.

When the technical controls in this investigation's policy sample are contrasted against the data in the UK government's survey, there is a noticeable discrepancy in policy content. It is apparent in Table 8 that the controls reported by the schools are not reflected in many of the surveyed policies. This may be because some of these controls are not listed in schools' IS policies as these policies are primarily drawn up for staff members who are perceived as not needing to know the technical details. If this is the case, then these schools are taking a centralised approach to security that relies heavily upon the background technical controls and the competence of the IT managers to handle IS in the school.

Table 8. Relative age focus proportions for UK schools' policy content and UK government survey content [32]

Rules or controls in place	Primary schools	Primary schools (government)	Secondary schools	Secondary schools (government)
Patching	24%	97%	46%	99%
Anti-virus/malware	64%	94%	54%	100%
Firewalls	42%	100%	46%	96%
Strong password policy	85%	97%	100%	93%
Account control	54%	99%	46%	100%
Backup (physical)	53%	69%	46%	82%
BYOD restrictions	64%	84%	54%	56%
Monitoring	54%	77%	85%	93%

When considering both the breach and content data, it is clear that the largest number of breaches involve staff interaction with the broader IT environment (redirects, phishing, malware), while the least common items in the school IS policy (spam/phishing attacks, public Wi-Fi usage and awareness of IS threats) also deal with staff interactions. This implies that the current IS policies have a substantial weakness involving human-IT interactions that is leading to increased cyber-attacks directed towards the human elements of the school organisation.

6   Conclusion

For this paper, 100 IS policies from UK primary and secondary schools were collected and analysed for their readability and content. It was found that 98% of these policies contained technical content, with the most common content items focusing on technical solutions, like password security. While there were some encouraging examples of schools realising that there was more to IS than technical controls, items dealing with security issues around the interactions of staff with IT, like spam/phishing attacks and awareness of IS threats, were substantially less common.

Despite the high occurrence of content rich IS policies, relative to UK businesses, security breaches are still rising in UK schools and this suggests that these policies are not as effective as they could be. As noted by other researchers, the presence of an IS policy, even one which meets industry standards, does not mean it has any relevance to those whom it applies and they may choose to ignore or work around it [11]. The research from this investigation also suggests two other possible factors for this ineffectiveness. Readability analysis of these IS policies found that they are on average difficult to access or a substantial time commitment due to policy length. Additional comparison with UK IS breach data also found a mismatch between the policy content and evolving threats that target the human element within an organisation, such as phishing emails and website redirects.

This has created a possible scenario where UK schools have derived a false sense of security from the presence of a policy which is not up to date with the evolving threat landscape and which does not engage the staff it is meant to inform.

There are, however, some examples within the sample of IS policies which have high readability scores, cover evolving threats targeting the human factors and keep the policy within a manageable wordcount. Further research could be conducted into the writing style, particularly the tone, of these policies and how teachers engage with and implement the content. The lessons from these further investigations could then be used to inform and improve IS policy creation by UK schools.

References

1. Weidman, J., Grossklags, J.: What's in your policy? An analysis of the current state of information security policies in academic institutions. In: 26th European Conference on Information Systems: Beyond Digitization - Facets of Socio-Technical Change. ECIS 2018, pp. 1–16 (2018)
2. Laszka, A., Farhang, S., Grossklags, J.: On the economics of ransomware. In: Rass, S., An, B., Kiekintveld, C., Fang, F., Schauer, S. (eds.) GameSec 2017. LNCS, vol. 10575, pp. 397–417. Springer, Cham (2017). https://doi.org/10.1007/978-3-319-68711-7_21
3. Verizon: 2019 Data Breach Investigations (2019)
4. Department for Digital, Culture, Media and Sport: Cyber Security Breaches Survey 2019 (2019)
5. Department for Education: Statutory Policies for Schools and Academy Trusts. https://www.gov.uk/government/publications/statutory-policies-for-schools-and-academy-trusts/statutory-policies-for-schools-and-academy-trusts
6. Ponemon Institute: 2016 Cost of Cyber Crime Study and the Risk of Business Innovation, pp. 1–37 (2016)
7. Siponen, M.T.: Analysis of modern IS security development approaches: towards the next generation of social and adaptable ISS methods. Inf. Organ. 15, 339–375 (2005). https://doi.org/10.1016/j.infoandorg.2004.11.001
8. Coles-Kemp, L.: Information security management: an entangled research challenge. Inf. Secur. Tech. Rep. 14, 181–185 (2009). https://doi.org/10.1016/j.istr.2010.04.005
9. Furnell, S., Clarke, N.: Power to the people? The evolving recognition of human aspects of security. Comput. Secur. 31, 983–988 (2012). https://doi.org/10.1016/j.cose.2012.08.004
10. Kolkowska, E., Dhillon, G.: Organizational power and information security rule compliance. Comput. Secur. 33, 3–11 (2013). https://doi.org/10.1016/j.cose.2012.07.001
11. Sadok, M., Bednar, P.M.: Understanding security practices deficiencies: a contextual analysis. In: Ninth International Symposium on Human Aspects of Information Security and Assurance, HAISA 2015, Lesvos, Greece, 1–3 July 2015, Proceedings, pp. 151–160 (2015)

12. Coles-Kemp, L., Hansen, R.R.: Walking the line: the everyday security ties that bind. In: Tryfonas, T. (ed.) HAS 2017. LNCS, vol. 10292, pp. 464–480. Springer, Cham (2017). https://doi.org/10.1007/978-3-319-58460-7_32

13. Chen, Y., Ramamurthy, K., Wen, K.W.: Organizations' information security policy compliance: stick or carrot approach? J. Manag. Inf. Syst. **29**, 157–188 (2012). https://doi.org/10.2753/MIS0742-1222290305

14. Balozian, P., Leidner, D.: IS security menace: when security creates insecurity. In: 2016 International Conference on Information Systems. ICIS 2016, pp. 1–17 (2016)

15. Durgin, M.: Understanding the importance of and implementing internal security measures. https://www.sans.org/reading-room/whitepapers/policyissues/understanding-imp ortance-implementing-internal-security-measures-1901

16. Gordon, L., Loeb, M., Lucyshyn, W., Richardson, R.: 2006 CSI/FBI computer crime and security survey. Comput. Secur. J. **22**, 1 (2006)

17. Bulgurcu, B., Cavusoglu, H., Benbasat, I.: Information security policy compliance: an empirical study of rationality-based beliefs and information security awareness. MIS Q. **34**, 523–548 (2010)

18. Kolkowska, E., Karlsson, F., Hedström, K.: Towards analysing the rationale of information security non-compliance: devising a value-based compliance analysis method. J. Strateg. Inf. Syst. **26**, 39–57 (2017). https://doi.org/10.1016/j.jsis.2016.08.005

19. Albrechtsen, E., Hovden, J.: The information security digital divide between information security managers and users. Comput. Secur. **28**, 476–490 (2009)

20. Adams, A., Sasse, M.A.: Users are not the enemy. Commun. ACM. **42**, 40–46 (1999). https://doi.org/10.1145/322796.322806

21. Koppel, R., Smith, S., Blythe, J., Kothari, V.: Workarounds to computer access in healthcare organizations: you want my password or a dead patient? IOS Press (2015)

22. Paananen, H., Lapke, M., Siponen, M.: State of the art in information security policy development. Comput. Secur. **88**, 101608 (2020). https://doi.org/10.1016/j.cose.2019.101608

23. Chou, H.L., Chou, C.: An analysis of multiple factors relating to teachers' problematic information security behavior. Comput. Hum. Behav. **65**, 334–345 (2016). https://doi.org/10.1016/j.chb.2016.08.034

24. Moyo, M., Abdullah, H., Nienaber, R.C.: Information security risk management in small-scale organisations: a case study of secondary schools computerised information systems. In: 2013 Information Security for South Africa, pp. 1–6 (2013). https://doi.org/10.1109/ISSA.2013.6641062

25. Pusey, P., Sadera, W.A.: Cyberethics, cybersafety, and cybersecurity: preservice teacher knowledge, preparedness, and the need for teacher education to make a difference. J. Digit. Learn. Teach. Educ. **28**, 82–85 (2011). https://doi.org/10.1080/21532974.2011.10784684

26. Shen, L., Chen, I., Su, A.: Cybersecurity and data breaches at schools (2018)

27. Department for Education: Schools, colleges and children's services: school and college funding and finance. https://www.gov.uk/topic/schools-colleges-childrens-services/school-college-funding-finance

28. Department for Education: Schools, pupils and their characteristics, January 2019. https://www.gov.uk/government/statistics/schools-pupils-and-their-characteristics-january-2019

29. Feng, L., Jansche, M., Huenerfauth, M., Elhadad, N.: A comparison of features for automatic readability assessment. In: Coling 2010 - Proceedings of Conference on 23rd International Conference on Computational Linguistics, vol. 2, pp. 276–284 (2010)

30. NHS: Use a readability tool to prioritise content - NHS digital service manual. https://service-manual.nhs.uk/content/health-literacy/use-a-readability-tool-to-prioritise-content

31. McDonald, A., Cranor, L.: The cost of reading privacy policies. Isjlp. **4**, 543–568 (2008). https://doi.org/10.1136/bmj.c2665
32. Department for Digitial, Culture, Media and Sport: Cyber Security Breaches Survey 2020 - Education Annex (2020)

Organizing Cybersecurity in Action: A Pragmatic Ethical Reasoning Approach

Richard Baskerville[1,2], Paolo Depaoli[3,4], and Paolo Spagnoletti[4,5(✉)]

[1] Georgia State University, Atlanta, GA, USA
baskerville@acm.org
[2] Curtin University, Perth, WA, Australia
[3] Tuscia University, Viterbo, Italy
paolo.depaoli@unitus.it
[4] LUISS University, Rome, Italy
paspagnoletti@luiss.it
[5] Department of Information Systems, University of Agder, Kristiansand, Norway

Abstract. This paper contributes to the literature on cybersecurity governance by suggesting an approach based on pragmatism. As Jeffrey Sachs in his The Age of Sustainable Development, 2015, reminds us: "The essence of sustainable development in practice is *scientifically and morally based problem solving*". Cybersecurity deals with problem solving in complex socio-technical settings where ethics and organizational learning are tightly related. The paper draws on pragmatism because from its earliest formulation, pragmatist thought was anchored to a dual interest in ethics and science. Under this lens, pragmatic ethics cannot exist as a set of rules or principles, but rather requires a cyclical, empirical process whereby ethical principles and context interact to promote justice among stakeholders in the research of reliable solutions during the unravel of critical events. As a result, an Ethically oriented Cybersecurity Approach (ECA) based on Pragmatic Ethical Reasoning (PER) is proposed for managing unexpected critical events when organizations must learn on-the-fly and improve their security profiles.

Keywords: Cybersecurity · Pragmatism · Organizing · Action research · Design · Deming · ISO 27000

1 Introduction

A large number of cyberattacks are born on the Internet on a daily basis and even though most of them are harmless, some bear severe consequences: e. g. the stealing and manipulation of data, identity thefts, and taking over control systems with damages to the physical sphere (de Bruijn and Janssen 2017). Reflection and search for appropriate policies and security measures are being conducted by organizations to respond to these unexpected and often disruptive events. The effects of a cyberattack can be magnified, or even unwillingly supported by the lack of awareness of employees or by conflicting objectives of different organizational units (Ruighaver et al. 2010). Indeed, from the onset of the Internet to the expansion of broadband, a multitude of harmful incidents have taken

S. Za et al. (Eds.): ItAIS 2020, LNISO 50, pp. 190–203, 2022.
https://doi.org/10.1007/978-3-030-86858-1_11

place and a wide range of protection technologies and techniques have been developed and deployed. Yet, it is still difficult to have a clear understanding of how corporations and agencies are responding to threats by enhancing their security profiles, that is by nourishing their organizational and infrastructural characteristics towards cybersecurity (Baskerville et al. 2018). In this area of research this paper addresses one important support for organizational design and governance: cybersecurity in action, an approach and a process proposed to integrate organizational and ethical learning in a cybersecurity perspective.

Research on cybersecurity has shown that response and prevention strategies have to be balanced for developing effective security measures (Baskerville et al. 2014). The number and gravity of incidents concerning critical infrastructures - as for example healthcare, telecommunication, energy and transport systems - underscores the relevance of response strategies. The increasing diffusion of cyberattacks and the pervasive use of automated systems to control operation processes and physical systems (e.g. IoT) raise several interrelated issues: technical, organizational and ethical. In this paper, these three issues are approached from the perspective of normative ethics applied to cybersecurity by drawing on the works of the classic pragmatists (i.e. C.S. Peirce, J. Dewey, and W. James) and on recent commentaries on, and extensions of, their work (Ormerod 2006; Bernstein 2010).

A Pragmatic Ethical Reasoning (PER) process is proposed to support cybersecurity design and governance - that is to support organizations (management, CIOs, CISOs, employees) in understanding and then filling the gap between their pursued (or claimed) ethical behavior versus their actual ethical conduct. In the proposed approach, ethical reasoning is embedded in cybersecurity design and governance.

2 From 'Tool' to 'Process' in Ethically Oriented Cybersecurity Governance

The search for viable approaches to business ethics have led to the adoption of codes of ethics on the part of several companies worldwide (Adams et al. 2001; Long and Driscoll 2008). The research carried out on their efficacy shows that in most cases these formal statements of value are ineffective if they are not supported by other initiatives such as employee awareness programs and training to complement such tools (Velthouse and Kandogan 2007; Kaptein 2011; Garcia-Sanchez et al. 2015). Hill and Rapp (2013) acknowledge the positive effect of involving the whole organization in the development of formal artifacts by adopting a bottom-up approach: both their literature review and the results of their study show that not only participation is important "in the development and operationalization of moral standards for healthy ethical climates in businesses" but that "formal statements of values are ignored unless they are the product of the company as a collective" (ibid., p. 622). Similarly, specific codes of ethics for information systems have been found not to have significant effects on most employees (Siponen and Vance 2010; Harrington 1996) whereas security education, training and awareness (SETA) programs show better results (D'Arcy and Hovav 2009).

In some countries, as in Australia, research has shown evidence that ethical aspects have not been considered explicitly by organizations in their information security approaches (for example in developing acceptable use policies): the driver being lack of guidance in applying ethics in this field (Ruighaver et al. 2010). Specific proposals have been developed: some belong to ethics applied to the information security literature as in the case of Ruighaver et al. (2010) who suggest the adoption of consequential ethics rather than deontological ethics to reinforce proactive behavior by employees since motivation should not be underestimated with respect to deterrence. Other contributions do not refer explicitly to the discipline of ethics but do consider conduct: it is the case of Siponen and Vance (2010) who explain information policy violations through neutralization theory (whereby people justify behaviors that violate norms by minimizing the perceived harm of their violations) rather than deterrence theory (whereby severity and certainty of formal sanctions are believed to dissuade people from infringements). Also Spears and Barki (2010) do not refer directly to ethical theories when they suggest user participation to leverage organizational aspects other than technology-focused ones in information security risk management. Further, "security training via user participation is specific to business processes, [it is] therefore likely to have greater meaning, and perhaps interest, for users, encouraging greater commitment in protecting sensitive organizational information" (ibid. p. 519). Some authors have even proposed to paradoxically extend the traditional Plan-Do-Check-Act (PDCA) Deming's cycle, by developing integrating bricolage, improvisation, and hacking in IS security practices (Baskerville 2005; Spagnoletti and Resca 2008) and prepare organizations to address unpredictable threats.

This concise literature review shows the need to approach conduct in cybersecurity from a 'process' perspective rather than from a 'tool' perspective. Indeed, in a pragmatist perspective, any theoretical or practical action is value-laden because it is performed only if it is considered to be worthwhile by the agent (Dewey 1897). This observation bears important consequences when trying to understand and change the ethical orientation of an organization: its overall ethical performance is the outcome of the actions and interactions of a large number of agents with probably heterogeneous interests. Furthermore, all studies mentioned above underscore user participation and involvement for an effective implementation of policies in security and ethics, while some researchers insist on participation across the board even in the design phase. We take these suggestions not only as a way to deal with the dissimilarity of interests and purposes of agents but also as an effective way to leverage their experience. As is well known, pragmatism highlights the role of experience in advancing, in an iterative process, both knowledge and practice (Ormerod 2006). The next section explains further reasons for drawing on pragmatism to answer the following research question: *how cybersecurity can be organized within an explicit ethical perspective? Specifically: what processes better support effective cybersecurity in organizations?*

The answer to the research question is developed in the following way. In the next section the theoretical underpinnings of this work are explained. The fourth section presents Deming's cycle because of both its recursive nature, similar to the approach proposed in this paper, and its being the foundation supporting the ISO 27001 standards. Section five describes the Pragmatic Ethical Reasoning process (PER) and its connections with both Deming's cycle and the ISO standards to build the design and development of an Ethically oriented Cybersecurity in Action framework (ECA).

3 Theoretical Underpinnings

Through an extensive examination of the works of its founders and of its critics, Ormerod (2006) concluded that pragmatism is of interest to practitioners and academics alike because of the practical, commonsense and scientific approach embedded in it. From the perspective of an operational researcher and professional, he summarizes the main epistemological tenets of pragmatism arguing that knowledge is fallible and beliefs are theories developed through collective experience to support practice. *"Truths were held because they worked at that time in that context. Theories developed out of the need to shape, simplify and make memorable the multitude of contingent facts that action threw up"*. Likewise, pragmatism attributes judgement-of-value to any action performed in a specific context. *"Morality lies in outcomes rather than principles. Therefore, it is the means that should be considered rather than ends. Whereas ends can be debated purely rationally, means always have a factual content." (ibid. p. 907–908).*

Ten years later Ulrich (2016) argues that pragmatic reasoning makes possible to selectively deal with validity claims of both empirical (scientific) and normative (ethical) nature. *"For all practical purposes, the meaning and scope of valid application of a concept or proposition depend on our boundary judgments as to what "facts" (observations and forecasts) and "values" (worldviews, ideals, ends, and norms) are to count as relevant, and these judgments (as the word is meant to suggest) are not given to us by nature or dogma but are a matter of pragmatic selection in the concrete situation." (ibid. p. 9–10).* Therefore, pragmatic reasoning is a suitable approach to address ethical issues in the design of complex sociotechnical systems when unobservable events, such as cyberattacks, raise the need of situational understanding.

Drawing on the cited works by Ormerod and Ulrich, complemented by another extensive analysis of pragmatist authors' work by Bernstein (2010), and by referring directly to some works of classic pragmatists (that will be cited further on when appropriate), we propose a Pragmatic Ethical Reasoning (PER) process applied to cybersecurity governance. The process is based on five principles of pragmatism: (i) inquiry and experience are intertwined; (ii) ethics permeate practice; (iii) in ethics context matters; (iv) principles are methods for action; (v) convergence on truth through critical reasoning.

First, for pragmatists 'inquiry' and 'experience' are intertwined. Experience can prove present results of inquiry false through 'surprises': fallibilism is one of the pillars of their philosophy (Ormerod 2006; Bernstein 2010). Within a pragmatist perspective, cyberattacks can be considered as 'surprises' capable of questioning the results of previous 'inquiry' i.e. an occasion to revise both prevention and response measures thus revising also deterrence.

Second, for pragmatism ethics permeate practice. According to Dewey (1897), every act contains a judgment of value because it is performed only if it is considered to be worthwhile by the agent – for this reason the conduct of a person can be evaluated only from her acts. At the same time, "every judgment about conduct is itself an act" (ibid. p. 2) because it affects conduct. Since information security relevant acts permeate the organization, it is crucial that responsibility and accountability are modulated across the organization together with the evaluation criteria to be adopted thereof (in the case at hand for example, through the process of information security audit).

Third, in pragmatic ethics context matters. Dewey (1897) underlines the role both of historic antecedents and of the physical and social environment in shaping conduct (ibid. p. 8). The agent is affected (both consciously and unconsciously) by education into certain habits of thinking, feeling and acting. Furthermore, "our acts are controlled by the demands made upon us. These demands include not simply the express requirements of other persons, but the customary expectations of the family, social circle, trade or profession; the stimuli of surrounding objects, tools, books, etc.; the range and quality of opportunities afforded." (ibid. p. 7). The consequence is that any idea or act or plan can become action but through the forces of the environment: in their respective roles both end users and cybersecurity operators set the scene for acts that affect information security.

Fourth, sets of ethical principles have been proposed in the information systems literature (e.g. Myers and Venable 2014). In pragmatism 'principle' is different from 'rule' or 'fixed precept': the former is "a method for action, [the] latter a prescription for it; former experimental, latter fixed; former orders in sense of setting in order, latter in sense of commanding" (Dewey 1897, p. 5). According to a pragmatist approach, ethical principles constitute experimental methods for action. For an organization this approach is vital because: (i) it supports critical discussions on the methods of action (principles) that better represent the different judgments of value of the people that make up the ethical profile of the organizational units; (ii) it allows for the convergence towards the identification of common principles (guides for action).

Fifth, for pragmatists (i.e. Peirce) there is a 'convergence' through critical reasoning on truth rather than a 'consensus' (Bernstein 2010, p. 228 and Ulrich 2016). This convergence is realistic because it rests on the experiences of the different organizational units which have to pursue both their business objectives and their information security objectives. It should be noted that this is not a 'relativistic' stance ("anything goes") but a 'pluralistic' one (different perspectives from which to consider a phenomenon); as Bernstein (2010) recalls, pragmatism in ethics and society supports pluralism.

The development of the Pragmatic Ethical Reasoning (PER) process is built on these five basic concepts. Other supportive notions, drawn from pragmatist literature, will be introduced along the description of the process. Given the importance of practice in pragmatism, we describe PER from the perspective of an actor (e. g. CIO, CISO, hereinafter referred to as PER Promoter) who, drawing on her theoretical background and experience, is engaged in designing and implementing an ECA based on the ISO 27001 process. As in all ISO standards, the process is based on the Deming cycle which is introduced and explained in the following section.

4 Knowledge and Improvement as an Iterative Process in Management Practice: The Deming Cycle

Deming's cycle (Deming 2000) is known in the business literature on quality management as the PDCA cycle or as the PDSA (Plan, Do, Study, Act) cycle (Sokovic et al. 2010). As Moen and Norman (2006) have noted, Deming considered the term 'check'(which became extensively used) to be originated from a wrong translation into Japanese of his term 'study'. Here we use his original acronym (PDSA) both because it is present in all of his work and because it better emphasizes the 'learning' aspect of the cycle. In his words, the PDSA cycle is "the flow diagram for learning, and for improvement of a product or of a process" (Deming 2000, p. 131).

The PDSA cycle starts with an idea for improving a product or a process. In this planning stage (Plan), a number of goals are suggested and compared on their feasibility and on the expected gains in terms of knowledge or profit. In the following step (Do), a test, comparison, or experiment is executed, preferably on a small scale. The results are analyzed (Study) to see if they correspond with hopes and expectations and possible causes of failure are identified. Finally, decisions are made on whether to adopt/abandon the change (Act), or run through the cycle again, possibly under different environmental conditions, different materials, different people, different rules (ibid., pp. 122–123).

According to some authors, Deming has a pragmatic vein through the influence of C.I. Lewis (Moen and Norman 2006; Canard 2011) whereas other authors underscore that "Deming's energies … have not been expended to espouse or to verify theories… The purpose of Deming management method has been and continues to be the transformation and improvement of the practice of management…" (Anderson et al. 1994, p. 473). It is beyond the scope of this paper to establish a direct philosophical affiliation of Deming; however, because of his highlighting experimentation and experience, Deming's approach chimes with two of the basic propositions of pragmatism mentioned above: the first (inquiry and experience are intertwined) and the fourth (principles are methods for action). It is indeed the recursive character of his approach to be aligned with the pragmatist viewpoint.

5 Principles of Pragmatic Ethical Reasoning (PER) to Design and Implement an Ethically Oriented Cybersecurity Approach (ECA)

Since inquiry in pragmatism has an iterative nature (Singer 2010, p. 484) and Deming's cycle also has a recursive character, in this section our presentation of the PER process refers both to the four phases of the PDSA cycle and to the clauses of the ISO 27001 standard, namely: the PLAN phase includes clauses 4 (context of the organization), 5 (leadership), 6 (planning), and 7 (support); the DO phase is clause 8 on 'operations'; the STUDY phase (the original Deming term for 'check') is the clause on 'performance evaluation'; and the ACT phase is clause 10 on 'improvement' (Kosutic 2014).

Each of the following sub-sections has two aims: (i) to situate the PER Promoter in a pragmatist perspective, that is to describe how this perspective affects her approach to relevant issues; (ii) to highlight the add-ons of the PER process to the ISO 27001 standard together with their practical implications (methods and artifacts) for the design and implementation of the ECA.

5.1 PER, Phase 1: 'Plan' the ECA

Three activities are important in an ISO 27001 process for building and maintaining an effective Information Security Management System (ISMS): planning, support and operations (clauses 6, 7, and 8 respectively of the ISO directive). This sub-section shows the web of relations that have to be understood by the ECA Promoter for her to undertake successfully the first two activities necessary to carry out the 'Do' phase (operations) described in the following sub-section. 'Requirements' in ISO and 'principles' in PER are different but not separated. The former are standards to comply with because they are built on factors considered relevant by the information security practice. The latter leave more room for interpretation and are the backbone of the guidelines for actions in the different contexts of the organization.

In designing and developing artifacts to implant an ECA in (and for) a socio-technical context, the Promoter brings her own individual experience to bear. Pragmatist ethics privileges the actor's engagement with her design context. This follows from the pre-eminence pragmatism attributes to experience over universal conceptions: experience improves conceptions. Further, classic and contemporary pragmatists assign to reasoned agreement through critical confrontation in the process of inquiry the way to convergence on new truths (Bernstein 2010, p. 118). This recalls Deming's observation in planning: "Somebody has an idea for improvement of a product or of a process. This is the 0-th stage, embedded in Step 1. It leads to a plan for a test, comparison, experiment" (Deming 2000, p. 122). Indeed, pragmatism does not completely overturn previous experience: on the contrary, it builds on it, it revises it in the light of 'surprises' (e.g. incidents). New ideas are adopted as true while preserving "the older stock of truths with a minimum of modification, stretching them just enough to make them admit the novelty, but conceiving that in ways as *familiar* as the case leaves possible." (James 1907, p. 60 emphasis added). The value of pragmatist conceptions is instrumental. "Beliefs, in short, are rules for action; and the whole function of thinking is but one step in the production of active habits" (James 2002, p. 430). But because action based on rules-for-action nets new experience, pragmatism is iterative: "since belief is a rule for action, the application of which involves further doubt and further thought, at the same time that it is a stopping-place, it is also a new starting place for thought" (Peirce 2001, p. 199). Furthermore, as mentioned above in the section on the theoretical underpinnings, pragmatism attributes judgment-of-value to every action because it is performed only if it is considered to be worthwhile by the agent.

In pragmatist planning settings, understanding is the reciprocal effect of actions taken in the context. In terms of pragmatism, the planner (our Promoter) gains a situated understanding of the ethical principles as part of her experience in making judgments about her actions in a socio-technical context. In other words, experience and agency are shaped by the interaction of the agent (the Promoter) and the planning context. Her actions not only change the context, they change her understanding and the ethical principles in use. A hermeneutic circle is at work here: the PER Promoter goes back and forth from the specific context to the ethical frameworks arising from preceding experience (especially significant incidents). But in this situation, the hermeneutic circle is finalized to ethical action in revising the relevant security strategy and procedures, and not just to acquire a deeper and deeper understanding of them, as in an interpretivist approach (Goldkuhl 2012).

The ethical understanding is only one component of the Promoter's broad pragmatic understanding of the socio-technical context. The ethical conduct of a Promoter is not only affected by her inclinations and background but also by the contextualized conditions for her project. Pragmatic ethics involve both deciding what actions to perform in the context and estimating the consequences of these actions. Both decisions and estimates are products of the agent's beliefs *and* values. The Promoter in the inquiry (planning) phase gains an understanding of how the context can revise her ethical perspective on both the means and the ends of her actions. The ethical elements in this understanding may extend to such outcomes as the ethical situation created for other actors in the socio-technical context. In terms of the outcomes of the planning actions that operationalize the ECA, there are two aspects that a pragmatist promoter-planner should consider relative to the ethical behavior of others in the organizational context: the existence of competing ideas and the interplay of assignments.

Competing Ideas for 'Planning' in a Socio-Technical Context. The Promoter-planner does not work in isolation, but interacts with other actors in a socio-technical context. This context can include clients, users, suppliers, sponsors, and other individuals working in her same team. When she intervenes in such a socio-technical context through action, three classes of practice can compete as ethical frameworks for ideas. First, there will be the class of practices relating to the information security discipline. Second, there will be the class of practices that are defined by the context or organizational setting, e.g., system developer practices around the present information security artifacts. Third, there will be the class of practices defined by the users of the information systems that have to ensure confidentiality, integrity and availability, e.g., in the case of a health care system, medical practices. Practices are: "a web of actions that are related and combined in a meaningful way" (Goldkuhl 2004, p. 17). They are made up of human actions, shared practical understandings within a common language, material objects or artefacts and ethical principles. Because these classes of practices may differ even within a single organization, they illustrate how ideas within the socio-technical context may compete in shaping and reshaping the ethics of pragmatist design and planning. In an ethical process of pragmatist planning, the foundation in principles such as those present in the code of ethics will interact contextually with other frameworks of ethical principles within the community around the design context. Ultimately the soundest ethical principles "should correspond with the actual feelings and demands of the community, whether right or wrong." (Holmes, quoted in Hantzis 1989, p. 584). When this does not happen, problems in the application of any institutional code of ethics emerge (they become a mere window dressing exercise) and security management will suffer because of the gap between the declared values and the real conduct of individuals and groups. Further, incidents are managed with greater uncertainty because the ethical *humus* that feeds the conduct during unexpected events is unknown. Further still, the 'scapegoating syndrome' is more likely to take place in order to "protect" the structure from questioning present procedures or top managers from questioning their own conduct or the way they manage their staff. We are underlining that a PER development process to build an ISMS has to take into account both the identification *and* the application of principles in order to solve dilemmas and orient real conducts. To this end, the planning phase has to consider what are the key aspects to make the organization become an 'ethical learning' organization.

Implications for Organizing. According to ISO 27001, when planning the ISMS, the organization shall determine: (i) the risks and opportunities that need to be addressed (clause 6.1, p. 3); (ii) the information security objectives and how to achieve them – including resources, responsibilities, and evaluation of results (clause 6.2, p. 5). The design and planning of the ECA supports these objectives and develops its specific activities and tools. The main actions and artifacts proposed are the following:

Identification of the PER Promoter who collates internal and external information on security theory and practice and guides the interaction (critical confrontation on ethical issues) among the Organizational Units (OUs) to build the ECA.

Organizing the ECA Teams. Different from Ethical Committees which are permanent and cross-functional, they are temporary and made up of the representatives of the 'communities': one per each function and organizational unit. Parallel to the definition of the opportunities/threats, ECA teams have a purposeful interaction with the Promoter and the information security units/experts to identify the 'threshold' of accountability of individuals and of the OUs concerning security in both prevention and response. One of the aims of this critical reasoning and confrontation is to define an appropriate mix of deterrence and motivation-based leverages. Supported by diffused leadership, the spreading of awareness and responsibility (on emerging ethical dilemmas for example) would increase resilience after incidents and favor the emergence of bottom-up innovative security practices.

Definition of the Structure of the Ethical Action Plan that will be Prepared by Each ECA Team. Basically, it should contain three areas where to describe: (i) the interpretation of the general ethical guiding principles of the organization applied to the specific activities conducted by the OU with the relevant implications for information security; (ii) the business objectives that the OU is pursuing together with the relevant information needs, dilemmas, and critical issues; (iii) the possible competence gaps in addressing security issues.

Outline of the Architecture of a 'Consolidated Ethical Action Plan'. It combines the ethical action plans prepared by the ECA teams. The name underscores the importance of identifying an ethical "bottom line" for organizations interested in going beyond formal statements: an ethical action plan is an operationalized code of ethics.

5.2   PER, Phase 2 and 3: 'Do' in the ECA and Purposeful Interactions in Operations During the 'Study' Phase

The organizational set up of a company that intends to go from business-as-usual to an ethically sustainable business conduct includes the arrangements between the different agents in carrying out their respective tasks and activities. These different agents may have different purposes in mind that motivate the conduct of the PER Promoter and the other actors implementing an ECA. As a result, the evaluation of the adequacy of an action in the implementation phase is a form of purposeful interaction between the actors involved in the identification and application of the principles adopted by the organization. However, these agents also interact with regard to deciding ethical values in light of potentially conflicting purposes. This interaction, which may be regulated by formal arrangements (i.e. the ECA teams and the Ethical Action Plans), means that the ethical meaning of a pragmatic outcome evolves during the intervention. The various actors in the socio-technical context interact in their evaluation of the research process and outcome. Thus, the ethical aspects of the socio-technical context may seem unstable as the design and the action research unfolds, and the pragmatist Promoter may find the ethical outcome is less a product of principles and more a moving target of conflicting justice. This is why a 'consolidated ethical action plan' is provisional, an open system related to a time horizon: the forces that move it both internally (intra-organizational conflicts) and externally (market, regulatory frameworks, digital innovation, and the upsurge of critical events such as the present pandemic) may induce changes both in the structure and in the aims of the ECA.

Interplay of Assignments: Implications in Terms of 'Support' in Both 'Do' and 'Study' Phases. Since an ECA is an evolving process, specific care should be given to find out 'who' decides 'what' and 'how' in the organization. That is, it is important to evaluate the organizational setting from the perspective of the allocation of power among the different agents. Design (or re-design) interventions may intentionally or inadvertently shift power relationship in the context (Markus 1983). As with competing ideas, there may be at least three power groups involved: the staff in charge of cyber-security operations, IT developers, and users (other stakeholder may be added to the analysis as needed). While each of these groups will exercise certain kinds of power, the actions of each group in the socio-technical context can reshape the power of each of the other groups. The PER Promoter (who acts also as a designer and a facilitator) should be aware of the ongoing interplay in the assignment of power that arises from the re-design interventions needed: (i) to implement the ethical turn of the organization; (ii) to keep information systems of the organization abreast with continuing digital innovation. ECA teams are an important support for the (re-)design and implementation of the ECA: power assignments in a specific context should be ethical for that context and, through specific reasoning and confrontation, should converge towards the general ethical principles pursued by the organization.

5.3   PER, Phase 4: 'Act' in the Open ECA

Because PER is an iterative process the Act phase is the synthesis of what has been planned, critically understood and acted: it is action research applied to information security (ethically oriented). Consider Fig. 1 which concisely illustrates such a process. "Ethical principles" (top bubble to the left) are only the opening context for a PER Promoter starting to work at an ethical reorientation of cybersecurity governance (Plan phase). These principles are a combination of her personal beliefs and judgments of value with the ones that, in her perception, are implicitly or explicitly implanted in the security policy and in the organizational context of the company (organizational behavior in operations). As mentioned above, in pragmatism complications in handling ethical issues have to be scouted and resolved or, at least, mitigated. Difficulties include appraising the intensity and solving the conflicts among principles that might arise in practical security situations (e.g. during or right after incidents). For example, understanding and negotiating the meaning of phrases such as 'severity of potential risks' or 'minimize negative consequences' (phrases taken from Myers and Venable 2014, p. 2) in the different contexts of the organization. The Promoter moves along the path described in Fig. 1 while interacting with different components of the organization and making sense of the different ethical, professional, and business aims and interests of the different stakeholders.

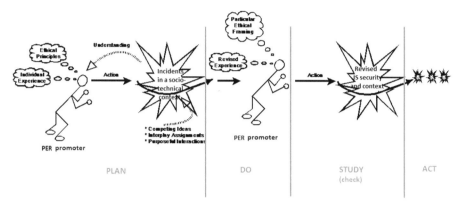

Fig. 1. The PER based ECA

6 Concluding Remarks

Because of its anchors in Deming's quality cycles, ECA is quite a natural fit to cybersecurity actions oriented toward prevention of future incidents. In a preventative mode, it is an ethical learning cycle, oriented to cybersecurity, that revises IS security and its context. ECA has a relaxing fit with prevention because cycles span the time from incident-to-incident. However, ECA is a more important framework when applied within incident response, where timeframe is much shorter. In incident response, the ECA cycles from response-action to response-action. When an action is taken in response to an incident, another ECA cycle must revise experience and ethical framing (Do) in determining if the action resolved the incident ethically (Study). If not, further Act, Plan, and Do phases to develop better understanding of the interplay between the incident and the response action; and to plan actions that will resolve the incident.

We can see that ECA as applied in incident response is a high speed PER cycle nested inside a slower-speed prevention PER cycle. Not dissimilar to Argyris and Schön's double loop learning (1978), the rapid inner PER loop reflects learning about how to pragmatically respond to an incident, while the outer PER loop employs this learning in taking ethical actions to prevent a class of similar incidents from affecting the secured system in future. By applying PER to cybersecurity governance, we extend previous works on IS security theories for managing predictable and unpredictable threats (Baskerville et al. 2014). Moreover, PER can potentially contribute to the broader fields of High-Reliability Organizations and crisis management by providing a theoretical ground to develop theories on collective mindfulness (Fraher et al. 2017), mindlessness (Salovaara et al. 2019) and fragmented coordination (Wolbers et al. 2018).

Cybersecurity governance is a key priority of modern organizations. The paradoxical nature of cybersecurity limits the effectiveness of policymaking in this domain. Ethical dilemmas emerge at multiple levels when hierarchical structures of human and automated systems are implemented to control operational processes. Effective cybersecurity governance and design cannot overlook the importance of ethical reasoning. An Ethically oriented Cybersecurity Approach is proposed as new way to design and manage cybersecurity operations. The philosophical underpinnings of pragmatism are discussed to present the model. Our conceptual analysis shows the applicability of the proposed model to cybersecurity design and governance.

Future research will explore how the PER based ECA approach can help addressing the several paradoxes and dilemmas affecting cybersecurity and pointed out in the literature (de Bruijn and Janssen 2017). Empirical cases of ethical learning in cybersecurity practices will validate the ECA approach and offer guidance to cybersecurity professionals. For instance, with data breach notifications companies can be damaged by making security problems visible but visibility is also necessary to create a greater sense of urgency and initiate action (Flak et al. 2019). Further, paradoxes trouble decision makers in organizations when deciding investments in cybersecurity: too little spending might indicate a lack of protection, while substantial spending might indicate a perceived high risk of attacks. Governments are to face privacy versus security adjustments as they decide to access data of individuals and organizations for prevention purposes. Further, the orientation of governments on these questions also depends on how experts, practitioners and advisors to governments conceive digital technologies (Depaoli et al. 2020): for some this technology is considered just a powerful tool to improve efficiency for the entire set of government interactions with citizens and relevant policies thereof (Hood and Margetts 2007); for other ones there is a transformative processing power of digitalization which is changing the very fabric of policy setting and making (Hildebrandt 2015). The purpose of successive explorations is therefore to further develop the potential of connecting ethical reasoning and organizational learning in the making of cybersecurity, so that coping with paradoxes and dilemmas will become more explicit and manageable.

References

Adams, J.S., Tashchian, A., Shore, T.H.: Codes of ethics as signals for ethical behavior. J. Bus. Ethics **29**(3), 199–211 (2001)

Anderson, J.C., Rungtusanatham, M., Schroeder, R.G.: A theory of quality management underlying the deming management method. Acad. Manag. Rev. **19**(3), 472–509 (1994)

Argyris, C., Schön, D.: Organizational Learning: A Theory of Action Perspective. Addison-Wesley, Reading (1978)

Baskerville, R.: Information warfare: a comparative framework for business information security. J. Inf. Syst. Secur. **1**(1), 23–50 (2005)

Baskerville, R., Rowe, F., Wolff, F.C.: Integration of information systems and cybersecurity countermeasures. ACM SIGMIS Database: DATABASE for Adv. Inf. Syst. **49**(1), 33–52 (2018)

Baskerville, R., Spagnoletti, P., Kim, J.: Incident-centered information security: managing a strategic balance between prevention and response. Inf. Manag. **51**(1), 138–151 (2014)

Bernstein, R.J.: The pragmatic turn. Polity (2010)

de Bruijn, H., Janssen, M.: Building cybersecurity awareness: the need for evidence-based framing strategies. Gov. Inf. Q. **34**(1), 1–7 (2017)

Canard, F.: "W. E. DEMING, pragmatism and sustainability. In: 17th Annual International Deming Research Seminar, pp. 1–17. HAL Archives-Ouvertes, New York (2011)

D'Arcy, J., Hovav, A.: Does one size fit all? Examining the differential effects of IS security countermeasures. J. Bus. Ethics **89**(SUPPL. 1), 59–71 (2009)

Deming, W.E.: The New Economics, p. 235. MIT Press, Cambridge (2000)

Depaoli, P., Sorrentino, M., De Marco, M.: Social and ethical shifts in the digital age: digital technologies for governing or digital technologies that govern? In: Metallo, C., Ferrara, M., Lazazzara, A., Za, S. (eds.) Digital Transformation and Human Behavior. LNISO, vol. 37, pp. 315–327. Springer, Cham (2021). https://doi.org/10.1007/978-3-030-47539-0_21

Dewey, J.: The Study of Ethics: A Syllabus. Georg Wahr, Ann Arbor (1897)

Flak, L.S., Sæbø, Ø., Spagnoletti, P.: Privacy violations in light of digital transformation: insights from data breaches in Norway. In: Proceedings of the 14th Pre-ICIS Workshop on Information Security and Privacy, Munich, Germany, pp. 1–7 (2019)

Fraher, A.L., Branicki, L.J., Grint, K.: Mindfulness in action: discovering how US navy seals build capacity for mindfulness in high-reliability organizations (HROs). Acad. Manag. Discov. **3**(3), 239–261 (2017)

Garcia-Sanchez, I.-M., Rodriguez-Dominguez, L., Frias-Aceituno, J.V.: Board of directors and ethics codes in different corporate governance systems. J. Bus. Ethics **131**(3), 681–698 (2015)

Goldkuhl, G.: Pragmatism vs interpretivism in qualitative information systems research. Eur. J. Inf. Syst. **21**(2), 135–146 (2012)

Harrington, S.J.: The effect of codes of ethics and personal denial of responsibility on computer abuse judgments and intentions. MIS Q. **20**(3), 257–278 (1996)

Hildebrandt, M.: Smart Technologies and the End(s) of Law: Novel Entanglements of Law and Technology. Edward Elgar Publishing, Cheltenham (2015)

Hill, R.P., Rapp, J.M.: Codes of ethical conduct: a bottom-up approach. J. Bus. Ethics **123**(4), 621–630 (2013). https://doi.org/10.1007/s10551-013-2013-7

Hood, C., Margetts, H.: The Tools of Government in the Digital Age. Macmillan International Higher Education, Basingstoke (2007)

James, W.: Pragmatism: A New Name for Some Old Ways of Thinking. Longmans Green and Co., London (1907). http://catalog.hathitrust.org/Record/001382943

James, W.: The Varieties of Religious Experience - A Study in Human Nature. (Ed. by, J. Manis). The Electronic Classics Series, Hazelton (2002)

Kaptein, M.: Toward effective codes: testing the relationship with unethical behavior. J. Bus. Ethics **99**(2), 233–251 (2011)

Kosutic, D.: Has the PDCA cycle been removed from the new ISO standards? 27001 Academy, The ISO 27001 & ISO 22301 Blog (2014). https://advisera.com/27001academy/blog/2014/04/13/has-the-pdca-cycle-been-removed-from-the-new-iso-standards/

Long, B.S., Driscoll, C.: Codes of ethics and the pursuit of organizational legitimacy: theoretical and empirical contributions. J. Bus. Ethics **77**(2), 173–189 (2008)

Markus, M.L.: Power, politics, and MIS implementation. Commun. ACM **26**(6), 430–444 (1983)

Moen, R., Norman, C.: Evolution of the PDCA cycle (2006). https://rauterberg.employee.id.tue.nl/lecturenotes/DG000%20DRP-R/references/Moen-Norman-2009.pdf

Myers, M.D., Venable, J.R.: A set of ethical principles for design science research in information systems. Inf. Manag. **51**(6), 801–809 (2014)

Ormerod, R.: The history and ideas of pragmatism. J. Oper. Res. Soc. **57**(8), 892–909 (2006)

Peirce, C.S.: How to make our ideas clear. In: Lynch, M.P. (ed.) The Nature of Truth: Classic and Contemporary Perspectives, pp. 193–209. The MIT Press, Cambridge (2001)

Ruighaver, A.B., Maynard, S.B., Warren, M.: Ethical decision making: improving the quality of acceptable use policies. Comput. Secur. **29**(7), 731–736 (2010)

Salovaara, A., Lyytinen, K., Penttinen, E.: High reliability in digital organizing: mindlessness, the frame problem, and digital operations. MIS Q. Manag. Inf. Syst. **43**(2), 555–578 (2019)

Singer, A.E.: Integrating ethics and strategy: a pragmatic approach. J. Bus. Ethics **92**(4), 479–491 (2010)

Siponen, M., Vance, A.: Neutralization: new insights into the problem of employee information systems security policy violations. MIS Q. **34**(3), 487–502 (2010)

Sokovic, M., Pavletic, D., Pipan, K.: Quality improvement methodologies–PDCA cycle, RADAR matrix, DMAIC and DFSS. J. Achiev. J. Achiev. Mater. Manuf. Eng. **43**(1), 476–483 (2010)

Spagnoletti, P., Resca, A.: The duality of information security management: fighting against predictable and unpredictable threats. J. Inf. Syst. Secur. **4**(3), 46–62 (2008)

Spears, J.L., Barki, H.: User participation in information systems security risk management. MIS Q. **34**(3), 503–522 (2010)

Ulrich, W.: Philosophy for professionals: towards critical pragmatism. Rev. Version of 20 March 2016. Reflections on critical pragmatism, Part 7. (Orig. Version in: J. Oper. Res. Soc. **58**(8), 1109–1113 (2007)). Ulrich's Bimonthly (2016)

Velthouse, B., Kandogan, Y.: Ethics in practice : what are really doing? **70**(2), 151–63 (2007)

Wolbers, J., Boersma, K., Groenewegen, P.: Introducing a fragmentation perspective on coordination in crisis management. Organ. Stud. **39**(11), 1521–1546 (2018)

Digital Enabled Mission Command and Control Systems in Military Operations

Andrea Salvi[1(✉)] and Paolo Spagnoletti[1,2]

[1] Department of Business and Management, Luiss University, Rome, Italy
`asalvi@luiss.it`
[2] Department of Information Systems, University of Agder, Kristiansand, Norway

Abstract. High Reliability Organizations (HRO) need to devise and implement organizational processes aimed to minimize the risk of failure, facing high risks and high stakes. In this paper, we look at the case of military HRO operating under Mission Command principles. Mission Command is a doctrine born to address unexpected circumstances through diffused leadership. Nonetheless, digital enabled Command and Control (C2) systems may challenge this doctrine. Remote-control technologies, automatic arms systems and tracking tools have seen a widespread application in modern warfare. Such advancements may favor purely vertical approaches whereby commanders can monitor and control the battlefield from afar. We investigate the tensions between digital enabled Mission Command and Control systems and the centripetal force of purely vertical C2 structures. This scenario contrasts with Mission Command as leaders may veer to more task-oriented approaches, which in turn may lead to a progressive decrease in accountability of subordinates. This is problematic for the entire command pyramid. We contribute to the HRO literature by shedding light on the paradoxical role of digital technologies in mission-oriented organizing.

Keywords: Mission Command · Digital command and control systems · Resilience · HRO

"If an execution of an order was rendered impossible, an officer should seek to act in line with the intention behind it."
(Oetting 1993, p. 86)

1 Introduction

Uncertainty is an ever-present factor in military operations. In this conceptual paper, we investigate the role of digital Command and Control (C2) systems as means to circumvent uncertainty in extreme contexts. Frontline military organizations, in fact, need to face crises characterized by high risks and high stakes in the form of losses of human lives, strategic fiascos and loss of sensitive information. They can be framed as High Reliability Organizations (HRO) [1] as they need to achieve a nearly error-free functioning through an organizational mindfulness processes [2] amid the "fog of war". Clausewitz (1982), back in 1832, defined war as intrinsically bound to *chance*. Such a peculiarity posits the need for military organizations to devise structures, processes and practices apt to engage with unexpected circumstances striving for a victorious outcome and for nearly total minimization of errors. Reliability is thus key. Information systems in this context are ideal enablers of increased reliability. Yet, such mediums need to fit the peculiar cognitive and structural features of military organizations. In this contribution we focus on Mission Command (*Auftragstaktik*), a doctrine born to address environmental constraints through diffused leadership to attain strategic objectives set by the higher ranks. In other words, in Mission Command the goal is identified and indicated at the top of the command chain, how to reach said goal is delegated to lower ranks and to specialists. Decisions in this context are a by-product of a thorough situational analysis that encompasses evidence from the battlefield condensed in tactical decisions and abiding the strategic address laid out by high-rank decision makers. This collective way of organizing requires high levels of trust and a shared understanding at multiple levels of the command structure. Operators, lower officers as well as support personnel needs to trust the command and be actively aware of the strategic address. Contemporaneously, Mission Commands requires horizontal trust within and between units.

The literature has highlighted a marked contrast with military scholars call the "managerial approach". This doctrine was a major organizational feature of US Army until the Vietnam War [3]. Such approach heavily relies on more "business-oriented" practices and processes. Decision-makers sat at the top of the command pyramid calculating strategic and tactical needs with large volumes of data from the battlefield originated by reports and previous experiences. Shamir [3, p. 649] describes this approach as "characterized by centralization, standardization, detailed planning quantitative analysis and aspires for maximum efficiency and certainty". Simply put, the doctrine of command was mainly vertical: compliance with the most fine-grained details of the orders was highly rewarded, while on the other hand variance originated by initiative was highly discouraged.

The eighties brought new ways of conceiving Command and Control as both the American and the British Armed Forces started to adopt a more decentralized organizing [4, 5]. This change was mainly reactive as a decentralized command structure was deemed better suited "to contend with the demands, uncertainties and frictions of command in war"[6] and with the new security challenges. This new way of organizing has been codified in doctrinal and technical documents[2] and most organizations quickly interiorized such changes in their training programs and in the way they organized tactical maneuvering. Not surprisingly empirical evidence shows – or at least points towards the finding – that Mission Command brought an increase in operative efficacy on the ground [6]. Furthermore, this collective mission-oriented organizing provided flourishing ground for a wider engagement in tactical assessments and in mindful concerted operations. As "no plan survives the first contact with the enemy" [7], flexibility and tactical initiative to seize the momentum are path to be actively encouraged. However, "this requires understanding your superior commanders' intentions, flexibility of mind, rapid decision-making, good organization and good communications" (UK Ministry of Defence, 2014, p. 31).

---

[1] British Army Doctrine Publication, Volume 2, 'Command'; Army Code No. 71584, April 1995.

[2] Among others, see [8, 22, 23].

Real-time control systems provide the opportunity to centralize decision-making and revitalize direct supervision as the main coordination mechanism in military operations [9]. Enhanced informating and automating capabilities result from the application of digital tools in modern warfare. Digital data streams convey information from the front-line to the control centers and offer the possibility to enhance situational awareness through advanced analytics and visualization tools. Moreover, cutting-edge remote-controlled technologies such as automatic arms systems, perform tasks in the battle-field and complement the activities of front-line operators. Therefore, high-rank officers have an opportunity to oversee the battlefield from great distances. These opportunities brought to the resurgence of a traditional "Command and Control" (C2) approach in technology-intensive armies [10]. This is due to the fact that digital command and control systems provide commanders with a clear picture from the operative functions of the organization and "intimacy previously reserved for the men in the trenches" (Shamir 2011, p. 166). However, such informating and automating functions in military operations are also associated to a progressive de-responsibilization of the frontline, which results in poor flexibility and limited initiative in extreme contexts [11]. Thus, digital C2 seems to be systematically opposed to the diluted organizing of Mission Command as "C2 leaders" would possess incentive to centralize the decision-making.

In this piece we provide a conceptual illustration of the tension between the centripetal effect of digital enabled C2 systems and the mission-oriented – agile – organizing offered by Mission Command. In first place we provide a review of the literature. Secondly, we focus on the affordances of digital systems that favor mission-oriented organizing. That is, these tools – with the proper design – can be implemented and used as enablers of tactical awareness. In the first part of the paper, we discuss the origins and the implementation of Mission Command in military organizations. Subsequently, we illustrate the constraints and limits of Mission Command in conjunction with digital C2 systems. Finally, we evaluate a point of equilibrium that stabilizes the opposing forces between structure and flexibility [12] as required by the contingencies of the battlefield. In order to do so, we discuss the affordances of the Blue Force Tracking 2 (BFT), a digital tracking system widely used by land forces. This article aims to contribute to the larger literature of organizational studies and military studies. It may constitute a first conceptual and foundational step towards of the design of a new generation of digital enabled C2 systems to attain reliability in extreme contexts.

2   Framing Mission-Oriented Organizing

The peculiarity of Mission Command lies in its same foundations upon diffused leadership. Through mission-oriented organizing – as opposed to more task-oriented approaches – its aim is that of fostering initiative and flexibility. Tactical decisions are therefore conceived in a state of situational awareness from frontline personnel, driven by the strategic address of higher ranks. Its core is three-fold: shared responsibility, intent and trust are the pillars that enable increases in efficacy [9]. The theory behind this approach reside within the so-called "manoeuvrist approach" [6, 13–15]. The latter has been fully incorporated in the Joint Doctrine Publication 0–01 (2014) that describes its main features and aims. Specifically, it aims to apply "strength against identified vulnerabilities, including predominately indirect ways and means of targeting the intellectual and moral component of an opponent's fighting power" (p. 29). The document delves further into this approach highlighting three synergic significant features from an organizational standpoint: momentum, tempo, and agility. The combination of those traits is used to build up shock and surprise.

Historically, Mission Command originated within the ranks of the Prussian Army in the aftermath of the defeat of Jena. Specifically, the Prussians heavily relied on a rigid model of command that was proven obsolete and ineffective on the battlefield [3, 5]. Conversely, the more "utilitarian" and agile nature of French military organizations, had a decisive competitive edge [6, 15]. Bungay [15] resorting to McGregor's [16] theory of X and Y organizations, conceptualized the organizational models of the two forces [6]. The Prussians exhibited the traits typical of the "X": direct management, a more rigid control structure and a strong emphasis on command and control from a tactical standpoint. Soldiers were given – and needed – detailed orders to operate. On the other hand, the French forces showed the traits of "Y": markedly utilitarian, tactically proactive and relatively self-controlled. In fact, in the extensive review on models of leadership offered by Yardley, the work Cameron and Quinn (2011) frames the Prussian Army as traditionally hierarchical in terms of organizational culture. On the other hand, the French Army took the form of an "adhocracy": an organizational culture that system that incentivizes bold, innovative and creative leaders.

The lesson learnt on the battlefield enabled a series of deep structural changes: Von Moltke in the middle of the nineteenth century started a series of reforms that were condensed into new model of leadership [17] under the name of "Auftragstaktik". It placed preeminent emphasis on initiative, aggressiveness, and tactical freedom of action [18]. The new organizational culture was progressively formalized and institutionalized into the military and found its way into Kriegsacademy as a novel paradigm to shape their new leaders [3].

The change of paradigm reverberated even into the World Wars with the Wehrmacht becoming an example of prime tactical efficacy [9][3]. On the contrary, the American tradition was still centered on a more centralized and managerial structure of command: "the hunger for information at the top produced an information overload resulting in long lead times needed in order to prepare and launch operations" [2, p. 652]. Constant communication was an operative need given the vertical nature of command [19]. This feature was even more evident in the American forces in case of the Vietnam War. Commanders directed the strategic address as well as the tactics and tasks on the frontline: order were issued analysing daily reports and fine-grained data (e.g. Hamlet Evaluation System). Several author in the military scholarship points out how the US army relied more on numbers, attrition, firepower and vertical control than on tactical finesse [3, 20].

The late seventies and the early eighties marked a turning point in the Anglo-American tradition as well. The British Joint doctrine - developed by General Bagnall - placed a new emphasis on mission-oriented organizing. Similarly, the American Army progressively turned toward a more decentralized philosophy of command [4, 5] better suited to deal with emerging security quandaries. In fact, these organizations needed a novel approach to engage in asymmetric warfare such as peacekeeping operations and

---

[3] See for instance the battle of Caporetto (1917) which is regarded as an example of Auftragtaktik.

counterinsurgency [21]. In those years, after being tested "boots on the ground" Mission Command found its place in several doctrinal documents across Western Armed Forces [8, 22, 23].

In terms of functioning and implementation Mission Command required a shared and diffused understanding of the rationale behind an operation. The strategic objectives - that embody the intent of commanders – must be clearly communicated to subordinates. In this way, operative personnel can circumvent uncertainty and exert diffused leadership adapting to contingencies and environmental constraints. As mentioned in the introduction, this course of action is based on multiple levels of trusts between units, within units and towards the strategic address. This organizational feature is achieved - as Yardley, Kakabadse and Neal [24] note – through a long process, in fact: "the glue that holds mission command together is the culture and values of the organization (p. 74)". Culture therefore becomes a systemic enabler of trust that – in turn - render the implementation of Mission Command possible.

In operational term, a key requirement of Mission Command is situational awareness (SA). The latter creates a space of action that enables operative functions to take ownership of tactical decision-making. Being aware of the contingencies and correct for them, in fact, is one of the main determinants of the increase in efficacy. In accordance with the superiors' intent, troops on the ground can exploit their "intimacy" with the battlefield to accomplish the mission. This approach shares many similarities with scholarly works on first-responders [25]: frontline operations need a certain degree of independence to achieve cooperation in fragmented and extreme scenarios. The two figures below represent the decay curve of a plan effectiveness over time illustrating the concept presented by Bungay [15] and discussed by Yardley and Kakabadse [6].

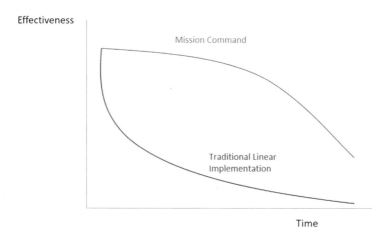

Fig. 1. Mission command and its adaptive effectiveness over time reproduced from [4, p. 74].

Figure 1 shows how in an "unaware" scenario – with no specific knowledge of the situation - a plan devised through Mission Command loses effectiveness at a slower rate over time. The reason for that is that Mission Command makes plans more flexible and agile: it allows for a more efficient switching of priorities if the contingencies dictate so. Nonetheless, even mission-oriented operations as time passes, suffers from loss of effectiveness if lacking of SA. That is, even a flexible plan can be deprecated when the operative conditions on the field change: a plan developed at t_0 will inevitably not be as effective at t_1 and even less so at t_2. Figure 2 conversely, shows the effect of situational awareness on Mission Command. The linear planning will perform exactly as in the previous case since it is not possible to update it when needed. A second plan needs to be developed, but it will inevitably decay over time when the conditions change again. Instead, Mission Command - in a space of SA- enables the actors to adapt the plan over time, correcting for contingencies and striving for the "higher intent" as conditions change.

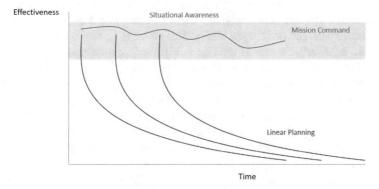

Fig. 2. Mission command and its adaptive effectiveness over time in a context of situational awareness. Reproduced from [4, p. 74]. [6]

This peculiar merits of Mission Commands in correcting for contingencies have led several authors to analyze its viability as an organizational theory for the private sector [6, 14, 24]. Such an agile approach may be ideal in scenarios where unexpected threats – or simply known unknowns - are common. Yardley and Kakabadse [6] points out that "competitive advantage is often to be found in narrow margins and innovative solutions rapidly developed and brought to market (p. 76)". That requires a proactive training of leaders towards what these works spells out as "controlled risk-taking" in tactical decision making.

In sum, mission command seems particularly relevant in facing threats stemming from uncertainty and from "the unexpected". While the military literature mostly emphasizes its doctrinal implications, we argue that from an organizational standpoint Mission Command is a conceptually compelling approach to foster hallmarks for increased reliability in extreme contexts. It ensures coordination in fragmented settings and fosters switching between structure and flexibility as required by the battlefield [12]. Furthermore, it solves the so-called "entrenchment problem". That is, by allowing for a more flexible approach to crises, it avoids over-reliance on Standard Operating Procedures (SOPs) [26] ultimately enabling the organization for graceful coping with surprises and learning from mistakes [26].

3   Mission Command and Control Systems: Conceptualizing the Tension

As sketched in previous section, throughout history armed forces have shown marked tendencies towards managerial approaches "inspired primarily by the scientific and quantitative school represented by Frederick Winslow Taylor (1856–1915) and Henry Ford (1863–1947) among others, as well as by the theories of operations research and system analysis" [2, p. 646]. The US Army held this tradition particularly dear offering a promising case for comparison with mission-oriented organizing. Shamir [3] instantiates his comparison starting from an analysis of the military academies and on training facilities whereby organizational culture is crafted and passed on. Most military academies indoctrinated future officers to seek efficacy through centralized processes and practices of command and control. Conversely, the German Army placed its bet on a more "fragmented" model centered on independent tactical prowess, initiative and flexibility. That made the Kriegsakademie one of the first modern mission-oriented formative institution [27]. The American effort in the World Wars marked this contrast further [28] due to the influence of private sector practices onto military organizations. The latter provided a further boost to centripetal forces. Yet, the Vietnam Fiasco showed that a purely centralized model was hardly the optimal approach to tackle complex and asymmetric security challenges. Mission Command found its way within the Anglo-American ranks and expanded to most Western Armies given the changing nature of their frontline operations.

Yet, the emergence of digital systems to enhance C2 presents mission-oriented organizing with a set of challenges. These systems have seen a wide range of applications in contemporary armed forces in the form of remote-controlled technologies, automatic arms systems and real-time data intelligence. In principle these applications provide commanders with virtually unlimited control over the battlefield. Being able to monitor the battle from afar, and assess what frontline operators experience, may provide commanders with incentive to deviate from their role of strategic directors towards a more tactical dimension. In other words, organizations may face the risk of an over-prevalence of the structure at the expenses of flexibility. Control rooms may become the cockpits from where the maneuvering is orchestrated moving away from mission-oriented organizing towards a micromanagement approach [9].

Due to this potential pitfall scholarly contributions have considered the rebirth of a purely vertical C2 culture as an archetypal model for technology-intensive armies [10]. This element is further reinforced by the implementation of automated systems for firepower in the form of drones, guided artillery and remote-controlled devices. These tools are extremely common in operative scenarios and often time provide a vital support to frontline operators. Their importance notwithstanding, these systems are largely managed and directed by the central structure of command: the risk is that of hampering tactical discretion of frontline troops in the use of these support systems. In short, strategic directors and commanders can benefit from an increased intimacy with the battlefieldm which in turn may provide an incentive to "impose their preferences on tactical units" [27, p. 1430].

This may be an inherent risk for the Mission Command model. The centralizing effect that these systems could exert, can have repercussions on initiative and penalize flexibility over a more structure-oriented approach. Augier et al. [29] further this argument suggesting how cultural changes brought by the implementation of digital systems may impact the ability of the organization to learn and adapt from tactical scenarios. Consequently, frontline operators may progressively be led towards deresponsibilization [11].

This envisaged process would emerge as a result of the lack of "practice in choosing" tactical addresses. That is, not exerting discretionary decision-making may lead to a progressive desensitization to contingency. This is a risky scenario as support systems alone do not substitute the need from plans' adaptation and corrections given the contingencies of the battlefield. While highly reliable in principle, digital systems may still suffer from malfunctioning or rely on incomplete or outdated data. The consequences of over-reliance on these tools as opposed to tactical adaptation of operators is inherently risky and may pose serious risks to frontline personnel. Simply put, "if the confidence of senior leaders outpaces the efficacy of the technology" [27, p. 1430], the operational space for correcting and adapting for contingencies or sudden changes may be severely reduced.

In conclusion, we presented how depriving tactical units from the capacity of making choices to accomplish the mission may have a negative impact on SA. In the long run that would cause a progressive, steeper, decay of plans' effectiveness over time in case of changes of the conditions on the battlefield. Furthermore, purely vertical approaches are not efficient catalyst of multidimensional trust as compared to Mission Command approaches. We can formalize such observations in a "performing and organizing" tension [30] at the organization level that becomes salient when the technological systems are implemented. Specifically, there is a pre-existing latent tension between vertical and decentralized command that is somewhat balanced by the need to operate with partial and imperfect information. Therefore, Mission Command is preferred. Yet, the implementation of a digital control system becomes a factor that renders the tension salient. A GPS tracking system, for instance, produce incentives for high rank officers to adopt a more task-oriented approach to command. In the next section we will provide an example on how these technologies can be used along to the line of the tension to offer a preliminary empirical context[4].

4   Two-Fold Empirical Evidence: Blue Force Tracker 2

An empirical instantiation of the above-mentioned tension can be found in the adoption of the Below-Blue Force Tracker 2 (BFT). The BTF mainly serve as a tracking tool to boost SA. It provides the Tactical Operation Centre with the GPS coordinates and real-time tracking of units' movements. Terminals were originally fitted on transport vehicles allowing for clearer insights on the location of dispersed units [31]. The system was made to allow a more agile maneuvering at the tactical level vis-à-vis the fine-grained disaggregated data. The affordance of the system is thus that of merging situational awareness and command and control information [31] with the aim of maximizing

---

[4] Offering a fully-fledged empirical test is beyond the scope of this conceptual paper. Further work on this line of research will expand on the examples proposed here and consider other family of technologies implemented in military organizations.

reliability and efficient maneuvering. The literature on decision-making framed its core capability as "combat identification" (CID) [32]. The latter includes processes such as managing the available resources, maximizing the utility of target actions and – most importantly - discerning friends from foes to avoid friendly fire [33].

Technologies able to foster such processes are crucial particularly in counterinsurgency and urban frontlines scenarios as the battlespace makes achieving CID considerably harder. Accordingly, the large-scale use of BFT in operation Iraqi Freedom and in the subsequent conflict has yielded promising results. Its implementation seems to have brought a reduction of Blue-on-Blue events[5] of almost 25% in scenarios of urban maneuvering. According to military scholars it has had the merit of providing commanders with SA towards the movements and positions of enemy forces, as well as those of allied forces in contexts where discerning friends from foes is hardly a trivial task [29].

Nonetheless, over-reliance on technology may posits several organizational tensions. The literature recount that the BFT has been used to to "punish" idled units that did not adopt an aggressive maneuvering [34]. On the same line, surveys on US Marine Corp units seem to suggest that in several instances the system was used to provide tactical units – at the platoon level - with direct orders. These elements suggest a progressive centralization of the tactical decision-making [35]. Furthermore, simulation studies have shown that most of the beneficial effect stemming from the system associates with a timely and flawless transmission of the data [32]. That is, over-reliance on the system may generate dangerous spillovers by hampering combat identification judgments of platoon members and leaders as discussed in the previous section.

Therefore, the affordances of the BFT seem to insist on the tension between Mission Command and Centralized Command. On the one hand, it provides invaluable benefits in terms of tactical awareness and in terms of reliability and enhanced maneuvering. On the other hand, evidence shows how it has been used also as a C2 tool for direct supervision.

5   Conclusion and Future Studies

Our multi-field review of previous works on digital technologies in frontline military operations highlight the tension between the centripetal force of vertical command and the principle of diffused leadership that constitute the foundation of Mission Command. This tension is made salient at the organizational level by the implementation of digital systems in operative scenarios. At the same time, we suggest that C2 systems can effectively support Mission Command, instead of contrasting its foundational elements. However, this goal can be achieved only upon certain conditions. Our conceptual model illustrates that advanced data-driven coordination tools can foster responsibility and tactical awareness in extreme contexts. We argue that the informating and automating capabilities of digital C2 systems do not necessarily threaten the applicability of the Mission Command doctrine. On the contrary, we claim that they may constitute powerful enablers of organizational mindfulness. Therefore, we argue that a design theory is needed to explain how digital technologies can successfully support military operations.

---

[5] A "Blue-on-Blue" – in NATO terminology - is an inadvertent occurrence of friendly fire.

The Mission Command doctrine can inform the design of digital enabled C2 systems fostering organizational mindfulness in extreme contexts. This may translate in providing different operative functions with ad-hoc systems based on their operative necessity with the aim of enhancing tactical SA reinforcing their incentive to take mission-oriented initiative.

Our analysis suggests how C2 decisions are embedded in the institutional fabric of military operations and highlights affordances and constraints of digital systems that serve this purpose [36]. Future studies can focus on other tensions to build a design theory on digital enabled C2 systems. For instance, a fragmentation perspective can be applied to coordination in extreme contexts [25]. By focusing on tensions between data integration and fragmentation, a design theory [37, 38] can identify the principles of form and functions to craft digital tools that successfully support frontline flexibility, sensitivity to operations, and improvisation in military operations. Moreover, the design principles can be applied to other domains such as crisis management and business resilience [39, 40] with the aim of extending the validity of the design theory to other managerial contexts characterized by fragmented coordination [25].

Aside from highlighting the value of fragmented coordination, our work poses emphasis on the affordances of digital systems. A careful examination should be carried out on the affordances that emerge from the use of these systems in training and simulations. Military organizations in fact operate in high-risks scenarios where extreme events are associated with extremely high stakes. The latter translate in harm for organizational members and risk for non-hostile actors as well as serious reputational and economic damages. At the same time, military organizations are on the frontlines less frequently as compared to first responders and trauma organizations. Such sparser nature of extreme events posits the need for frequent and more extensive training to attain tactical preparedness. Furthermore, the possibility of casualties in combat, shapes the nature of training that often times encompass redundancies and cross-functional components to account for contingencies. Given that replacement of injured operators or of casualties is hardly an option in extreme contexts, tactical teams must prepare for an efficient switching of roles and for proactive leadership is the austere operational conditions dictate so. In practical terms, this necessity posits the need to find a balancing stance between generalization and specializations. Operative units, and even more so special forces units which operate in even smaller teams, go through advanced training, realistic simulations and continuous rehearsal and training. That paradigm seeks to ensure development of leadership skills as well as preparedness under a plethora of different operative circumstances. In this context, further studies would need to consider contingency approaches to conceptualize and test the interactions between data technologies and leadership in frontline scenarios [41].

As a final note, our contribution aims to provide the long-standing centralization and decentralization debate [42] with renewed salience vis-à-vis emerging digitally shaped processes and practices. We built a case to highlight the tension between data intensive digital systems seen as both centralized hierarchical control systems and as decentralized internal control and interfaces supporting semi-autonomous units. Further empirical studies should allow to fully evaluate and appreciate how these systems interact with organizational effectiveness in frontline scenarios [43, 44].

References

1. Weick, K.E., Roberts, K.H.: Collective mind in organizations: heedful interrelating on flight decks. Adm. Sci. Q. 357–381 (1993)
2. Fraher, A.L., Branicki, L.J., Grint, K.: Mindfulness in action: discovering how U.S. navy seals build capacity for mindfulness in high-reliability organizations (HROs). Acad. Manag. Discov. 3(3), 239–261 (2017). https://doi.org/10.5465/amd.2014.0146
3. Shamir, E.: The long and winding road: the US army managerial approach to command and the adoption of mission command (Auftragstaktik). J. Strateg. Stud. 33(5), 645–672 (2010)
4. Farrell, T.: The dynamics of British military transformation. Int. Aff. 84(4), 777–807 (2008)
5. Shamir, E.: Transforming command: the pursuit of mission command in the US, British, and Israeli armies. Stanford University Press (2011)
6. Yardley, I., Kakabadse, A.: Understanding mission command: a model for developing competitive advantage in a business context. Strateg. Chang. 16(1–2), 69–78 (2007)
7. Hughes, D.J.: Moltke on the Art of War: Selected Writings. Random House Digital, Inc., New York (1995)
8. UK Ministry of Defence: Joint Doctrine Publication 0-01, UK Defence Doctrine. Forms and Publications Section, LCSLS Headquarters and Operations Centre (2014)
9. Storr, J.: A command philosophy for the information age: the continuing relevance of mission command. Def. Stud. 3(3), 119–129 (2003)
10. Connor, W.M.: Emerging army doctrine: command and control. Mil. Rev. 82(2), 80 (2002)
11. Bateman, R.L.: Force XXI and the death of Auftragstaktik (1996)
12. Salovaara, A., Lyytinen, K., Penttinen, E.: Flexibility vs. structure: how to manage reliably continuously emerging threats in malware protection. In: 2015 48th Hawaii International Conference on System Sciences, pp. 4980–4989 (2015)
13. Hooker, R.D.: Maneuver Warfare: An Anthology. Gower Publishing Company Limited, Aldershot (1993)
14. Pech, R.J., Durden, G.: Manoeuvre warfare: a new military paradigm for business decision making. Manag. Decis. (2003)
15. Bungay, S.: The road to mission command. Br. Army Rev. Defence 137, 22 (2005)
16. McGregor, D., Cutcher-Gershenfeld, J.: The Human Side of Enterprise, vol. 21. McGraw-Hill, New York (1960)
17. Widder, W.: Battle command: Auftragstaktik and Innere Fuhrung: trademarks of German leadership. Mil. Rev. 82(5), 2 (2002)
18. Echevarria, A.J., Antulio, J.: Auftragstaktik. In its proper perspective. Mil. Rev. 66(10), 50–56 (1986)
19. Van Creveld, M.: Command in War. Harvard University Press, Cambridge (1985)
20. Boot, M.: The new American way of war. Foreign Aff. 41–58 (2003)
21. Army, US and Corps, US Marine: Counterinsurgency Field Manual, no. 3–24. Cosimo, Inc., New York (2010)
22. NATO: AJP-01 (D): Allied Joint Doctrine. NATO Standardization Agency Brussels (2010)
23. Department of the Army: ADP 6-0, Mission Command. Headquarters Department of the Army (2014)
24. Yardley, I., Kakabadse, A., Neal, D.: From Battlefield to Boardroom: Making the Difference Through Values Based Leadership. Palgrave Macmillan, London (2012)
25. Wolbers, J., Boersma, K., Groenewegen, P.: Introducing a fragmentation perspective on coordination in crisis management. Organ. Stud. 39(11), 1521–1546 (2018). https://doi.org/10.1177/0170840617717095
26. Salovaara, A., Lyytinen, K., Penttinen, E.: High reliability in digital organizing: mindlessness, the frame problem, and digital operations. MIS Q. Manag. Inf. Syst. (2019). https://doi.org/10.25300/MISQ/2019/14577

27. Van Creveld, M.L.: The Training of officers: From Military Professionalism to Irrelevance. Free Press, New York (1990)
28. Gabriel, R.A., Savage, P.L.: Crisis in Command: Mismanagement in the Army. Macmillan, London (1979)
29. Augier, M., Knudsen, T., McNab, R.M.: Advancing the field of organizations through the study of military organizations. Ind. Corp. Chang. 23(6), 1417–1444 (2014). https://doi.org/10.1093/icc/dtt059
30. Smith, W., Lewis, M.: Toward a theory of paradox: a dynamic equilibrium model of organizing. Acad. Manag. Rev. 36(2), 381–403 (2011). https://doi.org/10.5465/amr.2009.0223
31. Chevli, K.R., et al.: Blue force tracking network modeling and simulation. In: MILCOM 2006 - 2006 IEEE Military Communications Conference, October 2006, pp. 1–7 (2006). https://doi.org/10.1109/MILCOM.2006.302050
32. Bryant, D.J., Smith, D.G.: Impact of blue force tracking on combat identification judgments. Hum. Fact. 55(1), 75–89 (2013)
33. Doton, L.: Integrating technology to reduce fratricide (1996)
34. Gordon, M.R., Trainor, B.E.: Cobra II: The Inside Story of the Invasion and Occupation of Iraq. Pantheon, New York (2006)
35. Dreier, M.J., Birgl, J.S.: Analysis of Marine Corps Tactical Level Command and Control and Decision Making Utilizing FBCB2-BFT. Naval Postgraduate School, Monterey (2010)
36. Orlikowski, W., Barley, S.: Technology and institutions: what can research on information technology and research on organizations learn from each other? MIS Q. 25(2), 145–165 (2001)
37. Gregor, S., Jones, D.: The anatomy of a design theory (2007)
38. Gregor, S., Hevner, A.R.: Positioning and presenting design science research for maximum impact. MIS Q. 37(2), 337–355 (2013)
39. Spagnoletti, P., Tarantino, L.: User centered systems design: the bridging role of justificatory knowledge. n: Baskerville, R., De Marco, M., Spagnoletti, P. (eds.) Designing Organizational Systems. LNISO, vol .1, pp. 105–121. Springer, Heidelberg (2013). https://doi.org/10.1007/978-3-642-33371-2_6
40. Tarantino, L., Spagnoletti, P.: Can design science research bridge computer human interaction and information systems? In: Spagnoletti, P. (ed.) Organizational Change and Information Systems. LNISO, vol. 2, pp. 409–418. Springer, Heidelberg (2013). https://doi.org/10.1007/978-3-642-37228-5_40
41. Hannah, S.T., Uhl-Bien, M., Avolio, B.J., Cavarretta, F.L.: A framework for examining leadership in extreme contexts. Leadersh. Q. 20(6), 897–919 (2009). https://doi.org/10.1016/j.leaqua.2009.09.006
42. Bloomfield, B.P., Coombs, R.: Information technology, control and power: the centralization and decentralization debate revisited. J. Manag. Stud. 29(4), 459 (1992). https://doi.org/10.1111/j.1467-6486.1992.tb00674.x
43. Mikalef, P., Krogstie, J., Pappas, I.O., Pavlou, P.: Exploring the relationship between big data analytics capability and competitive performance: the mediating roles of dynamic and operational capabilities. Inf. Manag. 57(2), 103169 (2020). https://doi.org/10.1016/j.im.2019.05.004
44. Mikalef, P., Pappas, I.O., Krogstie, J., Giannakos, M.: Big data analytics capabilities: a systematic literature review and research agenda. Inf. Syst. e-Bus. Manag. 16(3), 547–578 (2017). https://doi.org/10.1007/s10257-017-0362-y

Public Perspectives. Exploring Issues in Public Government and Research

A Lack of Smart Governance in the Public Sector: The Italian Case Study

Marco Berardi[(✉)] and Andrea Ziruolo

G. d'Annunzio University, Pescara, Italy
{marco.berardi,andrea.ziruolo}@unich.it

Abstract. Part of the international literature highlights the need of the public sector to change its managerial approach towards choices oriented to the so-called "Smart governance" [1] or *"an abbreviation for the ensemble of principles, factors, and capacities that constitute a form of governance able to cope with the conditions and exigencies of the knowledge society"*. This work will focus on the analysis of the digitization process of the public sector in Italy through the "digital administration codex" (CAD), highlighting the effects produced in terms of the introduction of the so-called new technologies to optimize investments in the area and attract them with innovative financing instruments. The analysis has been also considering the effects of the "Pandemic lock-down" showing that, despite the efforts made by the central government, the Italian public sector should not be considered as an exemple of "Smart Governance" as it seems to be still committed with "New Public Management Paradigm" [2, 3].

Keywords: Italian public sector · Smart governance · New technologies

1 Introduction

In Italy, there is evidence of attempts at introducing NPM-inspired reforms, especially during the 2010's, that have resulted in an "implementation gap": there seems to be a certain distance between the contents of what was prescribed by a spate of reform laws and the actual diffusion of the corresponding management tool and there seems to be an even larger distance between the mere presence and the actual utilization of the management tools oriented in a "smart governance" scenario [2, 4].

International literature agree that, all over the world, the public sector is adopting many different innovations in order to be "a smart government" to improve information sharing and interoperability [5, 6] such as: becoming an open government, engaging and interacting with citizens, opening up the budgeting process, facilitating accompanying culture shifts and capability enhancements, simplifying information management, facilitating access, compliance and analysis of government regulations, to responding to barriers imposed by local authorities concerning data release, enhancing service infrastructures, creating programs that contribute to a more efficient, effective, transparent, and collaborative city government, or executing total quality management initiatives [7, 8].

© The Author(s), under exclusive license to Springer Nature Switzerland AG 2022
S. Za et al. (Eds.): ItAIS 2020, LNISO 50, pp. 219–232, 2022.
https://doi.org/10.1007/978-3-030-86858-1_13

Being a smarter government seems to require having a forward-thinking approach to the use and integration of information, technology, and innovation in the activities of governing [3].

Authors such as Coe, Paquet, and Roy [9] document early examples of smartness from Canada's 'smart communities' initiative, where they draw from Eger's [10] definition of 'smart communities': "a geographical area ranging in size from a neighborhood to a multicounty region within which citizens, organizations, and governing institutions to transform their region in significant and fundamental ways" [9].

On the other hand, authors such as Kliksberg's [11] and Key and We [12], focuses on government's strategic role in society and the development of managerial capacities that enable it to perform its roles in a highly effective manner, which as bring to the distinction between government and governance.

Moreover, Bingham, Nabatchi, and O'Leary's [13] underline the thin difference between Government and Governance: "*Government occurs when those with legally and formally derived authority and policing power execute and implement activities*" and "*Governance refers to the creation, execution, and implementation of activities backed by the shared goals of citizens and organizations, who may or may not have formal authority or policing power*" underlying the importance of introduce new technologies even in the public sector.

As highlighted by part of the literature, the transition to "Smart Governance" must be accompanied by the introduction of new technological tools that allow the public sector to overcome critical issues such as excessive bureaucracy, emprove the speed in the transmission of information even the ability to generate "open access" to stakeholders [14].

In the last decades, Italy has introduced several reforms in terms of accountability, digitalization, and open government by attempting to introduce that digital innovation that is most indispensable to allow the transition to "Smart Governance" [15] in the attempt to reduce the enormous gap with other Eu's country and to finally introduce a new "state of mind" based on innovation and Digital Technologies.

The 25 of May 2005 "The Economist" indicated Italy has "The sick man of Europe" describing a country where the public sector was still conducted with "old rules" not based on innovation technologies or digitalization: a perfect mix of "economic crisis", corruption and political instability. After 15 years, many reforms occour in Italy trying to change the "rest of the world state of mind" about Italy of reform the situation in Italy is completely changed.

In terms of digitalization, the main legislative intervention undertaken was the introduction in 2010 of the "Digital Administration Codex - CAD" on the attempt to support public services with mobile-oriented public services, to participate effectively to the administrative procedures electronically also promoting the integration and interoperability between public services provided by public administrations citizens and businesses.

So, this paper will analyze the effort of the CAD in the Italian public sector analyzing his contribution to the introduction of new technologies in the public sector to allow the transition of the public administration towards a "smart governance" approach.

After describing the regulatory excursus that introduced digitization and new technologies in the Italian public sector, the state of the art regarding the main interventions required by the legislator will be shown, showing how public administrations have partially disregarded the expectations of developments technological expectations of the objectives set with the "Digital Agenda" [15].

Moreover, using the Carter and Belanger [7] framework, we investigated the effectiveness of digitalization in the public sector during the three months of lockdown (March-May 2020) due to the Covid_19 pandemic. Semi-structured interviews have been conducted to 36 managers of Italian municipalities to investigate the contribution of CAD and more in general of digitalization during the lock-down period. Interviews had emphasized and confirmed a generalized lack of "smart governance" [3].

So, the research questions of this paper are:

RQ1: What are the main reasons that lead to the failure of the Smart Governance in Italy?
RQ2: In the light of the recent pandemic, were there any changes that affected the Italian Smart Governance?

2   Digitalization and New Technologies in the Italian Public Sector

In the context of the Italian public sector, the process of defining and promoting the Information and Communication Society to achieve "Smart Governance", developed simultaneously with the more general international process of reform of public administrations [16].

The introduction of the new information and communication technologies (ICT) has appeared as a tool facilitating the reformulation of the organization and functioning of the public administration, often starting from the application of new laws and provisions [17].

The late 1980s and early 1990s was a period characterized by strong legislative action aimed at creating a regulatory "platform" on which to build public sector change [18]. In this regard, the enactment of Law 142/90 marked an important step in the management of local public services, introducing, among other things, the possibility of adopting new forms of management for the provision of the same. At the same time, the Legislator has introduced some regulatory guidelines in support of the computerization of the public sector.

In particular, with the legislative decree n.39 of 1993, the AIPA (Authority for Information Technology in the Public Administration, later transformed into AGID, Agency for Digital Italy) was established as an autonomous agency whose purpose consists of the promotion, coordination, control, and management of automated information systems within public administrations.

The Bassanini reform (in particular Law 59/97), provided for the creation of a network of public administrations (Unitary Public Administration Network - RUPA), favoring close coordination and synergistic integration of the work of different administrations, thanks to the integration of the corporate information system of the various entities, which also allows overcoming organizational fragmentation. This objective aimed at the redesign and integration of document flows (information and organizational workflows) and electronic filing techniques [19].

In this regard, introducing and managing IT protocols appears to be fundamental, as required by Presidential Decree 20/10/1998, and the provisions on digital signature. In 2000 with the publication of the "Action Piano for Italian E-Government" many of these objectives were taken up and made explicit in finalized lines of action.

Only in 2002, the implementation phase of the interventions to realize the e-government plan started, when Italian central Government started to work the guidelines of the so-called "Second phase of e-government". The main priorities consist of encouraging greater democratic participation of citizens and including of small municipalities.

In 2007, Minister Luigi Nicolais presented the *"Strategic lines of the national e-government system"*, from which the so-called "Innovation Directive" followed.

The national guidelines underlined the importance of technology as a factor in support of administrative change, arguing that "the modernization of public administrations will lead to the revitalization and development of Italy's competitiveness".

The innovation should have rested on these pillars:

- the redefinition of management applications and organizational processes;
- the deepening and acceleration of the technological innovation process as well as the develop of human capital capable of implementing it and transforming it into a decisive factor of sustainable growth and development.

Finally, with Law 69/2009 the Digital Administration Codex (CAD) was proposed, introducing innovative tools such as:

- recognition for the citizen of the right to use technologies in communications with all public administrations;
- the right to make any payment electronically;
- the right to use certified electronic mail (PEC);
- the right to find all valid and updated forms and forms online;
- the establishment of the Index of public administration addresses.

In January 2011, the CAD was formalized (Legislative Decree no. 235/2010) which constitutes the second pillar on which the renewal process of the Public Administration is based, together with Legislative Decree no. 150/2009 (the so colled "Brunetta Reform) which introduced principles of meritocracy, reward, transparency and accountability of managers into the PA.

The new CAD renews the regulatory framework for digital administration defined in 2005 with Legislative Decree no. 82, updating the reference rules concerning an evolving technological landscape introducing and adjusting:

- authorization to use free or open-source code software;
- managerial and disciplinary responsibility for failure to transmit documents electronically;

- the right for citizens to have their certified e-mail address, to which public administrations and managers of public services are required to send communications from 1 January 2013;
- the establishment of the national index of certified e-mail addresses (INI-PEC) of companies;
- the establishment of the national registry of the resident population.

In addition to the establishment of new rights and responsibilities, regulatory interventions also aimed at rationalizing the organizational structures functional to the pursuit of e-Government objectives.

Subsequently, in line with the Digital Agenda for Europe launched in 2010 to develop a digital single market to lead Europe towards smart, sustainable and inclusive growth, at a national level, starting in 2012, the Italian Digital Agendahas been promoted which updates annually specifies the macro areas on which to focus the interventions with the aim, among other things, of improving the PA's company performance but also of improving citizens' satisfaction and promoting transparency, reducing the possible pockets of systemic corruption [20–23]:

- digital identity;
- digital PA and open data;
- digital education;
- digital healthcare;
- digital divide and electronic payments;
- digital justice;
- research innovation and smart communities.

Finally, with Legislative Decree December 13, 2017, no. 217, the supplementary and corrective provisions were issued to the Legislative Decree no. 26 August 2016, 179, concerning changes and additions to the Digital Administration Code (CAD), on the reorganization of public administrations, the last intervention requested by the legislator. This intervention became necessary following the 2017 AGID report where it was shown that at the level of decentralized administrations, the much-desired epoch-making change towards digitalization was a chimera [20–23].

From this brief excursus, emerges that the stimuli to technological innovation in the public sector have been subjected, over the the past decades, to multiple regulatory interventions aimed at seeking the best ways of governing public intervention in terms of programs and policies aimed the introduction of technological innovations and facilitate their adoption and use to meet the needs expressed by the internal (public system) and external (citizens and businesses) environment [16, 17].

As will be seen in the next pargraph, despite the enormous effort made by the central government to introduce digitization and new technologies in the Italian public sector towards a "Smart Governance" logic, the state of the art the digitization process seems to be only in an initial phase, feeding the GAP, in terms of technological innovation, with others EU member states [21].

3   Methodology

Having analyzed the legislative effort of the Italian central government to introduce a "smart governance governmenatality" we tested the efforts of CAD in the Desi Agenda 2019 through a documental analysis of the report conducted by ISTAT and AGID. This methodology has been inspired by the framework suggested by Heeks [3]: by examining numerous cases of IS and e-government failure in developing countries emerges that: "major reason for failures is the mismatch between the current reality and the design of the future e-government system can be summirised in three points":

1. Hard-Soft Gaps: the difference between the actual technology (hard) and the reality of the social context (people, culture, politics etc.) in which the system operates (soft);
2. Private-Public Gaps: the difference between the private and public sectors means that a system that works in one sector often does not work in the other, due to gaps between systems designed for the private sector and the reality of the public sector into which the system is transferred;
3. Country Context Gaps: the gap that exists when trying to use the e-government systems for both developed and developing countries, which arises from the gap between a system designed for one country and the reality of a developing country into which the system is transferred.

The documentary analysis carried out, as will be seen in the conclusions, has outlined an Italian public sector that is far from the logic of "Smart Governance". To further investigate what are the causes of misalignment between what is suggested by the reference literature [3] and what emerged from the analysis, we proceeded, as will be seen in paragraph 5, to carry out semi-structured interviews on a sample of 36 municipalities equally divided on the Italian territory using the research sample provided by Deidda Gagliardo [14].

The interviews conducted highlighted a lack of "Trustworthiness" or a Trust of Internet and Trust of Governance combination in line with what has already been highlighted by some of the international literature [7, 24, 25].

4   Digitalization and New Technologies in the Italian Public Sector: A Documental Analysis

As shown in paragraph 2.0, the digitization process in Italy is inspired by over 10 years of administrative reforms concluded with the establishment of the CAD and in line with what has been done by the European Union.

The Italian Digital Agenda [20–23] follows the principles outlined by the European agenda, adapting them to national priorities and needs. Italy has thus developed its national digitalization strategy, translating it into a document, the "Italian strategy for digital growth 2014–2020", which has outlined the plan for the pursuit of the objectives proposed by the European Commission.

In 2017, a further step was taken by the Italian Government, introducing the "2017–2019 Three-Year Plan for Information Technology in the Public Administration" (Table 1) with the goal of defining and agenda with the main goals to be achieved within the public sector. The local authorities included in this agenda have been indicated in the IPA 2020 database for a total of 19,882 local authorities:

- 19,882 local public administrations;
- 2,239 central public administrations;
- 22 national pension funds;
- 92 companies in the consolidated income statement;
- 611 public services

Therefore, at the end of the digital agenda reference period (three-year period 2017–2019), the expectations of digitalization and introduction of new technologies in the public administration sector were "*per se*" very high and in line with the requirements of the European guidelines (Table 2).

From the reports provided by AGID [22], it emerges that Italy made important steps forward in the digitalization process, laying the foundations of an "*operating system for digital development*" by speeding up the dissemination of the National Registry of Resident Population (ANPR), with 4,300 municipalities that took over the platform and 35 million Italians involved.

Furthermore, it has approached the target of 150 million payments on pagoPA by 2020, with over 63 million transactions carried out and 15 thousand active PAs, even if only 4,200 have received at least one payment, it has released 13 million Electronic Identity Cards (CIE) to 21% of the Italian population. Five million digital identities were provided via SPID allowing access to 4,200 online services of over 4,000 PAs, even if the level of actual use is still limited.

On the other hand, there are over 140 million electronic invoices to the PA and more than 1.5 billion to private ones. The Electronic Health Record is active in all regions, fully operational in 18 and covers 22% of patients, and more than 63% of reports produced. More than 27,000 Open Data has been published in databases created by the central government (the main ones: OpenBDAP, Transparent Administration, Public Money).

As for the creation of the Italian Internet, only 44% of the entire territory within the peninsula is covered. In this regard, it is appropriate to underline how in 2017 the Authority for the Guarantees in Communications adopted the first Italian system of mapping the access networks (fixed and mobile) to the internet, or the "Broadbandmap".

Based on the provisions of Law no. 9/2014 (the so-called "Save Italy decree") the Italian Communication Authority (AGCOM) has made available to the entire population, an interactive map that can be consulted from a fixed or mobile location using a smartphone or tablet. The aim is to collect extremely detailed information on existing infrastructures and on the services available throughout the national territory.

The AGCOM online portal provides statistically processed data on coverage (in copper, optical fiber, wireless technology, on 2G, 3G, and 4G cellular networks) and the speed of networks (copper and optical fiber) as well as on the number of internet subscriptions (national, regional, provincial and municipal) [20–23].

Table 1. Digitalization Main Goals 2017–2019, AGID.

Goal	Description	Expected Results
National Registry of Resident Population	Establish a digital registry of the entire Italian population	Establishment of the Digital Registry for all Italian citizens
PagoPA	Establish a platform for payments to the public administration in order to reduce the costs for the PA	Digitize all payments to the public administration (at least 150 million by 2020)
SPID system	Creation of a unique digital profile that allows access to the online services of the Public Administration with a single Digital Identity (username and password) that can be used by computers, tablets and smartphones	Profiling of the entire Italian public sector (22845/22845)
Electronic identity card	Replacement of paper identity documents with digital cards equipped with an electronic recognition code	Full digital replacement of all identity documents (achive goal until 2020)
Use Open Source software	Replacement of software on payment with Open Source software and free share of the programming codex	Full use by the public administration of Open Source software (achive goal until 2020)
Use shared facilities and cloud services	Use shared databases to guarantee Open Access through "cloud" type services	Creation of shared databases and cloud services for all public administrations (achive goal until 2020)
Offer citizens digital services (Citizen services, electronic invoicing, electronic health record)	Complete digitization of all services offered by the public administration	Digital conversion of all public administration services (achive goal until 2020)
Establish the " internet broadband" throughout the Italian territory	Introduce new broadband internet browsing technologies	Introduce new broadband internet browsing technologies (achive goal until 2020)

The most relevant aspect is the possibility for anyone who uses the map to leave their valuable comment according to the so-called model. crowdsourcing (Brabham, 2015). AGCOM shows that in the period 2017, 2019, about 650 reports were received, which contributed to a sort of permanent development of the functionality of the platform, thus consolidating its reliability for the benefit of all public and private stakeholders.

The interaction with users is precisely the element that, from the launch of the map-to-date, has guaranteed and guarantees the enhancement of the total coverage of the service. In fact, on several occasions, the map has been modified and implemented based on user reports compared to what was communicated by operators (for example, due to the different coverage of one side of a road).

Table 2. Digitalization Main Goals 2017–2019, results achieved. Source: Agid: 2019

Goal	Description	Expected Results	Results achieved
National Register of Resident Population	Establish a digital registry of the entire Italian population	Establishment of the digital registry for all Italian citizens	22,375,226 inhabitants re-corderd over almost 60.36 million (37%)
PagoPA	Establish a platform for payments to the public administration in order to reduce the costs for the PA	Digitize at least 150 million payments by 2020	63m of financial transactions out of the 150m expected (40%)
SPID System	Creation of a unique digital profile that allows access to the online services of the Public Administration with a single Digital Identity (username and password) that can be used by computers, tablets, and smartphones	Ensure the use of SPID on 22846/22846 public administrations	4,000 out of 22846 public administrations were achieved by SPID profiling (17.5%)
Electronic identity card	Replacement of paper identity documents with digital cards equipped with an electronic recognition code	Full digital replacement of all identity documents (achive goal until 2020)	9,636,063 electronic identity cards issued against a population of around 63 million inhabitants (15.2%)
Use Open Source software	Replacement of software in use by public administrations with Open Source Software	Full use by the public administration of Open Source software (achive goal until 2020)	Datas not available (Objective has been added only in 2019)

(*continued*)

Table 2. (*continued*)

Goal	Description	Expected Results	Results achieved
Use shared structures and cloud services	Use shared databases to guarantee Open Access through "cloud" type services	Creation of national databases and shared cloud services for all public administrations	More than 27 thousand Open Data published in specific databases created by the central government (OpenBDAP, Transparent Administration, Public Money). The Italian Government has not yet estimated the Goal to Achieve
Offer citizens digital services (Citizen services, electronic invoicing, electronic health record) through new digital app such as "IO"	Complete digitalization of all services offered by the public administration in particular: electronic invoicing, electronic health record and then extending digitalization to all services aimed at citizens	Complete digital conversion of all public administration services also through the "IO" app	140 million electronic invoices to the PA and more than 1.5 billion to private ones. The Electronic Health Record is active in all regions, fully operational in 18, and covers 22% of the assisted and over 63% of the reports produced. The Io APP has not been yet realized
Establish the "broadband" on the whole Italian territory	Establish broadband (at least 30mbps per sec) throughout the Italian territory	Total coverage of the Italian territory	Percentage of coverage equal to 44% of the Italian territory

Although the results achieved seem to be positive, the comparison with the other member states of the Union of Europe appears to be somewhat unforgiving. From what emerges from the Digital Economy and Society Index (DESI), which measures the state of implementation of the Digital Agenda in European countries, Italy ranks fifth, with a delay in particular in the areas of digital skills and use of the Internet [21].

Although the gap with the others European has been eliminated for infrastructure and digitalization of the PA, there is the need to increase the effective use of technologies by citizens and businesses: Italy ranks 20th for efforts to achieve the Digital Agenda [21].

In this regard, part of the literature underlines the need to "*accelerate the switch-off of its services to citizens and businesses, enhancing collaboration or with the latter by rethinking procurement processes, experimenting with emerging technologies with prag-matism and defining digital transformation roadmaps*"(Digital Agenda Observatory, 2020).

5   A Lack of Digitialization in the Public Sector: Interviews

As is known, following the pandemic caused by Covid_19, the Italian government imposed the lockdown on the entire Italian territory from 9 March to 4 May 2019. During this period, local public administrations (municipalities) represented the contact point between the central government and citizens. To minimize contact between people, public administrations have adopted the logic of smart working: for the first time in Italian history, the public sector has had to rely almost completely on the digitalization of administrative procedures. At this stage, the shortcomings already highlighted by the Desi 2019 report have had concrete feedback on the daily activities of employees in the public sector and consequently on the services guaranteed to citizens.

Due to monitor the effects of the "lack of digitalization" in the public sector, 36 semi-structured interviews were carried out which involved 36 different managers of local authorities (municipalities) equally distributed throughout Italy (12 in the Northern area, 12 of the Center, 12 of the South) and considered as the best practices of digitalization in Italy [21]. As requested by the interviewees, in this work we will omit the names of the municipalities and managers involved in the survey, limiting ourselves to providing general information:

- All the municipalities considered are considered by the DESI 2019 report in line with the requirements of the CAD in terms of digitalization in the public service;
- The municipalities are equally distributed throughout the territory: 10 in the north, 10 in the center, 10 in the south, 6 on the islands (3 Sicily and 3 Sardinia);
- Municipalities have economic and social characteristics such that they can be compared with each other (Deidda Gagliardo, 2012).

Interviews were conducted by telephone and lasted 35 min each. The Nvivo software was used for the analysis of the interviews, the most significant data processing is shown in Table 3.

From the elaboration of the interviews, it emerged what the literature defines a lack of "trustworthiness": one of the elements that allow the transition towards the so-called smart governance is the "trust" that citizens show towards public governance and the use of digital tools and more generally trust in the use of the Internet [7].

It emerges that, even in those local authorities that during the quarantine ensured the regular performance of services for the citizen through specific smart-working methods or through mobile-phones apps (in example "Municipia") that allow the online management of certain services, part of the citizens showed a general lack of interest in the innovative ways in which municipal services were offered.

The analysis of the interviews (conducted by telephone and lasted 35 min each), conducted with NVivo, made it possible to identify clusters of "frequent words and sentences" used by the interviewees. Expressions such as "*Citizens have a lack of confidence in the services offered online"* or *"Citizens have little confidence in the use of municipal apps"* or *"Citizens prefer to contact a physical user directly rather than a virtual one"* show in fact, as even where Smart Governance appears to have been accepted by the administrations, what is lacking is a "Smart - governability" on the part of the citizens (Table 3).

Exclusively in a municipality in Northern Italy, problems have arisen related to the lack of a "broadband connection" capable of satisfying the needs of smart working (In particular the province of Bolzano has not yet even projected the possibility to realize the broadband connection and more in general unless 2349 local authorities are not in the "broadband connection") [21, 24, 25].

Table 3. Interviews analysis

Question	Word numerosity	Most significant answers
Did citizens use the digital tools deployed by your institution during the lockdown?	Lack of trust in Governance – 28 times over 36 interviews	"No as they do not trust to communicate their personal data via the App" "No as they prefer to go to the municipal offices and have direct contact with us" "no as they are afraid that the data communicated may be disseminated or manipulated"
Have citizens found the use of the municipal apps created by your institution during the lock-down to be comfortable?	Lack of trust in Internet – 26 times over 36 interviews	"No, because in some areas of the city you don't have a fast connection" "No, since they never used the app, they didn't think it could work"

6   Conclusions

What emerges from this work is a huge gap between what planned and what has been realized in the Italian public sector in terms of implementation of new technologies and digitalization to let the switch of local authorities into "smart communities" and "Smart Governance" [10].

So, answering to Rq1, while the importance of introduces new technologies even in the public sector [26, 27] seems to be clear in the "Digital Agenda" of the Italian Central

Government, at the state of art, goals are partially realized because of the gaps emerged in the literature framework cited [3] and confirmed by the report "Digitalization Main Goals 2017–2019" results achieved by AGID [21].

From the reports produced by AGICOM and AGID, it emerges that the gap generated between Italy and Europe is attributable to the failure to switch to "Smart governance" and inappropriate use of the so-called "new technologies" [6]. The partial achievement of the objectives set out in the 2017/2019 Agenda (Rq1) is attributable to a public administration that struggles in terms of Smart Governance, effectively preventing what are the minimum preconditions essential for the advent of the so-called new technologies regardless of the use for which they are intended, following the excessive bureaucratization of the Italian system [27].

The scenario described confirms what is supported by part of the international literature. Ciborra [28] holds the view that the notion of e-government on its own is not suited for developing countries to obtain the associated benefits and that instead political and social changes are required alongside the implementation of electronic mediums. Moreover, he indicates that an economy will be required to develop to a service delivery state or a minimal state, (where failures due to governance breakdown, corruption, rent seeking, distortions in markets and the absence of democracy are addressed before e-government can be im iplemented within it [27].

According with Heeks and Ciborra [3, 27, 28] it seems that in the Italian public sector scenarios, the gap between the design proposal for New eGov and the Current reality is far to be accomplished.

Moreover, when local authorities are "on time" with digitalization, interviews evidence that during the lock-down period the introduction of new digital tools such as "smart working" or specific App (Rq 2) has not positively affected the Italian Smart Governance due to a "lack of Trustworthiness" as a mix of Trust of Internet and Trust of Governance do not confirm what suggested by Carter and Bélanger [25].

So, Italy seems not ready to split into a "new technological era" pre-conditioning the possibility to introduce, in the public sectors, new elements such as "Crowdfunding" or "Business angel operation" to attract new forms of investment [25] as well as to adapt the public governance.

As far as the "new technology revolution" provided by the "Digital Agenda Goals" will not guaranteed the minimum conditions to split into an "E-governance" equally spread all over the Italian Peninsula, and the *Italian citizens state of mind and approach on digital innovations*" change, the public management dogma seems to be still the once provided by the New Public Management reform agenda "public expenditures are financed with taxes, contributes, private investments, public debt" [2].

References

1. Willke, H.: Smart Governance: Governing the Global Knowledge Society. Government Information Quarterly. The University of Chicago Press, USA (2002)
2. Hood, C.: A public administration for all seasons. Public Adm. Rev. **2**(69), 13–19 (1991)
3. Heeks, R.: Information systems and developing countries: failure, success, and local improvisations. Inf. Soc. **1**(18), 101–112 (2002)

4. Willke, H.: Smart governance: governing the global knowledge society. Gov. Inf. Q. **3**(31), 1–8 (2007)
5. Gil-Garcia, J.R., Pardo, T.A.: E-Government success factors: mapping practical tools to theoretical foundations. Gov. Inf. Q. **2**(22), 187–216 (2005)
6. Nam, T., Pardo, T.: The changing face of a city government: a case study of Philly311. Gov. Inf. Q. **1**(31), 1–9 (2014)
7. Carter, L., Bélanger, F.: The utilization of E-Government services: citizen trust, innovation acceptance factors. Info Syst. J. **3**(15), 5–25 (2005)
8. Dawes, S., Nelson, M.: Pool the risks, share the benefits: partnerships in IT innovation, technology trendlines: technology success stories from today's visionaries. ACM **1**(95), 125–135 (1995)
9. Coe, A., Paquet, G., Roy, J.: E-Governance and smart communities: a social learning challenge. Soc. Sci. Comput. Rev. **19**(1), 80–93 (2001)
10. Eger, J.: Cyberspace and cyberplace: building the smart communities of tomorrow. San Diego Union-Tribune **2**(17), 13–21 (1997)
11. Kliksberg, B.: Rebuilding the state for social development: towards "smart government." Int. Rev. Adm. Sci. **66**(2), 241–257 (2000)
12. Key, T., We, C.: Smart IT. IEEE IT Pro **27**(2), 20–23 (2009)
13. Bingham, L., Nabatchi, T., O'Leary, R.: The new governance: practices and processes for stakeholder and citizen participation in the work of government. Public Adm. Rev. **65**(5), 547–558 (2005)
14. Deidda Gagliardo, E.: La creazione del valore nell'ente locale, 1st edn Giuffrè, Milano (2012)
15. Casalino, N., Armenia, S., Medaglia, C.M., Rori, S.: A new system dynamics model to improve internal and external efficiency in the paper digitization of Italian public administrations. In: EURAM Proceedings, pp. 12–25, Roma (2010)
16. Asgarkhani, M.: Digital government and its effectiveness in public management reform. Public Manag. Rev. **3**(5), 465–487 (2009)
17. Vial, G.: Understanding digital transformation: a review and a research agenda. J. Strateg. Inf. Syst. **28**(2), 118–144 (2019)
18. Lappi, T.M., Kirsi, A., Jaakko, K.: Project governance and portfolio management in government digitalization. Transform. Gov. People Process Policy **13**(2), 159–196 (2019)
19. Nam, T.: Suggesting frameworks of citizen-sourcing via Government 2.0. Gov. Inf. Q. **29**(1), 12–20 (2012)
20. AgID: La spesa ict nella pa italiana: considerazioni sui principali trend e mappatura dei percorsi in atto, Roma (2019)
21. AgID: Piano Triennale 2019-2021 per l'informatica nella pubblica amministrazione, Roma (2019)
22. AgID: Agenda Digitale, Roma (2017)
23. AgID: Strategia per la crescita digitale 2014-2020, Roma (2014)
24. Pavlou, P.: Consumer acceptance of electronic commerce: integrating trust and risk with the technology acceptance model. Int. J. Electron. Commer. **7**, 69–103 (2003)
25. Van Slyke, C., Bélanger, F., Comunale, C.: Adopting business-to-consumer electronic commerce. The effects of trust and perceived innovation characteristics. Data Base Adv. Inf. Syst. **35**(1), 32–49 (2004)
26. Scholl, H.J., Scholl, M.C.: Smart governance: a roadmap for research and practice. In: iConference 2014 Proceedings, pp. 163–176, iSchools, Illinois (2014)
27. Heeks, R.: Most egovernment-for-development projects fail: how can risks be reduced? iGov. Work. Pap. Ser. **14**(1), 13–27 (2003)
28. Ciborra, C., Navarra, D.: Good governance, development theory, and aid policy: risks and challenges of E-Government in Jordan. Inf. Technol. Dev. **11**(2), 141–159 (2005)

A Framework to Achieve Cybersecurity Accountability of Critical Infrastructure Providers – A Design Science Research Approach

Barbara Krumay[1(✉)] ⓘ, Edward W. N. Bernroider[2] ⓘ, and Roman Walser[2] ⓘ

[1] JKU Linz, Science Park 3 – 1, Altenberger Straße 69, 4040 Linz, Austria
`barbara.krumay@jku.at`
[2] WU Vienna, Building D2, Entrance C, Welthandelsplatz 1/D2/C, 1020 Vienna, Austria
`{edward.bernroider,roman.walser}@wu.ac.at`

Abstract. Today's pervasive use of information systems (IS) not only comes with many opportunities but also with considerable risks especially in relation to cyberattacks, which become increasingly sophisticated and dangerous. Especially organizations providing critical infrastructures are at risk, which are held to account by governments to ensure sufficient protection. Governments request information to monitor cybersecurity levels of critical infra-structure providers over time, which are today subject to respective nation-wide legislation in developed economies. Following guidelines of design science research, this study offers a generic framework that supports continuous monitoring and benchmarking of an organization's cybersecurity status. It is generic allowing application by different critical infrastructure providers and usage by government institutions to help achieve oversight of the nation-al cybersecurity status. Our design proposition is supported by an extensive review of academic literature, the consultation of relevant industry standards, and two main rounds of field interactions. The framework includes 15 major risk areas, and a collection of associated metrics and controls, which cover material and social mechanisms. We would like to note that our domain of study would require more design work that targets knowledge accumulation spanning academic research and industry practice.

Keywords: Cybersecurity · Critical infrastructures · Design science research

1 Introduction

The ubiquitous use of information systems (IS) has changed the world as a whole. We depend on IS in our daily life as governments and societies rely on IS in many ways. Not surprisingly, IS are particularly threatened by attacks from the cyberspace and therefore require adequate protection [1]. From the viewpoint of governments, a special group of organizations, called critical infrastructure providers, are of particular importance to the society, such as hospitals, energy providers, and internet service providers [2, 3]. These organizations need to operate on external accountability [4]. Meaning, critical infrastructure providers are held to account to implement the required measures to improve cybersecurity and also report on their current state of cybersecurity. Such measures, however, are manifold and exist in a vast number, either as stand-alone measures or as part of well-established frameworks, guidelines or standards. What is more, existing frameworks and standards seem to run short in specifically helping such organizations to assess how well they are prepared to protect against cyberattacks [5]. In this study, supported by a governmental funding scheme, we therefore aimed at developing a framework to help these organizations to assess their current cybersecurity status and to ensure those insights can be used by the government to gain oversight about the nationwide cybersecurity status of critical infrastructures.

Specifically, our objectives were to (i) to design and test a framework that can help to provide transparency in terms of the preparedness of critical infrastructure providers against cyberattacks, (ii) which allows for combining the results of all participating organizations applying the framework. The former objective (i) is internally oriented to allow organizations, in particular critical infrastructure providers, to assess their cybersecurity status regarding their main risk areas. For this purpose, we focused on assessing threats, vulnerabilities and their level of preparedness. The second objective (ii) is externally oriented and should allow governmental authorities to compile the information into a landscape showing and comparing the status of cybersecurity among critical infrastructure providers. The scope of factors considered was intentionally not limited to technical perspectives, but also includes additional social and contextual (e.g. environmental) aspects, which are likely to have an influence on cybersecurity.

In terms of methodology, we followed a design science research (DSR) approach [6, 7]. We started with a structured literature review to identify indicators related to our assessment related objectives in relation to cybersecurity. Based on this and further empirical sources and methods (i.e. workshops, focus groups), we designed and evaluated the framework in multiple iterations. Additionally, we observed how experts from the field (i.e., security experts from business) were able to apply the framework in practice and observed them while operating it.

2   Conceptual Background

2.1   Cybercrime and Cyberattacks

Hardly any organization has not fallen victim to attacks out of the cyberspace, and even private people are not untroubled by such attacks. The resulting costs for the society seem to be enormous, however, hard to measure [8, 9]. Of course, cybercrime is a complex phenomenon, as it is global with no boundaries, it is innovative, as cybercriminals seem always to be one step ahead and it is ubiquitous, as it may target and compromise any computer [2, 3, 8, 10]. New technologies and services, such as the Internet of Things (IoT), cloud computing, blockchain or smart grids [11–13] increase the complexity of protection, as newly adopted technologies are less proven and thus often more vulnerable. Besides, terms like cyberterrorism or cyber espionage [14] blur the understanding of what cybercrime is. Cybercrime covers "different criminal activities where computers and IS are involved either as a primary tool or as a primary target" [15]. Cybercrime reflects on one hand traditional crime (e.g., theft, fraud, discrimination), often with a specific IS-related component (e.g., theft of cryptocurrency) but also crime uniquely related to IS and the infrastructure of such (e.g., distributed denial of service attacks, malware, ransomware) [15–17]. Since computers have become ubiquitous and smart systems control substantial parts of the production, logistics and industrial systems [18–20], the number of targets is constantly growing. Cyberterrorism is mainly related to bringing down the infrastructure of a nation to put pressure on a government, but could also occur with terroristic intentions [14, 15]. Recent statistics show that attacks from cyberspace against different targets have not only increased in quantity, but also in severity [21]. Cyberattacks, defined as any "deliberate actions to alter, disrupt, deceive, degrade, or destroy computer systems or networks or the information and/or programs resident in or transiting these systems or networks" [22], try to exploit vulnerabilities of organizations on different levels. Vulnerabilities in this context have been defined as "a weakness in design, implementation, operation or internal control" [23]. This definition seems to focus mainly on the technical level, such as built-in software and hardware problems [24, 25]. However, the individual (personal) level is at least equally important since flourishing techniques such as social engineering and phishing make use of limited knowledge, low awareness and laxness regarding cybersecurity issues [26–29].

2.2 Cybersecurity and Risk Management

Measures to fight cybercrime are often subsumed under the term cybersecurity or information security. However, it has been argued that the difference between the two is the human dimension: in information security, the human factor is bound to the process, whereas cybersecurity integrates human beings as targets that have to be protected [30]. According to the International Telecommunications Union (ITU), "cybersecurity is the collection of tools, policies, security concepts, security safeguards, guidelines, risk management approaches, actions, training, best practices, assurance and technologies that can be used to protect the cyber environment and organization and user's asset" [31]. As this is a very holistic definition, it covers not only technological but also social, organizational and legal aspects. Therefore, it is necessary to form activities addressing these threats in a holistic way, covering relevant social, organizational and legal aspects. The NIST framework further divides activities into different groups: "Identify, Protect, Detect, Respond, Recover" [32]. It can be argued that these activities show a chronological relationship with cyberattacks, in particular pre-attack (prepare, prevent, deter, identify), during the attack (protect, defend, respond) and post-attack (repair, recover) activities. The framework AVOIDIT differentiates attacks according to their attack vector, operational impact, defense, informational impact and target [33]. An often-used approach is to identify activities in relation to confidentiality, integrity and availability of information [34]. Besides the already mentioned NIST framework, other frameworks aim to support organizations in handling the complexity of information security and cybersecurity management. The ISO 2700x family [35] is a widely adopted framework with standards for implementing an information security management system to measure, analyze and evaluate information security issues and activities. In central Europe and German-speaking countries, in particular, the so-called BSI IT baseline protection ("Grundschutzkatalog") [36] was the de-facto standard methodology to identify and implement computer security measures in organizations for a long time. Anyway, a more holistic approach is needed to handle the increasingly challenging task of assuring a reasonable level of cybersecurity. With regard to technical threats, numerous measures are reflected by frameworks and applied by professionals, from encryption to access management, from firewalls to software updates. Putting the human being as a major 'weak point' more into focus, awareness building activities and training seem to be the appropriate approach [28, 37]. What the frameworks have in common is the idea of measuring indicators to be able to manage the challenges [1]. This is a challenging endeavor, as IS highly depend on and influence each other, hence testing and assessing where the problem is, is a complex task [9]. Again, frameworks and guidelines provide metrics or so-called Key Risk Indicators, which should be selected based on distinct criteria such as impact, effort to implement, measure and report, reliability and sensitivity [23]. However, measuring or assessing the organizations' cybersecurity status is also a precondition for calculating their risk. In the current version of ISO 31000, risk is described as "effects of uncertainty on objectives" [9]. An often stressed basic formula for calculating risk is the combination of likelihood times consequences [38]. Regarding cybersecurity, the relationship between threats and vulnerabilities and factors like consequences, asset value or likelihood and impact on the organization [39–42]. Besides assessing the risk level, there are several ways to cope with risk, such as risk avoidance, risk reduction or mitigation, risk-sharing or transfer as well as risk acceptance [23]. In the NIST Special Publication 800–30, risk mitigation is defined as "a systematic methodology used by senior management to reduce mission risk" [41]. The possibilities include risk assumption, avoidance, limitation, planning, transference as well as research and acknowledgment [41]. Whereas most of the risk mitigation possibilities are clearly within the scope of organizations, transferring and sharing risks extend the scope beyond the companies' boarders. On one hand, it integrates supply chain partners for sharing the risk, on the other risk insurances have become a common instrument of transferring risks [43, 44]. Summing up, organizations have to invest in cybersecurity activities on all levels – hardware, software, and employee - to reduce IS vulnerabilities [45].

2.3   Critical Infrastructure

Although cybersecurity is an issue for all organizations, it becomes a menace to the public when attacks negatively impact infrastructure supporting our daily life, such as power grids [46], hospitals [47], or smart cities [48]. This shift from a rather company or micro-level to a wider and global macro level induced governments but also organizations like the European Union to strengthen their efforts towards fighting cyberattacks, in particular when threatening critical infrastructure providers [49–51]. What defines a critical infrastructure is its importance for a nation when failure or reduction of service may menace security, economy, public health or safety [5, 32]. This includes energy (electricity, oil and gas), transport, banking, financial market infrastructures, healthcare, water supply as well as digital infrastructure such as internet exchange points [5]. Organizations – obliged to it or not - follow these frameworks in order to establish their internal cybersecurity activities and risk management. In our further examination, we focus on the two already mentioned directives, published by the US government and the European Commission due to their importance. The NIST Cybersecurity Framework has first been published in 2014, the current version (1.1) dates back to April 2018, aiming at supporting providers of critical infrastructures to handle cybersecurity-related issues holistically [32]. Consisting of best practices, standards and guidelines for appropriate action, it has soon been adopted not only by providers of critical infrastructures but also IT and security professionals in general [52]. The NIST framework comprises of five functions (identify, protect, detect, respond, recover), consisting of 23 categories and 108 subcategories, structuring activities in accordance with the functions. In Europe, on the other hand, the European Union had published the so-called EU NIS Directive on cybersecurity in 2016, which had to be implemented by Member States 2018 [5]. It obliges providers of critical infrastructures to continuously monitor threats from cyberspace, assess imminent risks and implement according technical and organizational activities to secure their IS. The NIS Directive sets goals on three levels, in particular increased cooperation at EU-level, improved cybersecurity capabilities at the national level, as well as the implementation of incident reporting and risk management obligations for providers of critical infrastructures at the organization level. The derivative duty of the national government includes identifying providers of critical infrastructures (by November 2018) and improving their cybersecurity capabilities. This is, of course, a very complex endeavor, as the basis are the organizations doing business in the country, and their internal and external circumstances, interdependencies and not at least IS are heterogeneous. Breaking it down to the organizational level, as requested by the NIS Directive [5] means requesting providers of critical infrastructures to measure their cybersecurity status based on specific criteria. At the most detailed level, this means measuring activities' performance in absolute (e.g., number of employees entrusted with security activities), relational (e.g., number of attacks per device) or time-related (e.g., money spent on security issues per year) indicators, be they monetarized or not. They have to be aggregated and reported to the according governmental or non-governmental point to allow for a further assessment of the nation's current cybersecurity status.

3 Methodology

As the goal of this study is to design and test a framework to allow organizations considered as critical infrastructure providers to assess their cybersecurity status, a Design Science Research (DSR) approach was an appropriate choice [6, 53]. The so-developed framework can be considered an artifact based on design as the research maxim, being relevant, as it is designed to solve real-world problems and rigorous, as it is rooted in the existing knowledge base [6, 53]. This requires iterative circles of design and evaluation regarding validity, utility, quality and efficacy [53]. In our problem-centered approach, we adopted the well-established six-step DSR process proposed by Peffers et al. [7]. The six steps include problem identification and motivation (step 1), definition of objectives for a solution (step 2), design and development (step 3), demonstration (step 4), evaluation (step 5) and communication (step 6) [7]. The research process involved different sources and methods, developing two different versions of the framework, both through several iterations within each sub-process. However, for the sake of clarity, we describe the first iteration (for developing framework V1) and second iteration (for developing framework V2) in a linear way. Iteration 1 mainly covers the first four steps in the process and involves a structured literature review of academic sources, resulting in more than 50 academic sources related to the topic. Next, we analyzed documents from non-academic sources (standards, guidelines, regulations). This rich knowledge set was the foundation for a workshop with ten participants from different fields (i.e., academia (3), private research institution (4), representatives of the ministry (1), security experts from business (2)), with the aim to develop the first version of the framework. In the workshop, we used the term impact area, which is defined for this study as the interrelationship between metrics and controls for specific cybersecurity issues. In addition, the consequences of impact areas for the organization or society are at least on medium level. Next, we identified three dimensions – (A) hardware and software supplier or manufacturer, (B) provider of critical infrastructure, (C) government – reflecting the context or to be more precise, who can influence the context or is most directly influenced by it. For example, the impact area 'Cyberwarfare' is related mainly to the government. Overall, 40 different impact areas were defined in this first iteration. However, in the workshop, the experts came to the conclusion that the framework should focus on impact areas influencing dimension B - the critical infrastructure provider - directly. Based on the result of the workshop, iteration 2 required going back to the literature and reflecting our findings. In parallel, we started the process of mapping and further defining the impact areas. We split up the impact areas into four groups and assigned each of it to two team members of the funded project. After four weeks, we discussed the results and designed a refined draft of the impact areas regarding definitions and indicators. Next, we conducted two focus groups with five to six experts. In the first focus group, we aimed at selecting impact areas with medium to high consequences, leading to 15 impact areas and assigned according indicators from academic and non-academic literature to it. In the second focus group, we demonstrated the 15 impact areas and tested it regarding utility, reliability, validity and efficacy. Although this testing is normally related to evaluation [53], we decided to integrate it into the demonstration step, but to retest it during the evaluation. Results from the focus groups were used to further shape the framework. None of the impact areas had to be excluded, but definitions and indicators were adopted. Another result from the focus groups was a discussion about who is applying the framework, as not all indicators may be assessed correctly on all levels of people involved. Therefore, the following roles were designed: Chief Executive Officer (CEO), Chief Information Security Officer (CISO), IT technician and auditor. In accordance with role descriptions, indicator sets were assigned to the impact areas per role. For example, business-related indicators such as the assessment of monetary aspects of cybersecurity issues are assigned to the roles of CEO, cybersecurity management indicators are assigned to CISO whereas indicators covering technical issues such as downtime of a system to the role of the IT security expert or the technician. The auditor role has been assigned more or less with the same indicators as the CISO, but from an external perspective. As the final step in this iteration, we invited experts from academia and business to apply the second version of the framework, observed them and conducted a post-hoc interview based on an interview guideline. We were aiming at balancing experts from academia and business per role, resulting in nine experts (Table 1). First, the participants received a short introduction including a declaration of confidentiality and the information that they will be observed. They were asked to express verbally what comes to their mind while applying the framework. This so-called think-aloud method provides more information compared to standard observations [54]. Verbally expressed thoughts as well as the whole process were documented by the observer in an observation protocol. After this, a post-hoc interview based on a rough interview guideline was conducted to further evaluate utility, reliability, validity and efficacy of the framework with according questions, such as comprehensibility, completeness, balance to name just some. Some minor changes evolved from this step (e.g., shorten long sentences), but the framework in general had not to be changed. The so-evaluated framework has already been communicated to various stakeholders as the national government, security experts and stakeholders in general.

Table 1. Participants in the evaluation step (5) in the DSR process [7]

Role	Sex	Age	From	Expertise in years
Auditor	Male	20+	Academia	2 years **
Auditor	Female	40+	Business	5 years
Technician	Male	30+	Business	7 years
Technician	Male	30+	Business	7 years
Technician	Male	50+	Academia	15 years
CEO	Male	30+	Academia	3 years *
CEO	Female	30+	Business	2 years
CISO	Male	30+	Academia	7 years
CISO	Male	40+	Business	12 years

* Interview via skype, ** self-reported

4   Results

As one key result of the above described DSR process, the designed and tested framework consists of 15 identified impact areas with potentially medium to severe consequences for critical infrastructure providers (see Table 2 with definitions). For an effective application of the framework and to strengthen its reliability, a common understanding of these impact areas among the stakeholders and security experts in the respective critical infrastructure provider is required. The assessment regarding organizations' cybersecurity status relies on indicators able to reflect an impact area (IA). In the framework, we differentiate between metrics and controls. Metrics are linked to threats and vulnerabilities, thus often defined by a lack of or something missing. Furthermore, it is something that can be measured (quantitatively or qualitatively) by comparing it to a reference point [55]. For example, in impact area 1 'Negligent Use' the slow or non-acceptance of cybersecurity policies by employees [56, 57] is such a metric related to a reference point in time, expressed in a rather qualitative, descriptive way (e.g., immediately, fast, medium-fast, slow, no acceptance). This metric indicates that such behavior makes the company vulnerable. A set of metrics, related to an impact area, can be used to assess the current threat and vulnerability status regarding this area. By contrast, controls are safeguards or countermeasures [58], which should be in place to mitigate risks in each impact area and can also be assessed to judge the preparedness of organizations. Controls are related to risk management covering different types of measures such as policies [58]. To give an example, establishing a process to revoke access rights when the status of an employee requiring access to a system has changed [59, 60] is a control related to impact area 1, as it fights negligent use. We consulted leading industry practice frameworks to support the initial selection of metrics and controls. However, we also added other sources, e.g. from academic literature, where appropriate. Interestingly, some impact areas are completely covered by one or two frameworks, (e.g. IA 3 fully covered by the BSI IT baseline protection framework [36]). The most prominent frameworks are the ISO 2700x family [35, 61, 62], the BSI IT baseline protection [36] and the NIST frameworks [32]. Particularly interesting is IA 11 as it is informed solely by academic literature. Table 2 gives examples of according metrics and controls, and their main sources. In our analysis, we used far more sources, however, due to page restrictions we just provide the most relevant ones. As already described, we processed metrics and control in conjunction with the identified roles (CEO, CISO, Technician, Auditor). The number of indicators (metrics, controls) assigned to impact areas and roles varies, e.g. the CEO, CISO and technician roles were assigned to 5, 11 and again 11 controls for IA 13, respectively. The CISO received the main load with 70 metrics and 97 controls.

5   Discussion

The aim of this study was to develop and test a comprehensive framework that allows critical infrastructure providers to evaluate and report their cybersecurity status in a way that allows governmental agencies to further process results to provide a nationwide assessment. The focus was on identifying the main risk areas and relate these with most common threats and vulnerabilities as well as capturing levels of organizational preparedness. Relying on a DSR approach, we based our framework on academic and non-academic sources (standards, guidelines, regulations), conducted workshops and consulted professionals through an iterative approach, which resulted in a holistic set of 15 risk areas (termed impact areas) with related metrics and controls. As intended, the framework can be used by organizations to assess and monitor their cybersecurity status, and by governments to build a 'landscape' of the current cybersecurity situation based on aggregating these organizational applications. It would also allow organizations to cooperate and create benchmarks of their individual performance as compared to other market operators. Thus, our framework serves as an innovative generic design for such evaluations, which is also seen as a pre-condition for DSR studies. The framework was also well-tested and documented thoroughly to allow for such an intended application in the given cybersecurity domain. Our results indicate that the final framework design is sufficiently stable in terms of utility, reliability, validity and efficacy. We, thus, contribute to research and practice, especially to national legislators in terms of obtaining and compiling the relevant data to hold critical infrastructure providers to account for their performance in the context of cybersecurity.

Table 2. Definition of impact areas - * refers to parts not or only partly covered by NIS/NIST

Impact Area (IA)/Definition	Metrics (M)/Controls (C)
IA 1: Negligent use: Lacking or inadequate diligence when using IS (examples: insecure passwords, opening spam emails)	M: the slow or non-acceptance of cybersecurity policies by employees * [36, 57]/C: establishing a process to revoke access rights when employees' status has changed [32, 36, 57, 59–61]
IA 2: Lack of prioritization and focus regarding cybersecurity activities: Lacking awareness (knowledge) of responsible actors regarding what has to be protected or how high the probability of certain threats is as well as ranking risks by their severity, hindering the organization to prioritize cybersecurity activities in a reasonable way for assigning resources and capabilities appropriately	M: a well-defined cybersecurity strategy is missing [32, 35, 61]/C: resources to develop a cybersecurity strategy exist [32, 35, 61, 62]
IA 3: Lacking general cybersecurity awareness: A general lack of awareness and knowledge regarding threats and attack vectors. In addition, the knowledge regarding appropriate and effective handling of such challenges is missing	M: no cybersecurity training specifically designed for the needs of the target group * [36]/C: cybersecurity trainings, specifically designed for the target groups, are conducted on a regular basis * [36]
IA 4: Insufficient awareness and appreciation regarding external cybersecurity situation: Knowledge, information or technical resources, processes and capabilities for developing a clear appreciation regarding the external cybersecurity situation is missing. This hinders the organization from reproducing and assessing the external situation	M: no structured analysis of incidents or attacks, affecting the organization or other organizations in the same industry [32, 35, 61, 62]/C: a defined process for the exchange of knowledge and experience with other experts or computer emergency response teams (CERTs) exists [32, 35, 61]
IA 5: Missing or insufficient Business Continuity Management (BCM): The insufficient preparation to handle possible damaging events, as the goal of BCM of an organization is to be back to normal business conduct as fast as possible (also often referred to the term disaster recovery)	M: defined responsibilities and list of involved parties for business continuity management processes are missing [36] */C: well-defined business continuity management processes and measures exist [32, 63]

(*continued*)

Table 2. (*continued*)

Impact Area (IA)/Definition	Metrics (M)/Controls (C)
IA 6: Insufficient attack recognition: The lack of capabilities to recognize in time attempt or successful malicious activates (i.e., cyberattacks) against the organization to be able to react appropriately with the according countermeasures (often subsumed under the term incident response)	M: last year attempted attacks have been recognized very late [36] */C: network traffic is continuously monitored using a software [36, 61] *
IA 7: Legacy systems: IS, which exist due to historical reasons although they are outdated, deprecated and not further supported by the manufacturer (vulnerable against new threats, as security updates by the manufacturer are not provided)	M: critical business processes depend on legacy systems [35, 61, 64] */C: a list of all legacy systems (incl. possible threats) exists [35, 61, 62, 64]
IA 8: Natural catastrophes: Massive natural catastrophes such as floods, earthquakes or fires threaten the infrastructure of IS	M: no emergency plan in case the infrastructure (in particular the data center) is not available due to a natural catastrophe [57, 65, 66] */C: concepts for backup and restore are constantly adopted in the business impact analysis considering impacts of natural catastrophes on IS [57, 65, 66] *
IA 9: Changes in the ownership structure: Changes in the ownership structure may push cybersecurity activities in the background leading to a decrease of investments and unclear responsibilities	M: changes in the ownership structure may hinder the continuation of cybersecurity processes [67–69]/C: the systems have been prioritized to allow appropriate continuity in case of changes in the ownership structure [67–69]
IA 10: Social engineering: Target towards exploiting interpersonal relationships to evoke a specific behavior, in particular, insecure activities to undermine existing cybersecurity policies and precautionary measures	M: employees are not familiar with the common social engineering techniques and attack vectors * [36]/C: technical measure to prevent social engineering attacks established * [36]
IA 11: Misuse of digital identities: Misusing digital identities (i.e., user accounts) facilitate unauthorized access to IS and malicious activities by using the identity of the betrayed user	M: no processes established to force secure passwords [40, 70] */C: least privileges principle established * [36, 40, 61, 70]
IA 12: Unavailability of systems: Distributed denial of service (DDoS) attacks make service unavailable to regular users or reduce their availability	M: no technologies in place to automatically fight DDoS attacks * [36]/ C: sufficient resources are provided to detect, fight and overcome DDoS attacks * [36, 61]

(*continued*)

Table 2. (*continued*)

Impact Area (IA)/Definition	Metrics (M)/Controls (C)
IA 13: Data theft or data manipulation: Data theft leads to loss of confidentiality whereas data manipulation degrades the integrity of data, hence both compromise two main goals of cybersecurity	M: there were data leaks in the last year [35, 61, 64]/C: there is an insurance covering possible risks evolving from data theft and data manipulation [35, 61, 62, 71]
IA 14: Cyber espionage: Politically or ideologically motivated attacks, technically very mature, aim at eavesdrop or wiretap data with high strategical relevance (e.g., business secrets) to gain strategic advantage	M: there have been watering hole attacks with the goal to steal valuable information in the last year [35, 61] */C: there is a strategy to fight cyber espionage accompanied by appropriate measures [32, 35, 61, 62, 64]
IA 15: Cybercrime: Illicit activities conducted via or on information technology and networks. IS foster as an instrument to conduct illegal activities and increase their distribution as well as elicit exponential material or non-material damage	M: there had been incidents relating into ransomware infection last year [61] */C: trainings on a regular base with all employees to increase awareness regarding cybersecurity issues * [35, 61, 62, 71]

Regarding research, the framework adds to the existing literature by providing a compilation of various sources of knowledge, initially informed by a structured literature review. Although we found overlapping contents between well-known frameworks such as NIST and the German BSI IT baseline, we could identify some relevant aspects that were only covered in the academic body of knowledge. Obviously, the impact areas cover technological and social (or individual) issues, yet social issues seem to dominate over pure technical issues. In almost all impact areas, metrics and controls related to social issues can be found. Especially, metrics regarding the lack of training (IA 3, IA 10), awareness (IA 2, IA 3, IA 15) and knowledge (IA 2, IA 3) are important. On the other hand, controls addressing the individual level (training, awareness, knowledge) characterize many impact areas (IA 2 - IA 5, IA 10, IA 11, IA 15). The framework, thus, is consistent with the notion that the human being is becoming the focus of holistic cybersecurity approaches [72], is equally important, in particular the time needed to comply. This has already been discussed in research and considers factors influencing the adoption process such as clear language, up-to-date policies and access to the documents [57]. Regarding the impact areas, we were surprised to find that some of them were not reflected in the well-known practice frameworks but discussed in the literature, in particular natural catastrophes (IA 8) and change in the ownership structure (IA 9). Both have been suggested by prior work [57, 65–68] with a clear focus on the negative effects they might have on the providers of critical infrastructures. Natural catastrophes threaten the facilities and infrastructure of organizations; thus, they should be a vital part of cybersecurity activities to protect IS.

Regarding contributions to practice, we seek to emphasize two key results. Firstly, the well-established standards used in practice do not cover all our identified impact areas completely. As already discussed above, natural catastrophes and changes in ownership structure are two under-documented examples, which all consulted experts from business and the officials of the national government classified as being especially important although not directly cyber-related. Additionally, other impact areas were mainly covered by metrics and controls from academic literature, for example IA 1 and IA 11. Our framework, thus, integrates knowledge from academic research to help to solve our field problem. Secondly, by assessing the number of metrics and controls and putting them into relation to roles, which strengthens responsibility, it became clear that the CISO occupies a particularly important position in this context. This role which combines managerial and technical tasks contributes to the application of the framework more than the technician. The high number of controls (97) assigned to the CISO reflects the importance of this role for the successful implementation and execution of cybersecurity controls. Thus, the CISO can be seen as mainly responsible for the cybersecurity preparedness of an organization.

Finally, in terms of legislation and policymaking, the framework may serve as a blueprint or starting point for governing cybersecurity assessments across the critical infrastructure sector. It suggests the key impact areas and their assessment mechanisms (metrics and controls) to strengthen cybersecurity and its awareness in a country. While the fifteen impact areas seem to define an adequate scope for developing a landscape of the cybersecurity situation among critical infrastructure providers, they are also generic enough to be of value to other organizations.

6   Conclusion, Limitations and Further Research

From the perspective of design science research (DSR), we designed and tested an innovative and well-documented framework consisting of impact areas and their associated metrics and controls, which can be applied by different types of organizations (and operators of critical infrastructures in particular) to assess their cybersecurity situation. Moreover, it can be used as a guideline by governmental institutions to generate national oversight and allow for comparison of different industries' level of cybersecurity. We thereby provide a design science research proposition covering a field problem (prevention of cybercrime and cyberattacks), a design artifact (the developed framework), expected outcomes (assessed and controlled cybersecurity and risk management), and the material and social mechanisms (implementation of metrics and controls covering social and technical issues, including roles and responsibilities) providing these outcomes in our domain of study.

We developed and tested an artifact to address the need of protection of IS that are threatened by attacks from cyberspace, which provides a generic answer on how to accomplish the comprehensive assessment and ongoing monitoring of cybersecurity and related risk management. The contribution of a generic design can be considered as a key requirement of DSR, which in our case was also a mandatory research condition for this study. We based the development and testing of the framework on the six-step DSR process proposed by Peffers et al. [7]. In particular, we used the relevant bodies of literature and standards provided by academia and practice to provide the foundation of the framework, which we amended and corroborated through fieldwork including two main developments and testing iterations. We thus produced a saturated body of evidence supporting the framework. The included metrics and controls shed insights not only on the material (technical) but also on social mechanisms needed to produce the assessment outcomes. Our work is therefore highly relevant in practical and academic terms. It should be stated that our empirical data is limited to one central European country. Although we do not see any deviating cybersecurity requirements as compared to any other developed country, additional empirical insights at a larger scale might be insightful. We are aware that assessing metrics and controls in binary format (yes or no) hinders a more fine-grained assessment. However, we deliberately refrained from a more sophisticated assessment to increase usability. In terms of future research, it would be interesting investigating the role of company characteristics such as size or age in the context of metrics and controls. We would like to note that our domain of study would require more work which targets the daunting process of knowledge accumulation across perspectives and rests on the pair of shoulders incorporating both, academic research and industry practice.

Acknowledgements. This study was funded by the KIRAS Security Program of the National Austrian Research Promotion Agency (FFG) as part of the project CRISCROSS (No. 10652570).

References

1. Krumay, B., Bernroider, E.W.N., Walser, R.: Evaluation of cybersecurity management controls and metrics of critical infrastructures: a literature review considering the NIST cybersecurity framework. In: Gruschka, N. (ed.) NordSec 2018. LNCS, vol. 11252, pp. 369–384. Springer, Cham (2018). https://doi.org/10.1007/978-3-030-03638-6_23
2. European Political Strategy Centre: Building an Effective European Cyber Shield. p. 16 (2017)
3. The Whitehouse: International Strategy for Cyberspace. Prosperity, Security, and Openness in a Networked World. The President of the United States Washington, DC (2011)
4. Hall, A.T., Bowen, M.G., Ferris, G.R., Royle, M.T., Fitzgibbons, D.E.: The accountability lens: a new way to view management issues. Bus. Horiz. **50**, 405–413 (2007)
5. European Commission: The Directive on Security of Network and Information Systems (NIS Directive). In: Union, O.J.o.t.E. (ed.), vol. L194, pp. 1–30 (2018)
6. Hevner, A.R.: A three cycle view of design science research. Scand. J. Inf. Syst. **19**, 4 (2007)
7. Peffers, K., Rothenberger, M., Tuunanen, T., Vaezi, R.: Design science research evaluation. In: Peffers, K., Rothenberger, M., Kuechler, B. (eds.) DESRIST 2012. LNCS, vol. 7286, pp. 398–410. Springer, Heidelberg (2012). https://doi.org/10.1007/978-3-642-29863-9_29
8. Anderson, R., et al.: Measuring the cost of cybercrime. In: Böhme, R. (ed.) The Economics of Information Security and Privacy, pp. 265–300. Springer, Heidelberg (2013). https://doi.org/10.1007/978-3-642-39498-0_12
9. Pfleeger, S.L., Cunningham, R.K.: Why measuring security is hard. IEEE Secur. Priv. **8**, 46–54 (2010)
10. Kraemer-Mbula, E., Tang, P., Rush, H.: The cybercrime ecosystem: online innovation in the shadows? Technol. Forecast. Soc. Chang. **80**, 541–555 (2013)
11. Weber, R.H.: Internet of Things - new security and privacy challenges. Comput. Law Secur. Rev. **26**, 23–30 (2010)
12. Khurana, H., Hadley, M., Lu, N., Frincke, D.A.: Smart-grid security issues. IEEE Secur. Priv. **8**, 81–85 (2010)

13. Kandukuri, B.R., Paturi, R.V., Rakshit, A.: Cloud security issues. In: 2009 IEEE International Conference on Services Computing, pp. 517–520. IEEE (2009)
14. Lewis, J.A.: Assessing the risks of cyber terrorism, cyber war and other cyber threats. Center for Strategic & International Studies Washington, DC (2002)
15. European Commission: Cybersecurity Strategy of the European Union: An Open, Safe and Secure Cyberspace. In: European Commission (ed.) (2013)
16. Chohan, U.W.: The problems of cryptocurrency thefts and exchange shutdowns. Available at SSRN 3131702 (2018)
17. Lau, F., Rubin, S.H., Smith, M.H., Trajkovic, L.: Distributed denial of service attacks. In: 2000 IEEE International Conference on Systems, Man and Cybernetics, pp. 2275–2280. IEEE (2000)
18. Cherdantseva, Y., et al.: A review of cyber security risk assessment methods for SCADA systems. Comput. Secur. **56**, 1–27 (2016)
19. Knowles, W., Prince, D., Hutchison, D., Disso, J.F.P., Jones, K.: A survey of cyber security management in industrial control systems. Int. J. Crit. Infrastruct. Prot. **9**, 52–80 (2015)
20. Humayed, A., Lin, J., Li, F., Luo, B.: Cyber-physical systems security - a survey. IEEE Internet Things J. **4**, 1802–1831 (2017)
21. Cybercrime Magazine. https://cybersecurityventures.com/cybercrime-damages-6-trillion-by-2021/. Accessed 15 July 2019
22. Hathaway, O.A., et al.: The law of cyber-attack. Calif. Law Rev. **100**, 817–886 (2012)
23. ISACA: The Risk IT Framework. ISACA (2009)
24. Rostami, M., Koushanfar, F., Karri, R.: A primer on hardware security: models, methods, and metrics. Proc. IEEE **102**, 1283–1295 (2014)
25. Bishop, M.: What is computer security? IEEE Secur. Priv. **1**, 67–69 (2003)
26. Jagatic, T.N., Johnson, N.A., Jakobsson, M., Menczer, F.: Social phishing. Commun. ACM **50**, 94–100 (2007)
27. Krombholz, K., Hobel, H., Huber, M., Weippl, E.: Advanced social engineering attacks. J. Inform. Secur. Appl. **22**, 113–122 (2015)
28. Bauer, S., Bernroider, E.W.: From information security awareness to reasoned compliant action: analyzing information security policy compliance in a large banking organization. ACM SIGMIS Database: DATABASE Adv. Inform. Syst. **48**, 44–68 (2017)
29. Tadda, G.P.: Measuring performance of cyber situation awareness systems. Air Force Research Laboratory (2008)
30. von Solms, R., van Niekerk, J.: From information security to cyber security. Comput. Secur. **38**, 97–102 (2013)
31. International Telecommunications Union: Series X: Data networks, Open System Communcations and Security - Telecommunication Security, Overview of Cybersecurity. (2008)
32. NIST CSF National Institute of Standards and Technology: Framework for Improving Critical Infrastructure Cybersecurity Version 1.1. In: Technology; N.N.I.o.S.a. (ed.) (2018)
33. Simmons, C., Ellis, C., Shiva, S., Dasgupta, D., Wu, Q.: AVOIDIT: a cyber attack taxonomy. In: 9th Annual Symposium on Information Assurance (ASIA 2014), pp. 2–12. (2014)
34. Samonas, S., Coss, D.: The CIA strikes back: redefining confidentiality, integrity and availability in security. J. Inform. Syst. Secur. **10**, 21–45 (2014)
35. International Organization for Standardization: ISO/IEC27001:2013. Information technology – Security Techniques – Information Security Management Systems – Requirements. ISO, International Organization for Standardization (2013)
36. Bundesamt für Sicherheit in der Informationstechnik: IT-Grundschutz-Katalog. In: BSI, Bundesamt für Sicherheit in der Informationstechnik (ed.) 15. Ergänzungslieferung. BSI, Bundesamt für Sicherheit in der Informationstechnik (2016)
37. Furnell, S.M., Gennatou, M., Haskell-Dowland, P.: A prototype tool for information security awareness and training. Logist. Inf. Manag. **15**, 352–357 (2002)

38. International Organization for Standardization: ISO 31000 - Risk management. International Standardization Organization (2018)
39. Azuwa, M., Ahmad, R., Sahib, S., Shamsuddin, S.: Technical security metrics model in compliance with ISO/IEC 27001 standard. Int. J. Cyber-Secur. Digit. Forensics (IJCSDF) **1**, 280–288 (2012)
40. Jouini, M., Rabai, L.B.A., Aissa, A.B.: Classification of security threats in information systems. Proc. Comput. Sci. **32**, 489–496 (2014)
41. Stoneburner, G., Goguen, A., Feringa, A.: Risk management guide for information technology systems recommendations of the national institute of standards and technology NIST special publication 800-30 In: Computer Security Division (ed.) National Institute of Standards and Technology, Washington (2002)
42. ASME Innovative Technologies Institute: All-hazards Risk and Resilience: Prioritizing Critical Infrastructures Using the RAMCAP Plus Approach. ASME (2009)
43. Gordon, L.A., Loeb, M.P., Sohail, T.: A framework for using insurance for cyber-risk management. Commun. ACM **46**, 81–85 (2003)
44. Bojanc, R., Jerman-Blažič, B.: An economic modelling approach to information security risk management. Int. J. Inf. Manage. **28**, 413–422 (2008)
45. Nagurney, A., Shukla, S.: Multifirm models of cybersecurity investment competition vs. cooperation and network vulnerability. Eur. J. Oper. Res. **260**, 588–600 (2017)
46. Electricity Information Sharing and Analysis Center (E-ISAC): Analysis of the cyber attack on the Ukrainian power grid (2016)
47. O'Dowd, A.: Major global cyber-attack hits NHS and delays treatment. BMJ: Br. Med. J. (Online) **357** (2017)
48. Cerrudo, C.: An emerging US (and world) threat: cities wide open to cyber attacks. Securing Smart Cities, vol. 17, pp. 137–151. IOActive (2015)
49. Sridhar, S., Hahn, A., Govindarasu, M.: Framework for improving critical infrastructure cybersecurity, Version 1.1. vol. 100, pp. 210–224, Gaithersburg, MD (2018)
50. Alcaraz, C., Zeadally, S.: Critical infrastructure protection: requirements and challenges for the 21st century. Int. J. Crit. Infrastruct. Prot. **8**, 53–66 (2015)
51. Zio, E., Kroeger, W.: Vulnerability assessment of critical infrastructures. IEEE Reliability Society (2009)
52. Dimensional Research: Trends in Security Framework Adoption. A Survey of IT and Security Professionals (2016)
53. Gregor, S., Hevner, A.R.: Positioning and presenting design science research for maximum impact. MIS Q. **37**, 337–355 (2013)
54. Jääskeläinen, R.: Think-aloud protocol. In: Gambier, Y., van Doorslaer, L. (eds.) Handbook of Translation Studies, vol. 1, pp. 371–374. John Benjamins Publishing Company, Amsterdam/Philadelphia (2010)
55. Melnyk, S.A., Stewart, D.M., Swink, M.: Metrics and performance measurement in operations management: dealing with the metrics maze. J. Oper. Manag. **22**, 209–218 (2004)
56. Zammani, M., Razali, R.: An empirical study of information security management success factors. Int. J. Adv. Sci. Eng. Inform. Technol. **6**, 904–913 (2016)
57. Bernik, I., Prislan, K.: Measuring information security performance with 10 by 10 model for holistic state evaluation. PLoS ONE **11**, 1–33 (2016)
58. ISACA. https://www.isaca.org/Pages/Glossary.aspx. Accessed 01 Apr 2018
59. Andreasson, K.J.: Cybersecurity: Public Sector Threats and Responses. CRC Press, Boca Raton (2011)
60. European Union Agency for Network and Information Security (ENISA): Technical Guideline for Minimum Security Measures, Guidance on the Security Measures in Article 13a. European Union Agency for Network and Information Security, Brussels (2014)

61. International Organization for Standardization: ISO/IEC 27002:2005. Information Technology - Security Techniques - Code of Practice for Information Security Management, vol. 27002:2005. ISO, ISO, International Organization for Standardization (2005)
62. International Organization for Standardization: ISO/IEC 27005:2011 Information technology - Security techniques - Information Security Risk Management. ISO, International Organization for Standardization (2011)
63. Bundesamt für Sicherheit in der Informationstechnik: BSI-Standard 100-4 - Notfallmanagement. In: BSI, B.f.S.i.d.I. (ed.) BSI-Standard 100-4 - Notfallmanagement, (2008)
64. CIS CSC Center for Internet Security: Center for Internet Security Critical Security Controls for Effective Cyber Defense. Center for Internet Security (2015)
65. Baker, G.H.: A vulnerability assessment methodology for critical infrastructure sites. In: DHS Symposium: R and D Partnerships in Homeland Security (2005)
66. Stapelberg, R.F.: Infrastructure systems interdependencies and risk informed decision making (RIDM): impact scenario analysis of infrastructure risks induced by natural, technological and intentional hazards. J. Syst. Cybern. Inform. 6, 21–27 (2008)
67. Lohrke, F.T., Frownfelter-Lohrke, C., Ketchen, D.J., Jr.: The role of information technology systems in the performance of mergers and acquisitions. Bus. Horiz. 59, 7–12 (2016)
68. Wijnhoven, F., Spil, T., Stegwee, R., Fa, R.T.A.: Post-merger IT integration strategies: an IT alignment perspective. J. Strategic Inform. Syst. 15, 5–28 (2006)
69. Robbins, S.S., Stylianou, A.C.: Post-merger systems integration: the impact on IS capabilities. Inform. Manag. 36, 205–212 (1999)
70. Langweg, H.: Framework for malware resistance metrics. In: Proceedings of the 2nd ACM workshop on Quality of protection, pp. 39–44. ACM (2006)
71. OECD: OECD Risk Checklist. Risk checklist. OECD (2015)
72. Aurigemma, S., Panko, R.: A composite framework for behavioral compliance with information security policies. In: 45th Hawaii International Conference on System Sciences, pp. 3248–3257 (2012)

Exploring Political Connections and Board Interlocking Through Social Network Analysis

Sohail Mansha$^{(\boxtimes)}$, Stefano Za , and Gianluca Antonucci

Department of Management and Business Administration, "G. d'Annunzio" University of
Chieti-Pescara, Viale Pindaro, n. 42, 65127 Pescara, Italy
`sohail.mansha@unich.it`

Abstract. This paper focuses its attention on political connection and Board interlocking among firms. If abstractly, political connections and board interlocking influence is evident, its detection and disclosing appear very difficult. The idea at the base of the paper is that network science theories and data visualization technics might be suitable for political connection and board interlocking detection and disclosing. We investigate if and how Social Network Analysis (SNA) could be a revealing one. In particular we use SNA to 'explore the hidden relationship among corporate organizations. Using, as case study, the data of Pakistan stock exchange for the period of 2009 to 2015, this work found the deep penetration of political connections and its board interlocking. SNA techniques allow us to find the web of network in which corporations build their relationship with the political connected firms for the valuable access of resources. More than 70% of the investigated firms were found interlocked through the consecutive years. Results were found stronger with the increase of the number of political connections in the board.

Keywords: Board interlocking · Political connection · Social network theory · Social network analysis

1 Introduction

Creating relationship with the government is a widely debated topic in financial studies. Extensive literature indicates that the benefits of political connections (PC) are highly associated with country institutional environment, legal system, level of corruption, and government interventions. These connections allow corporate firms to attain benefits from the government such as subsidies, lower taxation, easy loan access, contract, and financial bailout at the time of financial distress [1–3]. Across 47 countries, Faccio [4] revealed that firms enjoy more political interest in developing economies as compared to the developed one's. Immature financial environment and unstable political environment encourage the businesses to build relationships with the government for competitive advantages as well as for protecting from external uncertainty.

To understand the phenomenon of political connections, literature uses different definitions and constructs dummy variables for the political connected firms according

© The Author(s), under exclusive license to Springer Nature Switzerland AG 2022
S. Za et al. (Eds.): ItAIS 2020, LNISO 50, pp. 249–262, 2022.
https://doi.org/10.1007/978-3-030-86858-1_15

to the country political power and authorities. Researchers measures the political connection through corporate lobbying activities for USA [5], executive and supervisory board members close to the ruling party in Germany [6], board member as politicians with respect to provincial or federal assembly member in Pakistan [3], CEO politician, government officer or military personnel in China [7], company board personnel from government committee members [8], industry regulators [9], top appointed bureaucrats [10], Chief of the state or closely related to the top politicians [11], and different level of political connection in Malaysia on the basis of government ownership, board of directors, family members and through businesses [12]. Moreover, Wong [12] highlight the importance of social networks and assemble political connections where vertices are the board members and edges represented the co-attendance of firm's participants at the same government institutions. It indicates that the benefit of political connections highly depends on the behavior of the politicians in the board and their respective power. But, direct connections with the government and appointment of political personnel on board are costly for firms [13]. In this regards, board interlocking is an important channel to build relationships with the political connected boards.

Board interlocking is a situation in which companies share their directors. These networks provide access to tangible (better trade terms) and intangible (counsel, support, subsidy) valuable resources under the resource based view. Interlocked directors provide a shield against external environment uncertainties [14]. Greater access to information, experience, and prestige due to holding multiple directorships, the demand of interlocked members increased in corporations [15]. Interlock directors come up with external resources, knowledge, information and competitive advantages to the firms. Extended literature declares the information more reliable in interlocked networks as compared to any other source and act as third party facilitator [16]. But, for interlocks, every corporate action is based on their social relations and connectedness with the outside environment. Director personal attributes and connections offer more help in firms' decision choices [12]. Under the social network theory, Prem Sankar [17] discovered that legal and financial experts have a more central location in Indian corporate networks due to professionalism, expertise and political or elite connections. Several other studies also enlighten the importance of board interlocking by using social network techniques [18–20].

If abstractly, political connections and board interlocking influence is evident, its detection and disclosing appear very difficult, due to the fact that it relies on different levels, being composed by links and connections, both at single person level and at single organization one, having multiple layers, at inter-personal level and at inter-organizational one. This study intends to investigate how social network analysis (SNA) could be a revealing tool to detect and disclose political connection and board interlocking under graph theory. To address this phenomenon, the study chooses the non-financial Pakistani firms for the period of 2009 to 2015 as a case. The choice to have that period and Pakistan as case of study relies on three relevant aspects. Firstly, the relevance of political elites had as an inheritance in the passage from an autocratic regime to a democratic one in those years. Pakistani institutional and financial environment allowed us to investigate the different levels of the board political connections. Secondly, the identification of the number of political connected directors with respect to their power. Thirdly, to examine the linkage between firms without any political member in the board with the political connected ones.

The paper is structured as follows. The following paragraph describes the importance of political connections and board interlocking. The third one briefly describes the characteristics of Pakistan as a valid study case. The fourth one presents SNA and data collection along with methodology. In the last one results are presented together with discussions of them. In the last one result are presented together with discussions of them.

2 Political Connections in Pakistan

Pakistan is an emerging economy where political connections raised their importance in the corporate world due to a still immature institutional setting and, high accessibility to government resources and legislations. This environment provides opportunities[1] to some politicians for various unfair activities such as rent-seeking, corruption, self-interest, etc. For instance Khawaja [3] found powerful politicians to default on bank loans due to poor bankruptcy law implementation. According to the Panama Papers[2], many politicians, civil-military officials, businessmen were found to be engaged in unlawful activities to promote personal benefits from government resources. Due to poor governance practices, dictatorship and unstable political governments in Pakistan, World Bank governance indicators scores are low: rule of law (21 percentile), regulatory quality (24 percentile), government effectiveness (23 percentile), voice and accountability (24 percentile), control of corruption (17 percentile) and political stability (0.95 percentile) [21].

On one hand, after independence in 1947, Pakistan faced highly unstable political conditions and no elected government could complete its electoral mandate until 2009. Most of the elected governments were dismissed through Presidential orders or military dictators on charges of corruption, nepotism, misconduct, and inefficiencies [22] and lead to an autocratic government. The last autocratic regime lasted from 1999, when a military regime took control over the country, to 2008, after strong movements of democratic political parties and the judiciary independent[3] movement. General elections were held in 2008. In 2013 an elected government completed his tenure, for the first time and shifted it to another democratic government [21]. Political stability provided the best opportunities to flourish economic activities, but the autocratic regime provided a platform for civil-military personnel to penetrate the corporate world. On the other hand, in the business environment, the financial sector is regulated by the State Bank of Pakistan while the non-financial one is governed by the Security and Exchange Commission of Pakistan. All

---

[1] Such as Statutory Regulatory Orders issued by the Federal Board of Revenue provides unlawful facilitations to powerful bodies [21].

[2] In April 2017, elected Prime Minister of Pakistan Mr. Nawaz Sharif was disqualified against the corruption charges in Panama case. Moreover, Salim Saifullah (politician), Hussain Dawood, Bashir Ahmed (businessmen) and many other were found in panama leaks.

[3] In 2007, President Parvez Musharraf declared the state of emergency rule across the country and fired the Chief Justice of Pakistan. After that Judiciary started a movement for freedom of justice in which all political parties participated.

the listed companies abide to follow the code of corporate governance of Pakistan. Apart from these strong theoretical regulations, practical implications allow strong politician, civil-military, and private officials to obtain private benefits [23]. During the autocratic regime, there was a high accessibility to loans for politically connected peers. In the whole economy network, 65% of total Pakistani banking credit is allocated to the giant interlocked network which contains only 5% of total firms of the economy [24]. Easily access to credit for connected peers, inside government information raised the importance of direct and interlocks political connections in the corporate world. Such practices encourage exploring the role of politicians and interlocks after the shift change from the autocratic to a democratic regime.

3   Social Network Analysis

Over recent years, Social network analysis (SNA) has become a major instrument to analyze the social structure apart from the quantitative methods of statistics. Extensive development in graph theory and SNA techniques [14, 25–27] allows researchers to explore the hidden social relationship of directors at a different level. Corporate networks are consisting of directors, organizations, and ties arising due to the interlock directors. These types of networks are called two-mode network or affiliation networks bipartite graphs. Two mode networks can be converted into one mode by suitable folding of graphs. One node network gives a clear picture of nodes of the same kind which are buried in the two-mode network and difficult to understand.

Researchers based on SNA techniques for studying corporate governance are evident [12, 17, 28], but these studies used SNA either to explore corporate network or political network separately. On the contrary, this study attempts to reveal the importance of SNA, as a valid tool, to explore the significance of political connections for board interlocking purposes in the corporate network under a regime change. Therefore, the study aim is:

To investigate the political connections in corporate networking due to regime change under the social network analysis.

4   Research Design

To investigate the aim of the study, various steps have been followed as described in Fig. 1 and explicated hereafter.

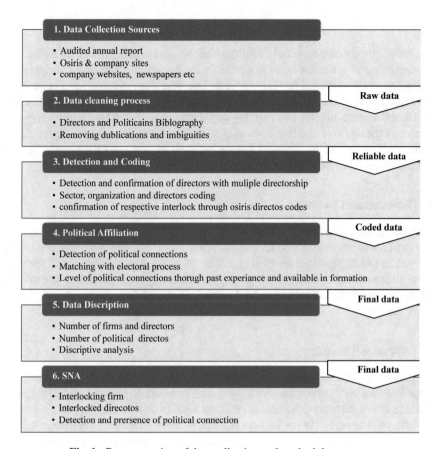

Fig. 1. Representation of data collection and methodology steps.

4.1 Data Collection and Sources

The study selected the non-financial firms listed on the Pakistan Stock exchange from 2009 to 2015 as per coverage of democratic regimes. After excluding the financial sector, 415 firms were found for the analysis. Board level data were obtained from the audited annual reports of firms downloaded from company websites. Furthermore, the director's bibliographies have been detected manually from the specific sections made available by companies in their annual reports and also from other reliable different sources such as Osiris, national newspapers, and companies' websites.

4.2 Data Cleaning Process

After data collection, we removed all the duplications and missing values for each firm in the respective year. To make data more reliable, for the network formation under regime change, the study excluded the firms whose data were not available for a consecutive three years period. In the data collection and cleaning process, on one hand, it has been found that the same director was working on different boards but his name spelling was different on the reports issued by the respective firms[4]. On the other hand, some different directors were working on different boards but their names were the same[5]. To solve these issues, we used another step to ensure data quality for the analysis.

4.3 Detection and Coding

To rectify data duplications and repetitions, we assigned a code to each director with the help of unique contact identifier given on Osiris site. But, some director codes were not given in Osiris data. The study also confirmed those directors "identity" searching reliable information from their bibliography and company site information to avoid any replication through the respective years. The study also issued a code to each organization and sector.

4.4 Political Affiliation

The benefits of political connections depend on the country's institutional environment. As the Political system consists of federal and provincial governments[6]. Parliament of Pakistan is a bicameral legislature that consists of the Senate (upper house) and the National Assembly (lower house). Each provincial government is composed of a provincial assembly and establishment division. Furthermore, both provincial and federal governments propose committees and commissions to formulate policies that consist of politicians, private officials[7], and civil-military[8] officials. In this regard, politicians have strong access to government contracts while the bureaucrat has legislation power [29]. Military personnel have good leading command and work experience [30] and also have a great influence in institutions, due to the penetration of the military in an autocratic regime. Moreover, the private official working on the government committee has a strong influence to draft policies and regulations.

---

[4] Mr. Shahid Aziz Siddique holds directorship in Mirpurkhas Sugar Mills Limited, Hub Power Company Limited,, Pakistan Cables Limited for the year of 2013 but his name is written as Dr. shahid Aziz Siddiqi, SHAHID AZIZ SIDDIQI, Mr. Shahid Aziz Siddiqui respectively.

[5] Mr. Mohammad Iqbal is the same name of two different directors working on Suraj cotton mill limited and Pakistan PVC limited.

[6] Representatives elected through electoral process.

[7] Mr. Arif Habib is the chairman of various firms listed on Pakistan stock exchange. He has served on various government committees such as privatization commission, board of investment, tariff reforms commission and security and exchange ordinance Review committee during autocratic as well as democratic regimes.

[8] Civil government officers are selected through the central superior services and army has his own structure to promote the officers.

For the political connection purpose, we constructed a second database, all electoral data of general and senate elections were obtained from the Election Commission of Pakistan website. After that, the study matched both databases in order to find the political linkages of firms. In addition to the matching process, it has been also checked each single director profile, through the annual reports and company sites for civil, military and government committee members. By following this procedure, the study constructed political connection (PC), as a dummy variable with 1 if director i was political personnel on board in year t otherwise 0. It has been noticed that most firms were connected to only one type of political connection but some firms had also different types of political connections. To explore the connections of politicians based on their current and past experiences, the study constructed the different levels of politicians according to their affiliation by following definition of [31] and assigning different values to the political directors.

4.5 Data Description and Limitations

After adopting the procedure, the study succeeded in finalizing the maximum sample of 287 firms in 2013 and a minimum of 240 firms in 2015 due to the availability of data. Furthermore, consecutive three years of data analysis for each firm allowed us to explore the firm position in the network during the coming years. Table 1 indicates the number of politically connected firms with a different level across the period.

The number of political connected firms significantly present in the Pakistani market. Some firms have more than one political board member. Finding indicates the significant penetration of military connections in the corporate world due to the autocratic regime. More than a half of PC firms are connected with MLC and GMC throughout the time periods in which most government committee members were appointed the first time during the autocratic regime[9]. Moreover CLC, FLC and PLC remain almost consistent even through the regime change. But, at this stage, it is hard to know how the political connections help another non-connected firm in network formation. To understand this phenomenon, the study used social network techniques for further analysis.

Table 1. Summary statistics of political connected firms for the period of 2009–15.

Years	2009	2010	2011	2012	2013	2014	2015
Number of firms	245	263	278	282	287	280	240
Total PC Firms	110	117	116	117	119	119	99
FLC firm	19	23	22	23	22	24	19
PLC Firm	24	23	23	24	24	24	23
CLC Firm	22	22	20	22	23	22	21
MLC Firm	41	42	43	39	41	43	37
GMC Firm	33	35	40	42	38	24	36

[9] Arif habib was first appointed as government committee member during the autocratic regime.

4.6 Social Network Analysis

SNA allows exploring the relationship among companies interlocking arising due to their director ties. It is very helpful to check the political director's presence in the companies and their interlocked firms. For this purpose, the study converted two-mode networks into one mode network for company networks. Descriptions of firms and directors network across the time period are given in Table 2.

Based on our data, we created a graph in which every node represents a specific company. Two nodes have a connection if there is at least one director sitting in both companies represented by those nodes. We considered only companies having at least one member of the board sitting in the board of another firm. In this way, we avoided to have any isolated node, since every node has at least a connection with another. The thickness of the tie between two companies (nodes) indicates the number of shared directors, those sitting in the boards of both companies at the same time. The size of the node is related to the number of connections (the degree). The label size of the node is proportional to the size of the node. Based on the connection among the companies, it is possible to identify a set of clusters (see Table 3 and Table 4 for 2009 and 2015 respectively). The colour of each connection and node depends on the cluster to which they belong. Moreover, the label colour of each node depends on the number of political members sitting in the board of the specific company (black if there is no political member).

Table 2. Summary statistics directors, directorships and political connections.

Years	2009	2010	2011	2012	2013	2014	2015
Number of board seats	1918	2073	2189	2215	2252	2233	1862
Number of directors	1466	1569	1650	1659	1690	1681	1463
Seats held by PC directors	170	177	187	189	189	202	154
number of PC directors	103	105	109	111	111	127	107
Avg. directorship held by other directors	1.28	1.30	1.30	1.31	1.31	1.31	1.26
Avg. seat held by PC director	1.65	1.69	1.72	1.70	1.70	1.59	1.44
Avg. seat held by FLC director	1.33	1.33	1.35	1.32	1.33	1.33	1.19
Avg. seat held by PLC director	2.50	2.00	2.18	2.27	2.27	2.27	2.18
Avg. seat held by CLC director	1.53	1.60	1.63	1.44	1.63	1.25	1.15
Avg. seat held by MLC director	1.67	1.63	1.55	1.68	1.68	1.60	1.44
Avg seat held by GMC director	1.56	1.95	2.13	1.96	1.82	1.71	1.50

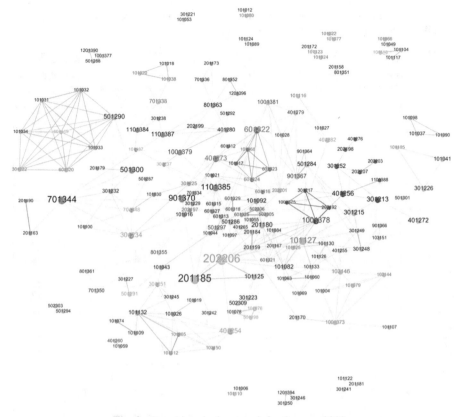

Fig. 2. Board interlock network for the year 2009.

Figure 2 represents the companies' network in 2009 and Figs. 3 the connections in 2015. The different colours of node labels provide information about the number of political members on the respective boards, for both years, specifically: Fuchsia-7, Red-4, Orange-3, Blue-2 and Green-1 for 2009 and Fuchsia-4, Red-3, Yellow-2, and Green-1 for 2015.

Table 3. List of clusters with the amount of companies distributed among the different number of political members in the board for the year 2009.

Cluster	Num. of companies with respect to number of political member present on board in each cluster						Cluster	Num. of companies with respect to number of political member present on board in each cluster					
	0	1	2	3	4	7		0	1	2	3	4	7
0	1	1					13	3				1	5
1	1	1					14	3					
2	1	3					15	1	2				
3	2	5	1			1	16	2		1	2		
4		2					17	10	2	1	1	1	2
5	14	6	7	1		1	18	2					
6	5	3	1	2			19	11					1
7	3	2	2	1			20	3					
8	4	1	3				21	3					
9	2	1	1	1			22	2					
10			2				23	3			1		1
11			1		1		24	28	2		4		1
12	2												

Most of the political connected firms are connected in the company network and other non-connected peers are also sharing their directors with PC firms. On the right side of the Fig. 2, we can consider cluster number 7 (see Table 3) where company 501290, which belongs to cement sector (sector code 501), is linked with four companies of textile sector (101), one company of chempharma sector (301), two companies of motor vehicle & auto parts sector (601) and one company of electric and machinery sector (1101). For this company, blue node colour represents the presence of two political connected members. SNA also helps to point out the position of firms. Node 101127 has significant influence because it helps this company (501290) to connect with other firms network. Although it has no political member in the board, it still has a great access to control the information, due to its unique position. Companies with more political members on board are highly connected to other firms. This increase the access to the resources with the presence of more political connected personnel and attract market players to get benefits. Figure 3 represents the company network for the year 2015; it is interesting that over the time, the number of political people decreases in the boards. In 2015, there is not a single company which has more than 4 political members on the board. In company board interlocked network, 53% of the firms are having not a single political member in the board while 31% of the companies have one political member in the board. But still presence and importance of political connected firms are very significant in the company board interlocked network. These structures are deep buried in the corporate world and cannot be easily measured, but SNA provides great facilitation to explore these relationships and find the unique characteristics of board interlocking phenomenon.

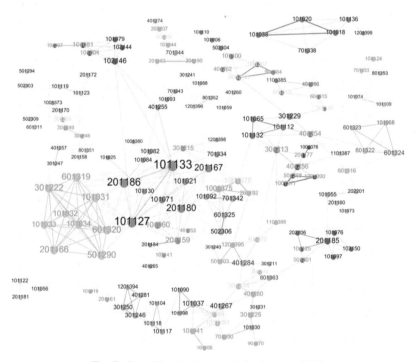

Fig. 3. Board interlock network for the year 2015.

260   S. Mansha et al.

Table 4. List of clusters with the amount of companies distributed among the different number of political members in the board for the year 2015.

Cluster	Num. of companies with respect to number of political member present on board in each cluster					Cluster	Num. of companies with respect to number of political member present on board in each cluster				
	0	1	2	3	4		0	1	2	3	4
0	3	3				13	5	2			
1	6					14	19	5			
2		9				15	1			1	
3	8	9	5	2		16		4	1	2	
4	3					17	7	2			
5	2					18	2				
6	5	1		2	2	19	2	2	1		
7				2		20	1	5			
8	2					21	4	3	2	1	1
9	4	2	1			22	2				
10	3	3	2			23	2				
11	3					24	2				
12	1	2									

5   Discussion and Conclusion

This paper investigated the relevance of the use of social network analysis tools to examine the presence of political connections in board interlocking phenomenon under a regime change. The data consist of the 287 non-financial listed companies of the Pakistan stock exchange for the period of 2009–2015. It encompasses 1690 directors sitting on various boards of directors. Social network analysis tools allowed to detect the various board members hold multiple directorships and form the giant network. The position of a company in the network has a significant impact on its access to market resources such as capital, status, prestige and legitimacy within the corporate environment. Moreover, social network analysis tools also important to indicate the presence of the number of political connected members sitting on board of directors. Apart of the direct intervention of political connected members, social network analysis also highlights the significance of indirect political connected firms by the interlocking phenomenon. Furthermore, due to the regime change from autocratic to democratic, social network analysis tools are helpful for the identification of the number of political connections which are deeper penetrated in the corporate network.

Apart of the importance of social network analysis tools, still there are various limitations such as, this study only highlights the network of two years. Due to data limitation, study could not identify the change in corporate network arising from the change of directorship.

References

1. Shleifer, A., Vishny, R.W.: Politicians and firms. Q. J. Econ. (1994).https://doi.org/10.2307/2118354
2. Faccio, M., Masulis, R.W., Mcconnell, J.J.: Political connections and corporate bailouts. J. Finance(2006). https://doi.org/10.1111/j.1540-6261.2006.01000.x
3. Khwaja, A.I., Mian, A.: Do lenders favor politically connected. Q. J. Econ. **120**, 1371–1411 (2005)
4. Faccio, M.: Differences between politically connected and nonconnected firms: a cross-country analysis. Financ. Manag. **39**, 905–928 (2010). https://doi.org/10.1111/j.1755-053X.2010.01099.x
5. Hill, M.D., Fuller, K.P., Kelly, G.W., Washam, J.O.: Corporate cash holdings and political connections. Rev. Quant. Finance Account. (2014).https://doi.org/10.1007/s11156-012-0336-6
6. Ferguson, T., Voth, H.J.: Betting on Hitler - the value of political connections in Nazi Germany. Q. J. Econ. **123**, 101–137 (2008). https://doi.org/10.1162/qjec.2008.123.1.101
7. Fan, J.P.H., Wong, T.J., Zhang, T.: Politically connected CEOs, corporate governance, and Post-IPO performance of China's newly partially privatized firms. J. Financ. Econ. **84**, 330–357 (2007). https://doi.org/10.1016/j.jfineco.2006.03.008
8. Han, J., Zhang, G.: Politically connected boards, value or cost: evidence from a natural experiment in China. Account. Finance **58**, 149–169 (2018). https://doi.org/10.1111/acfi.12215
9. Gao, W., Huang, Z., Yang, P.: Political connections, corporate governance and M&A performance: evidence from Chinese family firms. Res. Int. Bus. Finance **50**, 38–53 (2019). https://doi.org/10.1016/j.ribaf.2019.04.007
10. Boubakri, N., Cosset, J.C., Saffar, W.: Political connections of newly privatized firms. J. Corp. Finance **14**, 654–673 (2008). https://doi.org/10.1016/j.jcorpfin.2008.08.003
11. Faccio, M.: Politically connected firms. Am. Econ. Rev. **96**, 369–386 (2006). https://doi.org/10.1257/000282806776157704
12. Wong, W.Y., Hooy, C.W.: Do types of political connection affect firm performance differently? Pacific-Basin Finance J. **51**, 297–317 (2018). https://doi.org/10.1016/j.pacfin.2018.08.009
13. Du, J., Bai, T., Chen, S.: Integrating corporate social and corporate political strategies: performance implications and institutional contingencies in China. J. Bus. Res. **98**, 299–316 (2019). https://doi.org/10.1016/j.jbusres.2019.02.014
14. Mizruchi, M.S.: What do interlocks do? An analysis, critique, and assessment of research on interlocking directorates. Annu. Rev. Sociol. **22**, 271–298 (1996). https://doi.org/10.1146/annurev.soc.22.1.271
15. Pfeffer, J., Slancik, G.R.: Social control of organizations: a resource dependence perspective (1978)

16. Sankar, C.P., Thumba, D.A., Ramamohan, T.R., et al.: Agent-based multi-edge network simulation model for knowledge diffusion through board interlocks. Expert Syst. Appl. **141**, 112962 (2020). https://doi.org/10.1016/j.eswa.2019.112962

17. Prem Sankar, C., Asokan, K., Satheesh Kumar, K.: Exploratory social network analysis of affiliation networks of Indian listed companies. Soc. Netw. **43**, 113–120 (2015). https://doi.org/10.1016/j.socnet.2015.03.008

18. Samkin, G., Allen, B., Munday, D.: The social network of New Zealand directors: an exploratory study. Corp. Board Role, Duties Compos. **6**, 19–38 (2010). https://doi.org/10.22495/cbv6i1art2

19. Chuluun, T., Prevost, A., Puthenpurackal, J.: Board ties and the cost of corporate debt. Financ. Manag. **43**, 533–568 (2014). https://doi.org/10.1111/fima.12047

20. Blanco-Alcántara, D., Díez-Esteban, J.M., Romero-Merino, M.E.: Board networks as a source of intellectual capital for companies: empirical evidence from a panel of Spanish firms. Manag. Decis. **57**, 2653–2671 (2019). https://doi.org/10.1108/MD-12-2017-1238

21. Cheema, M.U., Munir, R., Su, S.: Political connections and organisational performance: evidence from Pakistan. Int. J. Account. Inf. Manag. **24**, 321–338 (2016). https://doi.org/10.1108/IJAIM-05-2016-0053

22. Syed, A.H.: Pakistan in 1997: Nawaz Sharif's Second Chance to Govern. Asian Surv.(1998). https://doi.org/10.2307/2645668

23. Siddiqa, A.: Military's economic role and beyond. RUSI J. (2007).https://doi.org/10.1080/03071840701863174

24. Khwaja, A.I., Mian, A., Qamar, A.: The Value of Business Networks (2008)

25. Newman, M.E.J.: The Structure and Function of Complex Networks (2003)

26. Wasserman, S., Galaskiewicz, J.: Advances in Social Network Analysis: Research in the Social and Behavioral Sciences (2012)

27. Scott, J.: Networks of corporate power: a comparative assessment. Annu. Rev. Sociol. **17**, 181–203 (1991). https://doi.org/10.1146/annurev.soc.17.1.181

28. Robins, G., Alexander, M.: Small worlds among interlocking directors: network structure and distance in bipartite graphs. Comput. Math. Organ. Theory **10**, 69–94 (2004). https://doi.org/10.1023/b:cmot.0000032580.12184.c0

29. Li, D., Eden, L., Hitt, M.A., Ireland, R.D.: Five year index issue, 2000–2004. Strateg. Manag. J. **27**, 1215–1228 (2006). https://doi.org/10.1002/smj

30. Lester, R.H., Hillman, A., Zardkoohi, A., et al.: Former government officials as outside directors: the role of human and social capital . Acad. Manag. J. **51**, 999–1013 (2016). Published by: academy of Management Linked references are available on JSTOR for this article: FORMER GOVERNMENT OFFICIALS AS OUTSIDE DIRECTORS: THE ROLE OF HUMAN A

31. Cao, X., Pan, X., Qian, M., Tian, G.G.: Political capital and CEO entrenchment: evidence from CEO turnover in Chinese non-SOEs. J. Corp. Finance **42**, 1–14 (2017). https://doi.org/10.1016/j.jcorpfin.2016.11.003

Literature Search Habits of MIS Academics: Empirical Evidence on the Discovery of Impactful Research

Chiara Francalanci[(✉)] and Paolo Giacomazzi

Politecnico di Milano, Milan, Italy
{chiara.francalanci,paolo.giacomazzi}@polimi.it

Abstract. The amount of academic literature published every year has increased at a steady 20% rate since the 1990s. With this impressive growth of available information, the discovery of *relevant* papers that are worth reading is recognized to be challenging. The search mechanisms of online archives are generally considered limited, as search keywords typically span multiple research areas and retrieve a large number of papers that are only partly pertinent to the user's interests.

The first research question of this paper is whether and to what extent academics perform their search online. The second research question is whether and to what extent academics use current advanced search mechanisms, as an indication of their commitment to online discovery. The third research question is on the role played by online search in different phases of the research process, that is choosing a research topic, finding readings on the topic, and selecting citations. To help answer these questions, the paper presents the results of an empirical survey conducted with academics in the MIS field. Findings from 326 respondents unveil interesting insights on the literature search habits of academics and, overall, indicate that despite the consensus on the low quality of current online search mechanisms, only a tiny minority of users seems to be willing to trade search simplicity for relevance.

Keyword: Online search · Search engine · Impact factor · h-index

1 Introduction

The number of academic papers published every year is continuously growing [23, 25] at an average 20% rate since the 1990s. With this impressive and steady growth rate, the size of the academic literature increases by a factor of 10 in 5 years. Although this demonstrates a growing interest towards research, previous literature has also pointed to some negative effects, which are summarized under the umbrella of a general *information overload* [4].

Efficient search mechanisms could obviate the risks of information overload by retrieving relevant papers irrespective of the size of the underlying archive. However, the search mechanisms of online archives are generally considered limited [4], as search keywords typically span multiple research areas and retrieve a large number of papers

© The Author(s), under exclusive license to Springer Nature Switzerland AG 2022
S. Za et al. (Eds.): ItAIS 2020, LNISO 50, pp. 263–277, 2022.
https://doi.org/10.1007/978-3-030-86858-1_16

that are only partly pertinent to the user's interests. Users entering search keywords can limit search results by selecting specific research areas, but it has been noted how the definition of research area provided by online archives is usually very broad and far from the more practical notion of research field [12].

This paper starts from the observation that working to improve online search is valuable only if the actual search habits of academics point to a tangible need for better online search mechanisms. To gather insights on this issue, this paper analyzes the search habits of academics by addressing the following research questions:

1. To what extend academics perform their search online?
2. To what extent academics use current advanced search mechanisms?
3. How to academics use online search in their research and, particularly, what is the role played by online search in different phases of the research process, that is choosing a research topic, finding readings on the topic, and selecting citations?

To help answer the three questions listed above, the authors of this paper have conducted a large-scale empirical survey with academics in the MIS field. Findings help understand whether and how online search can be improved to meet largely shared requirements.

The next section discusses the state of the art on search approaches and current online services. Section 3 presents our research hypotheses and testing results are reported in Sect. 4. Findings are discussed in Sect. 5 and conclusions are finally drawn in Sect. 6.

2   State of the Art

Online archives make a standard distinction among three types of basic parameters that users can specify to drive search: authors, publication outlets and content. Ideally, users entering a search would like to retrieve *all* the publications that are relevant to their search goals, possibly *ranked* by relevance. Users can set their search goals by specifying a value for the different types of search parameters, i.e. by formulating a query. This section reviews previous literature focusing on the main types of search parameters (authors, publication outlets, and keywords) and provides a comparative analysis of existing online archives in the last sub-section.

2.1   Authors as an Online Search Variable

The use of author names as a search criterion is a feature provided by all online archives and search engines. Some archives, such as Scopus, provide it as a basic search functionality, while others, such as Google Scholar, provide it as an advanced functionality. In both cases, entering the full name of an author or the last name only, as well as providing the first and middle name initials or the full spelling can return significantly different search results. These inconsistencies can be due to homonymies among different authors or to the standards applied by different publication outlets in recording author names.

The issue of homonyms is central to the literature on the *h*-index (cf. [22]). It has been observed that the calculation of the *h*-index is error-prone due to the inclusion of publications from homonymous authors, the exclusion of relevant publication outlets and missing citations [22]. From an online search perspective, the h-index can provide an assessment of the impact of authors especially when users do not specify any author names in their query. However, it should be acknowledged that the h-index is a controversial measure of impact. The h-index has been initially welcomed as a significant improvement in the assessment of an author's impact compared to the mere number of publications [10]. It has been noted how the h-index takes into account the number of citations and encourages the publication of fewer, but more impactful papers [10]. On the other hand, the more recent literature tends to be more critical of the h-index, introduces alternative measures of impact [6], such as the 37 variants of the h-index reviewed in [11], and emphasizes the need for complementing the quantitative assessment of impact with a more qualitative approach [10].

Most search engines and online archives, including Google Scholar and Scopus, provide the total number of citations of the papers that are returned in response to a query. The number of citations can be used as an indication of the impact of a paper and help select a few readings from a long list of search results. To the best of our knowledge, the h-index of authors cannot be used as a search criterion. In some cases, users can click on an author's name to be provided an assessment of the author's publications which includes the author's h-index. For example, Google Scholar provides the author's list of most recent publications, the h-index and the i10-index, that is the number of publications with at least 10 citations. Scopus provides a variety of analytics describing an author's productivity, including the h-graph, visually showing the calculation of the h-index together with a list the most cited papers above the h-threshold.

Calculating the h-index is computing intensive. Most online archives seem to store author records with descriptive statistics including the h-index. In theory, this would enable them to include the h-index among their search criteria without incurring the risk of exceedingly complex queries. Whether users could benefit from using the h-index as a search variable remains an open issue.

2.2 Publication Outlets as an Online Search Variable

Publication outlets or sources can be used as a search variable by specifying their *name* or their *type*. Most search engines support the incomplete specification of source name and use simple string matching algorithms to map the incomplete specification to actual source names. This mapping often results into multiple candidate sources and, once again, search engines aim at avoiding false negatives by considering all candidate sources, resulting into information overload.

The type of a source represents a categorization of its mission and style, such as "journal," "conference," "magazine," "patent," and so on. Source types vary across search engines, with no standard categorization. In general, search results include a number of different sources, even if they are restricted to a specific source type. The number and variety of sources increases when search is based on keywords that are inherently interdisciplinary. It cannot be expected that users have a precise idea of the reputation of all sources, especially if the search engine is general purpose, such as Google Scholar or Scopus. In theory, users may benefit from functionalities helping them assessing the quality of a source.

The issue of assessing journals is central to the literature on the *impact factor*. The impact factor represents a quantitative indicator of the impact that papers published on a given source have on average [9]. Similar to the *h*-index, the impact factor is based on citations and is highly controversial, both in principle and in practice. First of all, citations do not represent the only indicator of impact and, as a consequence, the impact factor does not provide a complete assessment of the quality of a source [14]. Furthermore, many researchers believe that they have published important research work in low-impact journals [14]. From a more practical standpoint, the impact factor is affected by several measurement problems. Self-citations represent the most widely discussed measurement problem. It has been noted how editors can increase the impact factor of their journal by inflating self-citations through editorials and readers' comments on published articles [13, 14]. A mismatch between citing and cited documents has also been observed, raising concerns on the precision with which the impact factor is measured [27]. An alternative metric to measure the impact of publication outlets is the *eigenfactor* [7].

Most search engines and online archives do not provide an assessment of the impact factor and none allows the impact factor to be specified among search parameters. Scopus is the only general-purpose engine providing three different measures of the impact factor of journals, the SCImago Journal Rank, the Impact per Publication, and the Source Normalized Impact per Paper. Including the impact factor among search parameters could be subject to strong criticism, as it would strengthen the role of a controversial indicator. Whether users would benefit from the practical use of the impact factor for search purposes remains an open issue.

2.3   Publication Outlets as an Online Search Variable

Search engines and online archives support the specification of a keyword-based Boolean expression as an input to search. Keywords are used syntactically by string matching algorithms that search for the specified keywords in the title, abstract or body of papers [9]. Papers are included among query results if they satisfy the Boolean expression entered by the user. This syntactic approach is recognized as a fundamental cause for the information overload experienced by users [26], who are returned papers that satisfy their Boolean expression, but are not relevant to their research domain.

The computer science literature provides several techniques to improve search, known as *semantic* or *content-based* search. The founding idea of semantic search is that keywords are ambiguous and need *disambiguation* to be used effectively. For example, the word "sustainability" has a different meaning in different domains, such as economics, agricultural sciences or computer science. Disambiguation can be achieved by understanding the meaning of a keyword, i.e. its semantics. Semantic search has been widely studied and experimented [26]. Semantic search engines have been proved to be effective, as long as a user provides the engine with enough knowledge for the engine to be able to disambiguate correctly. To the current state of the art, there is no general-purpose semantic engine that can be used effectively across different domains without prior instruction [5].

2.4 Comparative Analysis of Online Archives

The literature makes a distinction between general-purpose and domain-specific online archives and search engines [17]. Google Scholar, Scopus and Web of Science represent the main general-purpose engines. There is a vast literature focusing on the comparison among these three main general-purpose engines. The majority of papers in this stream date back in the years 2005–2007, when the comprehensiveness of general-purpose engines became necessary for the calculation of bibliometric indices, such as the h-index and the impact factor.

In 2005, Jacsò [19] noted how Web of Science should not be used alone for locating citations to an author or title, while Scopus and Google Scholar can help identify a considerable number of citations not covered by ISI citation databases [19]. However, Web of Science has been proved to have the best coverage of specific research areas. For example, Web of Science has been found to have the best coverage of South African scholarly research [1]. More recently, Scopus has been claimed to offer about 20% more coverage of citations than Web Of Science, while Google Scholar offers results of inconsistent accuracy [17]. In that same research contribution, authors conclude that Google Scholar can help with the retrieval of "even the most obscure information", but citation information is updated less often. A general answer on which archive provides the most complete set of citing literature does not seem to exist and authors of [4] conclude that the answer depends on the subject and publication year of a given article. Science mapping software tools have emerged to integrate citation information provided by different archives and obtain a citation coverage better than that of any individual archive. Science mapping tools are extensively reviewed in [16], including Bibexcel, CiteSpace, Sci^2, and VantagePoint.

There is substantial agreement in the literature on the superior quality of Scopus search functionalities [12, 19, 24]. A recognized strength of Google Scholar is its simple interface consisting of a query box, but an equally obvious shortcoming is its lack of reliable advanced search functionalities [24]. A comprehensive review of the "odd search behaviours" of Google Scholar's advanced search can be found in [20]. As an example, Page numbers and ISSN four-digit numbers are found to be often interpreted as publication year and, in some cases, the *OR* logical operator reduces the hit count compared to the *AND* logical operator. Scopus is acknowledged to provide a more complete and dependable set of advanced search functionalities organized in a clear and usable interface [12]. In particular, Scopus offers interesting analytics under the "analyze search results" button, which are unique to this archive.

3   Research Model and Hypotheses

We have adopted the three-step model of the research process shown in Fig. 1. Our model identifies three different search goals that emerge at different times along a research timeline: choosing a research topic, finding readings on a topic, and selecting citations on a topic. Our three-step model is iterative, as each search goal can emerge multiple times as research unfolds. For example, researchers may need to look for readings at the beginning of a new research as well as several times along the research process as new issues arise. It can be observed that our three-step model takes a search perspective and does not make explicit reference to any research method. In this research, the three-step model is considered general and is used to explore the search habits of academics independent of the research method that they use.

Fig. 1. Search-oriented model of the research process

The search habits of academics have been rarely addressed in the literature. The research efforts on search habits are summarized in [28]. None of these studies focuses specifically on the literature search habits of academics. However, they are reported to concur that as a general rule "poor quality queries are the main reason for low precision in search engines." Less than 3% of all queries are found to use query operators, such as Boolean expressions. Computer literacy is indicated as an important driver of users' commitment to search and, ultimately, query quality. In this respect, MIS academics can be assumed to represent a highly computer literate community and, thus, a best case scenario for the exploration of search habits and commitment to search.

As an exploratory study, this research considers two general variables describing search habits, namely usage and satisfaction. Different steps in our research model have different search goals that, in turn, may be associated with a varying degree of usage of online search and level of satisfaction with online search functionalities. Consequently, search habits have been separately explored for the three steps in Fig. 1.

Selecting a research topic seems to be a natural starting point of a research process. Academics need early insights on new and promising topics and, at the same time, they have to exchange views with colleagues to understand their opinions and interests. Participating in conferences, meeting with representatives from funding institution, visiting companies, and attending workshops and seminars seem more effective ways to choose new research topics. These considerations lead to our first research hypothesis.

H1 – The percentage of academics using online search to choose a research topic (in research step 1) is lower than the corresponding percentage of academics using online search to find readings on a topic (research step 2).

This need for knowing early about new and potentially hot topics as soon as they emerge is addressed by the literature on *weak signals* [21]. Weak signals are defined as hints of a new phenomenon that is growing quickly and, although currently small-scale, is likely to escalate in the near future [15]. In the scientific literature, weak signals represent emerging topics that have the potential to become mainstream soon. In research fields dealing with text analytics, such as information retrieval and social media analytics, weak signals can be discovered by measuring the occurrences of words or patterns of related words [5]. A word or pattern that has a number of occurrences lower than average (is not mainstream yet), but a growth trend higher than average (is growing fast) is a good candidate to represent a weak signal. Text analytic functionalities can support the discovery of weak signals [29]. These functionalities are not offered by online search engines and archives. In our second hypothesis, we posit that these functionalities represent a missing and potentially welcome functionality in the choice of a new topic step, especially among academics who use online search more often.

H2 – In research step 1, academics using online search more frequently rate the benefits from text analytic functionalities higher compared to academics using online search less frequently.

The second research step, finding readings on a topic, heavily involves literature search, in order for an academic to build a map of the state of the art and position her/his own contribution within previous literature. The search goals in step 2 can be considerably different from the search goals in step 1. Choosing a research topic can benefit from a wider breadth of readings, since the so called "weak signals" pointing to emerging and potentially interesting topics can be provided in multiple research fields and then develop into different research streams, each focusing on a specific set of research topics. Conversely, finding readings on a specific topic would benefit from more precise search results and, thus, in step 2 academics may come to the realization that online search, including advanced search, overloads them with information that is only partly related to their research issue. Accordingly, we put forward our third hypothesis:

H3 – In research step 2, academics using online search more frequently have a lower degree of satisfaction with online search and, particularly, with advanced search mechanisms to find readings on a topic, compared to academics who use online search less frequently.

As noted before, keyword-based search has evident limitations that cause information overload. To help cope with this overload, authors can rank search results according to different criteria. Publication time represents the default ranking criterion for several search services and is in fact useful to give higher priority to more recent publications. Other ranking criteria are the publication title or the so-called *relevance*, representing the percentage of matching criteria. None of these criteria guarantees that high-impact papers are ranked on top of search results. As a matter of fact, high-impact papers can be ranked low and be hidden below a large number of less impactful papers.

We have discussed in Sect. 2 how academics have strived to reach consensus on a quantitative definition of impact and how the *h*-index and the impact factor represent the most widely used quantitative indicators of impact of authors and journals, respectively. We have also noted that general-purpose search engines allow users to view the *h*-index of authors and the impact factor of journals as an aftermath of search by clicking on a specific paper. To the best of our knowledge, no search service allows to use *h*-index and impact factor as search criteria. Would academics appreciate the use of *h*-index and impact factor as search criteria to help filter results according to their impact and, thus, reduce information overload? In our fourth hypothesis, we put forward a negative answer to this question. Similar to H3, our fourth hypothesis is grounded on the observation that *h*-index and impact factors are widely criticized and, on the other hand, no quantitative indicator of impact has emerged as a widely accepted alternative.

H4 – In research step 2, finding readings is based on impact factor and h-index less than it is based on other impact assessment criteria.

We formulate a similar hypothesis also for research step 3 (selection of citations on a topic). Similar to H4, in H5 we hypothesize that selecting citations is based on impact factor and *h*-index less than it is based on other impact assessment criteria. The arguments leading us to this hypothesis start from the observation that there exists a common distinction between "strong" and "weak" citations [8, 18]. For example, a recent workshop where exploratory research results are presented is weaker to support a statement compared to a well-published survey paper providing more consolidated and conclusive evidence. It can be assumed that citations are chosen on the basis of their "strength", among other criteria.

There is no generally accepted definition of the "strength" of a citation. However, quantitative impact metrics may provide a measure of "strength" on the grounds that impactful papers constitute a stronger citation compared to less impactful papers and, similarly, impactful journals represent a stronger citation compared to less impactful journals. However, the criticisms raised against h-index and impact factor suggest that academics may choose their citations based on criteria different from impact metrics. For example, they may select citations because of their closeness to a research topic or to support specific statements. They may even select citations based on their personal knowledge (and judgement) of an author, rather than relying on quantitative indicators. These considerations lead us to our fifth hypothesis.

H5 – In research step 3, selecting citations is based on impact factor and h-index less than it is based on other impact assessment criteria.

4   Empirical Evidence

This section describes the empirical testing of our hypotheses. The data sample is described in the next section, while Sect. 4.2 reports testing results.

4.1   Data Sample

Hypotheses are tested on a data sample collected with an extensive survey submitted to academics in the MIS field. Interviewees have been selected as authors of papers published in one of the basket of 8 MIS journals [2] in the period January 2013 – February 2015. The selected MIS journal are: European Journal of Information Systems, Information Systems Journal, Information Systems Research, Journal of AIS, Journal of Information Technology, Journal of MIS, Journal of Strategic Information Systems, MIS Quarterly. A total of 3544 questionnaires have been submitted, collecting 326 complete responses with a 9.2% response rate. Figure 2 shows the distribution of respondents by continent.

Geographical Region		
	Count	Percentage
America	132	40.49%
Europe	138	42.33%
Asia	38	11.66%
Oceania	18	5.52%
Tot	326	100.00%

Fig. 2. Sample distribution by geographical region

The questionnaire has been piloted in the time frame March 1 – March 15, 2015 and then extensively submitted through Survey Face (www.surveyface.com) between March 20 and April 22, 2015. The questionnaire and a summary of responses are reported in Appendix (1). It can be noted that questions 6, 7, 10, 11, 15 and 16 address our research hypotheses directly, but the questionnaire includes additional questions that have been considered useful to gain an overall understanding of the search habits of academics. The qualitative results reported in Appendix (1) are discussed in Sect. 5.

4.2 Results

All hypotheses have been verified by testing for differences between mean values of two separate groups of respondents. All t-Tests have been performed with a significance value of 0.05 and assuming unequal variances, as f-Tests have indicated that the probability of equal variances was lower than that of having unequal variances. The hypothesized mean difference reported in the tables is the highest value that allowed the rejection of the null hypothesis. Figures 3, 4, 5, 6 and 7 report testing results for hypotheses 1–5, respectively. All hypotheses are verified with the exception of H3. H3 is not supported since the null hypothesis cannot be rejected (the *t Stat* is lower than minus *t Critical one-tail*). However, the mean values are different, consistent with H3.

	Step1	Step2
Mean	3.067692	2.169231
Variance	0.742317	1.363248
Observations	325	325
Hypothesized Mean Difference	1	
df	596	
t Stat	-1.2615	
P(T<=t) one-tail	0.103811	
t Critical one-tail	1.647414	
P(T<=t) two-tail	0.207622	
t Critical two-tail	1.963952	

Fig. 3. Testing H1: two-sample t-Test assuming unequal variances.

	More frequent usage	Less frequent usage
Mean	3.015748031	2.817258883
Variance	0.777527809	0.905210815
Observations	127	197
Hypothesized Mean Difference	0.35	
df	283	
t Stat	-1.463531791	
P(T<=t) one-tail	0.072215861	
t Critical one-tail	1.650255746	
P(T<=t) two-tail	0.144431722	
t Critical two-tail	1.968381923	

Fig. 4. Testing H2: two-sample t-Test assuming unequal variances.

	More frequent usage	Less frequent usage
Mean	1.669081884	1.92156851
Variance	0.215272006	0.289537625
Observations	69	255
Hypothesized Mean Difference	0.2	
df	122	
t Stat	-6.936483196	
P(T<=t) one-tail	1.03581E-10	
t Critical one-tail	1.657439499	
P(T<=t) two-tail	2.07162E-10	
t Critical two-tail	1.979599678	

Fig. 5. Testing H3: two-sample t-Test assuming unequal variances.

	Other criteria	h-index and impact factor
Mean	2.904615385	2.358461538
Variance	0.186475546	0.569411206
Observations	325	325
Hypothesized Mean Difference	0.6	
df	516	
t Stat	-1.116523842	
P(T<=t) one-tail	0.132358806	
t Critical one-tail	1.647812009	
P(T<=t) two-tail	0.264717613	
t Critical two-tail	1.964572029	

Fig. 6. Testing H4: two-sample t-Test assuming unequal variances.

	Other criteria	h-index and impact factor
Mean	2.552307692	1.792307692
Variance	0.204559926	0.486823362
Observations	325	325
Hypothesized Mean Difference	0.8	
df	555	
t Stat	-0.867245856	
P(T<=t) one-tail	0.193091057	
t Critical one-tail	1.647603773	
P(T<=t) two-tail	0.386182113	
t Critical two-tail	1.964247525	

Fig. 7. Testing H5: two-sample t-Test assuming unequal variances.

5   Discussion

The testing results presented in the previous section provide insights on the literature search habits of academics. First of all, H1 is verified, indicating that academics use online search to find readings on a topic rather than to choose a topic for their future research. Academics do not seem to make decisions on the direction of their research on the basis of information that they gather online. A possible explanation is that the publication process of research results requires a significant amount of time and, as a consequence, the information available from online search engines and archives is not timely. Other information sources, such as workshops, symposiums, and other real-time dissemination initiatives can provide fresh insights on emerging research issues and trends.

The second hypothesis is also verified, suggesting that academics using online search more frequently rate the benefits from text analytic functionalities higher compared to academics using online search less frequently. Answers to question 7 in Appendix (1) show that, on average, 76% of respondents think that it would be useful to have a tool that shows the most frequent topics in scientific papers. As per H2, this percentage is higher for academics relying on online search more heavily. This type of text analytic functionalities supports the aggregate analysis of information and is suitable for the exploration of large data sets. Given the size of online archives, the large-scale aggregate exploration of information is likely to represent a useful tool and our results show that academics are largely aware of this opportunity. The current lack of this type of functionalities may contribute to explain the less intense use of online search for the choice of a new topic (H1), as this research step requires the examination of a broader set of information with an exploratory approach.

Empirical data do not support our third hypothesis. H3 posits that academics using online search more frequently have a lower degree of satisfaction with the advanced functionalities of online search. The qualitative results reported in Appendix (1) show that respondents have a generally high degree of satisfaction with advanced search functionalities, as they rate them mostly *good*, although not *excellent* (question 11). This result contrasts with previous literature indicating a low degree of satisfaction with online search functionalities [3]. This contrast is partly mitigated by the fact that the mean values of satisfaction are different in the direction hypothesized in H3 (see Fig. 5), suggesting that users relying more heavily on online search might have a lower degree of satisfaction.

Results indicate that *h*-index and impact factor are used less than other criteria both to find readings (H4) and select citations (H5). In fact, most authors (73%) disagree on the statement that a publication is worth reading when at least one of the authors has a high *h*-index (see Appendix (1) question 15). The majority of respondents (60%) disagree on the statement that they select citations based on the impact factor of the journal where they are published. Almost all respondent (93%) disagree on the statement that they select citations based on the *h*-index of their authors.

Although H4 is verified, most respondents weakly (47%) or strongly (23%) agree on the statement that a publication is worth reading when it is published on a journal with a high impact factor (Appendix (1) question 15). This indicates that academics tend to trust information (the publication) if the information source (the *journal*) is impactful.

A more direct online interaction through academic social media, such as Academia.edu and ResearchGate, does not seem to be among the priorities of our respondents. More than 90% of our interviewees have answered that they do not use Academia.edu or ResearchGate to choose their research topic (Appendix (1) question 6). Similarly, less than 10% uses them regularly (at least once a week) to find readings (Appendix (1) question 10). Very few respondents (less than 20%) think that a publication is worth reading when at least one of the authors belongs to their research circle in either ResearchGate or Academia.edu (Appendix (1) question 15). Less than 10% uses ResearchGate or Academia.edu to disseminate their work, while going to conferences and working on common projects represent the most common dissemination mechanisms (see Appendix (1) question 17). Despite the success of social media in other domains, in academia the peer-reviewed publication system is still seen as the main mechanism for knowledge sharing and consensus building.

In summary, our results confirm that online search plays an important role in satisfying the literature search requirements of academics. They also indicate that academics mainly use Google Scholar and Google's general purpose engine and that they are generally satisfied with them. Advanced search mechanisms, including alerting services and the analytic functionalities of Scopus, are rarely used. This is consistent with previous literature indicating that users are not willing to put an effort into search [28].

6 Concluding Remarks

Our empirical survey conducted with academics in the MIS field has provided the following main results: MIS academics use online search to find readings on a topic, rather than to choose a topic for their future research. Academics using more frequently online search rate the benefits from text analytic functionalities higher than academics using online search less frequently. Both h-index and impact factor are used less than other criteria both to find readings on a research topic and select citations.

Query results provided by search engines can be made more precise, and information overload can be reduced, by applying semantic search techniques. However, improving search to reduce information overload does not seem to be a priority for MIS academics, especially if improvements must be achieved at the expenses of simplicity (at the current state of the art, semantic search places an additional burden on users).

The majority of respondents would welcome text analytic functionalities to identify new and potentially trending topics, by performing aggregate analyses on a large number of publications. Whether their need for simplicity applies to this type of functionalities remains an open question for future research efforts.

Acknowledgements. We would like to thank Marco Zamperetti, former Master student at Politecnico di Milano, for his assistance in the early phases of this research. This research has been supported by The Association of Information Technology Trust (AITT, London UK).

Appendix (1) – Questionnaire and Qualitative Analysis of Responses

How would you define a "hot research topic"?

		Strongly agree	Weakly agree	Weakly disagree	Strongly disagree
1	A research topic is hot if many researchers are working on it	38.65% (126)	48.47% (158)	9.51% (31)	3.37% (11)
2	A research topic is hot is many companies are investing in research on it	31.9% (104)	47.55% (155)	14.72% (48)	5.83% (19)
3	A research topic is hot if it is included in many calls for funded research	38.04% (124)	46.93% (153)	11.96% (39)	3.07% (10)
4	A research topic is hot if it is the focus of many research publications	32.21% (105)	46.63% (152)	18.1% (59)	3.07% (10)
5	A research topic is hot if papers focusing on it are more likely to be cited	26.99% (88)	43.25% (141)	24.54% (80)	5.21% (17)
6	A research topic is hot if it provides more opportunities to cooperate with other researchers	17.79% (58)	40.18% (131)	34.05% (111)	7.98% (26)
	answered question :	326			
	skipped question :	0			

How do you choose your research topics?

		Always	Frequently	Seldom	Never
1	I do research on what I think is a "hot topic" in my field	5.52% (18)	40.18% (131)	48.47% (158)	5.83% (19)
2	I do research on topics that are most likely to be cited	2.15% (7)	27.61% (90)	55.21% (180)	15.03% (49)
3	My research topics are a consequence of research contracts with companies	2.76% (9)	21.17% (69)	41.41% (135)	34.66% (113)
4	My research topics are a consequence of peer reviewed funded projects	6.44% (21)	28.83% (94)	41.72% (136)	23.01% (75)
5	I choose my research topics as a consequence of suggestions from peer/senior members of my research group	2.76% (9)	26.69% (87)	48.77% (159)	21.78% (71)
6	I choose my research topics according to my personal research interests	70.25% (229)	28.22% (92)	1.53% (5)	0% (0)
7	I choose my research topics according to cooperation opportunities with researchers outside of my research field	2.45% (8)	33.44% (109)	51.23% (167)	12.88% (42)
8	I choose my research topics according to cooperation opportunities with other researchers in my research field	7.98% (26)	57.98% (189)	27.61% (90)	6.44% (21)
9	I choose my research topics based on the directions provided by the most impactful authors in my field	2.45% (8)	23.01% (75)	48.16% (157)	26.38% (86)

4. How frequently do you change your set of research topics?

		Response Percent
1	Every year	4.29%
2	Every 2 years	10.43%
3	Every 3 years	22.39%
4	Every 4 years	18.10%
5	Every 5 years	21.47%
6	Between 5 and 10 years	21.47%
7	Never	1.84%

5. Why do you move away from a research topic?

		Strongly agree	Weakly agree	Weakly disagree	Strongly disagree
1	Because it is no longer a "hot topic" in my field	5.83% (19)	27.61% (90)	39.57% (90)	26.99% (88)
2	Because the related project has ended	27.61% (90)	46.32% (151)	17.18% (56)	8.9% (29)
3	Because of lack of funds	7.06% (23)	28.53% (93)	31.9% (104)	32.52% (106)
4	Because peer/senior members in my research group advised me to do so	3.37% (11)	10.43% (34)	27.61% (90)	58.59% (191)
5	Because I plan to move to a different research institution	3.68% (12)	15.64% (51)	21.17% (69)	59.51% (194)
6	Because I plan to move to a different research group	4.6% (15)	16.87% (55)	23.31% (76)	55.21% (180)
7	Because of a personal loss of intellectual interest	55.52% (181)	33.13% (108)	6.13% (20)	5.21% (17)

6. Do you use online archives and search engines to choose a research topic?

		Strongly agree	Weakly agree	Weakly disagree	Strongly disagree
1	I do not use them to choose a research topic	41.41% (135)	19.33% (63)	19.63% (64)	19.63% (64)
2	I use Google Scholar	30.67% (100)	26.69% (87)	14.11% (46)	28.53% (93)
3	I use Google's general purpose search engine	18.4% (60)	27.3% (89)	19.33% (63)	34.97% (114)
4	I use Scopus	3.68% (12)	10.12% (33)	17.48% (57)	68.71% (224)
5	I use the analytic functionalities of Scopus ("Analyze search results" button)	1.53% (5)	4.29% (14)	17.79% (58)	76.38% (249)
6	I use Web of Science	7.98% (26)	16.26% (53)	17.79% (58)	57.98% (189)
7	I use ResearchGate.net	2.15% (7)	15.34% (50)	26.38% (86)	56.13% (183)
8	I use Academia.edu	1.23% (4)	6.75% (22)	20.55% (67)	71.47% (233)
9	I use my field's vertical search engines (e.g. IEEE for engineering, Pubmed for medicine, etc.)	14.72% (48)	19.02% (62)	14.11% (46)	52.15% (170)

7. Do you think that it would be useful to have a tool that allows you to automatically gather the most frequent topics in scientific papers?

		Response Percent	Response Count
1	Yes	26.07%	85
2	May be yes	50%	163
3	May be no	11.66%	38
4	No	12.27%	40

8. How do you find readings related to your research topics? - Conferences

		More than 4 times	2-4 times a year	Once a year	Less that once a year	Never
1	I attend conferences in my field	10.43% (34)	49.39% (161)	29.14% (95)	11.04% (36)	0% (0)
2	I serve as a reviewer for conferences in my field	29.14% (95)	45.4% (148)	17.79% (58)	4.91% (16)	2.76% (9)

9. How do you find readings related to your research topics? - I serve as an editor for journals in my field

		Response Percent	Response Count
1	More than 3	9.20%	30
2	Three	8.59%	28
3	Two	16.26%	53
4	One	24.85%	81
5	None	41.10%	134

10. How do you find readings related to your research topics? - Other sources

		Every day	Every week	Every month	A few times in a	Never
1	I use Google Scholar	21.17% (69)	43.25% (141)	19.33% (63)	10.74% (35)	5.52% (18)
2	I use Google's general purpose search engine	22.7% (74)	30.98% (101)	21.47% (70)	14.11% (46)	10.74% (35)
3	I use Scopus	1.53% (5)	5.21% (17)	11.66% (38)	20.86% (68)	60.74% (198)
4	I use Web of Science	2.76% (9)	9.2% (30)	15.03% (49)	27.91% (91)	45.09% (147)
5	I use ResearchGate.net	0.31% (1)	10.12% (33)	17.79% (58)	26.38% (86)	45.4% (148)
6	I use Academia.edu	0% (0)	1.23% (4)	7.98% (26)	18.1% (59)	72.7% (237)
7	I use my field's vertical search engines (e.g. IEEE for engineering, Pubmed for medicine, etc.)	4.6% (15)	19.02% (62)	18.1% (59)	19.33% (63)	38.96% (127)
8	I select interesting readings amond the references of papers that I have read	17.48% (57)	43.87% (143)	25.46% (83)	10.43% (34)	2.76% (9)
9	I receive paper versions of the relevant journals in my field	3.99% (13)	10.12% (33)	17.79% (58)	23.31% (76)	44.79% (146)

11. How do you rate the effectiveness of the following tools to search for readings related to your research topics?

		Excellent	Good	Fair	Bad	I never use it
1	Google Scholar's advanced search	31.9% (104)	47.85% (156)	13.19% (43)	1.84% (6)	5.21% (17)
2	Scopus advanced search	3.68% (12)	15.95% (52)	12.88% (42)	1.84% (6)	65.64% (214)
3	Web of Science's advanced search	6.44% (21)	19.33% (63)	21.47% (70)	4.29% (14)	48.47% (158)
4	The advanced search of your field's vertical search engines (e.g. IEEE for engineering, Pubmed for medicine, etc.)	10.43% (34)	25.77% (84)	20.86% (68)	2.45% (8)	40.49% (132)
5	ResearchGate.net	0.92% (3)	10.43% (34)	26.69% (87)	5.21% (17)	56.75% (185)
6	Academia.edu	0.61% (2)	5.52% (18)	12.88% (42)	2.15% (7)	78.83% (257)

12. What type of readings do you look for?

		Always	Frequently	Seldom	Never
1	Academic papers	85.58% (279)	14.11% (46)	0.31% (1)	0% (0)
2	Company white papers	2.76% (9)	21.17% (69)	52.45% (171)	23.62% (77)
3	Patents	0% (0)	1.84% (6)	22.7% (74)	75.46% (246)
4	Slides	1.53% (5)	16.26% (53)	50.92% (166)	31.29% (102)
5	Videos	1.53% (5)	11.66% (38)	48.47% (158)	38.34% (125)

13. What are the characteristics of your readings?

		Always	Frequently	Seldom	Never
1	They discuss the results of theoretical research	33.44% (109)	54.29% (177)	11.96% (39)	0.31% (1)
2	They discuss the results of empirical research	33.13% (108)	63.19% (206)	3.68% (12)	0% (0)
3	They describe case studies	11.35% (37)	50.92% (166)	32.82% (107)	4.91% (16)

14. Do you use push services that alert you when new research is available that might be of interest for you?

		Always	Frequently	Seldom	Never
1	I use Scopus alerting services that let me know when there is a new publication that matches one of my searches	2.45% (8)	3.68% (12)	9.51% (31)	84.36% (275)
2	I use ResearchGate alerting services that let me know when a researcher in my network has uploaded a new publication	6.75% (22)	11.96% (39)	16.87% (55)	64.42% (210)
3	I use Academia.edu alerting services that let me know when a researcher in my network has uploaded a new publication	1.23% (4)	1.84% (6)	11.66% (38)	85.28% (278)

15. What are the drivers that make you think that a publication is worth reading?

		Strongly agree	Weakly agree	Weakly disagree	Strongly disagree
1	A publication is worth reading when it has a high number of citations	22.7% (74)	49.08% (160)	19.94% (65)	8.28% (27)
2	A publication is worth reading when it tackles a practical problem	34.36% (112)	49.39% (161)	14.11% (46)	2.15% (7)
3	A publication is worth reading when it tackles a theoretical problem	38.96% (127)	50% (163)	8.59% (28)	2.45% (8)
4	A publication is worth reading when it is closely related to your reasearch topics	80.98% (264)	16.56% (54)	2.15% (7)	0.31% (1)
5	A publication is worth reading when it presents research results that are practically applicable and useful	46.32% (151)	39.88% (130)	11.66% (38)	2.15% (7)
6	A publication is worth reading when at least one of the authors has a high h-index	4.91% (16)	21.47% (70)	32.21% (105)	41.41% (135)
7	A publication is worth reading when at least one of the authors is a well known established researcher in your field	15.34% (50)	48.47% (158)	26.99% (88)	9.2% (30)
8	A publication is worth reading when I personally know at least one of the authors	13.19% (43)	40.8% (133)	28.22% (92)	17.79% (58)
9	A publication is worth reading when at least one of the authors belongs to my research circle in either ResearchGate or Academia.edu	2.45% (8)	18.71% (61)	23.62% (77)	55.21% (180)
10	A publication is worth reading when it is published in a journal that has a high impact factor	22.7% (74)	46.63% (152)	20.25% (66)	10.43% (34)

16. How do you choose the citations to be included in your own publications?

		Always	Frequently	Seldom	Never
1	I choose citations based on their closeness to my research topics	62.27% (203)	33.13% (108)	3.37% (11)	1.23% (4)
2	I choose citations that provide important evidence to support specific statements in my publication	73.31% (239)	24.54% (80)	1.23% (4)	0.92% (3)
3	I choose citations based on my personal knowledge of at least one of the authors	3.99% (13)	19.33% (63)	45.4% (148)	31.29% (102)
4	I choose citations based on the impact factor of their publication outlet	7.36% (24)	32.52% (106)	31.29% (102)	28.83% (94)
5	I choose citations where at least one of the authors has a high h-index	0.61% (2)	6.44% (21)	25.46% (83)	67.48% (220)
6	I choose citations based on my target publication outlet	13.19% (43)	43.87% (143)	30.98% (101)	11.96% (39)
7	I make an effort to include highly cited papers among my citations	7.98% (26)	28.53% (93)	35.28% (115)	28.22% (92)
8	I cite authors who are most likely to cite me back	1.23% (4)	5.52% (18)	18.71% (61)	74.54% (243)

17. How do you work to disseminate your own research work?

		Always	Frequently	Seldom	Never
1	I personally go to the conferences where my papers are published	30.37% (99)	51.84% (169)	14.72% (48)	3.07% (10)
2	I reach out to other researchers in my field on ResearchGate	3.68% (12)	11.35% (37)	30.37% (99)	54.6% (178)
3	I reach out to other researchers in my field on Academia.edu	1.23% (4)	2.45% (8)	15.03% (49)	81.29% (265)
4	I create a network of contacts through cooperation in common research projects	11.66% (38)	44.79% (146)	25.15% (82)	18.4% (60)
5	I circulate my own papers before publication to get early feedback	8.59% (28)	32.21% (105)	39.88% (130)	19.33% (63)
6	I circulate my own papers before publication to engage other researchers	4.91% (16)	20.55% (67)	44.79% (146)	29.75% (97)

References

1. Adriaanse, L., Rensleigh, C.: Web of Science, Scopus and Google Scholar: a content comprehensiveness comparison. Electron. Libr. **31**(6), 727–744 (2013)
2. AISNET (2016). https://aisnet.org/?SeniorScholarBasket
3. Baez, M., Birukou, A., Casati, F., Marchese, M.: Addressing information overload in the scientific community. IEEE Internet Comput. **14**(6), 31–38 (2010)
4. Bakkalbasi N., Bauer K., Glover J., Wang L.: Three options for citation tracking: Google Scholar, Scopus and Web of Science. Biomed. Digit. Libr. **3**(7), 1–8 (2006)
5. Barbagallo, D., Bruni, L., Francalanci, C., Giacomazzi, P., Merlo, F., Poli, A.: Semi-automated methods for the annotation and design of a semantic network designed for sentiment analysis of social web content. In: Proceedings of 10th International Workshop on Web Semantics (WebS11), Toulouse, France, August (2011)
6. Belkadhi, K., Trabelsi, A.: Toward a stochastically robust normalized impact factor against fraud and scams. Scientometrics **124**(3), 1871–1884 (2020). https://doi.org/10.1007/s11192-020-03577-4
7. Bergstrom, C.T., West, J.D., Wiseman, M.A.: The Eigenfactor™ metrics. J. Neurosci. **28**(45), 11433–11434 (2008)
8. Boell, S.K., Cecez-Kecmanovic, D.: On being 'systematic' in literature reviews in IS. J. Inf. Technol. **30**, 161–173 (2014)
9. Boonyoung, T., Mingkhwan, A.: Semantic search: document ranking and clustering using computer science ontology and N-grams. J. Digit. Inf. Manag. **12**(6), 369–378 (2014)
10. Bornmann, L.: h-index research in scientometrics: a summary. J. Informetr. **8**(3), 749–750 (2014)
11. Bornmann, L., Mutz, R., Hug, S.E., Daniel, H.D.: A multilevel meta-analysis of studies reporting correlations between the h index and 37 different h index variants. J. Informetr. **5**(3), 346–359 (2011)
12. Bosman, J., van Mourik, I., Rasch, M., Sieverts, E., Verhoeff, H.: Scopus reviewed and compared. Utrecht University Library (2006)
13. CAIS, Special Issue on Self Citation (2009)
14. Campbell, P.: Escape from the impact factor. Inter-Res. **8**(1), 5–7 (2008)
15. Charitonidis, C., Rashid, A., Taylor, P.J.: Weak signals as predictors of real-world phenomena in social media. In: Proceedings of IEEE/ACM International Conference on Weak Signals as Predictors of Real-World Phenomena in Social Media (2015)
16. Cobo, M.J., Lopez-Herrera, A.G., Herrera-Viedma, E., Herrera, F.: Science mapping software tools: review, analysis, and cooperative study among tools. J. Am. Soc. Inf. Sci. Technol. **62**(7), 1382–1402 (2011)
17. Falagas, M., Pitsouni, E., Malietzis, G., Pappas, G.: Comparison of PubMed, Scopus, Web of Science, and Google Scholar: stengths and weaknesses. FASEB J. Life Sci. Forum **22**, 338–342 (2008)
18. Wu, H., Hua, Y., Li, B., Pei, Y.: Enhancing citation recommendation with various evidences. In: 2012 IEEE International Conference on Fuzzy Systems and Knowledge Discovery (FSKD 12), pp. 1160–1165 (2012)
19. Jacsò, P.: Savvy searching, Google Scholar: the pros and the cons. Online Inf. Rev. **29**(2), 208–214 (2005)
20. Jacsò, P.: Savvy searching: Google Scholar revisited. Online Inf. Rev. **32**(1), 102–114 (2008)
21. Rossiter, S., Noble, J., Bell, K.R.W.: Social simulations: improving interdisciplinary understanding of scientific positioning and validity. J. Artif. Soc. Soc. Simul. **13**(1), 1–34 (2010)

22. Schreiber, M.: A variant of the h-index to measure recent performance. J. Assoc. Inf. Sci. Technol. **66**(11), 2373–2380 (2015)
23. Scopus, Content Coverage Guide (2014). http://www.elsevier.com/__data/assets/pdf_file/0007/69451/sc_content-coverage-guide_july-2014.pdf
24. Shultz, M.: Comparing test searches in PubMed and Google Scholar. J. Med. Libr. Assoc. **95**(4), 442–445 (2007)
25. Thomson Reuters Community: Citation Impact Center (2016). http://community.thomsonre uters.com/t5/Citation-Impact-Center/Web-of-Science-Coverage-Expansion/ba-p/10663
26. Uyar, A., Aliyu, F.M.: Evaluating search features of Google Knowledge Graph and Bing Satori: entity types, list searches and query interfaces. Online Inf. Rev. **39**(2), 197–213 (2015)
27. Vanclay, J.K.: Impact factor: outdated artefact or stepping-stone to journal certification? Scientometrics **92**(2), 211–238 (2012)
28. Wells, J., Truran, M., Goulding, J.: Search habits of the computer literate. In: ACM Hypertext Conference 2007 (HT 2007) (2007)
29. Yoon, J.: Detecting weak signals for long-term business opportunities using text mining of Web news (2012)

The Italian Academic Research System and Its Evaluation: A Conceptual Framework Inception

Francesco Bertolotti, Angela Locoro, Luca Mari, Eliana Alessandra Minelli[✉],
Aurelio Ravarini, and Maria Rucsandra Stan

Università Carlo Cattaneo - LIUC, Castellanza, VA, Italy
{fbertolotti,alocoro,lmari,eminelli,aravarini,mstan}@liuc.it

Abstract. In this paper, we introduce the main topics and the initial settings of an Italian PRIN project aimed at investigating how the systematic adoption of systems for the evaluation of research in the Italian academic context may influence research outcomes. We motivate the need to adopt and adapt a conceptual framework, which may identify, define and describe the relevant entities involved in the evaluation process, their measurable properties and relations. We then present the first draft of an ontology derived from an existing ontology about the academic world, namely the VIVO ontology, and the criteria for its design. We report the steps taken to modify the received ontology in order to fit it to our purposes, with an interdisciplinary contribution to the selection and adaptation of entities. Novel considerations about the use of formal conceptual systems and the contribution of our work to the socio-technical view are finally drawn, and some further directions of the project are proposed.

Keywords: Research evaluation systems · Socio-technical model · Ontology design · VIVO ontology · Quality measurement

1 Introduction and Motivation: The Italian Academic Research Evaluation System

The increasing awareness of the strategic importance of academic research for national and regional development has led many countries to manage research for public policy purposes. Thus, given the complexity of the concept itself of 'quality of scientific research' and the connections between scientific research and public purposes, and given the level of autonomy recently granted to the academic institutions and the system of competitive funding that guarantees some sustainability to the endeavour (Whitley and Gläser 2007), several countries have implemented and are running a *research evaluation system*.

Such systems within European countries have often been inspired by neo-liberal principles, aimed at simultaneously fostering the steering capabilities of national policy makers and the accountability of the universities for the use of public resources (Neave 1991; Whitley and Gläser 2007). In Italy, weaknesses in the policy design together with poor implementation led to unintended consequences in the reform process for the access to public resources, and conflicts related to the introduction of a research evaluation system (Minelli et al. 2006; Reale and Seeber 2013; Rebora and Turri 2013; Capano et al. 2016).

The context of this paper is a publicly funded project "of national interest" in Italy (PRIN 2017), titled "The effects of evaluation on academic research: knowledge production and methodological issues". Its general purpose is that of investigating the effects of the research evaluation system implemented so far by the Italian government.

Since the 2000s, Italian governments implemented two parallel research assessment frameworks, which had a significant impact on academics' role and work: VQR (*Valutazione della Qualità della Ricerca*, in Italian) and ASN (*Abilitazione Scientifica Nazionale*, in Italian). Even though with some differences, both VQR and ASN aim at assessing the quality of the academic research outputs, using informed peer review and, extensively, either bibliometric indicators (Impact Factor and the number of citations) or a rating of national and international journals based on their quality (the so-called list of top 'A' journals). Both evaluation frameworks define academic quality excellence standards at a national and institutional level, whose achievement grants access to professorship, pushing academics to comply with such evaluation rules and criteria.

The PRIN project mentioned above focuses on the effects of the application of these evaluation frameworks on knowledge production in the Italian academic context, most of which were already pointed out by the relevant literature. Some open questions concern whether research evaluation drives research quality without creating distortions, and how measurable are both the quality of the research and the effects of an external evaluation of the research quality, whereby external research evaluation is intended as a control entity based on an authority who is placed outside (literally detached) the organization being evaluated and independent of it.

Given the complexity of the research process, the methodological aspects of the measurement of its characteristics and the evaluation of its output take on a specific significance. As a first instance of this investigation, it is crucial to rely on a core identification of an appropriate and relevant conceptual framework for this knowledge field.

Thus, the research questions addressed by this paper are related to: the initial identification and definition of the main entities of the Italian research system; how they relate to each other; whether it is possible to structure this knowledge to share unambiguous notions; and how to support the identification and measurement of the impact that external research evaluation can produce on these entities and research practices in general.

2 Towards a Socio-Technically Aware Ontology

The approach in unfolding the research questions took the perspective of a socio-technical system, i.e., a model defined by four interdependent variables: task, people, technology, and structure, where each of them influences the others (Leavitt 1965). In brief, the socio-technical perspective implies that all the activities considered under its framework regard both the social subsystems (human and structure) and the technical subsystems (technology and task), and requires that each of these elements is first of all identified, described and carefully considered alone and in interaction with the other ones. We employ a socio-technical approach to the research evaluation issue because we sustain that research products emerge from a network in which social entities, such as scholars and editors, interact with technical components of different complexity, and that the exploitation and the availability of such technical subsystems by social entities influence research quality. By these means, the idea of developing a conceptual framework revolved around the design of an ontology-based conceptualization followed, as already been established in the literature (Pinto et al. 2004; Kotis and Vouros 2006; Herrmann et al. 2007). This approach involves domain experts and/or end users as central actors. The literature further suggested initiating the development of an ontology not from scratch, but rather reusing already existing ontologies and managing the decision-making process about the ontology construction on consensus. Further advantages in adopting a socio-technical perspective to the development of an ontology were that knowledge sharing was encouraged since the early development phases of its conceptualization (Holsapple and Joshi 2004).

Research evaluation is intrinsically interdisciplinary in its conception, and its implementation is highly contextual. Hence its definition should go beyond organisations and disciplines. Moreover, as highlighted by Gläser (2007:246), "Scientific communities have their own distinct social order, which extends across all science policy institutions and organisations" and whose impact often prevails over governance practices within universities. These observations called for an effortful and rigorous process of definition, where the measurand of research (Mari 2003) should be identified, included what and how entities had to be measured in this domain, and how what had to be measured can be provided by an ontology that made measurands explicit and upon which different evaluation practices could be built in accordance with the requirements and the peculiarities of the scientific communities. In this sense, the conceptualization of an ontology, which can be defined as an "explicit specification of a conceptualization" (Gruber 1995), seemed to support the analysis of suitable research evaluation practices while formally defining the Italian research system from the point of view of evaluation, and shed light on its complexities and interactions with the evaluation practices.

The literature mainly provided examples of ontologies useful to build taxonomies in specific fields of knowledge, as shown in the following section. Instead, our approach aimed to reconcile interdisciplinarity and purposefulness in order to permit a large application domain. Interdisciplinarity is suited to be studied from a socio-technical perspective because the interaction of social with technical subsystems is transversal to different research areas. This purpose led us to focus on a specific ontology that assured a wide representation of entities and their properties within the Italian research system and thus provided interoperability across analysis methods and perspectives.

3 Background: Ontologies and the Organizational Field

In philosophy, the term "ontology" is used to refer to the fundamental studies of entities and their "modes of being" (their characteristics, their relations to other entities, and the like) (see for example Hofweber et al. 2014). As introduced above, an ontology is instead understood in an application context, as a suitably structured system of concepts, typically described by means of a computer-oriented formal language.

Many studies witness the application of ontologies to the field of management. A methodology called "Systematic Literature Network Analysis" (SLNA) (Colicchia and Strozzi 2012) was implemented to provide an overview of these applications in the following paragraphs.

In the context of organizational studies, until the first decade of 2000, the use of ontologies was limited to the description of organizational goals issues from the point of view of organizational processes, including elements such as sub-goal, task and resources (Fox et al. 1995). Later, ontologies were used to define competencies for learning activities by assessing the ever-changing knowledge needs within an organization (Sicilia 2005), as well as tools to facilitate the transfer of knowledge across organizations and reduce the learning curve by reusing acquired knowledge (Li and Chang 2009). Ontologies served also as tools in knowledge management when mapping the competencies of an organization (Zancanaro et al. 2013). Furthermore, ontologies enabled a common understanding of the organizational goals by identifying and evaluating the relevant organizational and social media data to achieve organizational goals, in addition to mapping their relationship with sub-goals, tasks and actions (Izhar et al. 2013; Izhar et al. 2017a, 2017b; Izhar and Apduhan 2018b). The efficiency and effectiveness of an ontology to act as a support in the decision-making, as well as in enabling the measurement of already achieved goals, resides in capturing data that allows to model relationships and knowledge within an organization, thus reducing irrelevant organizational data (Tengku Izhar et al. 2019). An ontology is, in other words, able to represent the dependency relationships of organizational entities to organizational goals and used for evaluating the level of organizational goals without affecting the organizational processes (Izhar and Apduhan 2018a).

Throughout the years, ontologies in the domain of organizations were used for different purposes, including organizational memory management (Paajanen et al. 2006), evaluation (Weinberger et al. 2008) and consolidation (Marian 2009); cross-organization knowledge transfer (Abou-Zeid 2002; White and Lutters 2007), retrieval of organizational knowledge (Yao et al. 2013) and compatibility check of cross-organization knowledge (Anjum et al. 2013). They were also used to federate virtual organizations for common goals achievement (Plisson et al. 2007).

3.1 Ontologies as Models for the Research Field

In the last twenty years, ontologies have been widely applied to the analysis of scholarly systems and to support activities related to academic research. To the best of our knowledge, it is possible to identify three main streams of research in this area. First, ontologies were used to classify specific research areas into taxonomies. A wide range of fields was characterized and defined through a set of objects and describable relationships among them, for example, computer science (Sanderson and Croft 1999; Salatino et al. 2018), economics (Cherrier 2017), biology (Lipscomb 2000) and physics[1].

Second, generic and wide ontologies were developed to represent the entire domain of academic research. Four main examples can be identified: VIVO, CERIF, SYNAT and FOAF-Academic. VIVO (http://vivo.library.cornell.edu/), a Virtual Life Sciences

---

[1] https://physh.aps.org/about

Library developed at Cornell University, describes the domain of scholars' activities, including not only the agents and the objects that compose it, but also a set of elements – like enterprises, libraries or students – that influence them.

The primary purpose of VIVO is to make a knowledge-based representation of the assortment of actors and activities taking place across the university's world (Caruso et al. 2006) as well as to support scholars' networking (Krafft et al. 2010). CERIF (Common European Research Information Format) describes elementary notions and properties for representing research information as semantic data (Lezcano et al. 2012). SYNAT describes information provided by the research system and covers notions and events related to scholarly work. The purpose of the project is to build comprehensive scientific content storage and sharing platform for anyone interested to use academic information (Wróblewska et al. 2012). FOAF-Academic (Kalemi and Martiri 2011) is an extension of the well-known Friend of A Friends[2], an ontology that specifies communications in scholarly communities and academic-related terms.

Third, ontologies were developed to support the evaluation of research, the quality measurement of the academia by aligning all the necessary information (Aminah et al. 2017), the conceptualization of qualitative factors that influence the performance of faculty members (Bai et al. 2014) and – through the CERIF ontology – the evaluation and the quantitative expression of scientific research results (Grace and Gartner 2010; Ivanović et al. 2011).

3.2 Interdisciplinarity and Quality: Our View

The use of domain ontologies is usually circumscribed within well-defined fields. However, as already stated, research evaluation is intrinsically interdisciplinary in its conception. Consequently, the paper proposes the use of an ontology at an interdisciplinary level (inspired also by the composition of the research group), with the aim of creating a tool that can better connect and support communication and comprehension. In other words, the authors proposed to handle an ontology from a socio-technical perspective, positioning knowledge sharing at the core of the process and putting domain experts and/or end-users at its centre, thus giving the design experience a more pragmatic angle.

Quality has always been relevant for the organizational world, for example in relation to compliance with internal specifications or to customer satisfaction. To this purpose, many tools (including ontology-based ones) were developed since the late 1990s. Ontologies have been used to enable quality problem identification by providing a shared terminology and defining semantics for the enterprise in a precise and unambiguous way (Kim et al. 1999). In this sense, the design of an ontology is driven by the interest to answer specific competency questions that characterise the decision-making. The academic research world is no exception to the practices of quality management; on the contrary, quality initiatives should be at the core of scientific endeavours, as this enhances knowledge and skills of humans (Rezeanu 2011).

---

[2] http://www.foaf-project.org

4 Management and Adaptation of the VIVO Ontology

The objective of this paper is one of the pillars for the development of the PRIN project introduced in the first Section, whose focus is "the investigation of the effect of research evaluation implemented by the government on the research work and knowledge production" in the Italian universities. Thus, the project aims at achieving three primary goals. First, the development of a methodological approach designed to measure the effects of evaluation. Second, the identification of the possible consequences of the measurement. Third, the elimination of the ambiguity for the evaluation, assessment and measurement concepts in the area of interest. By looking at the state of the art of literature, two research areas proved to be relevant to our analysis: one related to the specific use of evaluation (distributive, improvement, monitoring) (Molas-Gallart 2012); the other regarding the influence of neo-liberal approaches on the development of research evaluation reforms in Europe and how the implementation of such reforms has been affected by the institutional factors of the respective country (Gläser 2007; Neave 2012).

Consequently, the need for mutual understanding among peers as well as among partners in a project (Akyürek and Afacan 2018) has arisen. To overcome this limit, as well as to set a foundation for the research project, the use of an ontology was put forward. The literature already suggested the use of a domain ontology as a tool for knowledge elicitation (Kaiya and Saeki 2006). In fact, there was evidence of ontologies being used to support the evaluation of research and the quality measurement of academia (Aminah et al. 2017) and the conceptualization of qualitative factors influencing the performance of faculty members (Bai et al. 2014) as well as of scientific results (Grace and Gartner 2010), and to define unambiguously the main elements of a research system (Sure et al. 2005).

Taking into consideration that there are ontologies able to describe specifically the Italian research system yet, two alternatives were considered: the development of a new ontology from scratch (Wróblewska et al. 2012) or the adaptation of an existing one to fit the project's purposes (Kalemi and Martiri 2011). The latter choice enabled a solid foundation for the proposed work, as well as the chance to choose from numerous available alternatives. Accordingly, some existing ontologies were analysed, and in particular: VIVO, CERIF, SYNAT and FOAF-Academic. During the selection process two criteria were used: the number of applications of each ontology, in other words, the diffusion of the tools; the relevance of the ontology to our goal (the representation of entities and relationships that compose the Italian research system to support the assessment of the impact of evaluation criteria on academic outputs), underlining the preference for constant usage of the same tool through time. No quantitative analysis was developed for this decision, however, the information collected during the literature review was used to assign a qualitative judgment to each option.

As it can be seen in Tables 1 and 2, the tool that seemed to better fit the goals and purposes of our project was VIVO.[3] For this reason, we adopted this ontology as a starting point of our project.

---

[3] For documentation please follow the official VIVO link: https://duraspace.org/vivo/, where the last version of the ontology is available. At https://www.w3.org/community/vivo/ the official page of the VIVO as a W3C standard certified project.

Table 1. Application of the evaluated ontologies

Ontology	Level	Explanation
VIVO	High	Applied in more than 10 papers indexed on Scopus
CERIF	High	Applied in more than 10 papers indexed on Scopus
SYNAT	Low	Applied in less than 3 papers indexed on Scopus
FOAF-Academic	Low	Applied in less than 3 papers indexed on Scopus

Table 2. Relevance of the evaluated ontologies to our goal

Ontology	Level	Explanation
VIVO	Medium	Describes most of the entities and relationships we are interested in; needs only slight modifications
CERIF	Low	Describes only a small portion of the entities that are relevant for our goals; needs to be widely integrated
SYNAT	Medium	Describes most of the entities and relationships we are interested in; needs to be compared with VIVO for its redundancies with it
FOAF-Academic	Low	Describes only a small portion of the entities that are relevant for our goals; needs to be widely integrated

Once we selected VIVO, we defined some criteria to follow during the modification process[4]:

1. we removed entities considered not relevant for the evaluation of the quality of the research (for example, librarians and cities);
2. we removed entities considered not relevant to model the Italian scenario (for example, professor emeritus and US citizen);
3. we added entities considered relevant for the evaluation of the quality of the research, especially in the Italian scenario (for example, the research platforms and the research mindset).

Subsets of the VIVO entities that were identified at this round are reported in Figs. 1 and 2, from both original and customized ontologies. The figures, which exhibit a section of the VIVO before and after our intervention, exemplify how the modification criteria were applied to our work. As VIVO is a multilayer ontology using upper (more abstract) concepts borrowed from upper ontologies to frame proper domain concepts, we maintained the original VIVO structure and mainly worked at the first and more general domain entity level. In this context, we extended the ontology to include concepts that

---

[4] Both the inspection and modifications step of the VIVO ontology were done by uploading an.owl version of the ontology, available in the VIVO repository, into the Protégé tool, a Java-based specialized knowledge representation and reasoning tool freely available online (at https://protege.stanford.edu/).

are peculiar to the description of the Italian academic system and, on the contrary, pruned in width and in depth all those concepts that we deemed out of scope for our purposes or unnecessarily verbose and too detailed. We decided to show the modification criteria and an example of their application instead of reporting a list that includes every change. Thus, we tried to achieve better clarity and efficacy in the description.

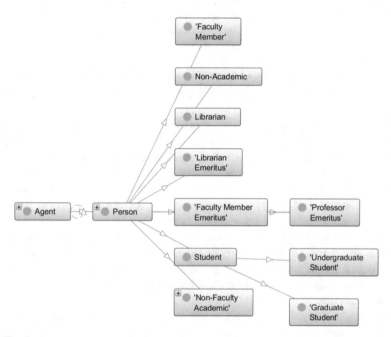

Fig. 1. Excerpt of the original VIVO ontology, with an overview of human entities.

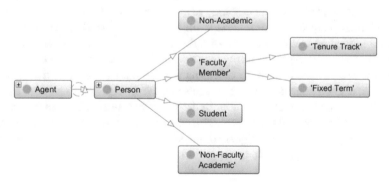

Fig. 2. Excerpt of the customized VIVO ontology, with an overview of human entities.

5   Discussion

As seen in the literature, it is not news that the academic research system could be analyzed through the lenses of a socio-technical approach (Singh and Han 2005). Our work puts once more in evidence the relationships between the social part of the system (like scholars, research groups and institutions) and the technical one (like laboratories and online platforms). The use of a shared vocabulary to define all entities involved in the evaluation of academic organizations under a sociotechnical perspective was a pragmatic choice. As a matter of fact, this vocabulary circumscribes the scope of the discourse and the horizon within which to observe and validate new routines. Likewise, a second goal was to showcase new approaches to the evaluation of research activities in the academic environment, by opening up to other validation pathways in the evaluation of scholarly practices.

The yielded ontology has the potential to support and help us pursue two goals. On the one hand, this tool could be relevant per se. On the other hand, it could help light up a debate about new ways of evaluating scholars, either inside the project or in the literature, helping other researchers and academic policy makers enrich their vision and take into consideration the existence of different points of view. For example, we already highlighted the introduction of research platforms in our version of VIVO. Nowadays, the score of a scholar on a platform such as ResearchGate[5] is not a discriminating factor in the formal evaluation of its research performance. We are not suggesting that a resort to these platforms should be the only way (let alone the main one) to assess the performance of a researcher. Rather a discussion about the relevance of this specific topic could help expand the boundaries of the debate and involve in the discussion very disparate research fields and traditions.

To conclude, this work gave to our goals a pragmatic attitude. Thus, we do not presume to revolutionize the way in which ontology-based techniques are applied, and neither to develop new theories related to socio-technical systems. Nevertheless, the approach to our research question is original and peculiar. To the best of our knowledge, it was never attempted to use an ontology to gaze at a national research system under a socio-technical perspective, nor to gaze at the effects of evaluation of academic results through a modelling choice. Furthermore, the peculiarity of our approach is given by the interdisciplinary perspective attributed to the design and the use of an ontology. This enables the user, as the creator, to reflect on a given purpose not just from her point of view, but also by considering all the facets that can be relevant to achieve a defined goal. This experience was also peculiar in the sense that, since the beginning, we tried to fill the inevitable gap between ontologies experts and non-experts by involving both interchangeably as users and designers of the same artifact, in that they were academic people and had a productive role in the project.

6   Conclusions and Future Work

Coherently with the PRIN commitment, results would first apply to the Italian research system. Nevertheless, a possible next step could be to test other academic systems. In

---

[5] http://www.researchgate.net.

conclusion, our customized version of VIVO could be a support in this process not only for an assessment perspective but also for other purposes.

The development of dynamical models could help understand the origins and the evolution of complex phenomena that emerged from evaluation activities, as well as the extension of the shared vocabulary towards a thorough examination of entities' measurable properties. This last endeavor is among our future work.

The idea is that of defining entities measurands, their kinds and their measurability. This conceptualization would extend the investigation of the entities defined so far to their measurable relata and their components, such as their algebraic structure and their unit of measure.

Lastly, the application of new-institutional theory to address the evaluation of research in the Italian academic system (Whitley and Gläser 2007).

References

Abou-Zeid, E.S.: An ontology-based approach to inter-organizational knowledge transfer. J. Glob. Inf. Technol. Manag. (2002). https://doi.org/10.1080/1097198X.2002.10856330

Akyürek, E., Afacan, Ö.: Problems encountered during the scientific research process in graduate education: the institute of educational sciences. High. Educ. Stud. (2018). https://doi.org/10.5539/hes.v8n2p47

Aminah, S., Afriyanti, I., Krisnadhi, A.: Ontology-based approach for academic evaluation system. In: Proceedings - International Conference on Data Engineering (2017). https://doi.org/10.1109/ICDE.2017.229

Anjum, N., et al.: Verification of knowledge shared across design and manufacture using a foundation ontology. Int. J. Prod. Res. (2013). https://doi.org/10.1080/00207543.2013.798051

Bai, S., et al.: Faculty performance evaluation system: an ontological approach. In: Proceedings of IEEE/ACS International Conference on Computer Systems and Applications, AICCSA (2014). https://doi.org/10.1109/AICCSA.2014.7073187

Capano, G., Regini, M., Turri, M.: Changing Governance in Universities. Changing Governance in Universities (2016).https://doi.org/10.1057/978-1-137-54817-7

Caruso, B., et al.: VIVO: case study of an ontology-based Web site. In: AAAI Fall Symposium - Technical Report (2006)

Cherrier, B.: Classifying economics: a history of the JEL codes. J. Econ. Lit. (2017).https://doi.org/10.1257/jel.20151296

Colicchia, C., Strozzi, F.: Supply chain risk management: a new methodology for a systematic literature review. Supply Chain Manag. (2012). https://doi.org/10.1108/13598541211246558

Fox, M.S., Barbuceanu, M., Gruninger, M.: Organisation ontology for enterprise modelling: preliminary concepts for linking structure and behavior. In: Proceedings of the Workshop on Enabling Technologies: Infrastructure for Collaborative Enterprises, WET ICE (1995). https://doi.org/10.1016/0166-3615(95)00079-8

Gläser, J.: The social orders of research evaluation systems. In: Whitley, R., Gläser, J. (eds.) The Changing Governance of the Sciences, p. 246. Springer, Dordrecht (2007). https://doi.org/10.1007/978-1-4020-6746-4_12

Grace, S., Gartner, R.: Modelling national research assessments in CERIF. In: CRIS 2010: Connecting Science with Society - The Role of Research Information in a Knowledge-Based Society - 10th International Conference on Current Research Information Systems (2010)

Gruber, T.R.: Toward principles for the design of ontologies used for knowledge sharing. Int. J. Hum. - Comput. Stud. (1995). https://doi.org/10.1006/ijhc.1995.1081

Herrmann, T., Loser, K.U., Jahnke, I.: Sociotechnical walkthrough: a means for knowledge integration. Learn. Organ. (2007). https://doi.org/10.1108/09696470710762664

Hofweber, T., et al.: Stanford encyclopedia of philosophy logic and ontology. In: Logic and Ontology, pp. 1–19 (2014). https://plato.stanford.edu/entries/logic-ontology/. Accessed 19 May 2020

Holsapple, C.W., Joshi, K.D.: A formal knowledge management ontology: conduct, activities, resources, and influences. J. Am. Soc. Inf. Sci. Technol. (2004). https://doi.org/10.1002/asi.20007

Ivanović, D., Surla, D., Racković, M.: A CERIF data model extension for evaluation and quantitative expression of scientific research results. Scientometrics (2011).https://doi.org/10.1007/s11192-010-0228-2

Izhar, T.A.T., et al.: Recent developments in the organization goals conformance using ontology. Expert Syst. Appl. (2013). https://doi.org/10.1016/j.eswa.2013.01.025

Izhar, T.A.T., Apduhan, B.O.: An ontology-based framework for organization information extraction. In: Proceedings - 2017 IEEE 15th International Conference on Dependable, Autonomic and Secure Computing, 2017 IEEE 15th International Conference on Pervasive Intelligence and Computing, 2017 IEEE 3rd International Conference on Big Data Intelligence and Computing (2018a). https://doi.org/10.1109/DASC-PICom-DataCom-CyberSciTec.2017.47

Izhar, T.A.T., Apduhan, B.O.: Configuring the relationships of organizational goals based on ontology framework. In: 2017 IEEE SmartWorld Ubiquitous Intelligence and Computing, Advanced and Trusted Computed, Scalable Computing and Communications, Cloud and Big Data Computing, Internet of People and Smart City Innovation, SmartWorld/SCALCOM/UIC/ATC/CBDCom/IOP/SCI 2017 (2018b). https://doi.org/10.1109/UIC-ATC.2017.8397479

Izhar, T.A.T., Torabi, T., Ishaq Bhatti, M.: An ontology-based goal framework to evaluate the level of the organizational goals achievement. Int. J. Organ. Theory Behav. (2017a). https://doi.org/10.1108/ijotb-20-02-2017-b003

Izhar, T.A.T., Torabi, T., Ishaq Bhatti, M.: Using ontology to incorporate social media data and organizational data for efficient decision-making. Int. J. Comput. Inf. Syst. Ind. Manag. Appl. 9, 009–022 (2017b)

Kaiya, H., Saeki, M.: Using domain ontology as domain knowledge for requirements elicitation. In: Proceedings of the IEEE International Conference on Requirements Engineering (2006). https://doi.org/10.1109/RE.2006.72

Kalemi, E., Martiri, E.: FOAF-academic ontology: a vocabulary for the academic community. In: Proceedings - 3rd IEEE International Conference on Intelligent Networking and Collaborative Systems, INCoS 2011 (2011). https://doi.org/10.1109/INCoS.2011.94

Kim, H.M., Fox, M.S., Grüninger, M.: Ontology for quality management - enabling quality problem identification and tracing. BT Technol. J. (1999). https://doi.org/10.1023/A:1009611528866

Kotis, K., Vouros, G.A.: Human-centered ontology engineering: the HCOME methodology Knowl. Inf. Syst. (2006). https://doi.org/10.1007/s10115-005-0227-4

Krafft, D.B., et al.: VIVO: enabling national networking of scientists. Technology (2010)

Leavitt, H.J.: Applying organizational change in industry: structural, technological and humanistic approaches. In: March, J.G. (ed.) Handbook Organizations. Rand McNally, Chicago IL, USA, pp. 1140–70 (1965). http://people.plan.aau.dk/~sh/SundTek2001/Tekster/Leavitt.pdf

Lezcano, L., Jörg, B., Sicilia, M.A.: Modeling the context of scientific information: mapping VIVO and CERIF. In: Bajec, M., Eder, J. (eds.) Advanced Information Systems Engineering Workshops. LNBIP, pp. 123–129. Springer, Berlin (2012). https://doi.org/10.1007/978-3-642-31069-0_11

Li, S.T., Chang, W.C.: Exploiting and transferring presentational knowledge assets in R&D organizations. Expert Syst. Appl. (2009). https://doi.org/10.1016/j.eswa.2007.10.024

Lipscomb, C.E.: Medical Subject Headings (MeSH). Bull. Med. Libr. Assoc. **88**, 265 (2000)

Mari, L.: Epistemology of measurement. Meas.: J. Int. Meas. Confed. (2003). https://doi.org/10.1016/S0263-2241(03)00016-2

Marian, M.D.: Ontologies representation and management, as a semantic tool for organizational memory consolidation, annals of faculty of economics. Univ. Oradea Fac. Econ. **4**(1), 976–980 (2009)

Minelli, E., et al.: The impact of research and teaching evaluation in universities: comparing an Italian and a Dutch case. Qual. High. Educ. (2006).https://doi.org/10.1080/13538320600916668

Molas-Gallart, J.: Research governance and the role of evaluation: a comparative study. Am. J. Eval. (2012).https://doi.org/10.1177/1098214012450938

Neave, G.: A changing Europe: challenges for higher education research. High. Educ. Eur. (1991).https://doi.org/10.1080/0379772910160302

Neave, G.: The Evaluative State, Institutional Autonomy and Re-Engineering Higher Education in Western Europe. 1st edn., p. 248. Palgrave Macmillan (2012). https://doi.org/10.1057/9780230370227

Paajanen, P., et al.: Folium - ontology for organizational knowledge creation. In: WMSCI 2006 - The 10th World Multi-Conference on Systemics, Cybernetics and Informatics, Jointly with the 12th International Conference on Information Systems Analysis and Synthesis, ISAS 2006 - Proceedings (2006)

Pinto, H.S., Tempich, C., Staab, S.: A case study in supporting DIstributed, Looselycontrolled and evolvInG Engineering of oNTologies (DILIGENT). In: Proceedings of the 4th International Conference on Knowledge Management (I-KNOW 2004) (2004). https://doi.org/10.1007/978-3-540-92673-3

Plisson, J., et al.: An ontology for virtual organization breeding environments. IEEE Trans. Syst. Man Cybern. Part C: Appl. Rev. (2007). https://doi.org/10.1109/TSMCC.2007.905842

Reale, E., Seeber, M.: Instruments as empirical evidence for the analysis of higher education policies. High. Educ. (2013). https://doi.org/10.1007/s10734-012-9585-5

Rebora, G., Turri, M.: The UK and Italian research assessment exercises face to face. Res. Policy (2013). https://doi.org/10.1016/j.respol.2013.06.009

Rezeanu, O.M.: The implementation of quality management in higher education. In: Procedia - Social and Behavioral Sciences (2011). https://doi.org/10.1016/j.sbspro.2011.03.237

Salatino, A.A., et al.: The computer science ontology: a large-scale taxonomy of research areas. In: Vrandečić, D. et al. (eds.) The Semantic Web – ISWC 2018 LNCS (including subseries Lecture Notes in Artificial Intelligence and Lecture Notes in Bioinformatics), pp. 187–205. Springer, Cham (2018). https://doi.org/10.1007/978-3-030-00668-6_12

Sanderson, M., Croft, B.: Deriving concept hierarchies from text. In: Proceedings of the 22nd Annual International ACM SIGIR Conference on Research and Development in Information Retrieval, SIGIR 1999 (1999). https://doi.org/10.1145/312624.312679

Sicilia, M.A.: Ontology-based competency management: infrastructures for the knowledge intensive learning organization. In: Intelligent Learning Infrastructure for Knowledge Intensive Organizations: A Semantic Web Perspective (2005). https://doi.org/10.4018/978-1-59140-503-0.ch011

Singh, M., Han, J.: Globalizing flexible work in universities: socio-technical dilemmas in internationalizing education. Int. Rev. Res. Open Distance Learn. (2005). https://doi.org/10.19173/irrodl.v6i1.218

Sure, Y., et al.: The SWRC ontology - semantic web for research communities. In: Bento, C., Cardoso, A., Dias, G. (eds.) EPIA 2005. LNCS (including subseries Lecture Notes in Artificial Intelligence and Lecture Notes in Bioinformatics), pp. 218–231. Springer, Berlin (2005). https://doi.org/10.1007/11595014_22

Tengku Izhar, T.A., Apduhan, B.O., Torabi, T.: Utilising ontology for "heteregeneous data analysis in organizational goals". Int. J. Web Inf. Syst. (2019). https://doi.org/10.1108/IJWIS-05-2018-0046

Weinberger, H., Te'eni, D., Frank, A.J.: Ontology-based evaluation of organizational memory. J. Am. Soc. Info. Sci. Technol. (2008). https://doi.org/10.1002/asi.20859

White, K.F., Lutters, W.G.: Structuring cross-organizational knowledge sharing. In: GROUP'07 - Proceedings of the 2007 International ACM Conference on Supporting Group Work (2007). https://doi.org/10.1145/1316624.1316651

Whitley, R., Gläser, J.: The social orders of research evaluation systems. In: Whitley, R., Gläser, J. (eds.) The Changing Governance of the Sciences, pp. 245–266. Springer, Dordrecht (2007). https://doi.org/10.1007/978-1-4020-6746-4_12

Wróblewska, A., et al.: Methods and tools for ontology building, learning and integration - application in the SYNAT project. Stud. Comput. Intell. (2012). https://doi.org/10.1007/978-3-642-24809-2_9

Yao, Y.G., et al.: Multi-perspective modeling: managing heterogeneous manufacturing knowledge based on ontologies and topic maps. Int. J. Prod. Res. (2013). https://doi.org/10.1080/00207543.2012.756152

Zancanaro, A., et al.: Mapeamento da produção científica sobre memória organizacional e ontologies. Perspectivas em Ciencia da Informacao (2013). https://doi.org/10.1590/S1413-993620 13000100005

Author Index

S. Za et al. (Eds.): ItAIS 2020, LNISO 50, pp. 291–292, 2022.
https://doi.org/10.1007/978-3-030-86858-1

Printed in the United States
by Baker & Taylor Publisher Services